THE DAY OF THE LION

The Life and Death of Fascist Italy

1922–1945

By Roy MacGregor-Hastie

THE MAN FROM NOWHERE
THE RED BARBARIANS

THE DAY OF THE LION

The Life and Death of Fascist Italy

1922-1945

ROY MacGREGOR-HASTIE

Coward-McCann, Inc.
New York

First American Edition 1964

Library of Congress Catalog
Card Number: 64-11923

MANUFACTURED IN THE UNITED STATES OF AMERICA

FOR ROMOLO AND MINOTT

CONTENTS

page

FOREWORD 11

1. LOTTA CLÀSSICA
   (CLASSIC STRUGGLE) 15

2. AUDÀCIA
   (AUDACITY) 50

3. ACCÊNDO FUOCHI
   (LIGHTING OF THE FIRES) 88

4. NORMALIZZAZIONE
   (NORMALIZATION) 131

5. UOMINI NUOVI
   (NEW MEN) 169

6. UN POSTO AL SOLE
   (A PLACE IN THE SUN) 212

7. MEGLIO UN GIORNO DA LEONE
   (BETTER A DAY AS A LION) 257

8. VIA SENZA USCITA
   (NO WAY OUT) 314

EPILOGUE (A NEED FOR NEW HEROES) 355

SOURCES OF NOTES 367

BIBLIOGRAPHY 374

INDEX 381

ILLUSTRATIONS

Following page 128

Newspapers edited by Mussolini

Mussolini the soldier

Offices of *Il Popolo d'Italia*

Communists take over factories

1922: The March on Rome; 1922: Street barricades

The London Conference; Visit of King George V

Mussolini the farmer

Pact with the Vatican and Talks with the Soviets

1931: Funeral of Arnaldo Mussolini; 1934: Visit of Hitler

Draining the Pontine Marshes.

Mussolini's New Towns 1929 and 1935

Italian women give their wedding rings

1931: General Galbiati; 1932: Recruiting drive

Il Duce petrified in the desert

More babies and better mothers for the regime

Mussolini—idol of the young

FOREWORD

In a book of this kind it is always important for an author to declare his interest.

I have been a member of the Labour Party since I was twenty-two, and no man should join when he is younger. I have been an active member: Ward Secretary and Agent; Borough Party Auditor; Delegate to numerous conferences. In 1953 I was adopted as prospective Parliamentary Labour Candidate for the Hall Green Division of Birmingham (where I taught Law). My only dispute with the Labour Party at the moment is over the specific gravity of its Socialism, and for this reason I pay my dues to the affiliated Party in Australia rather than to Transport House. In 1953 I was Joint Founding Secretary of the Birmingham Movement against Nazi Resurgence.

In 1956 I married an Italian lecturer and literary critic, the daughter of a formerly prominent Fascist. I have lived in Italy since 1959, writing and farming. In 1960 I was dragged through the courts for defying Mussolini's press laws, still in vigour, and my vicissitudes have been responsible for changes in the law. I write a column for the Left-Centre *Gazetta del Popolo*, for La Pira's *Politica*, and a number of similarly orientated magazines. As the best-known British journalist in Italy, I am continually under attack from all sides. My friends, colleagues and enemies are a mixture of Fascists and anti-Fascists, some repentant, others nostalgic. I speak Italian almost as well as I speak English.

I am, therefore, fortunate in having access to a cross-section of Mussolini's friends and enemies, not as a foreigner but as "one of the family". Because of my own involvement with Italian politics, things have been made much easier for me than they would have been for anyone unknown, or an outsider.

There is no substitute for personal interview and correspondence with the men and women who were involved in the principal events of the story of Fascism, and who determined the course of those events. I should have liked to have had long talks with Giuseppe Bottai, the creator of the doctrine of Fascism, so much of whose educational work survives. But he, alas, is dead, and I have had to be content with his letters and with conversations with his close friends and colleagues.

I have learned a great deal about Bottai from his friend, Senator Professor Vincenzo Buronzo, creator of the Fascist Youth Movement, on which so many countries modelled their own, and the former President of the Artigianato. My debt to Senator Professor Buronzo is especially great, as he first revealed to me aspects of Fascism I had never considered and in a way provoked this book. The public behaviour and pronouncements of other members of Mussolini's family (into which Buronzo married in 1905) seemed to me unsatisfactory as material. I therefore ignored them.

I am extremely grateful for long talks and correspondence with Major-General Enzo Galbiati, last commander of the Fascist Militia; General Giovanni Passerone, the war hero (who, in 1943, refused to believe that the Duce had been deposed and for eighteen months remained a voluntary prisoner-of-war, in British hands in India); with Baron Carlo Emmanuele Basile, godson of Crispi, former Prefect of Genoa and Under Secretary for Defence (his wife is a Bourbon, and he is typical of the young aristocrats who won over the Royal Family and nobility to Fascism); Dr. Ezio Maria Gray, first Fascist M.P., and architect of the Grand Design for a Mediterranean Confederation dominated by a Latin Alliance, which was frittered away in a scramble for colonies in Africa (I am especially indebted to him for notes from his unpublished Memoirs); Professor Roccardo del Giudice of the University of Rome, former Under Secretary for Corporations (he is typical of those intellectuals who still feel there might well have been an even greater disaster had Mussolini failed to seize power); Senator Luigi Federzoni, former Minister of the Interior, who merged the Nationalist Party with the National Fascist Party (P.N.F.); Senator Alberto de Stefani, former Minister for Finance and Minister for the Treasury, who balanced Italy's budget under Mussolini, for the first and last time in her history; Dr. Angelo del Boca, Italy's most brilliant political journalist and a former partisan commander; Signora Ada Gobetti, widow of the young Liberal martyr and former leader of the C.L.N.; Dr. Nicola Pistelli, Editor of *Politica*, and his young anti-Fascist friends; Senator Desana, On. Domenico Sartor; On. Brusasca of the present-day Christian Democratic Party, and a host of others.

I am also grateful to Sir Oswald Mosley for talks on many occasions about the exportability of Fascism; to Professor Luigi Salvatorelli, On. Palmiro Togliatto, On. Pietro Nenni and On. Walter Audisio, for their courtesy, correspondence or gifts of books. I owe a special debt to Monsignor O'Flaherty, who organized the escape route for Allied prisoners of war, via the Vatican.

For almost every reference, I have used Italian documents, published and unpublished. As source material, German records are often unreliable in spite of the fact that the Italo-German, Latin-Teuton Alliance ought to have been the most formidable in history.

My sources are listed in the Bibliography, and have been weeded out in consultation with the former members of Mussolini's Government and Opposition listed above. I might note in passing that I have found Pini's diary more reliable than Ciano's, possibly because Pini (as Editor of *Il Popolo d'Italia*) knew Mussolini the newspaper proprietor, while Ciano was a mere son-in-law, not always trusted even when he was Foreign Minister. I have used extensively notes made during talks with authors of source material.

I have had the good fortune to have access to hitherto unpublished Mussolini letters, *promemoria* and other documents in the possession of neighbours of mine in Italy, including the Duce's brother-in-law, whose personal assistance I have acknowledged above. Ezio Maria Gray, the only important leader who has not hitherto published his memoirs, also revealed for the first time the substance of conversations with Mussolini about his foreign policy. Between them, and with extra, so far unpublished, notes by General Galbiati, I have been able to reconstruct some hitherto obscure circumstances in Mussolini's relationships with his intimates, with the Militia, and with his Latin neighbours in the Mediterranean.

I have felt it necessary to go into some detail about conditions in Italy before 1922, the corruption, incompetence and misunderstandings, because these things have been glossed over during the recent celebrations of the Centenary of Reunification (1961). I have not entered into detail about Mussolini's personal influence on men like Baldwin, nor about the various pastiches of Fascism abroad, because to Mussolini and most Fascists these things were irrelevant. After 1936 the Italian Government worked on the principle that the régime was admired as a matter of course except by those consumed by envy, or "in the pay of the Bolsheviks". By 1940 Fascism had come to an end as a meaningful doctrine (the date is Bottai's). This book, then, contains only an expanded postscript about the war, though I do examine the reasons for loss of confidence in Mussolini and outline the legacy of Fascism to present-day Italy.

History's verdict will probably be that Fascism was best served by Bottai and Mussolini by his militia (which he treated abominably). Italy, as usual, came off worst.

I

LOTTA CLÀSSICA

CLASSIC STRUGGLE

The future Duce had this to say of his own beginnings: "I first saw the light of day at Varano di Costa in an old house in the village of Dovia, in the commune of Predappio. My father was at the local pub, the Osterìa del Moro, at the time, drinking and preaching revolution. It was 2:45 on the afternoon of July 29, 1883, a Sunday, feast day of the local squire, *padrone* of Camminate, the old ruined tower which, from the slopes of the Apennines to the hills of Ravaldino, dominates all the plain of Forlì. The sun had entered the constellation of Leo some eight days previously." [1]

Thirty-three years later, Professor Josef Garber, president of the Osterreichische Gesellschaft für Wissenschaftliche Astrologie, compiled a horoscope for Mussolini from this information. Garber wrote:

> The slope of the horizon at his birth renders Mussolini passionate and sensitive, but also closed within himself and strong willed, instinctively inclined to oppose force with force. Mars in the Heavenly Twins gives Mussolini courage, resolution, a quick mind, and never leaves him in peace. Mars in conjunction with Saturn gives him ardour and the capacity to throw himself into difficult enterprises, temerity. Mars in the Seventh House gives him aggressiveness, a ready sarcasm and excitability. Mars regent at his birth gives him eyes which speak, while Scorpio ascendant gives him a magnetic personality which explains his fascination for the mob. The Moon in the Heavenly Twins gives Mussolini, together with a love for Art and Science, the need for a varied and adventurous life. The Moon in the Seventh House makes it difficult for him to make up his mind about marriage. The Sun in the sign of Leo reveals in Mussolini a desire for greatness, for glory and power. Uranus in the sign of the Virgin gives Mussolini new ideas, brilliant improvisations about the road to follow. However, he must be careful of his foreign policy, which, because of the confusion of Saturn and Mars, shows a fatal tendency. [2]

Mussolini was christened Benito Amilcare Andrea, in honour of three revolutionaries—one Mexican and two Italian. The Andrea

Sources of quotations will be found at the end of the book beginning on p. 367.

was Andrea Costa, returned to the Italian Parliament by the local constituency, Le Romagne, on October 30, 1882. This electoral success for Socialism made nearly as much impression on the local revolutionaries as the death of Karl Marx that same year. It was perhaps inevitable that Benito should be named after Costa, like one in every three babies conceived in that moment of constitutional triumph.

It is not quite clear who or what Mussolini's ancestors were, the Duce himself having taken a great deal of trouble to confuse the issue, even to the extent of burning public records.

In his autobiography, written in Cell 39 in Forlì jail at the age of twenty-nine in 1912, he said of his grandfather that he was a small farmer who had fallen on hard times.[3] This more or less repeated the substance of the analysis of his family's past persecution and misfortune already published in *La Lotta di Classe*, the Socialist newspaper he edited in 1910. However, by 1928 he had decided that he stemmed from a noble family of Bologna, already well to do and well respected in the thirteenth century, which had moved out to the country sometime later and had lived well off the land. In fact, the archives of the city of Bologna contain references to a Mussolini family, supporters of the Pope's temporal aspirations at that time, which did move out to the country town of Argelate. It was a family of tailors and cloth merchants (hence the name Mussolini, from *mussolo*, *mussolina*, a sort of piled cotton cloth or towelling). Their town house in Bologna was in Via Saragozza. One branch of the family quit commerce for the academic life and politics, not always with scruples or success; Bettino Mussolini was banished and imprisoned in the Rocca Castelbolognese for conspiracy, at the beginning of the fifteenth century; Troilo Mussolini was indicted for the murder of Annibale Bentivoglio in 1445, outlawed, and had his property confiscated. In 1878 the city council of Bologna named an alleyway, which runs into the Via Saragozza, after the family, though the Communist administration of the city in 1949 renamed it Via dei Tessitori. There are, however, no records of the family's activities after the fifteenth-century misadventures of Troilo and Bettino. Benito claimed that the records had been destroyed by his enemies. He also claimed that in the eighteenth century one of his direct ancestors was a famous musician, a violinist who had an international reputation and performed in a Handel orchestra ("Perhaps it is from him that I inherit the love of the violin which even today—1928—in my hands, gives me comfort in moments of relaxation and creates for me moments of release from the realities of my days").

Benito's eventual choice of ancestors were "generations of humble peasants," and he put up a monument to them in 1935. From that time on, his Bolognese noble, or merchant, past lost favour. Perhaps, after an attempt to prove that he was descended from a "Jewish commercial traveller, much loved by the Prussians"—the work of one of the Duce's enemies—Benito thought it safer, as well as more praiseworthy in an age of self-made men, to have come from nothing, by nothing, out of nothing.

Mussolini's paternal grandfather was a semi-literate who spent his life in the National Guard. His academic attainments were so limited (two years at an elementary school) that even in the National Guard he never managed promotion beyond the rank of lieutenant. He retired at the age of fifty and lived on a small pension in the house he had inherited at Dovia. He habitually overspent his pension, sold most of his land and most of the house, leaving Mussolini's father only two rooms on the second floor. He spent his money on Republican—later Socialist—politics, red wine, food and women. At the age of seventy he chased a young rival around the village square, waving his rusty sword, and he was popularly supposed to be the father of forty children. His name was Luigi, known as Luison, and addressed by his fellow villagers with some respect as "Master."

Mussolini's father, Luigi's eldest son, was born November 11, 1854, in a house in a near-by village, the Mussolini house being under restraint for debt at the time. His uncle Pietro, who had been thrown out of a seminary, taught him to read and write. At the age of ten he was apprenticed to the local blacksmith. He soon followed his father's example and interested himself in local politics and local women. He joined the Internationale, founding a small study group at home and taking part in all the pitched battles between Socialists and Republicans, Socialists and the police, and Socialists, Republicans *and* the police. He wrote inflammatory articles for the local Red paper, *La Rivendicazione*, reading omnivorously to increase his vocabulary and improve his grammar. In 1876, at the age of twenty-two, he was noticed by the Office of Public Security which asked the mayor of Predappio for an "account" of him. The mayor replied briefly that Alessandro, alias Sandrein, was "twenty-two; height, low; forehead, regular; eyes, blue; nose, regular; chin, oval; colouring, brown; body, ordinary; no distinguishing marks; a subversive."[4]

In 1877 Rosa Maltoni was transferred to Dovia as an elementary schoolteacher, in the days of one-teacher schools. Miss Maltoni was the daughter of a self-appointed, unqualified veterinary surgeon, a family of almost suffocating respectability, which refused to speak in dialect, insisting on even conversations behind closed doors in prissy schoolteacher Italian. She is remembered today (1963) as a "holy woman." She was to marry the unholiest man in Dovia. Alessandro Mussolini was captivated by the young schoolteacher, largely because he found it impossible to seduce her. He spent a great deal of time in the woods with the local girls, and had in this way found marriage not only undesirable but unnecessary. He had to invent new tactics to win her, stopping her pupils in the street and inserting love letters in their homework. These tactics intrigued Miss Maltoni, and she agreed to meet the revolutionary blacksmith and bar-top politician. In 1877 they were engaged. To Mussolini's cousin she once remarked that she was neither fascinated by his reputation nor intrigued to find herself the only girl he wanted to marry. She was, she said, impressed by his ingenuity and skill at his trade, and felt he would have made a name for himself as an engineer if he had had any sort of opportunity for formal education. It is certainly true that Alessandro Mussolini was a born inventor, devised primitive "semi-mechanical" harrows, some of them ahead of their time, and showed more than average skill in adapting agricultural machinery of every type to local use. One of his inventions is preserved in Dovia by his son's admirers as evidence of inherited ingenuity.

In October 1878 Alessandro's smithy was raided by the police, and a large library of subversive literature was found there—pamphlets, manifestoes, books by Bakunin and Marx, leaflets calling on the peasants and workers to overthrow the government. The blacksmith was arrested, accused of being "a man inclined to acts of violence against the person, generally known to be such and therefore a danger to society." He was jailed for six months at Forlì, then put on probation for four years. Rosa Maltoni visited him every week in jail and saw to it that he did not break the terms of his probation. He worked hard in the smithy, suspended the activity of his Internationale cell, and courted his keeper. In December 1881 Alessandro was released from probation and asked Rosa to marry him. Her parents agreed reluctantly, but insisted that they marry in church. Alessandro protested, pointing out that he was an atheist. His friends told him that atheists in love could make concessions, and all turned up at church on March 5, 1882, to see him betray his principles. Benito Amilcare Andrea Mussolini was born seventeen months later.

The home life of the young Mussolinis was unlike that of the Queen. They were very poor. One room served as kitchen, store for firewood and bedroom for the children. It was furnished with a large wooden cupboard, bread-box, stove and a sideboard full of pamphlets, love letters from the blacksmith, and what linen would not fit in the cupboard. In the other room the young couple slept in a large iron bed, supposed to have been made by the blacksmith himself, but little different from the normal iron bedstead. A box, and a table on which Rosa used to correct homework, completed the furnishing of the bedroom. There was seldom much to eat (Rosa's salary of 50 lire a month and Alessandro's variable earnings never amounted to more than a subsistence income). The menu was invariable: a plate of thick vegetable soup at midday; a salad in the evening; on Sundays and holidays, mutton stew. From time to time Alessandro's relatives, some of whom were prosperous farmers, came to visit them or invited them over, and the whole Mussolini family gorged itself on free food for the day, to make up for the scarcity at home. But for all the privations, their life was reasonable and contented. Rosa even acquired a certain stoic tolerance of her husband's political extravagance. Alessandro was arrested again on June 2, 1884, for waving a revolutionary banner in the street, then hiding it under the altar in church when the local police force chased him away. He was discharged for "insufficient proof," the priest refusing to prefer any sort of charge against him, for fear he would set fire to the church. In 1885 the blacksmith founded a "Society of Drinkers" at the local pub, which was described by the mayor of Predappio in a letter to the Prefect of Forlì as: "Apparently for amusement only, but provided with a flag on which the words *Live Working, Die Fighting* are embroidered, thus leaving it in some doubt as to whether or not there is hidden there a political group." The Society of Drinkers became well known in the district, and many prominent internationalists attended its "Live Working" sessions.

On January 11, 1885, Rosa was given fifteen-days leave to have her second son, Arnaldo. On November 10, 1888, she gave birth to Edvige. Arnaldo and Edvige remained throughout his life Benito Mussolini's closest companions and confidants.

Edvige has made a pen portrait of the infant Benito. She says of him: "Benito was always, right from the start, an upsetting person; his mother and father did not succeed in getting any sort of sound out of his mouth for months. With all the love and apprehension imaginable, they repeated to him the simplest words, in every-day use, pointing to the things all around him in the house and in the countryside and trying to get him to repeat their names. Eventually they took him to a doctor, to several doctors in Forlì, who rated him a backward child. But his grandmother Marianna took him to a specialist who said: 'Don't worry, he'll talk all right. He'll talk too much.' At the age of three Benito started to talk, a strange mixture of Italian and the local dialect."[5]

At the age of seven the sullen boy showed traits of violence. A bigger boy had hit him, half jokingly, while they were playing in the fields. His father urged Benito to avenge himself, which he did, nearly breaking the boy's head open with a large, jagged stone. It took the intervention of the priest to prevent the mayor from sending him away. The boy remained sullen, taciturn, exploding into words only occasionally and then with considerable malice and anger. When he was not cursing his parents, beating up other boys or stoning the priest, he went for long walks with Arnaldo, declaiming as he went. But he was undoubtedly a clever, if difficult boy, and his mother looked for ways to improve his education and provide the discipline his father seemed unable to give him.

When Benito was nine his mother managed to persuade the Salesian Fathers at Faenza to take him as a boarder. He rode there on the back of a mule and arrived with his father, sore and angry. He got off the mule, cursing; cursed the college, cursed the Salesian Fathers and cursed his father. The priest at the gate remarked: "This seems to be a lively boy."

Benito was not happy at Faenza. He was a "poor boarder," sat at a different table and ate different food from the sons of rich merchants and lawyers. He became conscious of "the class struggle." He had only one friend, called Peter the Liar, who had an unusually hard head, and Benito used to amuse himself by breaking sticks and stones on it. At the end of his second year, in 1894, he knifed one of his fellow pupils and was promptly expelled. The records of the school have this to say of him: "Of a passionate and riotous nature, Benito Mussolini found it difficult to adapt himself to life at School, having convinced himself that he had been sent here as a punishment. He opposed the order and discipline of the School. He was solitary and preferred to be so. He was revengeful. He rebelled at every just punishment, so much that the Director, Don Giovanni Battista Rinaldi, was obliged to ask his parents to take him away after the final examinations of the year. This was in fact done, the boy by nature being not susceptible to the sort of education provided by the Salesian College."[6] The Fathers refused to receive Benito in later years, when he was seized (1910) with an urge to see his alma mater again.

For a year Benito studied at home with his mother and another schoolteacher friend of the family. His mother then managed to get him taken as a boarder at the Royal Normal School at Forlimpopoli. This entailed considerable sacrifice on the part of the whole family, even though the fees were low. On September 20, 1895, Rosa wrote to the Prefect of Forlì for a grant in aid for her "poor boy, according to his teachers a most promising pupil." But her husband's periodical occupancy of one of the Prefect's cells had exhausted that man's hospitality. In fact, the "promising pupil" lasted a year, then was expelled by the kindly, gentle headmaster, Valfredo Carducci, brother of the poet, for "having beaten up three schoolfellows at play." Rosa pleaded with Carducci, and Benito was allowed to continue as a day pupil. His father beat him unmercifully ("Whoever showed me kindness?" he was to write later), and Benito realized that it would be as well if he settled down to bloodless study.

For the next three years Benito was a better than average pupil and an average son. He went for long walks at home with his brother and sister, and alone in the house, read his mother's love letters, pages torn out of *Epoca*, Ardigo's *Positivist Morality*, Fiorentini's *History of Philosophy*, Victor Hugo's *Les Miserables* and the collected poems of Manzoni. It was a "general reading," typical of a child maturing fast to make up for a late start. Sometimes in the evening his father would lecture him about God and politics. He had an antitheistic sermon from the blacksmith when his grandmother died in September 1896, and a Republican sermon on the occasion of the marriage of Victor Emmanuel to Princess Elena of Montenegro. These sermons, he said later, were responsible for his reconciliation to both Church and Monarchy. At school Benito learned to play the trumpet in the school band, and in 1898 was allowed to return as a boarder. However, the academic honeymoon did not last, though there are no further records of violence; this was replaced by insolence, loquaciousness and an early inflated ego. On June 1, 1898, his headmaster wrote to his father: "Thursday morning your son had lessons in History, Italian, Calligraphy and Science. The history teacher being absent for a valid reason, the Italian teacher set the pupils of your son's 3rd year Technical class an essay: Time is Money. Your son quickly handed back to the usher a piece of paper on which he had written: 'If time is money, I am going home to study geometry, the exam being near. Doesn't this seem more logical to you? Benito Mussolini.' The Teachers' Council, meeting urgently to maintain the prestige of the school and respect to those who frequent it, has suspended your son from lessons for ten days. I let you know this so that you may take steps so that your son does not remain idle for so much time."[7]

One of Mussolini's pet hates at the Royal Normal College was his cap with a golden tassel, identical with those of the local firemen. When he was told he must at all costs wear this cap, he retaliated by wearing in addition an anarchist's flowing black tie. His friend Bedeschi has described the Mussolini of that time as:

> . . . unpleasant . . . mistrustful, timid, a set face and an iron will . . . in class among the best, undisciplined, widening his own studies without direction, including many books of history and philosophy and a political daily newspaper. He organised meetings of his schoolfellows, giving word of the time and place of meeting with secret code words such as "Come, little fish, to the freshwater". Mussolini would rant against false damagogues, parasites on the people. . . . The Rector was always on the alert and quickly walked over to any Mussolini meeting. Mussolini, seeing him coming, without changing tone of voice or posture, would carry on: "Cucumbers are cultivated for preference on well-manured land etc." One morning he organized a strike, in protest against the poor quality of the bread served at table. He was taken off to the Mayor for a reprimand, but the Mayor was impressed by the boy's mob oratory and was almost on the point of embracing him.[8]

On August 12, 1900, Alessandro Mussolini, on behalf of all the Left—whom he now represented on the town council—deplored the assassination of Humbert I, but added: "To be true to our principles we abstain from voting" on the Loyal Address of Regret.

On January 29, 1901, Benito Mussolini was reported by the local correspondent of *Avanti* as having made a commemorative speech in the town theatre on the death of Verdi, the speech being "much applauded." On May Day, 1901, he organized a stay-in strike at school, barricading the classroom doors and refusing to admit the teachers. The headmaster left the school in a huff, and for three days the school was run by Mussolini, his friends and the few teachers who were too lazy to argue with him. This incident was responsible for Mussolini's early graduation, on July 7, 1901, as a fully qualified elementary schoolteacher, with 132 marks out of 150. He set to work to find a job, applying for posts at Legnano (990 lire a year), Castelnuovo Scrivia (1,200), Tolentino (900), Ancona (1,452). He was interviewed in every case, but his aggressiveness and appearance (he was always dressed like a caricature of an anarchist, lacking only the smoking bomb to be fit for the front page of a comic paper) ensured his not being appointed. His father tried to get him a job in the town hall, but failed to do so, then succeeded in finding him a post as supply teacher in the commune of Gualtieri Emilia—"the reddest commune in Italy." His salary was fixed at 56 lire a month and he had forty pupils. He had to walk over a mile to school, which he did, balancing precariously on the railway line, his only pair of shoes tied around his neck. In the evenings on weekdays he held meetings in the nursery school, addressing the local Socialists on a variety of topics. Later that year he was elected chairman of the local Socialist club and a committee member of the workers' co-operative.[9]

On Sundays at Gualtieri, Mussolini always went dancing. He seems to have had a number of romantic interludes at Dovia before he left. He certainly tried to seduce his cousin Venusta and several of her friends, one of whom is said to have confessed that he made love to her "without even taking off his boots." In Gualtieri he had as his mistress the twenty-year-old wife of a soldier, absent on duty in the north, and kept her until her husband's family sent her away. She was soon replaced by other "violent and jealous lovers," though they cost him most of the 16 lire a month he had to spare after paying his room and board. When he was asked to go to the teachers' conference at Bologna, in 1902, he had to borrow 20 lire from Bedeschi to pay his fare. His father had just inherited 10,000 lire, but was in jail at the time and could not lay his hands on the "subsidy" for which his "loving son" asked him. At Bologna he made a speech condemning the whole educational system, which shocked the local education authorities represented there and ensured that Mussolini's present teaching career would be brought rapidly to an end. His Socialist friends kept his job intact for as long as they could, but in June 1902 Mussolini's contract was terminated and he was given his train ticket home. Before he left he made a speech, on June 2nd, celebrating the first twenty years since Garibaldi's death, opining that Garibaldi was better dead than alive in an Italy "of which he would be ashamed." On June 6, 1902, he wrote Bedeschi to tell him that he had decided to emigrate to Switzerland. He borrowed 45 lire from his mother and set off for "other shores on which to find my destiny." His father was still in jail, awaiting trial, though Mussolini always maintained that he did not know this.

Tired and already homesick, he arrived at Iverdon, via Lucerne, where a travelling companion had relatives, who he hoped would give him a job. They did not, but gave him something to eat and the address of a building site at near-by Orbe where they were hiring day labourers. He worked on the site for two days, ". . . leaving behind a pair of boots in tatters and the flesh off my hands," then took two days off. A week later he quit the job (July 20th) and took the train to Lausanne, where he had heard that there were 6,000 Italians, one of whom he hoped would find him something "more suitable" to do. At Lausanne he lived for several weeks, spending his wages from the building site, ". . . wanting to beg money for a bed from the rich English, glowing with gold and precious stones," but prevented by his pride from doing so. A man from near his home town gave him ten soldi one day, but it is not clear where the money came from to keep him alive until September, when he wrote to Bedeschi, reporting this itinerary. According to the letter, dated September 3rd, he then had only a nickel medallion with Karl Marx's head on it in his pocket. But he "arranged himself."

On December 20, 1902, his father appeared at the Court of Assize, Forlì, accused of having beaten up the local Popular Party's successful candidates at the July elections. The local Catholic weekly, *Lavoro di Oggi*, launched a tirade against "Mussolinism which has invaded the Council chambers" and urged the judiciary to be "stern and just." The Assize Court, thanks to the mildness of the principal prosecution witness, who put down the disturbance to the heat, gave Alessandro a suspended sentence and released him immediately. He had spent 167 days in jail and he was sick, ". . . sad, with my son Arnaldo at the Agricultural School at Cesana and my son Benito in Switzerland."

Meanwhile, Benito had fallen among fellow revolutionaries in Switzerland. A great many Russian and German Socialist emigrées lived—some well, some badly—in Switzerland, and the noisy Italian who introduced himself as a "refugee" found favour with many of them. He is supposed to have met Lenin, who certainly commented to a visiting delegation of Italian Socialists (Moscow 1923): "Mussolini is the only man capable of leading a revolution in Italy—why did you let him get away?" He met Angelica Balabanoff, the "Queen Mother of the *émigré* Marxists," whom he liked at first, but with whom he later quarrelled. He met Maria Rygier, whom he insulted, telling her that anarchism was not to be confused with not washing oneself.

The friends he made among the revolutionaries in exile helped to get him a part-time job as correspondent of *Il Proletario*, published in New York and Philadelphia, and of the Milanese *Avanguardia*

Socialista. He also worked as a "special correspondent" for the *Avvenire del Lavoratore*, the Austro-Italian Socialist newspaper. He wrote profiles of Lenin and other Communist and Socialist leaders, attacked monarchy in the person of his own King, and made enough money to send for his overcoat, which he had pawned in Gualtieri. He also wrote his first lengthy pamphlet, in prose as vile as his occasional verse, called *Man and Divinity* (47 pages, published Lugano, 1903).

He grew, if not rich, at least prosperous. In later years he would often refer to his stay in Switzerland as "months of unmitigated hardship," and recall his first few months, his job as a builder's labourer and his arrest for sleeping under the arches of the bridge at Lausanne, but the fact is that only for the first three months of his self-imposed exile did he suffer any hardship. For the rest of the time he seems to have lived quite well, to have had several Slav mistresses, and when he was not sleeping with them, slept in a room in a second-class hotel, not luxurious but comfortable. He always dressed well, and Angelica Balabanoff said of him that "in spite of the violence of his hate for every privilege, he did not consider himself as a proletarian, but as an intellectual, a leader; the contrast between his own opinion of himself and the humility of his everyday life had the effect of producing an enormous self-pity and a sense of social injustice." Paolo Monelli says of him that he wore "a suit, that of the elementary schoolteacher who wants to be taken for a professor, and the sort of tie proper for Easter visits to relations."

In October 1903, however, Benito Mussolini heard that his mother was ill, and he hurried back to her sickbed. It was the first long rest she had ever had. His father was greatly distressed, too, though he did not interrupt the campaign against the Church that he was waging in the *Pensiero Romagnolo.* Alessandro, proud of his son's police record as a subversive, would have liked Benito to stay at home and keep them company. He was mayor-elect and promised his son a job as a teacher in the next hamlet. But Benito was anxious to get back to Switzerland, the more so since he was due to be called up for military service and he had signed a pledge "not to serve those who want to bathe Italy in blood."

He was back in Switzerland for the winter. He spent the first months of 1904 consolidating his hold on the revolutionary press in exile and improving his mind. He left Geneva for a week, hearing that one of his friends had been expelled from the canton, but returned when word was passed to him that he was, for the moment, in no danger. He managed to get himself a reader's ticket for the library of the University of Lausanne, in which he worked on his French, translating several books. He was commissioned to do, among others, Koropotkin's *Words of a Rebel*, by a local group of anarchists. On April 6, 1904, he was arrested and expelled from Geneva, making headlines in the press for the first time in his life (*La Tribuna*, April 18th, reported that: "Today the Canton expelled the Italian Socialist Mussolini, from Romagna, the leader of the local Italian Reds"). However, he managed to persuade the police not to put him over the Italian frontier, where he would have been arrested as a deserter, but instead to leave him on the borders of the next canton.

He spent some time in Lausanne and Zurich, before being expelled from the canton of Zurich as an undesirable. There were few cantons left open to him, and he spent weeks hiding in Geneva and Zurich, in constant danger of imprisonment. When he heard that the King had declared an amnesty for Italians who had "deserted" or avoided military service by self-exile, he thought it better to return to Italy while the going was good. He crossed into Italy on November 15, 1904, and on January 14, 1905, joined the 10th *Bersaglieri* as an unwilling recruit. On February 10th, 1905, he received a telegram saying that his mother was seriously ill again. He was given compassionate leave and returned home in time to be at his mother's side, when on February 19th, she received extreme unction (in spite of his father's protest) from the local priest. She was forty-six.

Benito was very upset by the death of his mother. His father was lost without her. He stopped work at the forge and sat all day drinking at the Osterìa del Moro. The studied indifference he had shown during his wife's first illness vanished. He resigned from the local council; his contributions to the local press ceased. Benito, worried about his father's declining health, tried to get an early release from the army, but was not finally demobilized until September 1906. He was a good soldier—according to his discharge documents—anxious to please and with no visible sign of the old indiscipline.

Back again in civilian life, he told his friends that he felt: "The destructive time has passed, conditions are ripe for revolution and we must prepare for the assumption of power." He resolved to change his ways, take up a career, stop writing scabrous articles and generally take over the "cares and joys of the head of the family." He advised his father to sell his smithy and move to Forlì, a town large enough and Red enough to enable him to make a fair living as a hotel-keeper. His father took what he had not drunk of his legacy, sold what was saleable at the smithy, and moved to the provincial capital.

Benito, once he had seen his father settled, went back to Predappio to see if he could get the new mayor to help him find a teaching post or a job in local government. It was first of all necessary to get his record "adjusted," to have his dossier destroyed or at least amended. On his return from Switzerland, the Prefecture at Forlì had compiled, for the Italian Ministry of Foreign Affairs, the following testimonial: "He is an individual with a vivacious character, sometimes impulsive and violent. However, because of his above-average education, he is well thought of. He has a lively intelligence and modest culture. He spends most of his time in the company of workers, trying to convert them to his Party. He is in close contact with revolutionary elements in Romagna and in Switzerland and is marked in the records of the Swiss police as a fervent Socialist agitator. Towards authority he is either indifferent or contemptuous."

The mayor wrote to the Prefect of Forlì: "The young Mussolini, Benito, under my administration, lived for some time abroad (in Switzerland) where, for his somewhat warm ideas he was continually molested by the international police forces, in whose records he is noted down in unhappy colours. Repatriated, he completed his military service, with zeal and good conduct, had special praise from his officers, and now, having somewhat modified his ideas and become more mature and reflective, is trying to better himself."

With the mayor's help, Benito composed several applications for teaching and other posts. He had intended to stay in the shadow of the mayor's parlour until he succeeded, but his predilection for the local girls made this impossible. He fell in love, in his own overnight way, with the teacher Paolina Danti, who had come to Dovia to look after his late mother's school. A few weeks later he fell in love with another teacher, Virginia Salvolini, who had classes in the town hall itself. He wrote love letters to them both, stuffed with medieval declarations of eternal fidelity and sickness of heart, and took them into the woods whenever the opportunity presented itself. The mayor, still trying to help, told him to marry one or other of the girls or give them both up. When Mussolini declared that neither was possible without "destroying the soul," the mayor had the two girls transferred, Virginia to Osoppo, and Paolina to Resia in the north. He suggested to Benito that he go to stay for a while with his father in Forlì, where he could study and help the old man run the pub.

The young Mussolini did as he was told. Margherita Sarfatti has described the ménage: "An immense cauldron in copper smoked between the two men. Alessandro mixed the punch, according to some 'secret formula' which he held precious, adding herbs, some home grown, others from abroad, stirring the cauldron as he did so. At his side, Benito would put in the commas and full stops, reading aloud from the works of Machiavelli. Often the two men never went upstairs to their cold bedrooms to sleep in prosaic beds, but woke up in the morning where sleep had taken them. The young Mussolini drank it all in, punch, Machiavelli, Schopenhauer, Nietzsche and the Hellenes."[10]

In the daytime Benito left his father to his own devices and went down to the Macaroon Café, the rallying point for the "intellectuals" of Forlì. A student who was introduced to him there says:

> When I first saw him he was extremely thin, with a thin black moustache, brilliant black eyes, a three-day-old black beard, a fur cap on his head and a cape around his shoulders. He wore a flowing black *cravate à la La Vallière* under a sweat-stained collar. I was introduced to him by Torquato Nanni, then the two picked up their conversation where they had left off. They were talking politics and philosophy, throwing at each other the titles of the latest books they had read. Mussolini quoted the *Encyclopaedia of Philosophical Science* by Hegel, and Nanni quoted back at him the *History of Modern Philosophy* by Höffding. They talked of Bergson, Sorel, James, and the rival claims to greatness of Kant and Spinoza. Suddenly Mussolini turned to me and said: 'What do you think of monism?' I got the impression that they were just parading the half-digested reading of a few hours ago and trying to impress the merchants sitting at the next tables.

Nevertheless, hell bent for respectability, Mussolini did study. He studied Latin in the hope of further qualifying himself by taking out a diploma to teach in secondary schools. He wrote to his friend Calderara for textbooks, and for at least a year larded his letters with questions about declensions and conjugations. Paolo Monelli considers this was done to impress and without any genuine love for literature or philosophy, just as his coffeehouse talk was undoubtedly to impress. Certainly it was never possible to justify Fascism as the brain child of some student of philosophy and politics who had conceived the system, then set to work to put it into practice.

Shirer has shown, in his *Rise and Fall of the Third Reich*, how in Germany the economic and political ground was ploughed and generations of political thinkers had sown the ideas which fertilized Nazism. Mussolini fluttered from philosopher to philosopher, as he did from woman to woman, deriving nothing but momentary gratification from them. Hitler, characteristically, worked steadily at his own misinterpretation of nineteenth- and early twentieth-century political philosophers until *Mein Kampf* was ready in his head. Once *Mein Kampf* was written, the programmes of the Nazi Party were easy to deduce from it. Mussolini had neither philosophy, policy nor programme; he was *ad hoc* in these human disciplines as he was in any other. His superb *ad hoc*-ness eventually enabled him to create a party machine, and his intuitive understanding of the semi-literate masses enabled him to devise the trimmings, the shiny boots, the slogans and the noise. Hitler learned party organization from Mussolini, learned how to create the instrument of State, then used the instrument to forge his programme and implement an already existing policy. Mussolini had only the instrument, and his *ad hoc* genius was eventually insufficient. All he learned from his unselective reading was that much had been written about revolution, but little done since 1789. From Sorel he acquired a simple justification of violence. From Nietzsche he acquired the notion of the superman. From the Communist oracles he heard the testament of party organization and the secret of concealing hard work behind a curtain of jargon.

If Mussolini learned anything at all from his study of the "struggle classics," it was that the day of the learned revolutionary had arrived. Incapable of sustained study, he decided to gloss over his ignorance and hide his impulsive genius behind a façade of potted wisdom.

In the autumn of 1906 the mayor managed to find him a post as a supply teacher in Carnia, at Caneva di Tolmezzo. It is not difficult to follow Mussolini's movements from here on. It is sufficient to turn over the pages of his dossier at the Office of Public Security, Forlì. Police Message No. 1988 of November 28, 1906, notes that "the subversive Benito Mussolini is in Tolmezzo as an elementary schoolteacher, and a copy of his reserved biography has been sent to the Prefect of Udine for the necessary vigilance." At Tolmezzo, Mussolini tried to get on with his Latin (on March 6, 1907, he wrote to Calderara to ask him what was "the exact meaning of *quum* which I find so often in *Æsop's Fables*, and is *inquit* in the present tense or perfect?"). He seems to have persisted until the spring, then fallen by the wayside. He found a group of admirers at the local political café who had heard of his police record, and he spent most evenings holding forth to them. When he tired of his audience's immobility, he would oblige them to follow him up and down the main street while he discoursed à la Socrates. When they went home he would get drunk alone, then wander through the town singing revolutionary songs, before falling asleep where he dropped. He was found comatose in various places by the dawn patrol, in the public lavatories, in the cemetery, in school and in the middle of the street. In the late spring he was seen less often in public, having started a violent affair with his landlady Luigia, with whom he spent most evenings in bed. She was, he records in his autobiography, a very jealous woman and used to burn his books when she found them lying open at pages crammed with names which might have been those of other women. She must have had something of a hold on him, for when he left Tolmezzo at the end of the academic year, he returned to the town several times (a long train journey from Forlì) just for a night on the floor with her.

Mussolini's record at Tolmezzo was not impressive. He alienated the respectable citizens by his behaviour in public and by making inflammatory speeches attacking the priest. He was reported by some of his pupils for swearing in the classroom (his inspector, a Socialist, absolved him with the note "the teacher invokes only the name of Buddha"). Luigia's husband went about muttering dark threats. Police Message No. 3866 of September 8, 1907, records that he had left for Predappio and "ought to be watched," noting the relief of the population at his departure.

During his stay at Tolmezzo, Mussolini is supposed to have contracted syphilis, which remained uncured for the rest of his life. A law student, Dante Marpillero, is said to have found him one day with a pistol in his hand, shouting aloud his intent to kill himself. According to Marpillero, Mussolini, at his insistence, began a cure at the hospital at Tolmezzo, attended by a Dr. Cecchetti, some relation. Certainly in a letter to Calderara, Mussolini asks for a loan to cover the cost of treatment for "my illness" and refers in the same letter to his love affair with his landlady, presumably the source of the infection. This law student died under mysterious circumstances in 1928, a reported "suicide," which may have been Mussolini's way of suppressing evidence and eliminating witnesses.

Back home with his father at the pub in Forlì, Mussolini took up his studies again. He seems to have given up the unequal struggle with Latin and turned to French instead. On October 15, 1907, he applied to the rector of the University of Bologna for permission to take the examination in French, and an oral examination to fit him to teach in secondary schools. He told his friend Calderara that he could not live on an elementary schoolteacher's salary and "must arrange differently." He did not make any concessions to the rector or his august examiners, but turned up on November 17th in his anarchist clothes, a cigarette dangling from his lips, looking around him contemptuously at the other 200 candidates for the twelve diplomas available. However, he intrigued the rector—a man with some sense of humour—and he graduated fifth, with the rector's commendation.

Mussolini was now entitled to call himself "*professore*," and this he did without finesse. He was seized again by the desire to be respectable, and applied for several posts in boarding schools, including several run by priests. In January he was appointed French teacher and usher at a secular boarding school run by the Commune of Oneglia, on the Riviera, no priests having shown any enthusiasm to acquire his services. He arrived dressed soberly, without his cape or anarchist's hat, and for a few months posed as a reformed character. He even took his pupils on walks, explaining the beauties of nature to them in a style more orthodox than his usual mixture of oath and misquotation. At the suggestion of a humourless friend, he even tried to change his name to Benedetto, and scratched this new name on the wall of a church to which he had escorted his pupils. However, this flirtation with Church and State did not last. Mussolini always maintained that it was not his fault, that he was driven away from respectability by the police. The day he left home for Oneglia, February 24, 1908, the police had noted (Message No. 984) his departure, and had notified the Prefect of Porto Maurizio. The local police force at Oneglia was diligent if not tactful. Their attentions irritated Mussolini so much that he threw off his mask of conformity, made contact with the local Socialists and anarchists, and wrote, on June 27, 1908, an open letter to the police in the local Socialist weekly *La Lima*:

> To the Command of the Royal Carabinieri, Oneglia, the Delegate of Public Security and the Prefect of Rovadenda.
>
> The reserve which professional and personal reasons imposed on me has ceased with the end of the academic year. I am now in a position to submit for the judgment of all honest men, the conduct of the police in my regard. What I write cannot be denied.
>
> At the beginning of March, I came to Oneglia as French teacher at Ulysses Calvi College. I had not even got my suitcases open when the police went to the Administration of the College to pass on and receive information about me. The Administration did not lend itself to these

manoeuvres . . . After a few days the *carabinieri* went to see the Administration again and asked that I be dismissed. The Administration refused, and for this must be praised.

Now I limit myself to a single question: Is it not criminal to try to take the bread out of a man's mouth?

By July 2nd Mussolini had resigned and returned to Predappio (Police Message No. 2273). The interlude of sobriety was now over and there were no others for some time. His private and public lives became more hectic than ever. On July 6th he became part-time organizer of the local agricultural labourers, who at that time were fighting a fraternal civil war with the sharecroppers; for some never explained reason, labourers were thought of as natural recruits to the Socialist Party, and sharecroppers to the Republican, two parties which in any event would have involved them in a civil war. On July 12th Mussolini led a detachment of his labourers on a raid of the sharecroppers' farms and broke up their implements, ploughs, harrows and reapers. On the 13th a detachment of cavalry was dispatched to the valley to make sure that this raid was the last. On the 18th Mussolini was arrested for waving a club in the face of the leader of the sharecroppers and threatening to beat him up. Mussolini says of his arrest: "I was taken with an escort of half a squadron of cavalry to Forlì. This interest in my welfare I found touching. The nocturnal cavalcade was almost romantic. It seemed to me as if I had become suddenly famous, and I compared myself with my namesake the bandit Musolino who studied Greek at Portolognone."[11] When he appeared in court two days later, Mussolini was still under his own spell. He told the judge that he regretted nothing; that he had lived for several wonderful days in an atmosphere saturated with rebellion. He was condemned to three months imprisonment, without any benefit of suspension. He had the effrontery to ask for the return of the club with which he had been threatening the sharecroppers' leader.

This three-months sentence, of which he served fifteen days, was vitally important for the future direction Mussolini took in his search for fame and fortune. The sentence closed the door for him forever on any "respectable" career. It convinced him that his future lay in professional politics, either as an organizer, *agent provocateur*, or—more to his liking—as a professional political journalist. He closed the rooms in Dovia, Predappio, which he had kept open as a "souvenir" of his mother, and moved in again with his father at the pub in Forlì, the Bersagliere. He told his father that he was no longer just a customer, but "part of the direction of the enterprise."

He proposed to make the Bersagliere the political and economic centre of gravity of Romagna, much as his father had done with the Osterìa del Moro in the "good old days." Alessandro, delighted, prepared the best room and promised to supply wine for any anarchist or Socialist who cared to shout under his roof.

Benito found to his surprise that his father seemed to have taken a new lease on life. His arthritis had vanished, and he was a sprightly, violent, lecherous man, much as he had been in his youth. Alessandro confided to his son that his rejuvenation was due to "the most intelligent thing I ever did." He had hit on the idea of asking a former mistress to move in with him. He had heard that the woman, Anna Guidi, had been widowed (her husband was a peasant) and left with "a sackful of daughters." He had gone to see her and offered her his hospitality in return for her help and the help of her daughters in the bar. She had moved into his house and back into his bed, and her daughters were making the wine flow faster. There were three of the girls in the bar, Augusta, Pina and Rachele. Benito was delighted. He foresaw no need for excursions into the woods in the future. His bed looked as though it would be fully staffed for years to come, at no expense to himself. He set to work to woo Augusta. Unfortunately, Augusta said quite openly that she thought him off his head and refused to take him seriously. When he waylaid her at every hour of the day and night, trying to rape her, seduce her, talk her into marrying him, she set off one day and in her turn raped, seduced, or talked a poor agricultural labourer into marrying her. Not without a sense of humour, Augusta had heard Benito declare to his private army of agricultural labourers that they must "manifest solidarity, not taking each others' jobs or even each others' girls." Pina agreed with her sister that Benito was mad, and threatened him with a knife. Not dismayed, still without money to go elsewhere to satisfy his "lust and thirst for love," the young Mussolini turned to the youngest sister Rachele and offered himself at third hand, so to speak. His sister Edvige says of him:

The love affairs of my brother remain in my memory in an aura of surprise and astonishment at the way they were conducted. As soon as I saw the little signs, frequent visits, little presents, gestures of affection, I knew that once again Benito's perpetual readiness had made another conquest . . . But young Rachele Guidi, with her mass of pale gold hair, her incredible turquoise eyes and the contrast of her simple, working clothes and the delicacy of the proportions of her hands and feet, was ready, after falling in love with my brother, to follow him anywhere; as ready as he was to lose his head over her hair, her eyes, her whole personality[12].

Benito promised Rachele that he would marry her as soon as he had "found his road."

His road was found for him. He had not written for a job, being too busy wooing the girls in the Guidi family to set to and compose formal applications. He did not need to. The Socialist daily, *Avanti*, reported in full his "martyrdom" in jail, fighting against the "share-croppers, tools of the landlord class." The *Pensiero Romagnolo* described him as that "young man with the fervent wit, self-taught, with a frank and generous soul against whom the reactionary police pursue their vendettas." *La Lima* of Oneglia took his part. Even the clerical *Giornale Ligure*, perhaps the only testimony to his year of attempted respectability, said how sorry it was for the misfortunes of its "valorous adversary." In September 1908 Mussolini made headlines again when he held a meeting without police permission. He was immediately arrested, fined 100 lire—which he refused to pay—and dragged off to jail for ten days.

"I am not afraid of prison," he said to the magistrate in court. "My grandfather knew the Pope's prisons; my father those of the House of Savoy; and I know the prisons of the Swiss Republic and the Kingdom of Italy. I rate jail an excellent diet for the reinforcement of moral discipline and the strengthening of the will, as well as the refreshment of the soul."

In December 1908 Mussolini received several offers of jobs within the party and the Labour movement. He finally accepted, on January 21, 1909, the post of secretary of the trade-union council at Trent in Austria (then an Italian-speaking province), with which went the job of editor of the *Avvenire del Lavoratore*, its weekly newspaper. On February 16, 1909, the efficient staff of the public security office at Forlì sent to the Imperial Commissariat of Police at Trent a telegram:

MUSSOLINI BENITO IS A FERVENT SOCIALIST AND REVOLUTIONARY. A COPY OF HIS BIOGRAPHY FOLLOWS, WITH A REQUEST TO FURNISH THIS OFFICE WITH HIS DATE OF ARRIVAL, ADDRESS IN TRENT AND AN ACCOUNT OF HIS BEHAVIOUR THERE.

The Austrian police force, always ready to oblige, replied that:

BENITO MUSSOLINI LIVES AT VIA RAVINA 20, AS SECRETARY OF THE TRADE-UNION COUNCIL. WITH REGARD TO HIS CONDUCT, APART FROM

THE FACT THAT HE SEEMS TO BE AN ACTIVE PROPAGANDIST, NOTHING CAN BE SAID, AS HE HAS BEEN HERE FOR TOO SHORT A TIME.

Mussolini was not happy in Trent. He found the local Italian Socialists tame and, oddly enough, apparently enjoying the favour of the police and administration. He did not take long to discover that the administration considered the Socialist and workers' organization its allies against the nationalists who were agitating for the "return" of the region to Italy. Socialists, by definition, are internationalists. Though their leader in Trent, Cesare Battisti, declared that the "spiritual question, race, language and culture must take precedence over the material struggle for the stomach," these sentiments found little or no echo among his followers. Mussolini's workers were good, solid citizens for the most part, not disposed to sacrifice their well-being in any struggle for political supremacy or autonomy. There was no use in Benito's hanging up a sign above his bed with the motto LIVE FREE on it. His colleagues preferred to eat well, "oppressed" by the Emperor Franz Josef. Italians in Italy agitated for the "liberation of Trent," but those in Trent itself were not so enthusiastic. Mussolini lost patience with them, and from this time on nationalism and "liberationism" became inseparably confused with his Socialism. Socialism, according to Mussolini in the *Avvenire*, could only flourish in a free Italy, without priests and with its "natural frontiers." His readers thought the world of him, but did nothing. They offered him an increase in salary, but this infuriated him. He retaliated against their "comfortable Socialism" by wearing rags and eating beans and batter every day. When the trade-union council presented him with a new hat, he accepted the gift reluctantly.

Mussolini's only adversary in Trent was the clerical weekly *il Trentino*, edited by Don Giovanni Cheledi, with whom he conducted a private war in the best tradition of abuse and counter-abuse. On Mussolini's side the war was fought with every verbal weapon at hand, and he was arrested, imprisoned, and then released for "want of proof," on a charge of "threatening the clergy." He went in and out of jail quite regularly during the spring and summer. He also found time to write a very bad novel, entitled *The Cardinal's Mistress*, which he dedicated to Rachele, and which was published as a serial by Battisti in *il Popolo*. He tried to fight a duel with one of the contributors to *il Trentino*, Alcide de Gasperi, and when he had time on his hands he taught French to private pupils. In the early summer he had a violent love affair with a schoolteacher, Ida Delser, by whom he had a son later in the year. The child was always sickly, and both he and his mother died eventually in lunatic asylums from—it was said—the general paralysis of the insane which developed out of the syphilis Mussolini passed on.[13]

On August 2, 1909, he was appointed editor of *il Popolo*, a job he held down for just over a month. He wrote a series of articles in which his own variants of Socialism and Nationalism were apparent and in which some of the eccentricities of the Fascism of the future were faintly discernible. He inveighed against corrupters of the Italian language, which he himself spoke vigorously but imperfectly. He commemorated Garibaldi and the nation's Heroes (always printed with a capital letter). He hashed up a few articles about Sorel, Oriani and the "philosophers of violence," hinting that one day Trent would be torn from Austria by "men of good liver." This did not amuse the Austrian authorities, and they looked for a way to tear Mussolini from Austria themselves.

At the end of August the police raided and closed down the Nationalist newspaper *Alto Adige* and found compromising letters from Mussolini in its offices. On August 29th persons unknown hanged the effigy of an Austrian patriot from the monument to Dante in Trent. On the 30th the police raided Mussolini's office and found more compromising letters there, including the proofs of an article urging the Italian population to rise against their Imperial oppressors. They accused Mussolini of "agitation" and tried to find a way to charge him with the theft of 300,000 crowns stolen from a local bank by "Nationalists" for the "purchase of explosives," according to a sarcastic receipt left in the empty vaults. On September 3rd a quantity of dynamite disappeared from an army magazine. The police, convinced that this was all Mussolini's work, arrested him on September 9th and jailed him at Rovereto. On September 27, 1909, he was escorted to the frontier and put on a fast train for Milan.

The Italian press made much of Mussolini's expulsion, and for the first time the infant Nationalist Party took notice of him as "a patriot, mistaken in his Socialist ideas, but of an undoubted fervour."

Back in Forlì, at the Bersagliere, the young revolutionary found himself not only a local but a national hero. Rachele Guidi reminded him of his promise to marry her, and he could find no reason why he should not. He was told by the local Socialist leaders that "a place would be found for him where he could participate in the struggle." He had learned something from his seven years of journalism, if only how to reduce the academic arguments of the party's intellectuals to a system and terminology comprehensible to the man in the street. It was as a superior pamphleteer that the party decided to use him. While he was waiting for a definite appointment the Party made him a small allowance. On the strength of it and his prospects, he took Rachele away from her mother and set up house with her in Via Meranda 2, without the formality of any sort of wedding, but after a "Socialist betrothal."

On December 12, 1909, the president and secretary of the Socialist federation in Forlì formally invited Mussolini to "reorganize the federation to increase its efficiency and appeal, and to edit a new Socialist weekly *La Lotta di Classe*. The salary was fixed at 120 lire a month. Mussolini accepted the offer, and the first issue of *La Lotta di Classe* appeared on January 9, 1910. In many ways Benito Mussolini was an ideal comrade in charge. He lived openly and without benefit of clergy with a pregnant peasant woman. He declaimed against the Church and celebrated in his newspaper all the current anti-clerical riots and church burnings. He was always ready to speak in public and make inflammatory appeals to the mob. He showed no fear of the authorities, either at meetings or in the office of his newspaper. He ran the *Lotta* on a shoestring; built up its circulation until it started to show a profit. He had a fierce style all his own, at the same time simple and rich in better-known quotations from lesser-known Socialist oracles. He attracted readers away from the often stuffy theoretical Socialist journals and made the federation's paper a byword for fiery solvency throughout Italy. He refused any increase in salary as being "against his Socialist principles." He lived simply, in two rooms, with a bed, a stove and a violin, and asked for nothing more. Even when his daughter Edda was born, on September 1st, he found an excuse for not taking more money out of the party treasury, preferring to do translations in his spare time to balance his family budget.

In October 1910 Mussolini was sent to the Socialist Party congress at Milan as the delegate from Forlì. There, to his chagrin, he found he was not as well known nationally as he had believed. Some delegates had never heard of him. Others pretended not to know him and to confuse him with the bandit Musolino. But he made his first speech to the national congress. He astonished his audience by avoiding platitudes and attacking the Socialist Party in Parliament vigorously, saying that "if the party had to be run as a business they would all get the sack for inefficiency." The Republican daily, *Ragione*, noted that he had aroused a certain amount of mirth. *Il Giornale d'Italia*, a Nationalist paper, was kinder and praised his "accent of the genuine peasant." This did not please Mussolini, but did not dismay him either. He told his audience in the square at Forlì that he had made an impression, that Forlì had been named and would be "a place to watch for future leadership."

On December 20, 1910, Mussolini's father died. In the *Lotta* his son commemorated his passing: "My father knew all the joys and bitterness of party life." He promised to take up where his father had left off. He then took a few days' leave to settle his father's affairs, selling the Vallona farm his father owned, and dividing the proceeds equally between himself, Arnaldo and his sister Edvige. Most of the money he received he ploughed into the paper, increasing its size from time to time to eight pages, from the usual four.

There was plenty of work for Benito in Forlì. The class struggle was becoming more intense, if only in the few parts of Italy where classes were recognizable. Romagna was one. The Republican Party, which had lost many members to the Socialists, made common cause with them on occasion, when the landlords or bourgeoisie were due to be attacked. When they were not making common cause, they kept themselves alert by fighting each other. The class struggle proceeded in two directions—internal and external—and the casualties were considerable. Reputations made in the weekly pitched battles were also considerable, and for years the best agitators and mob orators in Italy were to be recruited from Romagna, men who had fought for or against Mussolini's newspaper and its guerrillas. Conscious of his position as the principal *agent provocateur* in the region, Mussolini listened to the blandishments of his "wife" and began to wash, shave and dress "stylishly." This was not so much a veneer of respectability as one of self-conscious superiority.

Throughout the spring and summer of 1911 Mussolini worked on his comrades, holding classes in Socialism for the workers and classes in philosophy for the party directorate. He boasted that he made personal contact with every Socialist voter in Forlì and "knew where to find them when they were needed." In the *Lotta di Classe* for the first week in September he hinted that they might be needed very soon. The government had embarked on the war in Libya, and Mussolini's anti-militarism was still stronger than his conviction that Italy had "things to do." Socialism might need a "liberated" Trent, Nice and Trieste, to grow to maturity. Nothing was to be gained from an excursion into the Libyan Desert. He urged his readers to be ready, and reminded them that "revolutions always follow wars."

No sooner had the first troops landed in Libya than the parliamentary Socialist Party and the General Confederation of Trade Unions proclaimed a general strike. But, as Mussolini pointed out, "it is one thing to proclaim a strike, another to organize one. The parliamentary party had done nothing to set up an efficient organization, in touch with the masses. The strike will be a magnificent fiasco in most parts of Italy. It is up to Romagna to show them how things should be done."[14]

Mussolini was true to his word. He did know where to find his followers and he called them all out on the streets. He made a temporary pact with the local Republicans and signed a secret "concordat" for the formation of a Republic of Romagna in which both Socialist and Republicans should have "leading rôles." He mobilized the least literate and most violent elements and sent them to break windows and destroy the property of the bourgeoisie. He sent the most vociferous to shout slogans. He had the railway blown up between Forlì and Mendola, and stopped the departure of local recruits to the army. He got his post-office workers to tear up the telegraph poles and cut off the province from the rest of Italy. He had his railway workers take over the station. He had his peasant followers burn the hay intended for the horses of the cavalry reinforcements sent to restore order. On September 24th he made a speech to a vast crowd—his best speech to date—urging his audience to fight to the last. On September 26th and 27th the city and province were effectively in the hands of the Socialists and Republicans, and all law and order other than their directives ceased. The correspondent of *Avanti*, when telegraphic communications were restored, cabled: THE GENERAL STRIKE AT FORLÌ WAS AN IMPRESSIVE DEMONSTRATION OF THE STRENGTH OF THE PROLETARIAT.

The police were as impressed as the correspondent of *Avanti*. Mussolini's dossier was transferred from Forlì to Rome—a sign that he had "arrived" as a public enemy. On October 14, 1911, he was arrested and jailed, together with Pietro Nenni. The local Catholic newspaper criticized the Prefect for having let the city and province fall into the hands of two social criminals like Mussolini and Nenni, and urged him to be severe. Nenni, then a Republican, and Mussolini were not dismayed. They spent five weeks together, cementing an easy friendship.

Nenni, in his memoirs written as an exile from Fascism, says of Mussolini: "We passed many hours of the day together shut in our cell, playing cards, reading and making plans for the future. Our favourite author was Sorel . . . with his contempt for parliamentary compromise and for reformism. Mussolini was not a Marxist fetishist. He was a Socialist by instinct and family tradition, and above all a rebel. . . . He was a model prisoner, indulgent to the habitual inmates of the prison, ready with excuses for everyone and everything and to justify their crimes in the name of social iniquity."

The *Lotta* listed in detail the charges preferred against the two men: resistance to the forces of public order; violation of the liberty of recruits to the armed forces; personal assault of public officials; forcing the closure of shops and industrial enterprises; breaking and taking away of telephone lines; obstruction of the railway. . . . "Comrade Mussolini looks forward to several centuries of imprisonment," added the acting editor.

On November 18th, handcuffed, Mussolini and Nenni were taken to be tried in the High Court at Forlì. The correspondent of the *Lotta* noted that: "Benito Mussolini was well shaven, his eyes sparkling more than usual. He was elegant, almost dandified. He spoke with his usual precision, incisively. Pietro Nenni is an endearing young man, rather shortsighted. He has an air of tranquillity, in spite of the fact that the police authorities had defined him as a little, fearful Robespierre."

Nenni was arraigned first. He said he was not guilty of provoking any disorders, that all he had done was to make a speech, then go to supper. "Then I went to the station and tried to stop the mob from taking over the telegraph office. I fell and was wounded by a scabbard."

Mussolini conducted his own defence. He had never had such an attentive audience. He told the president of the court that he was proud of the strike, but deplored vandalism. He said he was in favour of sabotage, but only "that which makes a protest more effective, and, as in any war, respects the rights of neutrals." The "noble civic end" of sabotage justified it as a means. The prosecution let Mussolini carry on, intending to insist on a much more severe penalty for him as "the ringleader, the man with the superior intelligence." Mussolini's friend Bentini, however, saw through this plan, and though he could not diminish Mussolini's intelligence in court, he told the court that if Mussolini were more severely punished for being an intellectual than others who had merely broken windows, then this meant the degradation of the intellectual. Mussolini argued from Marx, and used the occasional plea "to the mothers of Italy who will lose their sons in Libya." He rounded this off with an expression of contempt for the whole bourgeois process, declaring:

"If you let me free, you will please me. If you condemn me, you will do me honour."

The court did him honour, condemning both him and Nenni to a year in jail. But on February 19, 1912, after a number of debates in Parliament in which sundry Socialist members stressed "the essential patriotism of Mussolini," he had his sentence reduced and was set free, together with Nenni. They celebrated with an enormous banquet at the Vittoria Hotel, Forlì, having planned the menu in jail when there seemed to be few prospects of enjoying it.

On March 14, 1912, an anarchist tried to shoot King Victor Emmanuel III in Rome, wounding the major commanding the cavalry escort. The Rome mob celebrated the lucky escape with a great show of loyalty and affection. Crown Prince Humbert appeared on the balcony with his mother and was cheered enthusiastically. The Italian Parliament sent a message of "deep regret," and a delegation to the palace to convey their "relief and joy" in person. Three Socialists—Bissolati, Bonomi and Cabrini—formed part of the all-party delegation.

Mussolini, ever ready to spot an opening for both his extreme ideas and his newspaper, launched a protest at the participation of the three Socialist M.P.s. The protest spread from region to region, and the party was forced to bring the XIIIth congress forward to July and hold it in Reggio Emilia, the "Mussolini country." Mussolini himself, at the head of his protesting "pure" Socialists, mounted the rostrum and announced: "After the attempt on the life of the King on March 14th, the duty of Socialists in Parliament and out was to keep quiet. The attempt on the King's life was, after all, only one of the risks of his profession. Would the three Socialist M.P.s who showed such tender concern for the King's welfare take so much trouble over a bricklayer nearly crushed by a falling wall, or a railwayman nearly run over by a train? And one of these M.P.s not so long ago used to shout 'Down with the King.'"[15]

When he saw that he had the congress with him, Mussolini demanded the expulsion from the party of the three members. This was agreed by acclamation, and Bissolati retired to form a Moderate Socialist Party. Four other Socialist M.P.s were dismissed from the executive, though they remained in the party. Treves, one of the four, was forced to hand over the editorship of *Avanti* to Bacci, a friend of Mussolini and an extreme Left-Winger.

Mussolini's personal success at the congress enormously increased his reputation inside and outside the party. The Right-Wing press was hostile, scenting the rise of a formidable opponent. The *Resto del*

Carlino commented that Mussolini had "an abundance of gestures and mimicry which make him look like a Chinese juggler." The *Corriere della Sera* said he was "thin, bitter, speaking jerkily, with sincerity and pleasing the Congress who found in him an interpreter of its feelings." The *Giornale d'Italia* acknowledged him as the leader of the "intransigent element." The *Proletario* of New York, to which Mussolini had contributed for years, described him as "the complete revolutionary at the barricades." Another admirer was the editor of *La Folla*: "Mussolini is one of the best brains in revolutionary Socialism. He is temperamental. His style is his own. He writes as he pleases in a moving, angry, furious, tempestuous prose . . ."

Even his enemies inside the party admitted that he was a man with "a great future, a leader of our movement". (Sarfatti.)

His fiercest opposition came from the wives and mistresses of the Socialists he had either had expelled or removed from the executive. Turati's mistress, Anna Kulishchoff, accused him of being "neither a Marxist nor a Socialist, but just a minor poet who has read a bit of Nietzsche."

On December 1, 1912, the party offered Mussolini the editorship of the party newspaper *Avanti*. At a banquet in his honour, the party in Forlì described him as "the *duce* of our section, our *duce* for three fearful years." They saw him off to Milan, where the paper had its offices, with revolutionary songs, tears and presents. Rachele, bemused by her husband's rapid rise to power, stayed on in their small flat "until I am sent for." She did not wait for long, but took the train, with her mother, and walked into *Avanti* one day, fearful of the rivalry of the local girls. They set up house together at Via Castelmorrone 19, in a flat which would not have been thought fit for an out-of-work railwayman.

This was as high as Mussolini was to go in the Socialist Party. Editor of *Avanti* and an ex officio member of the party executive before he was thirty—many Socialists now agreed with those who spoke of his brilliant future inside the party. But Mussolini knew well enough, and so did his colleagues on the executive, that his brand of Socialism was becoming more and more personal.

The quarrels with his executive colleagues were still to come. His first task, as he saw it, was to increase the circulation of *Avanti*. It had degenerated over the years into an arid, unreadable, theoretical and discussion journal, bought only by the faithful and unread even by them. Most of the features were written by outside contributors, veteran Socialists whose styles were an echo of Marx and who wrote at Marx's inordinate length. Mussolini found old friends and enemies on the staff. Angelica Balabanoff, with whom he had quarrelled in Switzerland, had become deputy chief sub-editor of the paper; Margherita Sarfatti, a "floating contributor," and for many years Mussolini's mistress, said: "Balabanoff is angry with Mussolini because he never tries to make love to her, even though she is well known to be on offer generally and has a famous name among the old guard of the party as the Queen Mother of the exiles."[16]

Mussolini tried to get rid of Balabanoff, but failed. He did however sack all the old contributors and wrote most of the paper, including all the leaders, himself. He refused to accept long diatribes, even from the party president. He said once: "If Karl Marx sent me in a piece more than a thousand words long, I would put it in the wastepaper basket or spike it for Engels to see."

Avanti, under Mussolini's editorship, lost its old character of "sober informativeness, reflecting the decisions of the collective leadership." It became Mussolini's sounding board, a sort of de luxe edition of the *Lotta di Classe*. Just as he had made the *Lotta* solvent, so he took the circulation of *Avanti* up from 20,000 to 100,000 in three months. The paper may not have been a modern marvel of Marxist dialectics, but it was certainly the eighth wonder of the world of journalism. Mussolini attracted to his personal banner hundreds of journalists who were not, philosophically, interested in *why* he edited *Avanti*, but were professionally interested in *how* he did it. In later years a high percentage of the Fascist hierarchy were newspapermen of one sort or another, which is perhaps a fair comment on the nature of Fascism and Mussolinism. If there is nothing quite so dead, to a journalist, as yesterday's newspaper, then there is nothing quite so dead as yesterday's well-laid-out, well-made-up, well-illustrated political adventure. Only the readers and the masses remain, unconsciously, tied to the publicist's past efforts. In those days nobody in the offices of *Avanti* worried about the future of either Marx or the Socialist Party. The talk was of net sales and increasing circulation. When Angelica Balabanoff complained of the "scarce theoretical quality" of some of Mussolini's editorials, he told her to mind her own business. Stalin reproving Lenin, with a vengeance.

In January 1913 there were strikes all over Italy and clashes with the police. At Rocca Gorga, in the province of Rome, several strikers were killed. As soon as the news came over the wire Mussolini cleared the front page and published an editorial: "How is it that in Italy, a country which we dream of as the great teacher of civilization, we shoot old men, pregnant women and lost children?

Why is it that when the poor in Rocca Gorga ask for doctors, water, light and food, the government, bankrupt, sends instead the police to drown in blood the protest of the people?" Next day he took up his club again and told his readers that they had the right to take their revenge and "kill to avoid being killed." This was interpreted by the Ministry of the Interior as incitement to riot and the murder of the forces of law and order; once again Mussolini found himself on trial.

This time a "famous accused," he defended himself, as usual. The courtroom was packed. He did not disappoint them. He started his self-defence by stating baldly that it did not matter to him whether they condemned him or not, as he had grown used to prison life over the years. He accepted full responsibility for his article and urged the court to discharge his staff. But he said to the president: "You must set me free, not because I did not commit the so-called crime, but because I did commit it and because I promise to commit similar crimes in the future. My ideas may be unorthodox, but just imagine an Italy in which thirty million citizens all had the same brain and thought in the same way. Even the King, before thirty million monarchists, would feel the need of a Republican." He went on in this vein for half an hour to the applause of his audience and to the great amusement of the president of the court. He was declared "not guilty" of incitement to riot, and immediately set free.

The circulation of *Avanti* went up again. Mussolini also founded a magazine of his own, entitled, characteristically, *Utopia.* This was full of misquotation and ill-digested learning, and justified itself in his editorial: "The masses, called on to found a new kingdom, have not so much the need to know as the need to believe. Just as it is not necessary to be Christian to have understood theology, so it is not necessary to be a good Socialist to have read all the great works of Socialism. Socialist Revolution . . . is an act of faith." This editorial and the fact that he was able to found a magazine, without funds, in his spare time, sure of its success, infuriated Mussolini's rivals in the party. They started to try to undermine his influence on the executive, and to snipe at him in other Socialist newspapers. He was accused of all manner of "deviationism," and the rumour was put about that he was just a careerist, an opportunist who had climbed on to the Socialist bandwagon. These subterfuges on the part of his rivals did not enjoy much success with the rank and file membership of the party, who read Mussolini's papers and liked them, knew all about his family's record as revolutionaries, and considered his apprenticeship in jail to have been well served. Nevertheless, inside the party hierarchy the accusations of "careerism" had some effect, largely because most of the executive were jealous of Mussolini's meteoric rise to power. They did not even have any financial control over his professional activities, since he had made *Avanti* self-supporting.

On September 7, 1913, Mussolini accepted nomination as Socialist candidate in the general elections scheduled for October 19th. On October 18th he made his final speech at Forlì, his constituency. On the 21st he was told that he had been shatteringly defeated—that only 3,312 of the 13,698 Socialists on the lists at Forlì had voted for him. He did not make excuses nor attempt to justify his defeat as the result of "conspiracy, jealousy in high places and reaction," as some of his admirers did on his behalf. He laughed off the defeat, said that Italy was not yet ready for him and anyway he did not have enough suits to be a good M.P. However, he did react, and from then on *Avanti* showed a contempt for parliamentary manoeuvres and a preference for strikes, mob action, revolution and "no compromise." On January 1, 1914, he warned his readers that the forces of "militarism" were preparing war and that these forces could only be defeated on their own ground. "Certain problems can be solved only by violence."

On May 30th, in *Utopia*, he explained himself at length: "It is no use shouting Down with War. A man who shouts this is the most atrocious conservative . . . and in this sense nobody seems to be closer to the present regime than the Socialist Party which, instead of preparing a revolutionary situation at the cost of blood and battle, makes senile speeches about the horrors of war."

For Mussolini, violence was a concomitant of Socialism, of revolution. It was not violence in itself which was wrong, but the direction —militarism—in which it had thus far been used.

On June 9, 1914, the General Confederation of Trade Unions proclaimed another general strike, and so began the Red Week of clashes with the police. There were hundreds of deaths during seven days of rioting and insurrection. In Mussolini's home town of Forlì and in all Romagna the death and destruction exceeded every expectation. Church towers were pulled down or decorated with red flags. Priests were stripped and made to run naked through the streets (in Fusignano one was made to play the "Internationale," stark naked, on the trumpet). At Ravenna the police chief was lynched. Mussolini was delighted. He commented that this was "healthy violence."

When, on June 28, 1914, the news came through that the Archduke of Austria had been assassinated, Mussolini commented that it was "understandable; an explosion of hatred against the Austrian tyrant." Austria, according to Mussolini, represented one of "those forces which retard the revolution." He also suggested that, if a similar event occurred in those parts of Italy still under the Austrian Imperial Crown, every Italian's sympathies ought to be with the assassin. This was interpreted by some of Mussolini's enemies as an indication that Mussolini would support a war against Austria if necessary. The party was of course "internationalist and anti-militarist," and therefore classically anti-war. Mussolini was accused, before the executive, of "betrayal of the party's principles." However, in a note he sent to be read aloud at the meeting of the executive on July 1st, he quoted Marx and Lenin at his rivals, pointing out that "the classical struggle is essentially anti-pacifist." Though it was said that the distinction between anti-militarism and anti-pacifism was too nice and academic, the majority of the executive gave Mussolini the benefit of the doubt, and in a note sent to him after their meeting his colleagues said that he enjoyed their "undiminished confidence and gratitude for having revived the energies of the party."

On August 3, 1914, the German Army invaded Belgium. A few days later World War I had divided Europe into three camps.

The Italian Right took the view that Italy ought to remain faithful to her obligations in the Triple Alliance and go to the aid of Austria. Austria and Germany had certainly not been attacked, in the strict sense of the word, and so this obligation was more moral than legal, but nevertheless an obligation existed. For nearly half a century Italy had been an ally of Austria and Germany, and though this alliance had brought her little in return, an alliance was an alliance.

The Republicans in general, and some of the old Liberals who were now politically "Right," took the opposite view. They remembered the Risorgimento, the struggle to unite Italy, a struggle which took place for the most part against Austria, Austria's nominees and friends. They, too, looked at the Triple Alliance, but maintained that it had been a mistake from the start, that Italy's natural allies were Britain and France, and that this indicated quite clearly Italy's duty—to declare war on the Central Powers and repudiate the Triple Alliance. The Nationalists, who wanted a war at any price—to reinforce their dreams of a "newer, greater Italy"—added that all who "love the Queen, a Montenegran, ought to come to the aid of her fellow Balkans so long oppressed." Some of the Anglophile elements in the anti-Austrian party laid great stress on the moral certainty that Austria and Germany would lose the war, and that at the end of it Italy would have an opportunity to "widen her natural interests in the Adriatic, not to speak of re-incorporating so many Italian lands into the kingdom."

The Left in Italy was not deaf to the appeal for a war of liberation against Austria, in so far as the Italians of the Left were also Italians. However, for many years the Left had declared itself to be anti-militarist, had opposed the colonial misadventures of succeeding governments, and could not—so it seemed—go to war at any time for any reason. There were many Socialists, conditioned by Marx and Engels, who believed Great Britain—the "imperialist power par excellence"—to be the natural enemy of the Left, and could not stomach a war as Britain's allies. There were other Socialists who believed that it was "correct strategy" to let the British and French imperialists exhaust the German and Austrian imperialists, then step in to help the revolutions, which, according to Lenin, would burst into flame above the ashes of these empires.

The Socialist Party, at a meeting in the second week of September, decided that it ought to take a neutralist line, largely because its political opponents were agitating for a war on one side or another. All party officials were ordered to preach this line to the rank and file, and the editor of *Avanti* was ordered to conduct a "proletarian plebiscite against the war."

Mussolini organized this plebiscite with a sinking heart. He did not like Austrians, who had jailed him and landed him with an illegitimate, idiot child and its embarrassing mother. He had little faith in the revolutionary fervour of the Italians under Austrian occupation, but he felt that they should be helped positively. He felt, instinctively, that Austria and Germany would lose the war, were in the wrong, and ought to be fought; that the proletariat's and Italy's gains would be the greater if she did not wait. But the party had ordered him to preach against war, and the party had been the vehicle in which he had travelled to a position of enormous influence and prestige. Without the party, would Mussolini be able to survive? Was it not "a case of the wine being famous because of the label on the bottle"? He followed the party line, but in public expressed his doubts. On October 8th, in an editorial in *Avanti*, he confessed that "these past two months my thoughts have vacillated, have known uncertainty and trepidation. Who, inside Italy or out, has never felt such a crisis?"

Massimo Rocca, in the *Resto del Carlino*, seized on Mussolini's doubts and wrote that "the Socialist Party is hopelessly divided," indirectly attributing to Mussolini the statement that "the executive is not even unanimous." On October 10th and 11th Mussolini seemed to confirm Rocca's diagnosis. He wrote, in *Avanti*, that the government knew "that our hostility to war would have changed according to the circumstances; that we would have considered a war against France an act of violence; that we would have considered a war against Austria-Hungary legal and ideal."

On October 19th he enthused: "We have the singular privilege of living at the most tragic hour in the history of the world. Do we want, as Socialists and men, to be inert spectators of this great drama? Or do we, as men and Socialists, want to be protagonists? Beware of party dogma. We will not save the letter of the party's law if this means to kill the spirit of Socialism."

Mussolini's enemies on the executive again accused him of betrayal of the party's principles, and again an extraordinary meeting of the executive was called. This time they insisted that Mussolini appear in person to explain what was in fact a change in the policy of *Avanti* to a position from which the next step would be to openly advocate intervention in the war. Angelica Balabanoff, still an inveterate enemy and not in the least impressed by Mussolini's journalistic success, tried to organize an anti-Mussolini faction at the offices of the paper, but had little success. Most of the staff owed their jobs to him and admired his professional capacity.

On October 20th two resolutions were put before the meeting. One demanded his immediate expulsion and dismissal as editor of *Avanti*. The other, proposed by Mussolini, said that: "While reaffirming its opposition to the principle of war, the Executive of the Italian Socialist Party maintains for various reasons outlined in *Avanti* in the past few days, that the formula of absolute neutrality has become too rigid and too dogmatic before an international situation which becomes ever more complex . . . and reserves the right to decide, in the event of a war, its future actions."

Mussolini spoke, to the whistles of his enemies and the cheers of his friends. He was accused of betrayal, of secretly conspiring to destroy the party. He was ordered to resign as editor of *Avanti*, and his "anti-dogmatist" proposal was defeated by acclamation.

On October 21st he published his farewell in *Avanti*, saying that he went "with serenity, with pride, with my faith unchanged."

From October 21st to 24th his fate was debated by the executive, by his local party in Forlì and by the Milan executive, to which he was responsible as a resident of Milan. He was told he would have to appear before the full constituency committee and section membership of the Milan Party to defend his conduct. He did not care one way or the other. In his own mind he had committed himself to faction and bloodshed, "if by bloodshed we may bring the Revolution nearer." It seemed to him that as war fervour increased so the official Socialist Party widened the gulf between itself and the masses. He was no university-bred theoretician. He understood only action. He felt the party foolish to even think of expelling him—their only inspired leader—but suddenly he realized that "given the general, the troops will be found."

Hundreds of miles away a fellow revolutionary had had to face the same hostility from his colleagues. Lenin had chosen the road to violence. Benito Mussolini did the same.

2

AUDÀCIA

AUDACITY

Contrary to popular belief, Mussolini was not a man who made important decisions easily or quickly. He was always ready to make a *minor* policy statement; write, in a quarter of an hour, an article of minor, short-term significance; come to a decision which could easily be rescinded. But in both his private and his public life he always hesitated before taking a deep plunge. In his early years he nearly always waited until somebody helped him to make up his mind; in later years he became too lonely, a corpse inside the mausoleum of a myth. This time, however, Mussolini's comrades in the Socialist Party soon knew he was up to something. A suite of rooms was rented in his name at Via Paolo di Cannobio 35, and an office desk moved in. At first, rumour had it that he had gone over to the opposition and taken a job as Milan correspondent of a Nationalist newspaper. Then he gave an interview to *il Corriere della Sera*, and the story went the rounds that he was about to join the *Corriere*. Nobody knew quite what the office was for, but the local party executive knew that Benito was up to no good. Many of its members regretted the hasty decision of the national executive in Bologna to force Mussolini's resignation from *Avanti*—its circulation had already started to drop. Politicians, businessmen, journalists, went in and came out of the squalid flat in Via Castelmorrone, and nothing was revealed of the purpose of it all.

On October 28, 1914, the local party decided to hold a meeting of members to discuss Italy's neutrality in the war. The meeting was a baited trap for Mussolini. His old friends knew him too well to doubt that he would turn up to defend himself. They were not mistaken. In he strode and walked up to the platform. Whistles and cheers. He said:

> Listen. Then, instead of applauding, you can put up a monument to me. I will speak without reticence and without double meanings. There is no doubt about the fact that in the face of European conflict

> our party is not united [shouts of "Not *your* party!"]. The majority is still for neutrality. But neutrality is like a strait-jacket and I have freed myself from it. Even my friend Gustave Herve, who once wanted to plant his flag on a dung-heap, defends it today like a rabid Nationalist. The Nation, comrades, represents a stage in human progress [whistles and shouts of No!]. National feelings exist—you cannot deny it. Neither Marx nor Engels were against war, because they approved of the Seventy against France. We must not be afraid of intervention. By intervening in the war we are not appreciating the value of militarism . . . [deafening noise, making it impossible to speak] . . . Well, you won't let me speak . . . but I'll soon have a new way of expressing myself. . . . My new newspaper will let me speak every day . . . ![1]

The secret was out. A new newspaper. The local board of *Avanti* winced, looking forward only to further drops in circulation and financial liability. Mussolini's supporters cheered, then walked out of the meeting. His confirmed enemies either whistled, counter-cheered or sat looking glum.

On the foggy morning of November 15, 1914, out came Mussolini's new newspaper, *il Popolo d'Italia.* It was sold out in an hour.

Mussolini had chosen the title well. There had been a *Popolo d'Italia* published by Garibaldi from Naples in 1860. Flanking the name were two quotations, one from Blanqui and the other from Napoleon (a fair summary of the direction in which Mussolini's socialism was moving): MEN OF IRON HAVE BREAD, and A REVOLUTION IS AN IDEA WHICH HAS FOUND BAYONETS. The leader was headed *Audàcia* and carried Mussolini's by-line in bold, large type. Mussolini's leader read well:

> After the famous meeting at Bologna at which I was "burnt" . . . I asked myself: "Do I speak up or shut up?" . . . "Do I live or do I die?" . . . I was sure that time would prove me right, that it would shatter the dogma of neutrality as it has shattered many not less venerable dogmas of churches and parties. . . . In times like these not only the dead are in a hurry, as the poet said, the living are in an even greater hurry. To wait may mean to arrive late . . . and so I felt not only the necessity but also the duty of founding a newspaper. . . . Am I a deserter [from the party]? If, tomorrow, Prussian reaction triumphs in Europe, after the destruction of Belgium and the annihilation of France, it will lower the level of civilization, then all those who did nothing to stop it will be the deserters.

The executive of the local Socialist Party was furious. They consulted the national executive, then sent a formal invitation to Mussolini to appear on November 25th before the whole membership of the party in Milan, at the Teatro del Popolo, to try to show good cause why he should not be expelled for ever from the party.

Angelica Balabanoff was furious. She had told her friends that they had seen the last of Mussolini. Now here he was, back again, more influential than ever and taking the propaganda bread out of her mouth. The sales of *Avanti* dropped 25,000 in the first three days of publication of *il Popolo d'Italia.* Balabanoff, in an unsigned note in *Avanti,* sneered at Mussolini's description of his paper as a "Socialist daily" and wound up by asking her readers: "Who pays for it?"

All sorts of rumours went around about the "influential backers" of *Popolo d'Italia.* Some said it was financed by a group of armaments manufacturers. Others had certain information that it was paid for by Minister of Foreign Affairs San Giuliano. Another rumour went about that the French General Staff had transferred 20 million lire to a numbered bank account. Yet another had it that the British Government had transferred 50 million to Mussolini's own personal account. Everybody was sure that Mussolini was in the pay of somebody or other. There were, too, Socialists who were convinced that Mussolini had been in "somebody's pay for years" and had only "resigned" from *Avanti* when he was sure that he had another paper ready to take its place.

The Socialist Party even set up a commission of inquiry to establish "the facts." It was inevitably a hostile inquiry. Its terms of reference were to find out: (1) where the money came from; (2) if Mussolini knew whose money it was; (3) how long, if at all, before the Bologna meeting, this money had been "in the air." The commission did its worst. It hinted that Mussolini had been in contact with "the bourgeois" Filippo Naldi for months before November 1914, to discuss the possibility of help for a newspaper. It accused Mussolini of having closely collaborated with Naldi, an enemy of the Socialist Party. Naldi had tried to get money from the Swiss Haasenstein Publicity and Advertising Agency, in the form of a guaranteed sum per issue to cover advertising space which might or might not be taken up. This attempt having failed, another agency—an Italian one—"was set up especially to supply funds to Mussolini, guaranteeing him two months of life for his paper." But as for the "armaments cartels," the commission could find no evidence of funds supplied by them; and as for the British and French governments, the commission admitted that, far from finding stray millions in Mussolini's account, it found only promissory notes signed by Mussolini himself. The inquiry's report concluded: "All the money spent in the first three months of life of the newspaper came from: (1) the sales of the paper; (2) a sum of money advanced by a publicity and advertising agency; (3) loans from parents and friends and promissory notes to cover a bank loan."

The truth of the matter, according to documents which have just come to light, is that Mussolini had known Naldi for months as a political adversary and a personal friend, and had discussed with him the possibility of getting some advertising money for *Utopia*. Mussolini had never had to worry about getting any advertising revenue for the newspapers he had previously edited. The bills had always been paid by somebody else. But *Utopia* was his, it was costing more than it ought to have done, and Mussolini hated to see it go to the wall. Naldi, who thought the Mussolini of those days an amusing crackpot, advised him how to go about getting advertising revenue. He pointed out that with Mussolini's Swiss contacts he should have no difficulty in getting money from one of the Swiss agencies which habitually took space in magazines published in North Italy. This was as far as any of Mussolini's inquiries into the advertising business went before he was sacked by *Avanti*. In conversations[2] with his family at that time, especially with Vincenzo Buronzo, who disapproved of *Avanti*, Mussolini showed that he had never had any intention of letting go of *Avanti* or of exposing himself to suspension or expulsion from the Socialist Party.

When Mussolini found himself on his own, he had contacted Naldi again and asked him to repeat his advice. Naldi in turn had contacted the Swiss agency for him, but they were "restricting their advertising" (Mussolini got his own back with an attack on the Swiss in general some weeks later). Naldi also told Mussolini how to go about organizing the sale of the new paper he had in mind, and put him in touch with the Messaggerie Italiane, which did in fact distribute *il Popolo* (without any political interest, it distributed all sorts of newspapers of every political flavour, including an anarchist broadsheet). He also loaned Mussolini a sub-editor and a clerk—but made Mussolini sign promissory notes for their salaries. The agency, which was supposed to have been set up for the sole purpose of supplying Mussolini with advertising revenue, had in fact been registered months before, when there was no sign of the *Popolo d'Italia* and when Mussolini was still the party's "hope."

Actually Mussolini started *il Popolo d'Italia* with about 500 lire in cash, a lot of promises and promissory notes, a table, a chair, a flag with a skull and crossbones on it, which hung behind his table, and an unlimited confidence in his own ability to make the thing pay.

It did pay, and Mussolini soon cleared all his debts and redeemed all the notes. When Naldi, who had not helped Mussolini entirely disinterestedly, tried to get him to reprint articles from Naldi's own *Resto del Carlino* and follow the Naldi line, the "*duce*" wrote him a stiff letter and told him he always made up his newspaper with pen and ink and not with scissors and paste.

The success of *il Popolo d'Italia* kept the Socialist Party at boiling point. It also ensured a steady stream of defectors to Mussolini, who often insisted on calling at the office to pay their respects. At one stage there were so many callers that he had to put a notice on the door: IF YOU COME IN, YOU DO ME HONOUR. IF YOU DON'T COME IN, YOU DO ME A FAVOUR.

On November 25th Mussolini left the offices of *il Popolo d'Italia* with a small squad of Socialist defectors, all carrying their party cards. Admission to the meeting at the Teatro del Popolo was by membership card only.

Mussolini was invited on to the platform to defend himself. He seems to have been nervous, for after his opening sentence ("I see that my fate is decided, but you seem to want to complete the deed with a certain solemnity"), the official record notes that there were shouts of "Speak up!" This was the last occasion on which Mussolini was ever accused of inaudibility.[3] He went on to criticise the way they had gone about expelling him ("You are severer than bourgeois judges"), and resigned himself to be "guillotined according to the order of the day." "But," he added, "if you think you will lose me, you are mistaken. You hate me today because you still love me [cheers, counter-cheers and whistles]. But you will not lose me; you have not seen the last of me; twelve years of my life in the party are, or ought to be, a sufficient guarantee of my Socialist faith." Mussolini then went on to point out that Amilcare Cipriani, a Socialist idol, after whom he had been named, would be, in spite of his seventy-five years, the first in any trenches and so "ineligible to he a Socialist candidate." He concluded: "Don't delude yourselves that by taking away my party card you will stop me working for the cause of Socialism and the Revolution." Whistles, jeers and counter-cheers dissolved the meeting in confusion.

When Mussolini tried to address a meeting ten days later in Verona, he was again interrupted and eventually shouted down. But on December 10th the first-fruits of his interventionist campaign were gathered in. On that day Aurelio Galassi formed the first *fascio* of interventionists and asked for Mussolini's political blessing.

On December 12th, in *Avanti*, Marco Ramperti attacked Galassi, and accused Mussolini of "treachery, opportunism, and ingratitude." On December 13th Ramperti continued the attack, "underlining the dangers inherent in the formation of such *fasci*, to which Socialists might mistakenly adhere." At some time between the 12th and the 13th, the word "fascism" was coined. The word *fascio* was not new to Italian politics. The Sicilian Socialist de Felice-Giuffrida founded a *fascio di lavoratori* in 1890, and used it to agitate for better economic conditions for his peasants. The word *fascio* means simply "group," and de Felice's was simply a workers' group. Mussolini's inspiration was an "interventionist group." So the words *fascism* and *fascio* originally had none of the overtones eventually conferred on them by English-speaking Socialists.

It is perhaps a fair comment on Fascism that its style and title were essentially meaningless to Italians from the beginning. *Fasci* were simply groups of people, with other political qualifications, who happened to find themselves united on a single issue at a single time. It is interesting to contrast the word with that of its principal pastiche—Nazism, National Socialism—a style and title which gave from the outset a clear indication of where the party was going and why.

Mussolini's Fascist newspaper went ahead by leaps and bounds. Net sales at the end of December were 100,000. The editor himself used to go the rounds of the newstands to check up on progress, and was always delighted when he was told that sales were rising, "especially when that '*crapon*' Mussolini writes in it."

Mussolini wrote most of the paper and read all the readers' letters. From them he got a clear idea of the way the country was going—and not only that part of it which he had come to know as an orthodox Socialist. There is no doubt about the fact that during the first few months of 1915 he was at the centre of attention, a national figure. In January 1915 he formed his own *fascio*, which within a week had 5,000 members scattered up and down the country. The Socialist Party's commission of inquiry into the "backing" for his paper had the reverse of the effect intended and increased the number of his ex-Socialist supporters.

In March, when the commission's promoters thought fit to amend their "acquittal" by hinting that "it has been established that money is accruing to the newspaper from sources close to the French General Staff," this only had the effect of making the man in the street suspect that the party's fear of Mussolini must mean that Mussolini was right. Not only did money flow into the offices of *il Popolo d'Italia* from admirers at home, it came, too, from France, Switzerland, even England. But as fast as it hit the bottom of the tin trunk Mussolini used as a petty cash box, it was out again to be invested in more paper, more ink, more sensation. At the end of March Mussolini fought an "interventionist" duel with his former comrade Treves, and up went his stock again (he lost part of the lobe of his left ear).

The war was not going too well for France, England and their reluctant or willing allies. Incompetent generals tried to fight a highly trained homogeneous army with a rabble of courageous but ill-equipped civilians, uneasily co-existing in trenches with the oddly Victorian professional ranker. A new race of war profiteers, bred to a peak of commercial capacity, made the economic modernization of the armies of the Allies an impossibility. Russia, bankrupt and with the country's essential services disrupted by a mixture of incipient revolution and normal chaos, threatened to sign a separate peace if she were not advanced huge sums of money with which to purchase arms and recruit mercenaries.

The temporary discomfiture of the Allies affected Italy in two ways. The minority, which favoured war in the hope of "liberating" the northern provinces at the end of it, opened secret negotiations with Austria, convinced that there was a better chance of being paid these provinces as an ally than of looting them as a victorious enemy. Italian Foreign Minister Sonnino was in constant consultation with his Austrian counterpart, Bercholdt, and his successor, Baron Burian, well into the spring of 1915. Those who did not see in the Allied difficulties a good reason for renewing the Triple Alliance, saw in these difficulties an even more urgent reason why Italy should abandon neutrality and enter the war on the side of Britain and France. The number of Italians, in and out of government, who openly favoured neutrality was getting smaller every day. As might be expected in a country as theatrical as Italy, the fierceness of the interventionists was tempered by comedy and farce. At the end of March some thirsty porters at the railway station in Venice decided to push in the bungs of some 92 barrels of beer consigned to Tripoli, via Venice, from Berlin. But instead of beer they found 456 rifles and 27,300 bullets destined for Tripolitanian tribesmen still fighting the Italian Army of Occupation. The beer incident whipped up a war fury Mussolini never matched. The beer was on Mussolini's side; the barrels had come from Berlin, so this must mean that the Germans were "mocking Italy's neutrality."

On March 29th, in Rome, several parties organized a joint "Trent and Trieste" meeting, to demand a government policy, war or peace, which would ensure the return of these two Italian-speaking provinces to Italy. Barzilai spoke, assuring his audience that Trieste would rise at the waving of a flag. Ivanoe Bonomi, leader of the reformist Left, "confessed that he could not refuse to listen to the voice of national sentiment, the warnings of history and the hopes of the future." Enrico Corradini, for the Nationalists, attacked the "conservative bourgeoisie and conservative Socialists, men with their minds in their stomachs in a world which thinks too much of eating." The Garibaldi family, which had recruited, fought, then demobilized a Garibaldi legion, was also present and set up a shout of "*Arrivederci a Trieste*." Then the meeting formed into a procession and marched to the Prime Minister's office (breaking the windows of Gambrinus, Norddeutscher Lloyd and the *Popolo Romano* on the way). Underneath the Prime Minister's window the procession dissolved into a mob again and shouted: "*Viva l'Italia*. We want War!"[4]

On April 3rd a pro-interventionist general, Carlo Porro, was appointed deputy chief of the General Staff. On April 6th French General Pau was given a great welcome to Catania on his return from fighting the Turks in Greece, and was given an even noisier welcome to Rome on April 8th.

On April 11, 1915, Mussolini decided to try to organise a nation-wide "demand" for intervention on the side of the Allies. Each city which had a *fascio*, some called *fasci di intervenzione*, others *fasci di azione rivoluzionària* (Mussolini kept intact the Socialist jargon he had used for so many years, thus adding to the confusion of his enemies), organised its own demonstration. For a country which had only rudimentary communications, and for a "movement" which had only a rudimentary organisation, the April 11th demonstrations were a great success. The *fascio* in Rome issued a declaration accusing the government in "its dead intimacy" of suffocating the national aspirations of the people, calling the Germans the "pirates of Europe," and the Austrians "tormentors of the Italian people." The *fasci* in other cities addressed themselves to "patriots," "men of goodwill and strong hearts," "men of liver" and "men of the future." The Milan *fascio*, run by Mussolini from his home, appealed to the "proletariat." Their manifesto called on the workers to take note that the "great leaders of Socialism—Malato, Hyndmann, Plekhanov, Cipriani," were all in favour of a war against the Central Powers. The "German proletariat" had destroyed the

Internationale and released Italians from their obligations not to make war on it. "Neutrality is egoism, vested interests, cold calculation, cynicism."

More and more recruits to the interventionist "army" helped to swell its ranks, and, unkind critics said, helped to swell Mussolini's head. Famous names appeared on his manifestoes—D'Annunzio, the soldier poet, Maria Rygier, Cuardi, Olivetti, Marinelli. All sorts of men and women, of every party and of no recognizable party, hurried to sign petitions, make speeches, defend the leader of the "noble cause." Futurists, Nationalists, Socialists, Reformists, even some Catholic Party leaders. On April 12th Mussolini himself went to Rome, his paper in his hand, to wave it at the crowds and organise its sale in the capital. He was immediately arrested, together with Marinetti, the leader of the Futurists ("We are out to glorify War, the only health giver of the world, Militarism, Patriotism, the Destructive arm of the Anarchist, Ideas that kill, Contempt for Women . . . Italy has been too long the market place of the Secondhand Art Trade! Fire the libraries, flood the museums . . . we cast our challenge to the stars . . . we extol aggressive movement, feverish insomnia, the double quickstep, the somersault, the box on the ear" [5]). Mussolini was kept in a cell for eight hours, then released. Marinetti released himself, walking out of jail in a policeman's uniform.

On April 13th a declaration was made in Milan by the leaders of the Lombardy Democratic League, the National Italian League, the Reformist Socialist Party, the Democratic Liberal Union, the Secretariat of the Lombardy Radicals, the National Liberal group, the Patriotic Society for Trent and Trieste, and the Lombardy Committee for Italian Action. The declaration was quite simple: "We want an end to the present situation." [6] Coming from such a spectrum of parties, the declaration was impressive, though, as Professor Giudici says in his history of Italy: "The votes of parties and of associations were already suffocated by demonstrations." But the government still plodded on, hoping to gain Trent and Trieste, and so stifle the nationalist hard core of the interventionist movement without having to go to war. In negotiations with the Austrian Government, throughout April 1915, Sonnino tried to haggle, swindle and appropriate, and at the same time stop the mob from breaking his windows.

Eventually, at the end of April, the King called the Prime Minister to him and told him that "Italy wants to go to war, and wants to go to war against the Central Powers." He added that he would not hesitate to change the leadership of the country if the Prime Minister did not put the "will and interests of the nation above party interests."

On April 26th the government authorised the signing of the secret Treaty of London, under the terms of which Italy promised to enter the war on the side of the Allies, not later than May 26th—in return for Trieste, Trent, Istria and Dalmatia "at the victorious conclusion of the war."

On May 3, 1915, the Italian Ambassador in Vienna presented a note to Baron Burian, "regretting the intransigence of the Imperial Government and taking again full liberty of action, thus annulling all previously existing treaties."

On May 5th Gabriele D'Annunzio, addressing the King in his absence at an enormous rally near Genoa, gave a sermon, the burden of which was: "Blessed are the young, hungry and thirsty for glory, for they shall be satisfied."

The newspapers lined up for the last battle for Mussolini: the *Popolo d'Italia*, *Idea Nazionale*, *Corriere della Sera*, *Secolo*, *Mezzogiorno*, *Azione Socialista*, *Idea Democratica*, and a paper called, unfortunately *Asino* (the Ass); for the wavering government, which would not have hesitated to tear up the Treaty of London if it could have done so and stayed in office, *il Giornale d'Italia*, *Tribuna* and *La Stampa*; for the non-government neutralists, *Popolo Romano*, *Avanti*, *Osservatore Romano* (official Vatican newspaper), *Unita Cattolica*, *Perseverenza*, the unfortunate *Mulo* (the Mule) and *il Bastone* (the club).

On May 11th Mussolini launched a "Day of Intervention" which reduced the entire country to chaos. He invited the people to shoot members of Parliament in the back, but the whole of its membership retired to the country that day. Mussolini's editorial was described by his friends as "spirited," by his enemies as "libellous, vulgarly provocative." Mussolini wrote:

> While the country is waiting from day to day for a word from Rome, from Rome we get news only of revolting private misdeeds, and of the not less revolting manoeuvres of Parliament. The eve of the greatest enterprise in the history of Italy is spoilt by the regurgitating of every base [excuse and tactic] by the bemedalled tribe. Disdain and mortification alternate in our souls. These members of Parliament . . . ought to be put in front of courts-martial. Discipline must start from above, if it is to be respected from below. As for me, I remain firmly convinced that for the health of Italy it is necessary to shoot a few dozen members of Parliament in the back and put away for life a couple of ex-ministers, at least. I believe that the Italian Parliament is a pestiferous abscess which is poisoning the blood of the Nation. We must cut it out!

On May 12, 1915, Gabriele D'Annunzio arrived in Rome and made an interventionist speech from the balcony of the Hotel Regina. All pretence at public order ceased. The semi-literate and illiterate mob roamed the streets, stoning priests and chanting the poet's call to arms. The government, threatened by the King from his palace, and the mob from beneath its windows, resigned.

The resignation of the government caused consternation among the interventionists. At least Antonio Salandra, the Prime Minister had been a waverer. The only alternative to Salandra was Giolitti, who was quite rightly suspected of a firm conviction that Italy should intervene, but on the side of the Central Powers, against England and France. D'Annunzio reacted violently: "Listen to me! We are on the point of being sold like a flock of sheep." He urged the Roman mob to form itself into a militia, to make sure that "there will be no treason." Next day he attacked Giolitti by name, as a man "trading with the foreigner, in the service of the foreigner, to dishonour Italy to the advantage of the foreigner." Five days later Mussolini, in *il Popolo d'Italia*, celebrated "the poet's victory," assuring its readers that in the face of such opposition the King had had no alternative but to refuse to ask Giolitti to form a government, to refuse to accept Salandra's resignation, and order him to declare war immediately: "The terrible Passion Week of Italy has ended with the Victory of the People (May 17, 1915)."

But Mussolini was optimistic if he thought that either Salandra or Giolitti, for different reasons, had given up hope of avoiding a war against Austria. On May 18th the Hungarian Prime Minister commented: "I am convinced that if we succeed in eliminating the points of irritation, the sympathy between the Italian and Hungarian nations will reawaken in all its vigour." [7] As late as the evening of May 19th Sonnino and Salandra let it be known in Vienna and Berlin that they were still open to offers, and Giolitti was still hawking Italy through the expansionist market the next morning.

On May 20, 1915, the Italian Parliament reassembled. Both the members inside and the angry mob on the steps had learned of these last-minute manoeuvres. Like most state secrets, they had found their way into a newspaper almost before they had been sealed in a dispatch box. The members inside, many of whom had arrived via the cellars, knew that they stood little chance of sleeping that night if they did not make stirring speeches to pacify the mob outside. As the president of the Assembly pointed out, not even the police on duty were entirely trustworthy, nor could he guarantee members' safety. Marinetti and the Futurists had constructed a number of infernal devices which exploded during the sitting, doing little damage but causing consternation. Mussolini had written a threatening editorial that morning. Corradini, the Nationalist leader had sent the Prime Minister a letter, "fearing for his safety." Every party, except the official Socialist and the clericals, was by now committed to intervention by its leaders, even when those leaders did not "officially" act as spokesmen for their party executives. The Socialists, the clericals, the handful of waverers of uncertain allegiance, and the handful of Germanophiles owing allegiance to Giolitti, looked at each other and avoided overt acts. On a motion to accord the government the full powers necessary for the conduct of *a* War (*the* war was still not specific), the voting was 407 for, 74 against, abstentions 1. Ushers carried the news to the waiting crowd. The crowd broke into cheers and cries of "Long Live the King!" Inside, the members heaved sighs of relief and set off home again through the cellars.

War was not declared without the usual Italian element of farce. The declaration was drafted on the 21st, approved on the 22nd, and cabled to the Italian Ambassador in Vienna for immediate presentation to the Austrian Prime Minister. Five minutes after the last word of the declaration had gone over the wire, the lines either fell down or were blown down. The entire Italian Government sat throughout the morning, afternoon and early evening of the 23rd, unable to say whether or not the declaration had, in fact, been made. The Italian Prime Minister, at dinnertime on the 23rd, had to confess to a correspondent of *Corriere della Sera* that he could not say whether or not it would be "factual to bring the paper out the next day with the headline: *Italy at War.*" It was not until 11:30 P.M. that a reply was had from the Italian Ambassador, the Duke of Avarna. The burden of the reply was that the official declaration of war had found its way into Austrian hands, and he hoped that it had by now reached the Austrian Prime Minister. At any event, added the ambassador, "it is safe to assume that we shall be at war in the morning, because I have taken the liberty of consigning the text to the Viennese press."

Next day the King of Italy issued a proclamation: "The hour of national revindication has sounded." As a journalist commented when the proclamation was read out to foreign correspondents: "Only just."

Mussolini's editorial, which had already been set up before the government in Rome received confirmation of its declaration of war, said quite simply: "From today the Nation is called to arms. From today there exist only Italians. Now that steel is to meet steel, only one cry can rise from our breasts *Viva l'Italia. . . .*"

For many young men the interventionist campaign started by Mussolini was their initiation into politics. Giorgio Pini wrote as much in his memoirs: "Even without knowing Mussolini personally [he was later to become editor of *il Popolo d'Italia* and be in daily telephone communication with the Duce] or even knowing what he looked like, I had already met him spiritually." It is easy to laugh at the essential absurdity of Mussolini, scarcely in his thirties, sitting at a secondhand desk, with the skull and crossbones flag on the wall, forcing a government into war and five political parties to change their policies. Nevertheless, this is what he did, for good or evil. He made a reputation for himself which approached that of a latter-day prophet, when war was finally declared. By his success he discredited, not only the Socialist Party, but in a way all parties. His "above partyism" had already taken effect as early as January 1915 (Marinetti wrote then in *Terza Italia*, "The party is the negation of youth"). By May 24th Mussolini had succeeded in making all the experienced politicians in Parliament look either fools or cowards. He did not fully realise the extent of his popularity, even among men who should have known better. Had he attempted a coup at that time, he might well have succeeded in forming an extra-parliamentary "consultative committee," on the lines of the future Grand Council of Fascism, which could have run the war effectively from his office. Had he known the extent of Italy's unpreparedness for war, this idea might well have occurred to him, but it did not, and his understanding of war, like Marinetti's, did not go much beyond heroic images of heroic Italians storming redoubts with bayonets fixed. The heroic Italians were lucky to have any bayonets at all. There was a critical shortage of large and medium calibre shells, a scarcity of munitions in general, and too many "guns which exploded after firing a few rounds." There was a complete lack of equipment for engineers, including even such simple items as wire clippers. A shortage of machine guns was so acute that only half the regiments which ought to have had them did in fact have them in working order. There were only 70 aeroplanes in serviceable condition, and "the shortage of officers was so grave that many companies had only two officers, and whole battalions were commanded effectively by non-commissioned officers" (General Segato).

But few Germans or Austrians were disposed to believe that the Italian Armed Forces were so badly equipped. Their first naval and military campaigns were extraordinarily successful, largely because to the last the Austrians had refused to credit their own Intelligence, which had told them of the growth of "interventionism" and the inevitability of war. Italian industry set to work to fill the gaps in the equipment logs. Workshops and shipyards stayed open around the clock. The brilliance of Italian improvisation made shortages appear to be less, though none the less damaging. Volunteers flocked to the recruiting stations, after first parading through the streets. A semi-official history of Italy notes that: "Women did not show less enthusiasm than men. Women, even if in part they were not moved by a spirit of patriotism but by one of vanity or lechery, without distinction of age or class, hurried to lend their work of pity and patriotism at the stations, on the trains, in welfare committees, in hospitals in the rear and in the front line."

Mussolini's enthusiasm for the war he had in part provoked has been much debated. His adulatory biographers, and the encyclopaedias published during the Fascist era, write of him always as a volunteer. After the war he was nominated president of the Association of Volunteers. However, he did not rejoin his regiment, the Bersaglieri, until August 31st, three months after the declaration of war. Mussolini himself says that he went straight to volunteer, but was told that he could not as a reservist and would have to wait until he was called up "like all my category." It may well be that instructions had been given to the military authorities to keep him out of uniform, for fear of letting him see how acute were shortages of materials and munitions. It could be that Mussolini came to some sort of agreement with his former enemies to remain at the *Popolo d'Italia* and keep the flame of patriotism burning brightly throughout the summer months. It could be that the local military commander, who commented to his brother officers that he did not like the idea of being given work to do by a Red ignoramus, refused to allow Mussolini the distinction of being an early volunteer. Whatever the reason, Mussolini stayed on in Milan while his close friends and collaborators, Marinetti the Futurist and Corridoni the wild, renegade syndicalist, set off for the front line. The official Socialist Party, which remained neutrâlist, attacked Mussolini without pause in its newspapers, as was to be expected. *La Giustizia* reported that "one of the reasons why the *Popolo's* editor has not joined up is that he is afraid of reprisals by his former comrades already in the trenches." *Avanti* was even ruder. Mussolini, in his turn, attacked his detractors as vigorously as he attacked the Austrians. Of one, he wrote: "Zibordi is a worm. Harmless but repellent." Of another: "When the time comes, I know where I will be, but who knows what will become of such a stomach?"

On August 22, 1915, the government published a "summary of progress." It claimed that the Austrian Army was in retreat along the whole front. It denied the Austrian claim that 300,000 Italians were already *hors de combat*, and claimed that 18,000 Austrian prisoners had been taken. It concluded that the offensive continued "in spite of great difficulties." The difficulties were immense, not through any merit of the Austrian Army, but because of the continuing shortages of artillery and munitions which made any Italian advance almost impossible to consolidate. The Austrian claim that 300,000 Italians were out of action was not based on any estimate of killed, wounded or prisoners, but rather on a fair estimate of the number of Italian soldiers who could not be brought up to the front line, for lack of arms and ammunition, or who were immobile in the front line for the same reason.

On August 24th, Mussolini wrote Senator Barzilai, asking to be called up immediately. He was told again to wait until "the hour is assigned to you." On August 31st the call-up notice arrived, and Mussolini said good-bye to his colleagues at *il Popolo*. "Keep watch!" he ordered them. "Keep picking away and give no truce to the cowards at home."

On September 2nd he was already in the front line in Alto Isonzo. By September 18th he was in a forward trench being heavily shelled. In his war diary, cabled back to the *Popolo* from the front line and published daily, he commented on the every-day life of the ordinary soldier as he himself lived it.[8] From time to time he burst into heroics ("While I am writing the guns are sounding. In a few hours I shall be within a few feet of the enemy"), but for the most part he was, as even his enemies and political opponents agreed, "a disciplined, willing soldier with the simple enthusiasm of a student"[9] On occasion he was seen to behave with what might be described as "sentimentality," as when he ceremoniously drank the waters of the Isonzo as he crossed it, but these events he never chronicled, and they must be presumed the natural expression of an excess of enthusiasm from which he was never free. His officers found him adequate in all respects, and were intrigued to have him under their command. He went to dine in their messes quite often, but refused to be considered as an officer cadet. When a group of Alpini officers insisted on having their photograph taken with him, he struck an almost comic pose, with a grenade in his hand, the image of disrespect. He steadfastly refused to abandon the front line, even when invited by a general to become an official war historian. He was eventually promoted to lance corporal, "for his exemplary conduct, *bersaglieresque* spirit and serenity; first always in every aspect of work or daring; zealous and scrupulous in the discharge of his duties."

His fellow rankers liked Mussolini too. They considered him an amiable eccentric in many respects (he read poetry to them), but treated him with the respect the ranker always gives to the "gentleman." They had nothing to grumble at in his conduct, and he was always the first over the top of the trench, shouting verse intermingled with *Viva l'Italia.* They responded to his commands and once went to him in a delegation (when their officers had been killed) and asked him to take over their company.

Mussolini's enemies, however, did not let him stew in the mud in peace. His former mistress, Ida Delser, liberated from Trent, made a continual nuisance of herself at his home. His political opponents denigrated him in the press and even passed the word through the trenches that Mussolini was not a man to be trusted. One Socialist Party organizer saw to it that he always received the news of the death of his friends without delay and as brusquely as possible. Another sent a letter to one of his fellow Bersaglieri, which urged the man "to do me a personal favour, and a service to all our comrades, if you find the opportunity to kill the traitor."

At the beginning of December Mussolini was given a few days' leave. He went home and married Rachele, to her surprise, in a civil ceremony at the town hall. He went around to see his friends and colleagues, and found that the martial spirit he believed he had inculcated into all his readers was flagging. Enthusiasm for the war seemed to be diminishing, except among the profiteers. He was prompted to write a long article in *il Popolo d'Italia* (December 27, 1915) in which he commented:

> There are three sorts of Italians who can and do exercise a weakening influence, and a depressing influence on the morale of the Nation at war and these are: the alarmists, the unsatisfiable, and the zealots, who are more or less disinterested in metaphysical peace. About the first sort, it is not worth writing much; they never wanted the war, they "put up with" Italy's decision in May, hardly concealing their contempt and anger; they are for the most part "oblique men," a great many of them tied to Germany via the Marquis of Bulow, and they take their miserable revenge by diffusing rumours about huge and catastrophic losses by us. It is not difficult to get rid of these evil geniuses. We must start by expelling all the genuine Germans and false Swiss . . . and making an example of one of the alarmists. Next come . . . the unsatisfiable people. We must distinguish between those in bad faith

> who pretend to be dissatisfied with the war effort to render another service to *invincible* Germany. Their pessimism is political. And then there are those who . . . when we have occupied Trieste will complain because we have not occupied Vienna. The last category is more numerous but less dangerous . . . and consists of all those who, favourable in May, or still favourable to the idea of the war, start to be assailed by doubts . . . find that things are going slow . . .

Mussolini wound up his article by pointing out that the Italian army was the only one which had made considerable advances into enemy territory during 1915. He paid tribute to the "fierce resolution" of his fellow soldiers, and reproved all "waverers" for their doubts: "Today only strong and virile thoughts have a right to be expressed."

Mussolini went back into the line for the rest of the winter. By all accounts he was anything but pessimistic, in spite of the cold, the mud and the slush. If his superiors had any reason to reprove him, it was for his "excess of martial spirit." One evening he was guard commander in the trenches when he saw two cigarettes glowing in the Austrian trench opposite. Without hesitation he lobbed over a grenade and killed five men, so a prisoner reported the next day. His company commander reproved him for unnecessary cruelty ("They might have been talking of home, of their sweethearts"), to which Mussolini replied that if they took that attitude to war they might as well all go home, or for a walk under the Milan arcades. Mussolini's fanatical dedication to the war as a "national enterprise" parallels that of Hitler—" . . . never grumbled . . . the impassioned warrior, deadly serious at all times about the war's aims." Corporal Hitler and Corporal Mussolini had a lot in common.

The Holy See had still not made up its mind about the war. The Pope, Benedict XV, sent out a message welcoming 1916, in the hope that it would bring peace. The loyalties of the Curia Cardinals were divided between the belligerents. There were a number of French cardinals who suggested in their prayers that Divine Right was on the side of the Allies. They were, however, in a minority. Serbia and Russia, France's allies, were both Orthodox countries, and Britain, of course, even worse, was Protestant. On the other hand, Austria was a fervently Catholic country, and Germany had a substantial and powerful Catholic population, represented in the Vatican by numerous German and Austrian cardinals and monsignors. For most of 1915 the Curia wrangled with the government, backstairs and in the columns of *Osservatore Romano*, accusing the laity of having put pressure on the German and Austrian ambassadors to the Holy See to abandon their posts. The Vatican Secretary of State went straight to the point, and in negotiations with the government, conducted through General Porro, suggested that in return for spiritual comfort the government might see its way to modify the Law of Guarantees in the Vatican's favour, guarantee the independence of Vatican City as a separate state—together with a strip of land running from Rome to the sea—remove any jurisdiction Italian courts still had over Vatican territory, and return substantial lands and buildings to the Church's temporal care. The Italian Government did not respond favourably to what it called "spiritual blackmail," and retaliated by refusing to constitute a chaplain's corps in which ordained priests could serve. It was only with some regret that it later recognized the Vatican's chaplains corps and allotted the rank of major-general to its commandant, Bartolomasi. The government, largely liberal and anticlerical, obliged many priests to serve in the ranks of infantry regiments, or stay at home and point the obvious moral (Roncalli, the future Pope John XXIII, was a sergeant in the infantry, then in the medical corps).

Pope Benedict XV himself did not take part in any of the bargaining, but contented himself with references to it and his "faith" in the satisfactory outcome. He interested himself personally in the humane services which traced missing soldiers, helped the families of the killed and wounded, and supervised the women at work behind the lines. His only "grievance," he said, was that his letters were censored, as if he were the inmate of a reformatory or prison.

The directorate and executive of the official Socialist Party saw in the New Year as disgruntled as the Holy See. A number of students were beaten up in Florence for demonstrating in favour of the war. An Order of the Day went out "from the executive of the official Socialist Party, to underline the true nature of the present struggle," which made it an offence punishable by expulsion to attend military funerals or render the honours of war to fallen comrades. Anti-war demonstrations, and an incapacity to understand that Italy had closed its ranks and forgotten that its ephemeral parties existed, rapidly decimated the party.

Mussolini reproved both the Socialists and the Holy See for pacifism, and on occasion was unbearably righteous in his editorials. He replied to the pacifist Socialist executive by addressing his war dispatches to them and hoping they were well. He also attacked the Vatican indirectly in his war dispatches to *il Popolo d'Italia*, referring to priests who visited the front line as "almost a refreshing change," implying that there were few ready to take risks to comfort the dying. In one famous dispatch (February 20, 1916) he wrote: "The habit of wearing religious medallions is on the decline. When we first came out there were holy relics and sacred images everywhere. Soldiers carried them hanging around their necks, on their wrists, on their hats, on their fingers set into rings. Not any more. Experience in the front line has taught them that one lucky charm is as good as another . . . the latest in 'luck-bringers' is the habit of touching the stars on our badges or carrying about this cabalistic epigraph:

B I P Z1 R 16
C CH Z1 P S S

"Thousands of soldiers up here got hold of this epigraph on their way through the valley of the Natisone, but neither they nor I seem capable of deciphering it."

On March 2nd Mussolini came due for some leave. He was promoted to full corporal, sewed on his stripes, and set off to make trouble in Milan and see his family. His family had in fact grown, by a son Vittorio.

The government had managed to reorganize the economy in part on a war footing, but lacked information about how and when munitions and other war material reached the front line. The Finance Minister realized that almost every enterprise producing under government contract was filing false returns, in order to avoid taxation, increase profits, and make the best of the war. His colleagues told him he ought to be grateful that arms and ammunition were being manufactured and were reaching the armed forces at all. At a Cabinet meeting on March 4th it was decided that it was better not to inquire too closely into what was going on inside the war economy, but to keep the government's fingers crossed and hope all would be well. In fact, as a number of Socialists pointed out in the sitting on March 7th, the government did not even have reliable statistics on how many men it had under arms, much less where their guns had come from. The only way the government could avoid a debate which would have exposed the extent of their ignorance was to make the vote of the day one of confidence. The voting was 251 in favour, 25 against. Mussolini commented that the only reason why the vote had "shown such apparent approval of the government's policy" was that no one else had dared to take over the confusion which passes for the wartime administration. He added that it seemed to him to be an admirable thing under the circumstances for Salandra and his colleagues to remain ignorant, so that in the eventuality of the country going bankrupt they would remain ignorant of that, too, and continue to endorse the "heroic activity of the defenders of Italy's honour." On the visit of French Prime Minister Briand to Rome, Mussolini observed that it was a good thing he did not speak Italian, otherwise the government would have undermined his morale.

On March 31st Lord Asquith arrived in Rome. Mussolini was back up in the line and did not notice his arrival. Asquith soon left the governmental chaos in Rome, however, and went to inspect the Austrian front, not far from where Mussolini lay with his Bersaglieri. Asquith was impressed by the morale and discipline of the troops, and commented: "Without doubt it is the most difficult of all the fronts in this war. It is impossible to conceive the extent of the difficulties without seeing with one's own eyes. What you Italians are doing here is marvellous, marvellous, marvellous." He also commented that he had never seen so many incompetent generals and politicians sitting on the backs of so many brisk and business-like soldiers. Three days later General Zuppelli, the Minister of War, resigned.

The war went on in two phases. There was the perpetual struggle for a hundred yards of no man's land in the trenches. And there were the few "exploits," the acts of visible heroism which earned the medals and the congratulations of newspaper editors. Mussolini lived out the dull war in the trenches. D'Annunzio lived it out risking his neck in "demonstration flights over enemy territory and by recruiting a sort of private commando, the *arditi* ("the children chosen by death"). The activity of the Air Force and of the *arditi* was much more newsworthy than warlike, as Mussolini pointed out, with barely concealed jealousy, to his friends.

The record of the larger Austrian Air Force chronicled by the Italian Government gives some idea of the "danger and effectiveness" of the aeroplane in those days: "The Austrian Air Force made on an average ten sorties a month with one or two aeroplanes each time. On January 1, 1916, a bomb was dropped in Valsugana, killing nobody and doing no damage; on the 5th the same in Val Lagarina, Val Gogna and Alto Isonzo (narrowly missing Mussolini); on the 6th again over Alto Isonzo; and on the 12th a bomb in the middle of a flat, uninhabited plain; on the 13th a bomb was dropped in the sea off Rimini, the aeroplane being shot down by our artillery; on the 17th a person was killed by a bomb on Ancona;

on the 19th, 21st and 22nd bombs were dropped on Udine, Dogna and Valsugana, doing no damage; on the 26th a bomb was dropped in a lake."

A report filed by Mussolini in the same month (April, 1916): "After the heavy shelling of yesterday, we changed the guard in the forward positions before dawn. I woke at three. A grey morning. My dugout, No. 8, was the worst hit by enemy artillery. . . . Nine hours of snow. The hooded capes reissued to our troops give the place the look of a polar landscape. . . . Cold. Silence, melancholy. . . ." A note of optimism, and a clue to a future ambition in this particular report: "This war is really mixing up Italians. Regionalism is finished. In my squad Reali is from Milan, Balisti from Mantova, Tonini from Piacenza, Melosi from Lucca. . . ."

Marshal Conrad von Hotzendorf, the Chief of the Austrian General Staff, was, he said, "extremely angry and disappointed that we have not, in a year, already liquidated the Italian forces." On May 4th he launched what he called a "Strafe-expedition" against the whole of the Trentino Front, with 300 battalions of infantry and 2,000 pieces of artillery, some of them battle hardened in Russia and in the Balkans. His military ability was reinforced by a personal hatred for Italians which stemmed from an unfortunate affair he had had with an opera star touring the Empire.

The Italian generals facing him along the front had only 172 battalions and a handful of effective pieces of artillery; the infantry was still not perfectly equipped with rifles (many units had carbines tried out in Africa thirty years before), though its clothing was now adequate. The Austrian offensive pushed back the line, and it soon became obvious that their advance would continue to a line along the Po-Adige valleys, the nearest natural defensive position. The population of Milan, which swore it could hear shellfire, organized protest marches and demonstrations in the streets against General Cadorna, the Italian Commander-in-Chief. Prime Minister Salandra reacted immediately by suggesting to the King that Cadorna be relieved and made a duke. Salandra knew well enough that practically all of his most urgently needed supplies came from the Milan area, the population of which was quite capable of temporarily sabotaging the war effort to reinforce its demands for the dismissal of Cadorna. The King, however, and those of the ministers not from the north of Italy, opposed the "transfer of the Generalissimo." On June 5th the Italian Parliament reopened to the shout of a Socialist member, Ferri: "Honour a brave people, now paying for so much negligence!" Salandra immediately availed himself of the opportunity, taking a vote of confidence, which he won by 414 votes to 45. In a debate on June 10th, 1916, however, Salandra was apologetic about the fact that "after a year of fighting the war outside our frontiers, the enemy is now inside our territory . . ." and had to admit, in answer to Socialist questions, that: "Had our positions in Trent been better prepared, the enemy could have been held for longer." Salandra confided in a friend next day that he had "deliberately provoked the crisis" to force the Chamber to choose between him and Cadorna. Whether or not this was true, the Roman mob was certainly vociferous next day, shouting: "Down with the generals! Away with Salandra! Away with Cadorna!"[10]

On June 12th, defeated in a motion of confidence by 197 to 158 votes, Salandra resigned, and Cadorna soldiered on.

On June 16th Cadorna was urged by the King to launch a counter-attack, and the same day confirmed in office the first "national government, under the leadership of Paolo Boselli." Both the counter-attack and the national government enjoyed an early success, in spite of criticism of Cadorna by Salandra ("an extra parliamentary failure"), and of the government by the Socialists ("the government of Vegetable Soup, Minestrone Ministeriale"). In the first weeks of August the Duke of Aosta (Cadorna was sick with a bad liver) launched a series of successful attacks, capturing the city of Gorizia and a large amount of war material (18,758 prisoners, 30 heavy and 63 light pieces of artillery, 92 machine guns, 12,225 rifles, 5,000,000 bullets, 60,000 grenades, on the 14th and 15th of August alone). These successes were all the more remarkable because a great deal of the preparatory fighting and mopping up was done at an altitude of over 10,000 feet.

The Italian Navy's summer activities were not so successful. The *Orellana*, *Roberto*, *Ginestra*, *Cormillano*, *Principe Umberto*, *Erminia*, *Serpente*, *Dolmetta*, *Audace*, *Pviga*, *Mongibello*, *Pino*, *Roma*, *Città di Messina*, *Impetuoso*, *Balilla*, *Pullino*, *Letimbro*, *Angelo*, *Sirra*, *Siena*, *Sebastiano*, *Ida*, *San Guiseppe*, *Patriarca* and *Leonardo da Vinci* were all sunk. It was never quite clear whether these losses were the consequence of heroically fought actions at sea or of sabotage. Certainly the cruiser *Leonardo da Vinci* was found to have been "sunk from the inside" by "paid agents of the enemy" (with the loss of 20 officers and 237 men). It was widely believed at the time that a group of shipbuilders had organized the sinking of Italian ships, receiving in return not only cash prizes, but also profitable contracts for building other, larger ships as replacements. The prize money, it was said, came from Germany. This did not improve relations with Germany, with whom Italy was not yet formally at war. Profiting from this and promising unrestricted supplies of coal, the British Government urged the Italian Government to declare war on Germany, too, thus "formalizing an already existing situation." On August 27, 1916, the formal declaration was made.

The last four months of 1916 saw the arrival of a considerable quantity of coal at Italian ports, the dispatch of Italian troops to France, and the continued success of an Italian land offensive on all fronts. The nation's morale rose. The eighty-year-old Prime Minister made a number of tours of the country, launching new ships and new loans. On October 8th, at La Scala in Milan, Boselli said he had had a vision of "the fatherland, girdled with new glory, rising to new heights of Italian virtue." Attempts by the German Government—especially after the death on November 21st of the Austrian Emperor—to make peace with Italy alone were treated with "heroic contempt." Throughout November Boselli reinforced his appeals for greater patriotism with promises of pensions for the widows and orphans of the war dead, and better post-war conditions for the lower paid and neglected, especially the peasants. On December 5th Parliament reopened and the Socialists demanded that Italy should take the lead in trying to negotiate a peace. On December 12th the German Chancellor sent a note to the principal neutrals, urging them to "use their good offices" for peace. The Italian Socialists were immediately accused by the Nationalists of being in the pay of the Chancellor. On the 18th this was debated in all seriousness, the Socialists absolved of the charge, and a peace motion of theirs also discussed, voted on and rejected. On December 22nd both the Lower House and the Senate reaffirmed their intention to "pursue the war to its logical conclusion," then went off on holiday.

On December 24th the Pope made an appeal for peace, and was immediately suspected of Germanophilia, as his Socialist enemies had been a fortnight before.[11] Mussolini accused him of "undermining the war effort" and of using underhand means to sap the morale of troops in the front line. According to Mussolini, where the Pope was not trying to stop the war altogether in the interests of Germany and Austria, he was trying to make ecclesiastical capital out of it by preying on the front-line soldier's fear of death, to win recruits for "his extinct creed." "Peace or war," Mussolini wrote, "the Pope intends to be the last man on the battlefield to fill his pockets with the booty." On December 30th Mussolini wrote in his war diary for *il Popolo*:

Father Michele came through the trenches, handing out tricolour badges and pamphlets. I took a badge and had a look at the pamphlet. It was about "the solemn consecration of the soldiers of the Royal Italian Army to the Sacred Heart of Jesus." I do not comment, I transcribe. Inside the pamphlet there was an "instruction" which said: "Devotion to the Sacred Heart of Jesus is the great hope of our time. We can get anything and everything through faith and love for the Heart of Jesus. He himself, appearing to the Blessed Margherita Maria in France, has said: 'You will not lack help for as long as I have power.' Look at the French in the Battle of the Marne. All seemed lost, when General Castelnau had the inspiration to invoke the Sacred Heart and consecrate the Army to it. And the result was the marvellous victory which saved France. We all want victory—double victory, one over our political enemies for the greatness of the fatherland, the other over ourselves to purify and elevate us...." Then came a prayer. I repeat: I do not comment. I transcribe, I copy . . .

Next day Mussolini was annoyed by a "priest with a squeaky voice" who came to celebrate Mass. He was just haranguing a friend about the "tragic mistake" of the government in changing its mind about compelling priests to serve as rankers and recruiting them as chaplains, when a huge shell dropped at his feet, but failed to go off. Mussolini commented: "Tonight we leave this position. The Austrians have made something of the end of the year for me."

Parliament, still on holiday, was reported to be hurrying back to debate a series of notes from neutrals, urging an end to the war. Mussolini, in his paper, commented that a soldier returning from leave had told him that Italy had become "a brothel, full of old men and women talking about peace." He noted, on January 30th, that, like its predecessors, it was a government of national impotence. Promoted to lance-sergeant (*caporale maggiore*), he lost interest in government for a month while he trained on a new type of grenade-thrower. He was given this to experiment with in the front line ("I put out many cigarettes and smokers"), then pulled back to teach a squad how to use it. On February 23rd, with a lieutenant in command, he took out a squad, two boxes of grenades and the thrower, and started a demonstration. It went on lazily all morning, a long way back from the line. After two hours of continuous firing, at about one o'clock, Mussolini asked permission to fall the men out for lunch. The barrel of the thrower was red hot, anyway. The lieutenant looked in the box and saw two more grenades left. "Better finish these off," he said, "then we won't have to take them back." Mussolini saluted and popped a grenade in the barrel. The thrower exploded. Five of the soldiers in the squad were wounded.

Mussolini was thrown five yards, then landed on his back, with blood streaming from his legs and shoulder. The six men were hurriedly put on stretchers and rushed down to the field hospital at Busto Arsizio, after a first dressing at the ambulance station at Doberdo. Mussolini wrote later: "I have seen tragedy. . . . Next to me a dying man was shouting 'Give me red carnations. . . .'"[12]

The news of Mussolini's field accident quickly spread throughout Italy. The enormous circulation of *il Popolo d'Italia*, the "pioneer war paper," and of Mussolini's war diary in it, had made him as well known as the legendary D'Annunzio, the competent Duke of Aosta, the liverish Cadorna and old Boselli. His old enemies in the Socialist Party, who had tried to convince the diminishing readership of *Avanti* that their former comrade, the traitor Mussolini, was in fact having a cushy time in the rear, immediately changed their tactics and admitted that he had been in the front line, but was now "dying if not already dead, a fate such a man deserves."

The dying man himself sent a message to *il Popolo* the day after the accident, saying that he was happy to have reddened with his blood the road to Trieste. His assistant Giuliani went to see him on March 1st, and wrote:

> . . . At the entrance to the hospital . . . I was stopped. A non-commissioned officer had precise orders . . . "The doctors have forbidden visitors. He has a temperature of 40 C, this evening. He wants to be left in peace." I told him who I was . . . I asked to speak to the Director of the Hospital . . . the officer understood . . . Two minutes later I was near him . . . I did not know how to start . . . "How are you?" "I'm all right, I'll soon get better." I made him talk too much, realized this . . . I persuaded him to stay silent while I plunged my hand into an enormous pile of get-well telegrams and letters on his bedside table, from the aristocracy to the most humble worker. The minister Commandini had wired: "I am moved by your glorious baptism which has strengthened you. I send you my best wishes for a speedy complete recovery." . . . But to look through all the letters was impossible . . .

On March 7th the King visited the hospital. Garinei of *il Seccolo* was following the King around and sent back this dispatch to his paper:

> The King asked the Director of the Hospital if he could see Benito Mussolini and the others of his squad with him. A few minutes later he walked into the ward where Mussolini had been taken after the most agonizing of his daily activities, his daily medication. Mussolini was exhausted, the medication having been perhaps even more painful than usual. Mussolini recognized the King, who walked straight over to him.

The King asked: "How are you, Mussolini?"

"Not too well, Your Majesty."

Captain Piccagnoni, interrogated by the King, added precise details of his condition. The King listened, watching the face of the wounded man.

"You must have a bad time, even a strong man like you, immobile and in pain."

"One must be patient, Your Majesty."

After a brief conversation the King continued: "The other day, at Debeli, General M . . . spoke very well of you . . . Bravo, Mussolini."

By the middle of April Mussolini had partially recovered, though he still had to hobble about on crutches. Photographs of him in hospital and in convalescence were widely circulated by *il Popolo d'Italia*. He was lodged at a Red Cross convalescent home in Milan, from which he started to edit the paper again. He had plenty of targets. In spite of his prognostication (April 18, 1917) that the war would last only a few months more, he was determined to have it fought at fever pitch right to the end. The neutralism of the Church remained unaltered, though it manifested itself in both Italy and Austria in various patriotic guises. Mussolini had hoped that Socialism, his other enemy, had shot its last bolt and would bother him no more. He had seen the sales of *Avanti* drop. He had talked to Socialists in the line and confirmed his suspicion that most of them supported the war in principle, even though they would like to see it end as soon as possible. What Mussolini, the former revolutionary, had not foreseen was the second Russian Revolution of March 1917, its success, and the pressure brought by the Russian Social Democrats on their government to conclude an armistice. As 1917 wore on there was no doubting the success of the revolution, even though it seemed as yet undecided who would lead it when the fighting was over, Lenin or Kerensky. Socialists in Italy took heart and began to preach revolution and armistice in their turn. They concentrated on armistice and appealed to the bellies of Italians who grumbled at rationing (introduced in the first months of 1917), rather than to minds formed by Marx and Engels. Mussolini put his heart into combating the "revolutionary undoing of the country." On July 12, 1917, in *il Popolo d'Italia*, he wrote: "Christianity, which has seen in this war the failure of the evangelical precept of brotherhood of man, has not given to the world a single one of its followers who had the courage to make a gesture of negation and revolt. Socialism less still. These ideas have not provoked any sacrifice. No Christian and no Socialist has gone to his death in the name of Christianity or Socialism. A spectacular aridity, historical and moral, of Catholic mysticism and dogmatized historical materialism. . . . It is the Idea of the Fatherland which has had soldiers and martyrs, its consecration of blood and its glory. . . ."

On September 3rd, as rumours spread that the Army's morale was low and that part of the civil population was on the point of revolt, he wrote: "What does it matter if we have thousands of guns and machine-guns, if side by side with this increased efficiency of the instruments of war we see a spiritual deficiency in the souls of the people? The Order of the Day must be: this winter no more trenches. The Germans, before the winter, will do all they can to weaken the Allied nations, provoking as much opposition and discord as they can."

The words were prophetic. A few days later German and Austrian troops began a build-up of arms and ammunition for a big push to the south. The aim was to knock Italy out of the war once and for all, then attack with everything left on the Western Front (negotiations had already begun with the Russians for a separate peace in the east).

It was well known to the Austrians that the spring offensive had left the Italian Army weakened, and they knew all about the moral impact of the Russian Revolution. The Austrian press had commented at length on the "disturbances" in the northern cities of Italy, where most of the war material was either manufactured or made fit for use. In August there were Socialist-inspired riots in Turin, food shops were sacked, and effigies of the Prime Minister burned. Mussolini went to Turin, after order was restored, and toured the city with a table on his head, stopping to climb on to it to make speeches whenever he saw a likely audience. The Austrian High Command could not believe its luck when General Cadorna, back in action again, decided to launch yet another offensive, in August, with an exhausted army, a discontented civil population, and no guarantee that the Left would not take over the source of his supplies. Bearing these factors in mind, the Austrian High Command convinced the German High Command that it would be worth while pulling troops out of Germany, off the Western Front, and to concentrate on liquidating the Italian Army as soon as its offensive slackened.

On October 24th the Minister of War reported to the Chamber that he had information that a big enemy concentration was being prepared. He was one of the last men in Italy to hear of it, as a number of Nationalist members pointed out. The Italian offensive ground slowly to a halt, and Austro-German troops began pushing back along the whole north-eastern front. The minister said, in spite of sabotage at home, the blowing up of ammunition dumps and the derailing of trains: "Let the attack come, we are not afraid of it."

The attack came a few hours later. The Battle of Caporetto was the biggest military disaster in the long series of disasters contrived by governments since the reunification of Italy. It was caused, according to Pini, by a mixture of tactical errors, poor leadership and battle weariness. Certainly the men in the line were tired. Many of them had been fighting more or less continuously for months, while other regiments had spent uninterrupted months in the rear (their commanding officers used to arrange these dispositions by bribing the planning officers—the richer the commander, the easier a time his men had). However, the injustice of authority, especially of military authority, was nothing new for Italians, who had grown up in the belief that without a bribe or a "recommendation" it was impossible to get anything done. Possibly the incompetence of the Supreme Command and interchief jealousies were equally responsible for the scale of the disaster. Cadorna quarrelled with General Capello, and Capello intrigued in turn with General Porro, the deputy chief of General Staff. General Cavachiocchi, Commander of the IV Army Corps, privately opined that Cadorna was an idiot, when, having been asked if he had sufficient men, he replied No, and was then told that Cadorna did not think there would be an offensive at all (meeting of Cadorna and Cavachiocchi, October 22nd).

General Segato commented that:

> The causes of the disaster were primarily of a technical character, and during the re-formation of the line the consequences of military errors were aggrandized by the organic and morale condition in which the armies found themselves on the eve of the battle. But the responsibility for the rout is not limited to military chiefs and politicians; it involves all those whose passive or active defeatism exercised a depressing influence on our soldiers; it involves all those who, having succeeded in avoiding military service, made as much profit as they could out of their reserved occupations; it involves all those who had nothing else to offer to the soldier on leave but a nauseating spectacle of waste and self-pleasuring.

The magnitude of the disaster of Caporetto and the subsequent rout captured the imagination of many people, from Mussolini to Ernest Hemingway. In the spirit of Hemingway, on his way to prepare *Farewell to Arms*, Mussolini addressed his readers, calling for a "unity of spirit." In the paper, on October 28, 1917, he wrote: "We bear in silence the pain and the humiliation. . . . When the house is on fire, though, we do not worry too much, for the moment, how it caught fire. When the Fatherland calls its sons to a fight for life or death, a curse on the man who is slow to respond. . . . Today the Nation must be the Army, just as the Army is the Nation."

But Mussolini did worry about who had started the fire. He began a campaign in his own paper, and in the whole chain of newspapers which now followed his lead, to avenge the "pain and humiliation." The government had to go, and the government went. On October 30th Orlando became Prime Minister, not a man approved of by Mussolini ("Your policy is that of a waverer"), but at least younger than the senile Boselli.

The retreat went on. Excuses began to multiply. On November 10th the King, in a proclamation, said: "The enemy has been favoured by an extraordinary combination of circumstances." Cadorna maintained that there had been some errors. Cadorna had to go, and Cadorna went, his place being taken by General Diaz.

Mussolini attacked the Ministry of the Interior and urged stronger measures against Socialist saboteurs, though he commented that the "Austro-German-Tartar coup has failed. The enemy hoped for much help from Italians themselves, but Italy is not Russia." On November 2nd even Mussolini made excuses:

> Well, so there was a moment of weakness and shame. But this happens to all peoples, at all times—it even happened occasionally to Roman Legions, who have been recorded as breaking up when they saw a flock of unlucky birds in the sky . . . but our soldier will be again tomorrow what he was yesterday. . . . Before the Austrian offensive, the third winter was our greatest worry. Who thinks of this today? Yesterday's questions were: "Will there be coal?" "Will there be bread?" "Will there be wood?" Today our citizens demand: "Will there be sufficient iron—grenade cases and bayonets—to exterminate the maximum number of Huns?"

On November 9th Mussolini urged his citizens to show more "discipline." There were still, it seemed, a large number of them worried more about coal, bread and wood than about exterminating Huns.

The retreat went on. The government, which had hoped that with the coming of the cold weather in December the Austro-German armies would lay up for the winter, found that it was to be disappointed. Britain and France, fearful of a separate peace treaty which would leave them alone against the Central Powers (notwithstanding the late entry of the United States into the war), urged the Italian Government to take urgent measures to raise the morale of its civil and military populations. When the Orlando government confessed that, though it was doing its best, it had to deal with "a number of insoluble problems"—the Church, as bitterly opposed to the war as the Socialists, the combined Left threatening revolution, a routed army, and a profiteering industry—the British and French governments insisted that they be allowed to send troops of their own to stiffen up the Italian north-east front. Orlando was forced to agree. On December 5, 1917, French troops took over from Italians in the zone of Monte Tomba. A day later British troops flanked them to the left and right. General Diaz proclaimed: "Once again we face the future with decisiveness, a future which will take us to victory side by side with the magnificent army that the inflexible will of the British people has known how to create . . ."

On December 6th the Austrian advance was halted. The battle blazed into life again all along the front. For the Austro-German armies this was a decisive battle and one which must not be lost, if the plans for a spring offensive in the west were to be fulfilled. Fighting did not even cease on Christmas Day, perhaps a sign that the Christianity of both sides had been suspended for the moment. The year ended with a small victory at Zenson, with Italian troops crossing again over to the left bank of the Piave, from which they had been driven after Caporetto.

British and French intervention on the north-east front did not constitute "taking over the war from the Italians," who remained in the vast majority. As far as the troops in the line were concerned, it represented a boost for morale and a sign that the other powers had not forgotten that there was a war going on along the Piave. But the great impact of Franco-British intervention was on the war profiteers, neutralists and pro-German, pro-Austrian minorities, and on the Socialists, who were seeking an Italian "Brest-Litovsk" (the Soviet Union's peace treaty with Germany) and a revolution to follow. The presence of British and French troops, as Mussolini pointed out, was a guarantee that no Bolshevik "defection" would still further weaken the Allies in the south of Europe; it also guaranteed immobility for the "peacemakers" and discouraged the profiteers from abandoning their factories. In Parliament a "parliamentary union" of the Left had been formed to promote an armistice.

This was immediately countered by the consolidation of the "fight-on" groups into a *Fascio* for national defence, hailed by Mussolini as "a firm base for the present and a good start for the future."

The year 1918 opened optimistically. Mussolini promised peace within the year; Lloyd George promised peace within the year (January 5th); President Wilson promised peace within the year (January 8th). All three "peacemakers" made conditions which the Germans and Austrians pretended to ignore. The German Chancellor found especially amusing the fourteenth point of Wilson's declaration, that of "an Association of Nations, based on a special convention with the scope of furnishing mutual guarantees of political independence and integrity." Mussolini in his "peace debates" in *il Popolo d'Italia* was critical of his rivals. He had an idea that somehow the British would find a way out of their obligations to Italy signed and sealed into the Treaty of London, Italy's ticket to war. He was as suspicious of America and President Wilson, especially when Wilson's Fourteen Points seemed to show an Anglo-French-American intention to turn the Austro-Hungarian Empire into a patchwork of *independent* states. Mussolini, like every Republican and Socialist politician since Mazzini, was enthusiastic about the break-up of the Austro-Hungarian Empire; it would deprive the Church of one of its strongest allies; it would be a revenge for the centuries of Austrian occupation of Italian-speaking territories; it would emasculate an enemy on the doorstep. However, Mussolini believed and wrote that it was essential that large slices of this empire become Italian, including that non-Italian-speaking part which, in fact, became the Kingdom of Yugoslavia. There was nothing new in Italian claims to Yugoslavia. From 1866 onwards Austria and Italy had always agreed that, should there be a "re-distribution" of Yugoslavia, it would be made with the participation of both countries, and it had been understood since 1872 that Italy would take Dalmatia (and most of Catholic Croatia), including Albania, and Montenegro, where the Queen came from. Wilson's speech seemed to deny Italy her "due." Mussolini found himself in agreement with Italian Foreign Minister Sonnino in his anger at the thought of the British, French and Americans plotting a betrayal. There was only one difference between Sonnino (an old man mentally alive in 1872) and the young Mussolini. Sonnino wanted to negotiate for Italy's territorial aggrandizement with a post-war Austrian government. Mussolini recommended Italy's walking into Dalmatia and helping herself.

Mussolini found out that talks had been going on in London

between the leaders of the projected Yugoslav State, the British, and some Italian politicians led by General Mola. Mola, Mussolini "revealed," did not believe it necessary to negotiate with the Austrians, but was against helping himself to Dalmatia; he proposed to negotiate with the "successor state" to Austria, the Yugoslav Government in exile. Mola, so Mussolini's informants told him, was "ready to concede independence as the right of the Yugoslav State," when the war was over, reserving for Italian annexation only the predominantly Italian-speaking areas. The *Popolo d'Italia* began to publish alarmist articles, prophesying that "Italy's enemies at home and abroad were conspiring to sell the peace."

The frenzied diplomatic activity which went on throughout the first months of 1918, with the prospective victors dividing up the booty before the Austrians and Germans had been vanquished, involved trips abroad by most of the Italian Government, including the Prime Minister. Every time one of the government returned from Paris, London or elsewhere, Mussolini gloomily prophesied that the return meant that yet another of Italy's "inalienable rights" had been sold for coal or cash. In fact, Mussolini under-estimated the Prime Minister, who, though less violent, was as determined as the editor of *il Popolo d'Italia* to see that Italy received at least no less than she had been promised as victor, in the Treaty of London. He told Lloyd George, on January 31, 1918, that he would on no account vary the treaty, and Clemenceau and Lloyd George were forced to assure him, in writing, that no such idea had ever entered their heads. A week later Lloyd George was in consultation with the Yugoslav Nationalists, discussing the new "state" with the Italophobe Croat Trumbic. The sessions of the Italian Parliament during February and early March 1918 were lively with debates about the future political status of the subject states of the Austro-Hungarian Empire. The Left denounced the Treaty of London as "imperialist." The Right denounced it as "weak." But when, on March 7th, the British press (including the *Manchester Guardian*, per Sir Arthur Evans) announced that it had already been agreed with the Italian Government that "all the suffering people under the Hapsburg yoke should be assisted to attain their ideal," both Right and Left denounced the government as unpatriotic. Actually the government had nothing to do with this "agreement" directly, though it had not disowned Barzilai, Ruffini Torre and Amendola, when they had opened negotiations, as the "Society for Relations between Italy and Yugoslavia," with the Yugoslavs in exile. On April 8th the Prime Minister promised doubts in the minds of members would all be resolved at the International Conference of the nations oppressed by Austro-Hungary, in Rome, in which Italy would take part. Members would see that the government's legitimate aspirations in no way conflicted with those of the Yugoslavs.

Mussolini, accredited to the conference, opined that it was a further demonstration of: (1) confusion in the government; (2) the fact that the government did not govern, but allowed policies—present and future—to be made by the pressure groups which maintained it. He addressed himself, in *il Popolo d'Italia*, to the special commando squads (*arditi*) in the Army and urged them to be ready to fight on after the war "in case of betrayal."

The conference dissolved in goodwill. There were no official British or American delegations present, and none of the conference's deliberations affected the British, French or American governments in any way. The fate of Yugoslavia had already been decided. It only remained to find a way to persuade an Italian government of one sort or another to accept it, even if this meant bribery on the grand scale.

Corruption was rife in 1918. It was not confined to normal profiteering, but had extended to involve nearly everyone who made, sold, or bought anything. Lazzari and Bombacci were arrested for suspected trafficking with the enemy. The Società Filatura Cascami di Seta was accused of being a front for the same traffic, and—as directors—Commander Gnecchi and Count Primo Bonacossa were arrested and imprisoned, together with Feltrinelli, Ceresa, Braida (all *commendatori*) and three engineers; in other cities in Lombardy, Piedmont and Liguria, arrests and imprisonment of profiteers and traders with the enemy were a daily occurrence.

During 1918, the last year of the war, some 362,000 people were sentenced to fines or imprisonment for "irregularities"; these figures do not include those who were able to corrupt the magistrates and were never brought to trial.

The war was fought now almost absentmindedly. The army, reorganized after Caporetto, had found itself competent commanders. Training was "rethought," and the first battle schools and assault courses were built. Minor Italian, French and British offensives were mounted during January, February and March, and minor Austrian counter-attacks were repulsed. Several mountains were exchanged four or five times, including the Col del Rosso and Sasso Rosso. In April and May activity on the Italian front intensified, though the German and Austrian high commands, after the check to their advance in December, had abandoned their grand design for a separate peace with a defeated Italy and were concentrating their efforts on the Western Front. On May 10th, *Arditi* took Monte Carno, strengthening the Italian line and making it possible to prepare for an offensive out of range of Austrian artillery. Italian planes, now more numerous, made a large number of sorties and dropped as much as 12,000 pounds of bombs a day. They could not, however, prevent German and Austrian dirigibles from flying more or less where they chose and, on April 29th, sinking thousands of tons of Allied shipping off Sardinia.

On May 24, 1918, Mussolini, who had intensified his own war on "neutralists, defeatists, profiteers and the bourgeoisie at home," made a speech to commemorate the third anniversary of Italy's entry into the war. To a packed Teatro Comunale in Bologna, he said:

> The coming of this war has been life, a jet of pure water for our people . . . We wanted it . . . we chose it . . . a war which was understood intuitively by two sorts of men, poets and industrialists—poets who saw the truth of it and industrialists who realized it would be a mechanized war . . . and between the two let us put journalists, too, who are sufficiently poets not to be industrialists and sufficiently industrious not to be poets . . . until today this war has been quantitative . . . now we must face the problems of quality . . . we young people, as I never tire of repeating, made one great mistake, we put our youth in the hands of old men.[13]

Mussolini's speech in the Socialist mecca was the first in which he suggested that once the war was over the "returned soldier" would have the right to rule; that the days of parliamentary rule by "old men, old in spirit" were over. The speech is also interesting for its description of England, France, Italy and America as "the true, the profound Internationale, the long-lasting one, even if it does not have the formula and dogma of official Socialism." This speech, too, was the first in which he did not attack the Church; it may well be that he had realized, as Hitler realized about this time, that no successful revolutionary party ever did itself any good by attacking an established religion; it may well be that the Church had already made overtures to Mussolini, seeing in him a potentially formidable adversary for Bolshevism.

On June 15th the Austrian armies suddenly launched an offensive under the command of General Boroevitch. It was to be the last offensive, the least successful. The Italian troops along the line of the Piave were now convinced, as Mussolini said, that "one good push and the Austro-Hungarian Empire will topple into the dust." They fought superbly and drove the Austrians steadily back, from June 22nd, with scarcely an interruption, to the last day of hostilities. There was no need for *il Popolo d'Italia* to exhort the troops to "stand firm"; they saw that the quickest way home was via Vienna.

The first Italian victories along the Piave affected the official Socialist Party in an unexpected way. The Executive was having troubles of its own with the extreme left-wing element, which wanted to launch a full-scale revolution the moment the troops returned home. But the executive, knowing its own peculiarly Italian Socialists and the mentality of the troops in the line, had realized that such a full-scale revolution was unlikely. The troops were just as likely to go to Mass the day after they got home, and spend the next few weeks sleeping and drinking, with never a thought of liberating themselves from oppression. Turati, for the executive, opined that the time had come to recoup the losses sustained when the party had declared itself against the war. By allying themselves with the victory, they could make the masses forget their moral responsibility for defeats. In the Chamber (at the sitting which fixed the length of its holidays), Turati made a speech when news of a victory came in: "Our hearts as Socialists beat in unison with men of all parties, while down there on the Piave men are fighting and suffering . . . When facts speak, when the blood flows, when a new Judgment of God comes on the people . . ." Turati was loudly applauded, and the Prime Minister declared that he was a sound man at heart.

Mussolini watched the manoeuvres of the Socialist Party with some alarm. He could not afford to let the party re-establish itself, or he—the heretic—would find himself a forgotten man. Who wants to pay tribute to heroes in time of peace? Who wants to remember the man who started a war, when the war has come to an end? His tours of Italy became more extensive, his appeal to youth and his "fellow soldiers" more exclusive.

Mussolini's fellow soldiers were slowly driving the Austrian Army out of the last Italian-speaking territory. Caporetto was far behind. By October 31st the decisive last battle of the war, that of Vittorio Veneto, had been fought and won. The government, moved perhaps by tact, had refused to publish the findings of the commission of inquiry set up after Caporetto; had refused not only to allot blame but also to reveal the extent of Italian losses in men and materials. Mussolini commented: "The Commission of Inquiry has shed no light on the matter. We must not be surprised. Inquiries in

Italy are made because it is a habit. It is a way of hushing things up. They do not apportion blame, but waft it away." On November 1st Mussolini attacked the government at length for refusing to publish enemy communiqués and casualty bulletins as British and neutral nations did: "A government not only afraid of its own shadow, but of the shadow of the dead." On November 2nd Mussolini forgot his feuds to celebrate the fact that the Austrians had asked for an armistice.

On November 4th a naval division occupied Fiume, which had a few days previously "declared its union with Italy," and on the 17th an army garrison was added. All along the north-eastern front, in Yugoslavia, in North Africa, the Italian Army took up its agreed armistice positions. On November 20th the Prime Minister announced that he was ready for the peace talks, that he was sure Italy would have her just desires fulfilled. But he added that, of course, Fiume had not figured in the Treaty of London, and, like other "liberated" territories, might have to be abandoned. At this he was howled down. Nobody in Italy was in a mood to evacuate anything. Where Italian feet were, there they were to stay.

Throughout November and December demonstrations in every city of the peninsula celebrated the victory. Under the guidance of Nationalists, Mussolini-Socialists and interventionists, the mob let the government know that from now on the word "retreat" would be unacceptable. The Prime Minister was urged to steel himself for hard bargaining with the Allies, to stand firm with his people behind him. "From now on," said Mussolini at a mass meeting in Milan on November 11th, "the Italian people will be the arbiters of their own destiny. We have reached our objectives; the Italian flag flies from the Brenner Pass to Trieste, at Fiume, at Zara."

Mussolini had no clear idea of his plans for the future, other than a determination to consolidate his popularity and turn it, if possible, into political power. He was convinced that, by putting himself at the head of the returned soldiers, he could win pensions for them, and for himself a permanent place in the councils of the nation, ". . . in which the voice of those who have shed their blood must be heard." He was disturbed by the news that Communists and Socialists appeared to be taking over the government in defeated Germany, with the Kaiser gone and other administration non-existent. He did not like the idea of an official Socialist revolution spreading to Italy, though he consoled himself with the thought that the official Socialist Party in Italy was not Leninist.

On January 18, 1919, the Prime Minister went to Paris for the opening of the Peace Conference. It was soon obvious that he was not competent to state Italy's case or refuse to accept compromise. He seemed ready to sacrifice almost all of Italy's territorial gains, even those agreed upon in advance in the Treaty of London. When, on February 11th, there were anti-Italian riots in Croatia and Dalmatia, he agreed to arbitration by President Wilson, which was construed by many Italians as a sign of weakness. The Italian press as a whole attacked the government for its lack of any clear direction at home or abroad. A British newspaper, with a misprint, unwittingly summed up Italian feeling for America in the headline: WELCOME TO PRESIDENT WILSON IN THE NAME OF THE TRADITIONAL LIES (TIES) OF DEMOCRACY.

As the winter of 1919 drew to a close Mussolini took heart from the fact that the succession to power appeared to be an open question. He realized that the first determined group to present some sort of policy statement, some sort of programme, to the masses would be well on the way to gaining their allegiance, if not their immediate support at the polls. With this in mind, he had talks with all the different interventionist groups, Nationalists, Reformist Socialists, his own friends and returned soldiers' representatives, and decided to set up a chain of "watchtowers" from which he could observe the political battlefield and decide upon the tactics to be adopted by those who "refused to see Italy betrayed at the conference table, or the blood of its young men spilled in vain."

On March 20, 1919, at the suggestion of some of his closest friends, Mussolini decided to go further and see if it were not possible to convert his *Fasci*, formed to advocate intervention, into some sort of permanent body which could act as a pressure group locally and nationally, and hold a watching brief for its members and the interests they represented. *Il Popolo d'Italia* acquired a new masthead ORGAN OF COMBATANTS AND PRODUCERS. On March 23, 1919, Mussolini called a delegate congress to a room in Piazza San Sepulcro 3, Milan, to discuss a draft programme for a league of "*Fasci di combattimento*." One hundred and nineteen people turned up. There were not sufficient chairs. There was neither paper nor ink for the delegates. There was only a great deal of enthusiasm and Mussolini, ready with a declaration—the charter of the *Fasci di combattimento*: [14]

1. The meeting of March 23rd salutes the memory of the fallen, the sons of Italy fallen in the name of Italy's greatness and the liberty of

the world, salutes the wounded, the invalids of war, all combatants, ex-combatants, and prisoners who did their duty, and the meeting declares itself ready to sustain energetically the material and moral claims of associations of combatants.

2. The meeting of March 23rd declares its opposition to the imperialism of other peoples to the detriment of Italy and accepts the clause of this League of Nations Charter which presupposes the integration of all nations—in Italy's case from the Alps to the Adriatic, with the annexation of Fiume and Dalmatia.

3. The meeting of March 23rd charges all Fascists to sabotage, with all means at their disposal, the candidature of neutralists of all parties.

The declaration was vague and necessitated by the agglomeration of different ideologies and parties represented at the meeting. But, as Mussolini said: "The important thing is to come into existence. Now we are a fact. From facts we will proceed to deeds."

There was some lively discussion, there were toasts, and patriotic songs were sung. Nobody remembered to take the names of those present, which caused some dissension in later years when up to 300 people claimed to have been there. At the end of the meeting, when the last song had been sung, the delegates left the salon, some to get something to eat and drink, others to go out and find Socialists to brawl with.

Outside in the streets it was noisy. Mussolini closed the windows and sat down to work out what to do next.

3

ACCÊNDO FUOCHI

LIGHTING OF THE FIRES

Mussolini found difficulty at first in explaining just what the *Fasci di combattimento* were and what was their ultimate objective. The name itself was not self-explanatory. Even in textbooks for elementary schoolchildren, published after the creation of Fascism (e.g. *Primo Libro del Fascista*[1]), there was a certain vagueness about the original aims and objectives, which may have been deliberate: "In the *Fasci di combattimento* there were grouped together Italians of all sorts faithful to the Fatherland and determined to fight against those who denied or threatened its unity of power. The *Fasci di combattimento* proposed to fight for the revindication of victory, against foreign imperialists who were suffocating Italy's rights, and against the disorder which was ruining, internally, the Fatherland, looking always to the well-being of the whole people in a régime of social justice."

The programme[2] for the *Fasci*, drafted by Mussolini late on March 23, 1919, is more specific, but still does not give any ideological direction. The programme was described in its preamble as "healthily Italian." It was:

> . . . revolutionary because it is antidogmatic and antidemagogic; an innovator because it is against prejudice. We will stress the supreme importance of the revolutionary war [which Mussolini maintained had put an end to democracy, the "nineteenth-century system of government"] and other problems—bureaucracy, administrative, judicial, scholastic, colonial, etc., problems—we will tackle later. *We want:*

1. Universal suffrage, proportional representation and votes for women, voting to be by regions.
2. Voting age lowered to eighteen and qualifying age for M.P.'s to twenty-five.
3. The abolition of the Senate.
4. The calling of a Constituent Assembly.
5. The formation of National Technical Councils for Labour, Industry, Transport, Social Hygiene, Communications, etc.,

elected by the various professions and trades themselves, with legislative power and with the right to elect a Commissar General with Ministerial powers.

For the social problem we want:

1. The eight-hour day for all workers.
2. Minimum rates of pay fixed by Law.
3. Participation by the workers in the running of industry.
4. The putting in order of all the transport industries.
5. Old-age pensions at age fifty-five.

For the military problem we want:

1. The institution of a National Militia with short periods of training and an exclusively defensive mission.
2. The nationalization of all arms and explosive factories.
3. A national foreign policy which will augment the value of Italian civilization to the world by peaceful competition.

This programme could have been drafted and published by almost any of the parties of the Left in 1919, and by almost any party in 1961. Mussolini himself, in *il Popolo d'Italia* (March 24, 1919), admitted that "examining our programme, you may find analogies with other programmes. You will even find things in common with the official Socialists . . . but we cannot permit an official Socialist experiment because the official Socialists want to import the Russian phenomenon, when all the best brains in Socialism from Branting to Thomas and Bernstein are contrary . . . we are against all sorts of dictatorship . . . we are not static, but dynamic, and we want to take our place in the *avant-garde*."

It is not even clear whether or not Mussolini wanted to form a political party. Most contemporary historians assume that this was his intention from the start, if only to revenge himself on the official Socialist Party which had expelled him. Friends of Mussolini's who talked to him in those days, however, remembered his saying that: "We do not want to fall into the error of becoming a rigid party, like all parties must be. We must be rather a pressure group, representing the most legitimate interests of the nation." During the years 1919–1921, Mussolini often said that he represented the "special interests" in Italy, while other political groupings represented only "vested interests" (of labour or capital). It is certain that Mussolini, in spite of his abuse of it, was impressed by the Russian Revolution. He was impressed by its success and by the fact that it seemed to have solved the "dilemma of democracy." Mussolini, who knew the working class and its leaders well as former colleagues and friends, had no faith in their ability to rule. They were good for riots and strikes, but lacked understanding of administrative compromise. Once given power, the mass—the democratic majority—transformed order into chaos, a lesser tragedy in Italy where chaos was the rule, but nevertheless an obstacle to progress. Mussolini recognized that universal suffrage and parliamentary institutions were inevitable, because they had been equated by the working class with better life and working conditions, but he was pessimistic about the prospects for workers' parliaments. He was all for mass participation in government, but the ruling of the country should be left to a small Executive, essentially undemocratic, and responsible not permanently and continuously, but only periodically, to the electorate.

According to Mussolini the strength of Lenin lay in the fact that he had transferred real power from the Tsar to the Bolshevik dictatorship of the proletariat, without ever having to give the proletariat a taste of that power. An out-of-date autocracy had been supplanted by a modern autocracy, an autocracy which was supported by the masses instead of undermined by them.

Mussolini, if his friends are to be believed, wanted to create something like a ruling clique outside government, a "representative Executive" which would rule without being obliged to reign. But he was not certain of the form, even if the content had already taken shape in his mind. In the end it was the weakness of the other parties in Italy which convinced him that it was necessary to "give the country" his own.

The war had left the "official" political parties in something of a dilemma. The government, which was not so much a party government as a coalition of individuals with followers, was in the hands of two old men—Orlando and Sonnino, Prime Minister and Foreign Minister respectively. "Traditional" politicians, they based their policies on assumptions which had been valid in 1861. "Traditional" right-wing foreign policy had been directed at the liberation of the Italian-speaking areas under Austro-Hungarian domination. The traditionally Republican, Mazzini, Left-Centre, had advocated not only an anti-Austrian line, but also a total dissolution of the Austro-Hungarian Empire and an Italian alliance with all the liberated national minorities. The Orlando-Sonnino government was composed in almost equal parts of men who owed political allegiance either to Mazzini or to the traditional "Right," Cavour, line. Orlando and Sonnino themselves were "Cavourian." They were glad to have liberated Trieste and Trent, but did not want to see the traditional balance of power in Europe upset, and were bewildered by the apparently spontaneous disintegration of the Austro-Hungarian Empire. Neither Mazzini nor Cavour were available for consultation, having been dead for half a century. Sonnino, at the negotiations for a peace treaty in Paris, found himself bewildered at the pace of events, and his bewilderment was reflected in an ever-increasing incompetence. Both Yugoslavia (which Sonnino did not recognize except as part of the Austro-Hungarian Empire) and Italy laid claim to Dalmatia and Fiume. The British and French, profiting from the confusion apparent in Sonnino's mind and anxious to make a new ally in the Mediterranean, supported Yugoslavia's claim to territorial integrity. Sonnino was treated so casually and informally that his nineteenth-century sense of the proper was outraged and he flounced out of the conference room in April, offended beyond his self-imposed limits. By all the rules of the diplomatic game, the other Allies should have adjourned the Peace Conference and invited him back, full of contrition. But they did not adjourn. They carried on as if Sonnino had never existed. *Il Popolo d'Italia*, reporting these contretemps, echoed the opinion of the whole country when it suggested that the fighting at Versailles was likely to be as tough as that on the Piave, and needed young men in the front line.

If the "traditional" parties, or agglomerations of individuals, demonstrated old-fashioned incompetence in their foreign policies, at home they were no better.

Italy had never been a rich country. According to Professor Chabod,[3] at the outbreak of war the average Italian ate 3,200 calories a day, as opposed to the 4,000 of the average Englishman. According to Colin Clark, the average Italian's earnings were 158 in international units, while those of the average Englishman were 481. The war diminished the average earnings and the total real income of Italy and impoverished the whole nation, excluding profiteers. The effort of fighting a war, without any efficient economic organization, after only 60 years of "unity" under unenviable governments, was too much. The trade deficit in 1918 was almost 25 per cent. Inflation followed every increase in imports over exports. From 2,051 million lire in 1913, the budget rose to 30,857 million in the fiscal year 1918–1919. The national debt stood at 95,017 million lire (1919). When the currency-control agreement between the Allies was ended (March 25, 1919) the lira collapsed; in 1914, in the month of June, the lira was worth just less than a fifth of a dollar—in December 1919 it had dropped to less than 12 cents. This was all the more serious because items such as petrol, coal and wheat had to be imported (home wheat production dropped by a fifth during the war). This financial tragedy had its impact on Italian foreign policy (added to Sonnino's caution was a reluctance to offend foreign banks and suppliers of raw materials), which still further weakened as 1919 wore on.

The first to suffer from the weakening of the economy and the devaluation of the lira was the middle class—the shopkeepers and smaller property owners in town and country. The Italian middle class had traditionally invested its savings in real estate, and lived in retirement off the rents or supplemented its earned income in this way. During the war rents were controlled and could not be raised to meet rising costs of maintenance. People who were living exclusively off fixed incomes derived from real estate were bankrupt at the end of the war. Even the *rentier* middle class, urban and rural, which had survived the rise in prices, froze commerce in 1919 by refusing to buy until prices fell. The shop-keeping middle class, on the contrary, increased its prices, thus dividing the middle class itself, as well as infuriating its working-class customers. That part of the middle class which was State employed—the middle and upper grades of civil servant—renting its town apartments, was hit by both landlords' refusals to do repairs and inflation in the shops.

The aristocracy in Italy "suffered," but by no stretch of imagination could they be described as in dire straits. They and the war profiteers enjoyed the chaos, and when prices rose too far and disorder became too general, they emigrated to the South of France for a few years. This caused no widespread regrets, except in the countryside, where the aristocracy had always acted as spokesman for the rural masses. Fifty-five per cent of the population of Italy lived off the land in 1914—the largest proportion among the Allies. Only a quarter of these "farmers" owned the land they worked, and only 1 per cent of the land was worked by its owners. Even those farmers who owned their land had only tiny plots—an average three to four acres. The rest of the land was farmed by sharecroppers or by labourers, and a minority by tenant farmers. During the war most of the land was farmed by women and old men, causing a decrease in total production (especially of wheat) and an increase in the price of the staple peasant food, bread. The landless majority of peasants came to the conclusion that after the war all their problems could be solved only by breaking up the estates of the absentee landlords and redistributing the land to family farmers. Those who stayed at home during the war shortsightedly sabotaged their landlords' farms in the belief that this would depreciate their values and depress their prices, thus making it easier for compulsory purchases. The government encouraged them in the belief that there would be a redistribution of land, just as it encouraged the middle class (which subscribed 30 per cent of its income to war loans) to believe that there would be a revaluation of the lira. When neither promise was fulfilled, economic and political discontent rose like a tidal wave.

The Italian worker did not suffer much material hardship during the war. Though prices rose in the shops, wages on the whole rose as fast or faster. The war effort depended on an increasing production of arms and ammunition, and though the workers were urged by their Socialist leaders to sabotage production, they were more interested in making money. It is important to remember that the working class was numerically small and not united. The skilled worker despised his semi-skilled colleague; the skilled worker at the Fiat factory in Turin despised everybody. The Fiat worker aristocracy was not "respectable," but dominated the extreme Left Wing of the Socialist Party and trade-union movement. In his newspaper *Ordine Nuovo*, Antonio Gramsci (later jailed by Mussolini) preached a Leninist revolution as the solution of the workers' economic problems. The employers—anxious to placate Gramsci and his friends and delighted to be able to divide them from the Socialist leadership, the more moderate Turati and Treves—raised wages in Turin, making the élite still more of an élite. The richer they became, the further Left these skilled workers moved, until a split in the Socialist Party and official trade-union movement was socially inevitable.

The "traditional" Republican and Liberal parties hoped to use these skilled workers as a club with which to beat the other discontented social groupings. This had been the domestic policy of Crispi and of Giolitti before the war, and there seemed to be no reason why it should not be possible to play off one interest against another after the war.

Of course, it would not be fair to indict the Republican-Liberal parties for ineffectiveness and "traditional" dishonesty without mentioning the young men who preached "Liberal Revolution."[4] Gobetti and his friends, most of whom lived in Turin where *Ordine Nuovo* was winning readers away from *Avanti*, believed in the necessity for revolution, for a purge of Italian public life. They did not believe that the Socialist Party, inspired by "foreign" theoreticians, could lead an Italian revolution, though they themselves were inspired by the success of the same foreign, Leninist, Russian Revolution. Gobetti believed that, whereas traditionally changes were made in Russian absolutism by assassination, so changes ought to be made in Italy by Piedmontese Liberals in Parliament. It only remained to find the formula, expel the dishonest, abolish corruption, and win the confidence of the masses. However, none of the young Liberals had any idea of how to go about winning the confidence of the masses, and the idea of "cleaning up" the Liberal Party was Utopian. The strong hand of the Republican-Liberal-Radical-Democrat Old Guard, Giolitti, had no training in honest administration. He still believed that it was possible to quiet things down inside his own party. The economic crisis would pass. All political groupings of workers would eventually melt into the official Socialist Party. The Socialists could be invited to join the government (they had already refused in 1903), and would eventually be "absorbed." A few years of the good life in Rome, and the fires in their bellies would be damped down.

Giolitti believed, and he was not far wrong, that every Italian worker or peasant aspires to membership of the bourgeoisie, and once in it becomes unshakeably loyal to his new environment.

However, times had changed. The day of friendly alliances and of arbitrary descriptions of these alliances as Left, Right and Centre, had passed. The Era of the Party had arrived. The old men in Parliament were not mentally or organizationally equipped to deal with mass parties, either in Opposition or under their own electoral insignia.

In 1919 the largest political party in Italy was still the official Socialist Party. The Reformist Socialist Party, formed by Bissolati after Mussolini had had him expelled from the official party, enjoyed an uncertain existence with a handful of parliamentary representatives. The official Socialist Party had won 883,409 votes in 1913, and had a nation-wide organization of full-time or part-time officials. It had several newspapers; it had a mass membership and a clear programme. The fact that its leadership was divided and of poor quality diminished its strength and unity, but these were nevertheless formidable.

The only alternative mass party was the Popular Catholic Party. This had been founded by Catholics who saw in it the instrument for a proper direct participation by the faithful in a government doomed to be dominated (they believed) by atheists. It was run by an unusually able priest, Don Luigi Sturzo, and enjoyed wide popularity, especially in the country. It had stolen much of the Socialist Party's thunder in the country by taking up the cry of "Land for the Peasants." There were twenty-nine Catholic Party

M.P.s in 1913, and one of them, Meda, served in the wartime coalition government.

In 1919 it seemed as if two-party government might become the rule in Italy, with the Popular Catholic Party in power, in uneasy coalition with the anti-clerical Liberals, and the divided Socialist Party in Opposition. Mussolini believed this to be the future make-up of the Italian Parliament, and said as much to Michele Bianchi in 1919. Mussolini believed that the function of the *Fasci* was to accelerate the fall of the present Orlando government, get Parliament divided between Socialists and Catholics, then play off the one against the other from *outside* the Chamber. If the *Fasci* could be made nationwide, at election time they could be used to help one side or the other in return for promises of specific aid for the "special interests" which the *Fasci* represented. Mussolini knew that the old "traditional" parties or groupings were doomed. He was not dismayed by the prospect of two-party government, government by a party which had expelled him, or a Church which he had attacked in print for ten years. He believed that a two-party system would give the "pressure group" a unique opportunity to develop and become a permanent, extra-constitutional supra-parliamentary institution, holding a parliamentary balance of power *outside* parliament.

In March 1919, he seems to have had no thoughts of founding a formal party nor of participating in elections. He seems to have been surprised by the range of political opinions owned by his supporters, and co-signatories of the Fascist programme. They seemed to have only one thing in common, their anti-Socialism. Some were anti-Socialist by conviction; others had been frightened into it by the Red marches and riots of February and March 1919 (on February 18, 1919, there had even been a march past the offices of *il Popolo d'Italia*, an assembly dispersed by Futurists who happened to be marching in the opposite direction). Mussolini's closest collaborators were unclassifiable.

Emilio Marinetti founded "Futurism" when he was thirty-one, in 1909. He was among the oldest of Mussolini's intimates and one of the weirdest. He was the inspiration of many of the slogans with which Mussolini decorated his office, such as: "ALL MEN ARE IDIOTS, SOME ARE AMUSING IDIOTS—GOD SAVE ME FROM IDIOTS WHO ARE BORES AS WELL. Futurism had something of a hold on the young intellectuals of the day. Giuseppe Bottai, who later became the "philosopher of Fascism" and was responsible for the invention of its creed after the Fascists had achieved power, was a Futurist and regular contributor to *Roma Futurista.* Marinetti believed in something like a distortion of Sorel, in the inherent virtues in force. The *Futurist Manifesto* sounds today like some lunatic catechism, with its declarations of love for "Racing motor-cars running on shrapnel," and insistence that "The past is a balsam for prisoners, invalids and men on their deathbeds, who see the Future close to them." In the sphere of art, Futurists insisted on the glorification of the machine and the depiction of action (creating the idea of action by painting an object at various stages of its movement from A to B). They were the forerunners of surrealism. In politics they believed in bombs. Marinetti himself always carried a few grenades in his pocket and gave them away to his friends like cigars. Mussolini used to keep these unwelcome gifts in the stove (and a pistol on his desk), and was nearly blown through the roof one morning when a new porter tried to light the stove without clearing it. Marinetti, though in later years he lost his influence over Mussolini, was important during the formative years of the Fascist mobs, and kept violence well to the fore in their activities. Marinetti founded an association of *arditi* in Milan on January 19, 1919 (Mario Carli had founded the first in Rome earlier in the day). The newspapers *l'Ardito* and *Roma Futurista* supported Mussolini and took their line from *il Popolo d'Italia.*

Mussolini's every-day office collaborators were Ferruccio Vecchi, Enzo Ferrari, Mario Giampoli, Michele Bianchi, Ferruccio Ferrandini and Carlo Meraviglia. This was the "Executive Committee" of the Milan *Fascio* (they subscribed the first 210,000 lire for the funds of the *Fasci*—the "Movement" as they called it). This inner council was composed mostly of adventurers, young officers and sons of rich Milanese businessmen. Bianchi was clerkly in appearance, hard working and an ideal secretary. Mario Giampoli was more typical, cracked many heads, rose to power with Mussolini, becoming party chief in Milan (*ras* of Milan, to use the Ethiopian title conferred unofficially), then was expelled from the party in 1929 after a great scandal involving women and party funds. This executive committee lost some of its power when the movement became nationwide.

The men Mussolini met outside the office of *il Popolo d'Italia* were in the long run more influential, and in the short term more useful. He had won the affection of a great many returned officers who felt that the government was deliberately frittering away the gains of war at the Paris conference, and who wanted a "strong" Italian foreign policy. The party which represented the older officer element was the Nationalist Party. Enrico Corradini, its founder, and Luigi Federzoni, were the ablest and most powerful of the party's leaders. Both of them became ministers under Mussolini, which is some measure of their influence. They both supported Mussolini in his interventionist campaign, 1914–1915, and were among the first to ally themselves with what they described as "postwar Nationalism." On January 12, 1919, at a meeting at La Scala, Milan, at which Bissolati tried to explain away the government's "international compromise," Nationalists allied themselves openly with supporters of Mussolini.[5] By the end of March 1919 the alliance had been confirmed in many brawls. There was as yet, however, no formal fusion between the Nationalist Party and the Fascist movement. Luigi Federzoni says: "The considerable Nationalist Party worked with the *Fasci di combattimento* but differed from them in its ideological premises and in its perfect legality. Fascism was not yet transformed into a party, but the principal field of action for Nationalists was the Chamber of Deputies."[6]

This did not mean that many Nationalists, as individuals, did not take part in brawls and noisy meetings and even join *Fasci.* It merely meant that the leadership of the Nationalist Party was biding its time, to see if anything would come of Mussolini's efforts. It was only later, when the Fascist Party was formed and won mass support, that it suited the Nationalists to sign a pact with them (the Nationalists never won the support of the millions and were always something of an aristocratic grouping).

The vast majority of Mussolini's "action groups" were formed of young officers without any political affiliations. Even the anti-Socialism which united them was not ideological, but a personal reaction to Socialist policy. The official Socialist Party, having opposed Italy's intervention in the war and counselled sabotage for its members, seemed to have been reconciled to the idea of war by the suffering at Caporetto ("closing the ranks"). During 1918 and the first part of 1919, however, they returned to their opposition to war and militarism, taking their cue in part from "classical anti-militarism" and in part from Lenin's directive to fraternal associations in Western Europe urging them to refuse to participate in any attempt to restore the Tsars. It was official Socialist policy to try to destroy the patriotism which flourishes after a successful war, and to exploit, instead, war weariness. They tried to discredit the victory, suggesting that only the rich had benefited from it. Few of their worker supporters had gone to war, so they readily abused those who had. Party propaganda played on the hurt and humiliation of the defeat at Caporetto, suggesting that in some way the private soldier had been betrayed. Federzoni wrote: "The signs of bravery on the chests of returned soldiers and the decoration of the streets with the national flag were considered as provocations which legitimized any sort of act of revolt. The situation became so acute that officers of the Armed Forces were advised not to wear their uniforms in public." Naturally enough, officers resented being (literally) spat on in public. This is not to say that they all joined or formed *Fasci di combattimenti*, though there were 82, with 14,000 members, by April 15, 1919. Many of them did, however, look to Mussolini as the man who had "saved the nation's honour with the interventionist campaign," and waited to see if he could save it twice.

In the early part of 1919 local veterans' associations which were not *Fasci* followed *Ardito* and *Popolo d'Italia* and took their line from these two papers. Enzo Galbiati, who later became Chief of the General Staff of the Fascist Militia, insists that Mussolini was not the "master" of the local officers' "self-defence" associations, but was seen as their "instrument." He himself, typical of many of the generation of subalterns, came from a family without definite political affiliations—a family which thought the Risorgimento and reunification had been a good thing, but was afraid that somehow they had gone wrong. Galbiati believed that it was possible to "make the nation healthy" by "giving Socialists a taste of their own medicine." He spent the early years of the *Fasci* in Romagna-Emilia, Mussolini's home ground, where there was even more habitual violence than in Milan.[7]

Some of the young Army officers who formed themselves into anti-Socialist commandos, and later formed the hard core of the Fascist Militia, were, to say the least, picturesque. Giovanni Passerone, later one of the most influential consuls, stood every morning in the streets of Casale, with an Alsatian dog at his heels and a bull-whip in his hand, challenging the Socialist workers to spit on his uniform. In the later spring of 1919 a circus came to Casale. Passerone waited until the lion tamer brought on his animals, then walked into the ring with the lions and challenged any Socialist in the audience to come and fight him there.

There was nothing homogeneous about Fascism in its early days. In fact the word meant, to the man in the street, little more than organized violence in reprisal for the organized violence of Socialists.

It seemed at first as if the movement was to have no other scope. During the three weeks following the formation of the *Fascio* in Milan there were a hundred clashes between Fascists and Socialists in the city streets. On April 14th, Marinetti came rushing into the office of *il Popolo d'Italia* and told Mussolini that it was time to barricade the doors. He had heard, he said, that the following day Socialists were planning to march on the paper and burn down the building which housed it. The reason for the new attacks, he said, was that "Fascists and *arditi* had been strike-breaking and had to be taught a lesson." Mussolini was horrified. He knew what a sacred cow "strike-breaking" was and what a crowd he could expect outside his doors in such a cause. The day before there had been trouble in the streets, shops sacked, officers in uniform attacked, and public buildings stoned, but this was "normal." No man or woman had dared to go out into the streets of any Italian city after dark for many years. The railway station was said to be a hundred times safer than the square beneath the cathedral in Milan.

Mussolini sent Ferruccio Vecchi to appeal for help to the local officers' self-defence corps. He managed to recruit some 150 men by the evening of the 14th. Fifty of them slept that night on the floor of the editor's and sub-editors' offices. There was no furniture to get in the way. Mussolini considered armchairs a sign of softness, and furnished only slogans such as: THE DAY THE EDITOR PAGED UP, THE PAPER WENT TO BED ON TIME. By the morning of April 15th the atmosphere was tense. From the window Mussolini could see Socialist sentries posted a hundred yards away, presumably to make sure he did not escape.

The Socialists held a mass meeting in the arena, then formed into a procession which police estimates put at 20,000. Present-day Socialists, including Nenni (converted by Mussolini to Socialism, then to Fascism, then back again to Socialism), put the figure lower. There were certainly, to judge from the single photograph extant, at least 10,000 in the procession which set off to march to *il Popolo d'Italia* via the Piazza del Duomo. In Via Mercanto, the procession came up against a human barricade of Ferruccio Vecchi, in his uniform as a captain of *arditi*, and 750 Fascists. Then followed a battle royal. It seems certain that the police lent their help to the Fascists and reinforced them, otherwise there is no explanation for the fact that the 20,000 were put to flight. In the meantime the police were searching the offices of both *Avanti* and *il Popolo d'Italia* looking for hidden arms. They confiscated all they found and forbade both newspapers to barricade their doors. Neither paper took any notice. However, the attempt to set fire to *il Popolo d'Italia* seemed to have fizzled out with the dispersal of the crowd. Ferruccio Vecchi assumed that it was safe to leave Mussolini to himself, and held a counsel of war with the survivors of his command (150 wounded and three dead). They decided to turn the tables completely and march on *Avanti* to see if it was inflammable. It was inflammable, and Vecchi, with Marinetti supplying the fire bombs, did set fire to it. The police stood by laughing. The paper, publishing two days later, declared that it would "rise again greater than ever from the ashes."

To the correspondent of a Rome newspaper Mussolini said: "What has happened at the offices of *Avanti* was a spontaneous movement of the people against Leninism." He took the same line in *il Popolo d'Italia* which came out with banner headlines: NOT AGAINST THE PROLETARIAT BUT AGAINST BOLSHEVISM—TUESDAY MARKS THE END OF LENINISM IN ITALY—THE MOB SACKS AVANTI. It was a departure from the truth, but it was impressive. Mussolini managed to convince part of commercial Milan that he was in a position from which he could suppress strikes and protect them (as Chicago gangsters "protected" their clients). He avoided police reprisals by insisting on only "moral responsibility" for the burning of *Avanti*. However, he was pleasantly surprised by the rise in his prestige which followed the event, and he gave Marinetti, Vecchi and the ultra-violent element in his entourage their heads. It was like turning bulls loose in a china shop. In some way which nobody was able to imitate, Marinetti could always be relied upon to find arms and ammunition, and so the "squads" of avenging Fascists were always well armed. The police were reluctant to try to disarm them, because they feared resistance.

Throughout May and June, Mussolini fought vigorously against the "menace of Bolshevism." As a newspaper proprietor and working editor, he was well informed of events overseas and in other parts of Europe. The Bolshevik Revolution in Hungary, which had broken out in March, seemed to be getting under control, and Admiral Miklós Horthy was preparing for his march on Budapest. In Germany the Bolshevik and Social Democrat "government" was losing ground to associations of ex-officers, serving officers and politicians of the extreme Nationalist Right. Both these circumstances encouraged Mussolini. He was even more encouraged by the direct financial support he was now receiving from secret associations of shopkeepers, and from the unofficial "trade-union" of manufacturers, the Confederation of Industry (a counter-confederation to that of labour). The secretary-general of the *Confedindustria*, during Mussolini's rise to power and after, has steadfastly refused to discuss his part in it, but no such reticence is characteristic of Mussolini's friends on the receiving end of subsidies. Many of the

Futurists did not like the idea of being "in the pay of big business." Giuseppe Bottai was writing (in *Terza Italia* and *Ardito*) typical abuse of the bourgeoisie and of the working class which aped it. Marinetti had a dim belief that in some way revolutionaries were under divine protection and did not need money. Mussolini was not so proud. He toured the country between major brawls, making speeches and raising funds. On May 6th he addressed a mass meeting in Rome and discovered that, in the capital, the government was more unpopular for its foreign incompetence than for its inability to deal with inflation and shortage of foodstuffs at home. From then on until he achieved power, the policies he advocated alternated between the reckless and piratical overseas and the traditional, sub-Socialist at home. Throughout May and June he urged "expansionism," acquiring many "respectable" middle-class supporters.

On May 22nd Mussolini went to Fiume and told an enthusiastic crowd that it would soon be annexed by Italy—earning the admiration of D'Annunzio. Just as Mussolini always leapt into action when he could not think of what to say next, so D'Annunzio, whenever his poesy dried up, sought inspiration in adventures. The soldier-poet confided to Mussolini in a letter (June 15, 1919)[8] that it might well be "necessary" to "take the sword in our own hands before sheathing it at the side of the King." He started to recruit his own Foreign Legion with which to embark on private imperial adventures.

On June 20, 1919, conditions at home and abroad made the life of Orlando and Sonnino impossible, and they resigned. The King asked Nitti to form a government. Federzoni says of Nitti: "He was an illustrious economist and author, but was inclined to adopt a passive policy toward those who threatened public order." Nitti was, in fact, afraid of offending the United States, which was holding up the lira (having allowed it to fall to a record low) and supplying Italy with wheat. His government was predestined to have a short life. He was lucky to take office at all. The day after Orlando resigned, 600 ex-servicemen met in Rome to decide on what action they should take to defend their "special interests," i.e., whether or not they should form a party, or attach themselves to some already existing party. Bottai proposed that the 600 should walk into the empty Parliament building and take over the government. Had they done so, the *coup d'état* might well have been accomplished without an excess of bloodshed. But the 600 did not ride into any valley of death or political rebirth, but contented themselves with passing resolutions. At the end of the "congress" most of them decided to join Mussolini's *Fasci*. The squads and the *squadristi* grew in numbers. There were an estimated 25,000 Fascists by the end of June.

In July 1919 there were riots throughout Italy, the most serious to date. There were "routine" clashes between *squadristi*, Socialists and the police. Mussolini, wherever possible, informed the police of his plans, sure of their support against the Left. More serious and widespread were the "housewives' riots," led by trade-union and Socialist Party officials, who broke open shops, split shutters with crowbars, and looted entire shopping centres in Milan, Turin and Florence. On July 5, 1919, *il Popolo* reported: "In the night the invasion of the Florentine shops by the mob continued. Food shops and clothing stores—a large part of the loot was taken to the Chamber of Labour. There were some injuries to looters and police. From the surrounding Tuscan countryside there are also reports of violence against shops and shopkeepers. This morning the general strike is complete, except for one or two shops which are open, with prices much lowered (the Prime Minister had ordered a reduction by half). The tram service is suspended. The newspapers came out as usual . . . the cavalry patrols the city. The Prefect has published a call for calm." The following day *il Popolo* added: "The Town Hall has ordered a general reduction of prices by 45 per cent to 50 per cent, but this morning there were incidents in the market, with women overturning baskets of fruit and vegetables. . . ."

Giuseppe Bottai found Mussolini, on the morning of the 6th, delighted with the riots in Florence. He told Bottai he was convinced that this would mean the fall of the government, a general election, a Popular Catholic and Socialist two-party system, with the real power in the hands of his *squadristi*. Bottai was sceptical. In *Roma Futurista*, a week later (July 13, 1919), he wrote:

> A bandit frenzy is animating with unwonted courage the least warlike and most obtuse part of the Italian people. They have attached—to the chaos of sacked shops, goods scattered in the street, broken sacks, and houses turned upside down—the label REVOLUTION . . . but let us not exaggerate . . . The whole thing seems to us to be a good deal less than a revolution, and certainly less beautiful. Our people, even in this matter of the high cost of living, as in many other matters during the war, have stopped at the first pub on the way to revolution. A drop of weak wine has inebriated them and taken away the will and the strength necessary to look for the old wine hidden elsewhere. . . . This assault on commerce ought to be the beginning, not the end . . .

Bottai advised Mussolini to preach more and more violence. Then, according to Bottai, the mob would come down on the side of the greater violence, that of the Fascist *squadristi*. It was easier than waiting for elections, than playing the game of the anterooms.

Mussolini, if he were truthful, would have admitted that for the moment the situation was out of his control. His nominal "followers" were acting largely on their own initiative, and there was only a sketchy national tie-up with other secretaries of *Fasci* in town and country. He was sensitive for the moment about strikes, riots and internal disturbances, though he and his newspaper were responsible for many of them. There were riots in Fiume, demanding annexation by Italy (riots encouraged by agents of Mussolini and D'Annunzio, but certainly pro-Italian). The French and British police in Fiume reported a "deterioration in public order," and the British officer in charge suggested an international commission of inquiry. Mussolini and D'Annunzio, vying with each other to be the more aggressive and patriotic, urged the Nitti government to "reject such a shameful proposal." On August 4th Fascist-inspired riots in Trieste—the nearest Italian city to Fiume—provoked a head-on clash with Socialist-led strikers and gave the Fascists their first martyr, Carlo Polla, an eighteen-year-old worker of limited intelligence but undoubted violence. In other parts of Italy, in addition to the always brawling black-shirted officers' self-defence corps and their mercenary rank and file, new private armies formed, re-formed, and demobilized themselves.

Luigi Federzoni formed a "Blue Shirt" army, which, ironically, had the same motto (Always Ready) as the Soviet Union's Young Communists. It specialized in breaking up strikers' protest marches. In and out of the Blue Shirts and the Black Shirts, Marinetti, Bottai and the Futurists moved, offering bombs and pistols to all comers, writing manifestoes, urging the veiling of women and the "reinforcement of masculine prestige," making declarations of their "Intelligent non-intellectualism."

The Commission of Inquiry into the Retreat from Caporetto (Caneva, Bensa, Stoppato, Raimondo, Ragni de Orestis, Tommasi) had completed its hearing of evidence by the beginning of August and was ready to give evidence to the Italian Parliament. On August 16, 1919, *il Popolo d'Italia* exhorted its readers to insist on the firing squad for deserters, and in an open letter to the Prime Minister urged him to "hide nothing from the country." *Avanti* was conducting its own inquiry and urged that deserters be pardoned and only the generals punished.

Ultra-nationalistic rioters, urging not only the annexation of Fiume, but the sending of an expeditionary force to Split (Spalato), continued to embarrass the government, which had promised the United States that it would "reach an accommodation with Yugoslavia." On August 25, 1919, the Allied inquiry commission in Fiume recommended the "demilitarization" of the city—and the immediate withdrawal of all Italian troops, who were accused of "fomenting discord." The French wanted to use Fiume as a naval base, and had already signed a treaty with Yugoslavia under the terms of which they were to rent the harbour. The British government was supporting the French and helping them to "reach an agreement with the Yugoslav government and put an end to the disturbances in the city." Both the British and French governments maintained that their only concern was for the welfare of the people of Yugoslavia and in particular the citizens of Fiume. The reaction of the citizens of Fiume to the order to withdraw all Italian troops was to burn down the British police headquarters and haul down the French tricolour wherever it flew.

On September 2nd the Nitti government still further inflamed the "patriotism" of the *squadristi* and The Poet's friends (D'Annunzio was always referred to as "The Poet," in capital letters, just as Garibaldi was referred to in print as The Hero). A general amnesty was granted to the deserters of Caporetto. Mussolini was furious. The country as a whole reacted unfavourably. To pile "injustice" on "injustice," the founder of the Rome *Fascio*, Mario Carli (a captain of *arditi*), was arrested for "political activity while a serving officer." As *il Popolo d'Italia* pointed out, Carli, as a wounded war hero, ought to have been demobilized months before. Having refused to demobilize him, the military authorities ought to accept responsibility for the way in which he had been filling in his time (organizing meetings of ex-servicemen, burning Socialist newspapers, brawling with trade-union leaders, wrecking labour rooms).

D'Annunzio and Mussolini decided that the time was ripe for an act of super violence which would raise Italy's prestige abroad, show contempt for the government, and win the widespread approval of the populace at large. Both men had their eyes fixed on only one objective—Fiume. D'Annunzio's private army had grown to 287 men, all well armed. He launched a call for recruits to "clean Italy's banner of the spots of dirt which have accumulated on it." Hundreds of young men from North and Central Italy made their way up the peninsula to Ronchi where D'Annunzio had his "headquarters." On September 11th D'Annunzio wrote to Mussolini:

"My dear comrade, the deed is done. I am leaving now. Tomorrow morning I will take Fiume by force of arms. May the God of Italy be with us. I get up from my bed, feverish, but it is impossible to put the thing off. Once again the spirit will overcome the miserable flesh. . . ."[9]

On September 12th D'Annunzio, in a car with reinforced bumper bars, drove into Fiume at the head of his legion. He did not stop at the British control post outside the city, but drove straight through it. The population of Fiume gave him a hysterical welcome. He had defied his own government, the governments of France and Britain, and the President of the United States. The Allied police and army patrols wisely evacuated the city to avoid bloodshed. Even so, there were heads broken and innumerable windows smashed.

Mussolini was beside himself with delight, and published enthusiastic editorials in *il Popolo* (September 14, 1919) and in *Idea Nazionale* (which published the text of D'Annunzio's message to him).

Marinetti did not entirely approve of the venture. He felt that it diverted attention from the "fight against the fat-bellied bourgeoisie at home."

D'Annunzio proclaimed the annexation of Fiume in the name of the King. Bottai and Marinetti opined that the King stood in the way of Italy and greatness. Nevertheless, all Mussolini's friends and collaborators approved the public reaction to Fascist approval and participation in the enterprise. The number of *Fasci* rose to 140, and the number of Fascists to 43,000. When the Nitti government ill-advisedly ordered D'Annunzio to withdraw from Fiume (censoring *il Popolo d'Italia* on September 15th for criticizing the move), the mass of the middle-class and rural population sympathized with the *Fasci*, notwithstanding a certain disapproval of their violence. On September 18th Nitti blockaded Fiume and tried to starve D'Annunzio out. This was a very foolish move and resulted only in an upsurge of disloyalty in the Army and Navy, which refuelled and supplied D'Annunzio in secret for the next three months.

By the beginning of October the number of *Fasci* had risen to 149, and the registered Fascists to 45,000.

In the face of such open defiance, continued with impunity, Nitti had no alternative but to resign. He dissolved Parliament and called new elections for the middle of November.

Many Fascists, on hearing of Nitti's dissolution of Parliament, believed the moment had come for a Fascist "double triumph."

Some of the *ras* claimed that within the year the whole of Italy would be effectively under their control and that no other action was necessary. More moderate Nationalists and ex-Liberal Fascists urged the making of an effort to achieve "respectability" by fighting the elections as a "party." Mussolini was originally opposed to this idea, not because he believed that the same end could or should be achieved by violence, but because he was sure they would not win. The only part of Italy which was well enough organized to be electorally efficient was the city of Milan. Elsewhere there were *squadristi* aplenty, but no cohesion of activity. Mussolini knew that a minority in Parliament is often more ineffective than a noisy minority outside, and anyway, he did not want to give away the strength or weakness of the movement. The success of the Mussolini-D'Annunzio enterprise had given the impression that the influence of the *Fasci* in the country was vast, and Mussolini was content with that.

Unfortunately, the careerist, get-into-Parliament-at-all-costs section of the movement prevailed. They conceded to Mussolini that the only place they could possibly fight was in the Milan constituency, but there they felt they had a good chance of winning. Their argument was that if they could win three or four seats in this Parliament they would acquire so much extra respectability at the next election that they could even hope for a majority. Nobody listened to Mussolini's plea, in public and in the columns of *il Popolo d'Italia,* that "the characteristic of this post-war era is the disappearance of the direct representation of the individual or individual currents. Electoral success is now a matter of organization. There are only two parties with adequate organization—the Popular Party, with an agent in every pulpit, and the Socialist Party, with an agent in every workshop."

With a bad grace, Mussolini allowed himself to be put up as a candidate. With him stood Marinetti, Ferrari, Baseggio, Banfi, Arturo Toscanini the conductor, Bolzon, Aversa, Podrecca, Macchi, Romanini, Bellinato, de Magistris, Camillo Bianchi, Mazzuccato, Lanzillo, Fabbri, Galimberti, Pozzi. The election was fought with a great deal of noise but little or no enthusiasm on the part of the voters.

The results were published on November 16th. The Fascist list had suffered a resounding defeat, getting only 4,064 votes. As Mussolini had predicted, both the Socialist and Popular (Catholic) parties won great victories. The Popular Party had 100 members and the Socialists 156 (out of a total of 508).

The old régime had passed. Both victorious parties were run from outside Parliament by "amateurs," the Popular Party by Don Luigi Sturzo, a priest; the Socialist Party by the party's Executive Committee. It seemed as if the whole Fascist movement had collapsed. With no seats in Parliament and the electoral defeat to diminish the effectiveness of the pressure the *Fasci* could exert outside Parliament, many of the careerists burned their *Fasci* cards and "gave up politics." Mussolini remarked to Margherita Sarfatti: "I have been a journalist too long. But I've got other trades. I could become a bricklayer—I'm very good at laying bricks. Then I am learning how to fly (he had tried a flight to Fiume to see D'Annunzio, determined not to be outdone by The Poet, who had had a pilot's licence for years). Or I could travel around the world with my violin. . . . Bocca, the publisher, has made me a good offer for my book on *Myth and Heresy*. All I have to do is find fifteen days to get it on paper. I've got a three-act play ready—all I have to do is write it. . . ." [10]

For the next three months Mussolini found it hard to keep his spirits up and try to stop the circulation of *il Popolo d'Italia* from falling. The Socialist Party paraded up and down with effigies of Mussolini in a coffin. The local Popular Party leaders, lay and clerical, just smirked. Even Mussolini's late allies, the police, arrested him three times in November. But, as Bottai said, the masses have always been fickle and Mussolini must not be too disheartened. The tide would turn. He was right. Many people were shocked by the behaviour of the Socialists in the new Parliament, their discourtesy to the King and unnecessary lack of civility. After nearly two years of agitation, many rank-and-file Socialists were tired of march and countermarch. There was a feeling that little had been achieved. There were not sufficient Socialist M.P.'s to form the government of the people which was to put an end to the economic crisis, so the parliamentary party had only nuisance value. Many leading Socialists opined that Mussolini had been right to urge his Fascists to stay out of Parliament. This had been Lenin's practice, they pointed out. An alternative to Parliament, on the lines of the Soviets, should be worked out somehow. The parliamentary revolution had failed. The time was now ripe for "action," for "Lenin's road." In fact, during 1920 at the various local elections, Socialists fought for control of town councils as embryo soviets, and won control of some 2,000 communes. The trade-union movement, the C.G.I.L., controlled by the Leninist faction inside the party, had some 2,500,000 members, who were not always active or intelligent, but did at least furnish funds and allocate block votes. The party began to come apart at the crutch, one leg walking slowly toward Social Democracy and the other running after Lenin. In the growth of its unpopularity and disunity Mussolini would soon see his revenge.

The Popular Party had also reached its zenith. The Church had had mixed feelings about it since its inception and first electoral success in 1903. Now the party had 100 members; it could not be ignored by the Church. It represented a challenge to the authority of the Curia Cardinals. The cardinals could not even deal with the party's leader without some awkwardness in protocol. He was, after all, only a parish priest. The Vatican had been indulgent to the party, largely because Benedict XV had favoured it with his personal attention and had given its leaders ready access to him. But Benedict was a sick man. The Curia Cardinals had already decided that the next pope would be one with a different approach, a more "detached" man. There were old cardinals who felt it improper for Catholics to have anything to do with the government, which they still regarded as the usurper and hoped would go back to Turin. There were other, slightly younger cardinals, and the Vatican Secretariat, who felt that lay politics was, anyway, beneath the dignity of the Church, if not unnecessary.

To Mussolini's surprise, during the first months of 1920, he found himself courted again by rich industrialists and by Church leaders outside the Popular Party. In January there were two national strikes—by post office workers and transport workers. Between February and April there were 297 more at various levels, national, regional and local, each strike disrupting some sector of the economy and helping to precipitate the country still further toward bankruptcy. On March 31st the state-owned industrial enterprises struck, and on May 1st there was a little revolution. Some idea of the scale of the disorders may be seen at Viareggio, where strikers burned down the police barracks and forced all government officials to withdraw from the district. Nitti was powerless. It was to stress the impotence of Nitti that Mussolini's distinguished visitors came to see him, so they said. They were disturbed by the continuing and increasing public disorder, and alarmed by the prospect of the extremists in the Socialist Party igniting a Bolshevik revolution. The counter-revolution in Russia was, alas, not going too well. What could Mussolini do about it? Could he offer an alternative to disorder?

Mussolini was delighted to be able to offer some alternative to disorder. He had a newspaper which was solvent and even made a little money. He had a personal following, outside its readership, of about 600 men. Up and down Italy there were still 130 *Fasci* active, and they owed him some nominal allegiance, even if they only used his newspaper as a post office. But he was afraid that many of his *Fasci* were as violent and disorderly as the Socialists, and he did not have the organization to keep them under control. It was here, they said, that Mussolini's visitors could help. One of them, General Pecori Giraldi, promised immediate and nationwide assistance to help organize the *squadristi* into a paramilitary force. Falche, then on the staff of the Army corps at Trieste, told Mussolini that he had arranged to supply D'Annunzio and *Fasci* as far west as Milan with arms and ammunition in excess of those now filtering through via Marinetti. Milanese and Torinese businessmen left cheques on the editor's desk for spurious advertisements. One man donated half a million lire to *Ardito*.

In May a large number of officers were released from duty on full pay and detailed to local *Fasci* to act as secretaries, organizers and leaders of punitive expeditions against Socialist "peoples' commandos." On May 12th, at Trieste, the loyal Fascists were organized by Falche and others into squads, with boots and uniforms from local barracks. Arms, petrol and lorries were supplied by the Army. Collaboration became so open that a civilian employee of the divisional command attended all *Fasci* meetings in Florence as a shorthand writer. The police became friendly again. Local magistrates stopped prosecuting Fascists and concentrated on the Left. Nitti, unable to rely on the loyalty of the police, formed a royal guard, which for a time fought energetically on the side of the Socialists and periodical strikers (in Rome on May 24, 1920, they killed fifteen Fascists), but even their loyalty was suspect. Money, arms, ammunition and organization enriched the movement. Mussolini, who did not recover quickly from surprise at the speed and extent to which he had been "taken up" again by the Armed Forces and big business, lost control of the *Fasci* for a time. The local *ras*, though now disciplined and under surveillance, did little more to acknowledge his authority than make weekly reports on Army stationery.

On June 16, 1920, Nitti's place as Prime Minister was taken by Giolitti. Giolitti's attitude to Fascism was the same as his attitude to the Mafia and the Camorra. For many years he had kept control of the underworld by appointing or dismissing prefects, magistrates and other authorities, bribing his way into the confidence of the leaders of various criminal associations. He believed he could neutralize Fascism in the same way, and get hold of the reins of the Fascist-military alliance which was threatening to undermine the authority of the State. He was not lucky in his first encounter with Mussolini and his friends. The Italian garrison in Albania was vigorously attacked by the local Nationalists and forced to call for help. The other garrisons in the Adriatic, when the order was transmitted via Rome to proceed to Valona, thought it was a trick—that while they were away Fascist Fiume would be "purged"—so nobody went to the help of the Valona garrison, which was compelled to evacuate the city.

Mussolini was sarcastic about this in *il Popolo d'Italia* and accused Giolitti of spreading the rumour that anybody could help himself to a piece of Italy. But Giolitti let the insults go over his head and sent friends to "talk reasonably" to Mussolini. These same friends had failed to talk reasonably to the Socialist Executive, and Giolitti had an intense personal dislike for Don Luigi Sturzo. If he was to restore order by enlisting the help of one of the disorderly parties in the country—a policy which had worked well enough from 1902 to 1913—he had to make friends with Mussolini. The garrison in Ancona mutinied, shouting Fascist slogans.

On July 14th the *Fascio* of Trieste burned down the local Red headquarters, the Hotel Balkan. Two days later Giolitti offered Mussolini a place in the "national bloc" he was forming to contest a general election he intended to hold next year. Mussolini accepted.

In August 1920 the extremist leadership of the Socialist Party ordered a "revolution of the soviets." Throughout Italy workers occupied factories and workshops, putting out signs saying COMMUNIST FACTORY or taking down the names of the proprietors and substituting that of Lenin. In Turin the revolution went almost according to plan. The large numbers of skilled and well-educated workers made the running of factories by "workers' councils" a practicable proposition. There was also a large nucleus of intellectual Socialists willing and able to help, led by Antonio Gramsci and others. There seemed to be plenty of money available, though nobody knew quite where it came from. It was not until later in the year that the roubles started to arrive from Moscow. But elsewhere in Italy the occupation of the factories just brought production to a standstill. The most complete week of "soviets" was that from August 30th to September 6th, though the "revolution" went on until September 27th. By then the revolutionaries had had enough. Just as the shop looters had "stopped at the first pub"[11] in their revolt against the increasing cost of living, so the "nationalizers"[12] were satisfied with a month of anarchy.

Giolitti always claimed that he had provoked the extreme Left into starting this revolution and setting up the soviets, in the certain knowledge that they were not yet ready for such experiments. Historian Gaetano Salvemini says that Giolitti told him: "I wanted the workers to learn by experience, to see how impossible it was to keep production going without technicians, credit or capital." He added that he had kept the railway stations, post offices and the Bank of Italia under his control, and so always had the situation in hand. This may well have been a boast of relief when the last soviet disbanded. Nevertheless, the lesson was not lost on Mussolini, who told a visiting delegation of ex-officers, led by Giovanni Passerone, that he intended to "bring order with the co-operation of all classes—the time of classes is past; the class struggle belongs to history; its place has been taken by the struggle for the nation."

The lesson was not lost on the Socialist Party, either. Discontent multiplied, Pieraccini told Salvemini in December 1920 that "all is finished." Certainly many tens of thousands of workers and peasants deserted the Socialist Party and started flirtations with their local *Fasci*.

Giolitti turned his hand to "arranging" Italian foreign policy. In November he signed a treaty with Yugoslavia (the Treaty of Rapallo) under the terms of which he promised to hand over Fiume. This was easier said than done. D'Annunzio was still in possession. At Christmas, Giolitti, after declaring Fiume a free city, open to all, ordered the royal guard and regular troops to fire on D'Annunzio. The "Bloody Christmas"—five days of fighting—which followed was deplored throughout Italy, and the Army saw to it that legionaries who had left their units without permission to join D'Annunzio were not punished.

Nevertheless, Fiume was freed and Giolitti was—not for the first time—credited with a mastery of his fellow countrymen and the situations in which they contrived to find themselves. D'Annunzio made a funeral oration at the burial of the dead of the five days of Bloody Christmas in which he said: "These Italians gave their blood for the mysterious fact of Latinity." Mussolini commented on the dead to the living D'Annunzio that "It had been an enterprise in the name of liberty." The Poet was eventually persuaded to leave the city precincts on January 10th.

The New Year came in to the sound of revolver shots from one end of the peninsula to the other. At Coreggio there were 3 dead and

20 Socialists wounded. The Fascist *squadristi* based on Bologna, who had done the killing, were not prosecuted. The same pattern was repeated throughout Italy. Chaos seemed to be the resolution for 1921. It opened in Biella with the French shareholders of a textile firm ordering the dismantling of a mill and its re-erection in Switzerland. Foreign stock and shareholders withdrew their money so fast that Giolitti was obliged to place restrictions on the emigration of capital. The farcical element was much in evidence. The breakdown in the postal and communication services saved many firms from bankruptcy, keeping their capital intact by delaying requests from foreign creditors for immediate payment. This enabled firms heavily in debt to have cheques circulating which were never presented. Even *Avanti* commented on the vagaries of the postal and cable services, calling the delays "spectacular." In Turin the undertakers went on strike, leaving bereaved relatives to bury their own dead. The extreme Left took heart from the chaos and started to prepare for another revolution. Crucifixes were torn down from the walls of schools in Naples, and portraits of the royal family were burned in the streets.

However, the revolution had to be postponed for a week or two, because the leaders of the Left had already arrived in Livorno for the party congress. The congress soon promised to be lively. The party's official leader, Filippo Turati, was reproved for having published a critical history of the Bolshevik revolution in Russia without permission. The congress chairman, a Miss Argentina Altobelli, could not keep order. The first day's proceedings dissolved in shouts of "Long Live Communism," with Miss Altobelli deploring the fact that she was not allowed to throw bombs at the delegates. This was January 15th. It was not until a week later, on the 21st, that the congress was able to vote on a motion calling for a hardening of the Socialist line and the renaming of the party Communist. The motion was imposed on the congress in a circular signed by Lenin, Bukharin and Trotsky. It was lost by 57,783 votes to 98,028. After this the congress was carried on in two halves—the Communists in the Teatro San Marco and the Socialists of the Old Guard (in the majority), with their flowing beards, flowing ties, and overflow of resolutions, in the congress hall. The two assemblies decided on different plans of action, and the "Bolshevik threat" was over. The Socialist revolution had committed suicide. For a time, however, the fight was carried on in the streets. Violent men like Dino Grandi, the Fascist leader in Socialist Bologna (Nenni had left the *Fascio* there and gone back to official Socialism), burned down the headquarters and meeting rooms of the party. Warrants for their arrest (there were six current at one time in Grandi's name) were never executed. In other cities like Modena—even in Milan, Turin and Arezzo—Socialists and Communists, from long habit of working together, continued the day-to-day struggle with the *Fasci* in their "Soviet areas." Two Fascists were shot in February at Modena. Between January and March the Soviet Union spent nearly 60 million lire in Italy to assist the infant Communist Party during the first few months of its life. It was money thrown away. It came too late to reinvigorate the party and it was more than matched by the money big business was pouring into the hands of the principal Fascist leaders. Between January and March, 100,000 members of the Socialist and Communist parties refused to renew their subscriptions. The Communist mayor of Rocca Strada was forced to resign under a threat of murder by the local Fascist leader Compagni. The following day a group of Fascists under Francesco Giunta reoccupied Fiume.

On March 2nd somebody sabotaged the aeroplane in which Mussolini was still learning to fly, and he only just managed to escape.

On the morning of March 23, 1921, Mussolini noted that: "There is scarcely time to remember that this is the second anniversary of the foundation of the *Fasci di combattimento*. The battle rages everywhere."

On the afternoon of the same day a small group of anarchists from the suburbs of Florence gave themselves up to the guards outside the cellar beneath the offices of *il Popolo d'Italia* (the *cova* to which the staff retreated in times of emergency). They said they had been given 20 lire each too assassinate the editor. They were taken to Mussolini himself, who forgave them, gave them each another 200 lire and said: "I thought I was worth more than that, but, anyway, you won't have to go home on foot."

In the evening farce gave way to tragedy. A group of Communists let off a bomb in the Teatro Diana in Milan. It seems that they miscalculated the strength of the explosive, which was one they had not used before. They had intended, one of them said at his trial, to "give the bourgeoisie a fright." They killed 18, wounded a further 127. Some of the beauties of Milan who had gathered for a gala performance of the *Blue Mazurka* were horribly mutilated. Fascist squads "on duty" made straight for the offices of *Avanti* and *Humanita Nuova* and burned them to the ground.

This ill-advised Communist bombing only helped to increase the mounting irritation with which the general public regarded the

Left. It is disputable whether or not there was ever a real threat of "Bolshevik revolution"—Salvemini and other historians maintain that so many opportunities were missed that it must be presumed that the threat was imaginary. Nevertheless, the *fear* of a Bolshevik—or even Socialist—revolution was real enough, and the Left did nothing to diminish this fear. If anything, their incompetence as revolutionaries did them more harm than good. Had they been brisk and businesslike, they might have overcome the big business–Armed Forces–Fascist coalition (after all, the Bolsheviks in the Soviet Union overcame the Allies in the civil war). A businesslike revolution always has a chance of success in time of chaos. Salvemini notes that: "Even if there was never the objective danger of a Communist revolution, there was a verbal threat and a subjective fear on the part of the propertied classes; there was a general irritation with disorder; and an alienation of many intellectuals who would otherwise have been Left inclined." The disaster at the Teatro Diana acted as a recruiting drum for the Milan *Fascio*.

There was, of course, still the Popular Party, but its days were numbered. The Curia Cardinals who disapproved of Sturzo were in the ascendant, and Benedict XV was an ailing man. Nevertheless, with 100 M.P.'s it was still a danger to Mussolini. He was well aware of it. He told his followers that it was essential to reduce the amount of violence and create an image of respectability. The Socialist threat had been removed, the party having committed suicide. The Church's bright young men must now be fought, as he put it, "On Sundays in Sunday clothes." His financial backers approved of this drift toward respectability, and urged him to recruit more intellectuals, writers and artists to his movement, to act as counterpoise to the undoubtedly brave, but hooligan, element in the squads.

On April 5, 1921, Mussolini went to see Gabriele D'Annunzio at Gardone Riviera to discuss "plans for the future." D'Annunzio was for violence and disapproved of any plans for "respectability." Marinetti agreed with him. Michele Bianchi thought them both childish and said so, but commented that he believed it a good thing to frighten the bourgeoisie within limits. Bianchi knew that many of the *ras*—Grandi, Roberto Farinacci in Cremona, Italo Balbo in Ferrara—were outside these limits. If they could be persuaded to spill a little of each other's blood, no harm would be done. Balbo and Grandi, who were with Mussolini at Gardone, were told to "warn the bourgeoisie that they must defend themselves."[13] Giuseppe Bottai mistrusted both the pacification of the bourgeoisie and the bloodletting among the *ras*. He suspected treachery, that the "Fascist revolution was being betrayed." He did not say so openly, but wrote leaders in *l'Ardito*, recommending a Futurist solution, "the association of desperate ideas." Nobody, not even Marinetti, was quite sure what the Futurist solution would mean in practice. When Parliament was dissolved and elections fixed for May 15th, the Futurists, the *ras* and the "respectable element," all fought for places on the electoral list. This time they knew that everything was on their side. Giolitti had "arranged" elections before, secret ballot or no, and he would see to it that a good number of Fascists were elected. As far as Giolitti was concerned, every Fascist in the Chamber meant one less Socialist or Catholic.

Giolitti soon realized that he had made a mistake and underestimated Mussolini. He was shown photographs of a procession which had taken place in Bologna and Ferrara three days before he dissolved Parliament. According to reports, 20,000 Fascists had marched past Mussolini in perfect order. All of them were armed. The months of training by the Army were beginning to show results. Indeed, many of the Fascists marching had never been demobilized and had been fighting, foreigners or Italians, since 1915. A minority, like Farinacci, had fought only in the streets. The 20,000 were certainly well disciplined if not less violent. Italo Balbo had been given the responsibility for their formation into an hierarchy of para-military units, and he had found the right formula: two of guns to one of drums.[14]

The election campaign of 1921 was unlike anything Italy had ever seen, though the pattern was to become familiar in Nazi Germany. Processions by daylight and torchlight. Bands, silver and brass, playing military marches and songs of World War I. Gala performances at concert halls and theatres, with collection boxes discreetly available. Nothing was forgotten. If the stage management was any indication of the quality of government, the Fascist group (it was still not a party) deserved to be elected. Even The Poet, his bald head gleaming, put in an appearance, allowing a facsimile of his Fascist membership card (issued in Fiume on October 5, 1920) to be published widely.

In a report to Mussolini on the eve of the election, Balbo boasted that the movement now had 2,000 local sections and 300,000 registered, paid-up members. If it was still very much a personal thing, with the strength of *Fasci* depending largely on the strength of the personality of the local leader (it was strongest of all in Bologna, Ferrara and Milan, under Grandi, Balbo and Mussolini), it was not in any way a movement to be politically ignored. It was certainly the best-organised and most purposeful political entity, and in moments of national chaos and general uncertainty a man who has made up his mind (even wrongly) stands a good chance of being entrusted with power.

The election was, in fact, a "famous victory." The Socialist Party representation went down drastically. The "old parties" were dominated. The Nationalists, who had fought on a common programme with Mussolini, but in a different list, made substantial gains. The Popular Catholic Party, too, gained 8 seats, but Fascists won 35. Mussolini was elected twice; received 124,918 votes in Milan, more than twice the number given to his Socialist opponent; and was also returned by the Bologna-Ferrara-Forlì constituency by his old comrades, now nearly all members of local *Fasci*.

Mussolini was, however, not complacent about the victory. He knew that there was a movement to "constitutionalize Mussolini," and he urged his friends to resist any temptation to be domesticated. He urged them not to take their seats during the opening of Parliament while the King was present, because the "Fascist movement is slightly Republican, though without any prejudices." Mussolini did abstain from the State opening, though Farinacci and Bottai went along to brawl with the Minister of Labour on the floor of the Chamber.

On June 26, 1921, Foreign Minister Sforza announced the government's intention to cede the Italian-occupied territory of Porto Baros to Jugoslavia. There were Fascists still quartered openly in Fiume (Giunta had left the city to fight the elections), and they kept it in permanent revolt. Throughout the last week in June there were riots, Nationalist and Fascist inspired, all over Italy. The casualty list reached the thousands, and Giolitti, who had always prided himself on his ability to "keep order," promptly resigned. Mussolini was embarrassed by the violence with which Balbo, Grandi and Farinacci were fighting what often seemed to be private vendettas with local Socialist leaders. He urged them to show some moderation, and pointed out to them that if they did not, then the bourgeoisie who had voted for them in the recent elections would transfer their loyalty to the "priests' party."

On June 30th the King sent for Mussolini, to discuss the government crisis. Bottai, who accompanied him to the palace, urged Mussolini to ask for the principal portfolio himself and form a coalition with the Nationalists and the old Right. The King, however, did not believe the "Duce" capable of keeping order in his own ranks, much less in the country as a whole, and they discussed the possibility of a government headed by de Nicola or Bonomi. The King finally asked Ivanoe Bonomi, a mild "reformer," to form the best government he could.[15]

The moderate elements in the Fascist movement were disappointed. They had hoped to go from electoral success into office without delay. They were not even offered a single portfolio by Bonomi, and Mussolini decided that the policy of the movement should be to bring the government down. However, before he could put this policy into practice he had to have an alternative to present to the King. If possible, the 35 Fascist M.P.'s had to be transformed into a shadow cabinet. Talks were opened in secret with Federzoni and the Nationalists, to see how far they would go toward joining a coalition.

On July 21st there was what Fascist historians call the "massacre of Sarzana," a military ambush by Socialists of a Fascist procession. The police fired into the ensuing mêlée, without discrimination, and by some coincidence Fascist casualties were enormous (20 dead and 100 wounded), while the Socialists lost not a single life. The ambush was considered to be a reprisal for Fascist insistence that Misiano, a wartime deserter and Socialist M.P., be expelled from the Chamber (he was in fact removed from his seat). Grandi and the ultra-violent wing of the movement proposed a nationwide massacre of Socialists, with the burning of their meeting rooms and offices and the dynamiting of all their newspapers. In Parliament Grandi announced that he was "ready to die" and "do his duty."

Mussolini was impressed by the "massacre of Sarzana." He had believed the initiative in violence had passed to him. He deplored Grandi, but had believed him to be the "master of the streets." Now it seemed that the Socialists, who had opened tentative negotiations with Michele Bianchi for a truce after the elections, were in fact negotiating from some strength. Mussolini wanted office; now he was in Parliament. He did not want to face another election. A coalition with the Popular Party was personally as distasteful to him as it was to Giolitti, and the Nationalists were too demanding.[16] He told Bottai that it might be possible to come to some sort of agreement with the Socialists—a cease fire, if not a prelude to coalition. Above all, he insisted in a letter to Grandi, Farinacci and Balbo: "The time has come for regulation action within the framework of the Constitution, until we are strong enough to change the Constitution."

On August 2, 1921, much against the will of the *ras*, a truce was signed between the National Council of the *Fasci di combattimento* and the Executive of the Socialist Party. Mussolini made a speech at the signing in which he described it as a historic event. He was especially intrigued by the idea of a permanent accommodation which would enable him to rejoin the Socialism of his youth and early manhood, rejoining "at the top." But the *ras* would have none of the truce, and suspected Mussolini's tender feelings for his old comrades.

Grandi, behind the scenes, made contact with the other extremist leaders in the provinces and proposed that the National Council be forced to break the truce and declare war on the Socialist Party, to "avenge Sarzana." In Emilia, Venice and Romagna, Grandi found immediate agreement, if not on any ideological grounds or in the name of the purity of the movement, at least on the desirability of action and the reasonableness of bloodshed. The recent occupations and evacuations of Fiume, according to Grandi, represented a victory for Reason over an Idea, and Fascism, he said, ". . . is nothing if it is not an Idea."

On August 17th the opposition inside the movement had grown so vocal that Mussolini resigned from the executive. He said: "Only fools refuse to understand. I wanted the armistice with the Socialists. Now it seems that hundreds of Fascists do not want it and do not want me. I am not going so much as being forced by them to go."

The government press ran banner headlines on the CRISIS OF FASCISM. But Mussolini's backers had no intention of letting all their time, money and effort go to waste. After ten days of bribery, corruption and intimidation, the majority of the members of the National Council had been "convinced." On August 27th they rejected Mussolini's resignation and confirmed the armistice.

Grandi was not dismayed. Campagni sent Mussolini a telegram to the effect that he and the squads in the suburbs of Florence considered the armistice at an end. Grandi himself spent his days fomenting disorder and intriguing for support. Eight Black Shirts were killed at Modena by the royal guard on September 26th. Mussolini buried the armistice with his dead. He accused Prime Minister Bonomi of conspiring with the Socialists; of having undermined the armistice for his own ends. On November 2nd, as the body of the Unknown Soldier was being interred in the Altara della Patria, Mussolini declared that the resurrection of patriotism lay entirely to the credit of the Fascist movement, which would "always have something new to say."

On November 7th, in the Augusteo, the National Congress of Fascists met to discuss their future plans. Though there had been rumours, it was not until Mussolini went to the rostrum (cheers and whistles) that he revealed that it had been decided to transform the movement into a party, the National Fascist Party, that the period of struggle was at an end, that the fight on the benches of Parliament was to begin. The *ras* were bitterly opposed to the idea of "constitutionalization," the very process against which Mussolini had warned them. Around the Augusteo and in the evenings in the suburbs they deliberately provoked disorders, in an attempt to convince the congress that the fight was still on in the streets. Many young officers, like Giovanni Passerone and Enzo Galbiati, were opposed to the "partification" of the movement because "it would destroy this glorious spirit which has moved us." Sensitive to accusations of "careerism," which they had hurled at so many Socialists, their only aim—where they had a clear one—was to "purge the country," then go home. Mussolini said, on November 21st: "We are a voluntary Militia at the service of the Nation. We are with the State when it defends the interests of the Nation. We will take over from the State when it shows itself incapable of fighting. We will fight the State when it falls into the hands of those who threaten its existence."[17]

It was only by five votes that the National Fascist Party was born. In closed session the congress debated two alternatives. They could carry on as before, without Mussolini, under the leadership of Dino Grandi; or they could become a party under the leadership of Mussolini. It was only after sweat and toil in the anterooms that Bottai and Michele Bianchi managed to ensure the bare majority for the Mussolini line. If Grandi had won, nobody knows what might have been the future of Italy. The violence of the original movement might well have spent itself and *il Popolo d'Italia* become just an eccentric, excessively patriotic daily newspaper.

But the party was born, albeit with some trepidation on the part of the midwives, and Mussolini confirmed again as "Duce." Prime Minister Bonomi realized the significance of the change and warned Parliament, on December 6th, that its life "may well be limited." Mussolini's rivals were mysteriously attacked. Farinacci narrowly escaped assassination at Cremona. Lorenzo Palzani was shot in the face at Voltuna. Antonio Pagani died near Cremona. The new Fascist Party closed its ranks and prepared for constitutional victory in 1922.

In the Vatican a new Pope was enthroned. Benedict XV had died, and as had been predicted, Achille Ratti was chosen to succeed him. Ratti took the title of Pius XI. During his years as head of the Ambrosian Library in Milan he had conceived an extreme dislike for the Popular Catholic Party and its leaders. He disliked especially the vigorous young priests, among them Angelo Roncalli (later Pope John XXIII), who invigorated the party in nearby Bergamo.[18] He was determined to "dissolve" the Popular Party, which he regarded as an essentially unchristian enterprise. His first acts were to remove from office in the Vatican all the young progressive priests who had acquired key posts. Angelo Roncalli was removed from his post as head of Propaganda Faith, in which he had been invaluable to Sturzo. Pius XI, known as a "holy" man, was determined to keep the Church's own to itself. He would bargain with governments, but did not want to see his cardinals form part of one. His friends in Milan told him that the government would soon be in the hands of Benito Mussolini, "a sound if somewhat wild ex-Socialist." Had Pius XI continued Benedict's policy of aid and encouragement to the Popular Party, Luigi Sturzo might have been able to hold off Mussolini and his disunited, if disciplined, "militia." But neither Sturzo nor the effective leaders of the Left received any help from industry, the Church or the trade unions. The Church abandoned Sturzo. The trade unions and Moscow abandoned the Socialists. The Communists were too weak to fight.

Nenni and Mussolini met dramatically on a bench on the promenade at Cannes on January 7, 1922. They discussed, as old friends, the possibility of—if not an alliance—at least a renewal of the armistice. But the gap between them was too wide. More important than the ideological and sentimental differences which Nenni later chronicled, it was too obvious that Mussolini was on the winning side and Nenni a late convert to the losers. They parted without a handshake.

On January 8th Communists killed a Fascist university student at Borgiola. One of D'Annunzio's legionaries was beaten to death by Communists at Prato. On January 14th a sixteen-year-old Fascist was beaten to death with a hammer by Socialist teenagers. The *ras*, with Mussolini's blessing, hit back, burning down trade-union and labour council rooms, beating up officials. At the peak of the violence Mussolini issued the "Manifesto of Fascist Womanhood," in which he exhorted the fair sex to be gentle and forbearing and not to imitate men.[19]

In February the disorders multiplied, though under Mussolini's control (he held Grandi and the other *ras* on a tight rein, letting them go sporadically to relieve the tension, then reining them in again). It became impossible for Bonomi to govern. Mussolini hoped for an invitation to form a government with his brand-new party and shadow cabinet. On February 4th he spent four minutes with the King; on the 20th, thirteen minutes. On the 24th there was an anti-Bonomi demonstration in Florence, and on the 26th he resigned. His place was taken by a third-rate lawyer, Facta, who was universally recognized as a stopgap. He was, in fact, a creature of Giolitti, whose own candidature for the ministry had been vetoed by Don Luigi Sturzo. It has been suggested that had Sturzo supported Giolitti's candidature, the march on Rome would never have occurred. However, Giolitti had said many times in public that he preferred to retire rather than owe allegiance in part to a priest, and the real sources of power in the country had already decided to install a Fascist government to restore order. Mussolini was already sure of himself, and had begun the first of his triumphal tours, prophesying a "new glory for Rome." He felt sufficiently confident to go to Rome early in March, leave the party in the hands of Bianchi and Achille Starace (recovering from an attempted assassination), and confer with the German Right.

There is no record of Mussolini's consultations with the industrialists and army officers who were suppressing the Left in Germany, though they are known to have taken place. Mussolini always referred to them in later years as "nursery talks," but it seems certain that Italian businessmen arranged to have him "processed" by their colleagues in the north.[20]

The condition of the Socialist Party continued to grow worse. Forty-seven Socialists were put on trial in Moscow for "crimes against the Revolution," and Mussolini made much of this in his paper. On May 1st he wrote: "For thirty years in these parts we have not seen such a miserable May Day. How many months must pass before Italian Socialism forgoes its ridiculous proposals for revenge and its conviction that Fascism will never rise to power?"

On May 12th, without Mussolini's permission, Italo Balbo, with 40,000 armed Fascists in uniform, occupied Ferrara. On the next day, to regain the initiative inside the party, Mussolini was forced to show himself even more aggressive than Balbo, addressing meetings, writing sulphuric editorials, and fighting a duel with Mario Missiroli, the future editor of *il Corrierre della Sera* (he was wounded three times). On May 24th Mussolini told a crowd that he had thunderbolts in his pocket, ready to loose on the government. The crowd cheered. The *ras* opined that he had at last come to his senses. On June 4th he eulogized the strength of the *ras* at a meeting in Bologna, praising Grandi for his exceptional loyalty and "fiery patriotism," and noting to Bottai that he must be got rid of as soon as possible.

On June 7th Prime Minister Facta asked his private secretary to arrange talks with Mussolini. Rumours spread in the capital that the Popular Party was reaching agreement with the Socialists on a common front against the Fascists. The rumours were given little credence, but served to repair a temporary breach of confidence which had opened between Nationalists and Fascists. The Church, too, reacted to the rumour with a criticism of Facta (Cardinal Gasparri commented that, being a gentleman in politics, he deserved to be liquidated). Church leaders voiced the opinion that it "would be as well to seat Mussolini now as later." On June 13th Facta came into possession of a confidential instruction to the Rome *ras* to "hold himself ready for any eventuality." On July 19th, losing a vote in the Chamber of Deputies, Facta resigned. He told his wife that he had never been so happy in his life.

But on July 30th Facta was back in power again. Mussolini had told the King that only Giolitti could restore order, knowing that Giolitti no longer enjoyed anybody's support. The Socialists would have formed a government but were not invited. Mussolini was not yet ready.

The Fascist Party was, in fact, still divided about means and ends. On June 4th, in Milan, a congress of syndicalist corporations, prepared by Bottai, seemed to suggest that the party was aiming at peaceful conquest of power followed by the implementation of a declared programme. The programme discussed by the congress was one of reorganization of the industrial structure of the country, of worker participation in industry, commerce and government through corporations (workers and intellectuals would join according to their trades or professions), as well as through Parliament. However, side by side with the peaceful syndicalists sat representatives of the *ras* to whom the words peaceful and Parliament were anathema.

Farinacci disobeyed Mussolini's orders to "quiet down his boys," and occupied Cremona. Balbo took over civil power in Parma. By August 8th most of the key cities were in the hands of the local *Fasci*, with the civil authorities either banished or in office on sufferance.

On August 9th, Mussolini, anxious to restore confidence in his respectability, ordered the demobilization of the militia "until it should be needed again." In a communiqué issued to the press he said that the danger of a Socialist general strike and Bolshevik *coup d'état* (the one real; the other imaginary) had passed. D'Annunzio spoke from balconies, in support of riots, then pacification. An impression, not entirely accurate, was created in the country that Mussolini could manipulate, at will, riots, pacification, poets and *ras*, and was in some way comparable to a giant political switchboard operator. The Prefect of Milan sent several urgent telegrams to Facta, asking him what he was to do in the event of a Fascist *coup* in the municipality. The Crèdito Italiano was asked by Mussolini for a huge loan, and wired to Facta for permission to grant it (the Socialists had withdrawn their funds from the national banks).

Achille Starace and Michele Bianchi spent most of their time either interviewing Facta's private secretary and assuring him that no *coup d'état* was intended, or interviewing recalcitrant *ras* and trying to stop them from making one.

On August 24th the King asked Facta if he thought Mussolini could be trusted. The following day a group of ex-legionaries asked D'Annunzio what he thought would happen next. Did he think they ought to march on Rome as they had marched on Fiume? D'Annunzio answered: "A move on Rome is premature because it has to be made in enormous force, even for the Fascists, because they have not yet been able to give an organic unity to their own actions nor give any political or social content to what they call their programme."

Signs of a rivalry between The Poet and Mussolini were appearing. Mussolini stopped consulting D'Annunzio and sent him instead galley proofs of *il Popolo d'Italia*, recording action accomplished. The *ras* became impatient again. Farinacci accused Mussolini of "just using the Black Shirts to intimidate the government instead of giving the order to march and take it over."

On September 22, 1922, at Udine, Mussolini replied to his critics: "From the banks of the Piave we began the march towards the supreme end—Rome. There are neither men nor things which can stop us." [21]

But they were words. The country met in cafés and bars and wondered if and how the words would be translated into facts. There were rumours that Grandi was about to march on Rome himself (encampments of Black Shirts were springing up outside the city); that D'Annunzio would march; that Mussolini had accepted office in a coalition government. Farinacci told Mussolini privately that if he did accept such an offer he would shoot him himself, that the government would collapse like a house of cards at the first shot from a Black Shirt gun. In a statement to the press General Badoglio said that the Army was ready to defend the Constitution and that Fascism would collapse like a house of cards at the first shot from the guns of loyal troops.

Badoglio denied the statement next day, but the damage had been done. The hard core of *ras* was now determined to force the issue. They were, however, prepared to admit that without Mussolini they would not know what to do with power when they got it, and that they had to reorganize if they were not to be defeated by the first determined police patrol they met. In the Holland Hotel at Torre Pellice, Italo Balbo, Cesare Maria de Vecchi (the Piedmontese *ras*), and General Emilio de Bono discussed and perfected a complete "militarization" of the forces at the disposal of the party—an estimated 200,000 armed men. De Bono was a regular officer and his alignment with the *ras* caused an outcry, sponsored by the Socialists, in Parliament. De Bono's resignation was demanded, and he was threatened with a court martial by Minister of War Soleri (October 3rd).[22]

Mussolini took this opportunity of calling together the various leaders of the party and warning them that "the time was not yet ripe." When he was asked when the time would be ripe, he said he would give them an answer within fourteen days. On October 16th, at Milan, Bianchi, Balbo, de Vecchi, Teruzzi, de Bono (continuing to defy the Minister of War), Fara, Ceccerini and Igliori, met to hear the answer. Farinacci again demanded action and suggested Mussolini think twice before accepting a compromise solution to the problem, or any office in a "democratic pastiche of a government."

Italo Balbo, who made notes at the meeting, wrote that Mussolini made a speech in which he proposed that the party hand over control to a quadrumvirate of Balbo, de Bono, de Vecchi and Bianchi, as from Saturday next at noon. These four men were to remobilize the militia and occupy the main cities—Turin, Milan, Piacenza, Rimini (though these cities had never recovered from the Fascist occupation of August 4th). Three additional "armies" would be formed and billeted at Ancona, Orte, Citta Vecchia—surrounding Rome and blocking its approaches. At the Congress of Naples on the 24th, "they would see how it had turned out."

When he was asked by de Vecchi to name the actual day for the March on Rome, Mussolini said that de Bono was still working on the Army, Balbo was still working on the militarization of the militia, and all needed time. It was pointed out to Mussolini that the *ras* would not wait long, and eventually he agreed, "all things being equal," to start the march on November 7th.

On October 24th de Bono and de Vecchi (farcically Balbo stayed behind because he did not have a dark suit) called on the Queen Mother, who had been "working on" the King and urging him to depart from constitutional practice and ask Mussolini to form a government. De Bono assured the Queen Mother of Mussolini's loyalty and deplored the possibility that the royal guard might fire on marching Fascists, "her Majesty's most devoted subjects." She was told that the date of the march on Rome had been fixed for the 7th. The King, her son, was the only man who could stop it—by declaring martial law. De Bono pleaded with her to use her influence with the King "to avoid bloodshed." She told de Bono that she would do her best.

The congress of the Fascist Party that day was an enormous success. Those who did not travel to Naples marched past the local *Fasci* headquarters in their home towns. Naples itself was a circus of march and countermarch. The word had gone out on the 20th that there was to be no disorder, and the command was obeyed. The Prime Minister, observing this, wired to the King, who was in the country at San Rossore: INFORM YOUR MAJESTY FASCIST REUNION NAPLES OF NO IMPORTANCE.[23] The atmosphere at Naples was, however, so tense that the King's advisers told him that Facta had misread the situation and ought to be told so. Facta was cabled to attend the King, but regretted that he was busy in the capital. He had, in fact, had a bright idea. Knowing that a certain strain on the relationship between D'Annunzio and Mussolini had been placed by the Duce's insistence on the "premiership of the Revolution," Facta had decided to use The Poet as an anti-Fascist. He invited D'Annunzio to Rome on November 4th, the day celebrated in Italy as Armistice Day, to deliver an address at the Tomb of the Unknown Soldier. D'Annunzio immediately accepted this invitation. Facta was delighted—Mussolini and the *ras* alarmed when they heard of it. They all knew that D'Annunzio was capable of exhausting the reserves of national pride and patriotic enthusiasm on which the Quadrumvirate was counting for popular support.

On the morning of October 26th Mussolini brought the date of the march forward to November 3rd.[24] Mobilization was to begin next day, the 27th. They were to make camp around Rome on the 28th. In case of defeat on the 3rd, they were to retreat to Central Italy, protected by "reserves" in Umbria. A bill of exchange for three million lire signed by de Vecchi, Balbo, de Bono, Civelli and

Postiglione, was to be deposited with a bank, to finance any claim on the party made as a consequence of the march. The Rome correspondent of the London *Times* wired that "the occupation of Rome is a matter not of days, but of hours."

Mussolini, however, never had any intention of marching on Rome and allowing the *ras* and the militia to hold him to ransom ever after. He was in close consultation with the Queen Mother, and he was determined to show as much calm as the leaders of the Socialist Party, one of whom had left for Moscow with a declaration that he was confident that the good sense of the Italian people would prevail (Serrati). He knew that Minister of War Soleri had issued instructions for the Navy to resist by force and oppose any attempt to land Fascist reinforcements from Sardinia (in open revolt since March). General Badoglio had been ordered to take command in Rome under the instructions of Minister of the Interior Taddei. Taddei was receiving innumerable cables from the Prefect of Milan, asking for instructions and suggesting that a *coup d'état* was planned for the night of the 27th.

Mussolini was, however, assured by the Queen Mother that this was all "just to reassure some of the more delicate members of Parliament." She prevailed upon Facta to invite Mussolini, by phone, to come to Rome from Milan and discuss a "peaceful solution." Facta's price for recommending to the King that Mussolini be invited to form a government was a portfolio for himself and "certain compensations." Mussolini said he would think it over. He told his *ras* that he had "decided on the necessity for a show of strength." He told the prefect of Milan that there "would be no show of strength." He put about the rumour that he had come to an arrangement with Giolitti. Even de Vecchi believed this last rumour and phoned the palace to query it with a friend, the King's aide, General Cittadini.

At 4 p.m. on the 26th the cabinet met and issued a statement to the effect that the government did not intend to resign. Mussolini had already agreed to go to Rome by October 30th at the latest. He had confided to the staff of *Popolo d'Italia* that "it is a pity but there may well be no march on Rome. History is accelerating." Then, to show calm, he went to the theatre. His correspondent in Naples rang Milan later to tell him that in Naples everybody believed the march was to begin that night at midnight. Mussolini refused to even come to the phone.

At dawn on the 27th Bianchi rang the *Popolo d'Italia* to see if there was any news. He was told that "the date is still the third."

Mussolini lied to him that Giolitti had offered him four ministries in a coalition government, and he was tempted to accept—if only to spite Farinacci—then added that "the machine is in motion and maybe it cannot be stopped." Bianchi eventually hung up and got in touch with Farinacci, ordering him to mobilize and get ready for "an immediate blow at a minute's notice." Telegrams reached the Ministry of the Interior that morning from the prefects of Pisa, Venice, Genoa, Perugia and Forlì, asking for reinforcements and announcing that the final Fascist mobilization had begun. Facta immediately got in touch with Mussolini and asked him the meaning of this "betrayal." Mussolini's only reply was that he had been forced to "take a more urgent view of matters." He might have to go to Rome before the 30th, he said, and it might no longer be possible to speak in terms of compromise.

The King reached Rome at seven o'clock in the evening after a bad journey. He soon realized that the city was in a state of siege, and reproved Facta for refusing to come to see him or ask him to come to Rome before. At nine o'clock Facta told him that he did not believe any sort of coalition government was possible—that nobody would even speak to him on the telephone. The King's reply was "Nonsense," and he ordered Facta to send for Mussolini "for talks" immediately. It was raining heavily in Rome. The Queen Mother was omnipresent.

From the Hotel Brufani at Perugia, the Quadrumvirate, fearing that Mussolini would double-cross them at the last minute, decided to bring forward the date of the march to the 30th, and issued a proclamation signed by Mussolini: "Fascists of all Italy! The decisive hour of battle is at hand!"

Mussolini was furious. Early in the morning of the 28th he was already at the offices of *il Popolo*, busy checking the stocks of ink and newsprint for a special edition. He never lost the habit of wasting his time on details he could easily delegate to women. At five in the morning the cabinet met in Rome. The Prime Minister's private secretary told Facta that Bianchi had telephoned from Perugia to say that the "machine was in motion and could not be stopped." It was Facta's turn to be angry. He ordered all negotiations with Fascists to cease and said that he would never "even eat a meal with Mussolini, much less share the burdens of State with such a worthless adventurer." At six o'clock orders went out, signed by Facta and the Minister of the Interior, bringing the Armed Forces to a state of immediate readiness. At 6.05 and 6.35 a.m. Facta cabled to all prefects, asking them to confirm their loyalty to the constitution. At 6.55, the draft of a state of siege in his hand, Facta wrote out a proclamation addressed to the population of Rome, warning them to "oppose sedition."[25]

Luigi Federzoni, the leader of the Nationalists and the only man still on speaking terms with both Facta and Mussolini, phoned the Duce in Milan (using knowingly the tapped phone in the office of the Minister of the Interior). He spoke first to Aldo Finzi, and told him that General de Bono insisted that he come to Rome with Mussolini. Finzi told him that the Army in Milan seemed to be stopping them from going anywhere. Mussolini then came to the phone and told Federzoni that: "The action in Milan has begun. Other solutions are now impossible. The Movement is serious all over Italy. The solution of the crisis must come from the Right, from the Right . . ." When Federzoni asked him what he meant, he replied: "A Fascist Government or nothing."

At nine o'clock, just after Federzoni had told three of Facta's cabinet that Mussolini was now intransigent and that all hopes of a "deal" were off, Facta himself and Taddei came back from an audience with the King, and told the cabinet that the King had refused to sign the state of siege. Federzoni left the cabinet room and spent the next half hour talking to Davanzati and Grandi about "putting pressure on the Liberal Right." But both Facta's talks with his cabinet and Federzoni's cabinet, meeting at his house, were inconclusive, for the simple reason that Mussolini was in Milan.

At nine-thirty Facta asked the King again to sign a state of siege and proclaim martial law. Again the King refused. The rumour had just reached him that Mussolini was negotiating with his cousin the Duke of Aosta, and had promised to "save the dynasty even if it means dethroning the King." His reaction was to tell his wife that the Queen Mother was right—that "Mussolini is certainly the man of the hour."

At 9.45 a.m. Federzoni phoned Mussolini again to urge him to take the first plane or train to Rome. Again Mussolini put him off with vague promises, insisting on "a concrete offer," and saying that he had "no time for exploratory talks." A procession of Army, Navy and political leaders called on the King to offer their advice and help: Diaz, de Revel, Salandra, Tittoni, Orlando. They all told the King that he had no alternative: Send for Mussolini.

At eleven Federzoni phoned the prefect of Milan and told him that within a few hours Mussolini would have his telegram from the King, and that he was to tell the Duce to "hold himself ready." Outside the offices of *il Popolo d'Italia*, barricaded like those of

Newspapers edited by Mussolini, the greatest journalist of his day. As a politician he did not know how to keep himself off the front page.

La Lotta di Classe

Organo della Federazione Collegiale Socialista Forlivese

ESCE OGNI SABATO

Potenza

Minestrone

DOVE IL ROGO ARSE.

Per Mario Todeschini

Anno I. N. 1 — Milano, 22 Novembre 1913

UTOPIA

Rivista Quindicinale del Socialismo Rivoluzionario Italiano

Direttore: BENITO MUSSOLINI — Redattore: GIUSEPPE DE FALCO

SOMMARIO:

B. MUSSOLINI: *Al largo!* — J. GUESDE: *Pagine dimenticate (La rivoluzione come fatto storico)* — G. DE FALCO: *Il trionfo di un metodo* — NOI: *Costantino Lazzari* — G. BARNI: *I sofi dell'anarchismo* — G. BALDAZZI: *Augusto Blanqui* — IL FASTIDITO: *Vittoria molfettese* — L'AMMINISTRATORE: *Parole chiare* — *Riviste socialiste* (Neue Zeit — Sozialistische Monathshefte — Socialist Review — Vie Ouvrière — L'effort libre — Die Tat)

Abbonamenti: Anno L. 10 — Semestre L. 5

Direzione ed Amministrazione: MILANO — Via Castelmorone, N. 19

Il Popolo d'Italia

Chi ha del ferro, ha del pane. — BLANQUI

quotidiano socialista

La Rivoluzione, è un'idea che ha trovato delle baionette. — NAPOLEONE

ABBONAMENTI

Anno I. - N. 1 - Milano, domenica 15 novembre 1914

DIREZIONE ED AMMINISTRAZIONE — Via Paolo da Cannobbio, 35

AUDACIA!

La bandiera del Profeta al vento: tutto l'Islam in armi!

I Giapponesi in Egitto — I Greci in territorio bulgaro

Il bando della Guerra Santa — Tutto l'Islam in armi

Garanzie tedesche per la Libia — Anche il Profeta è agli ordini del Kaiser!

Palmi di terreno conquistati a caro prezzo

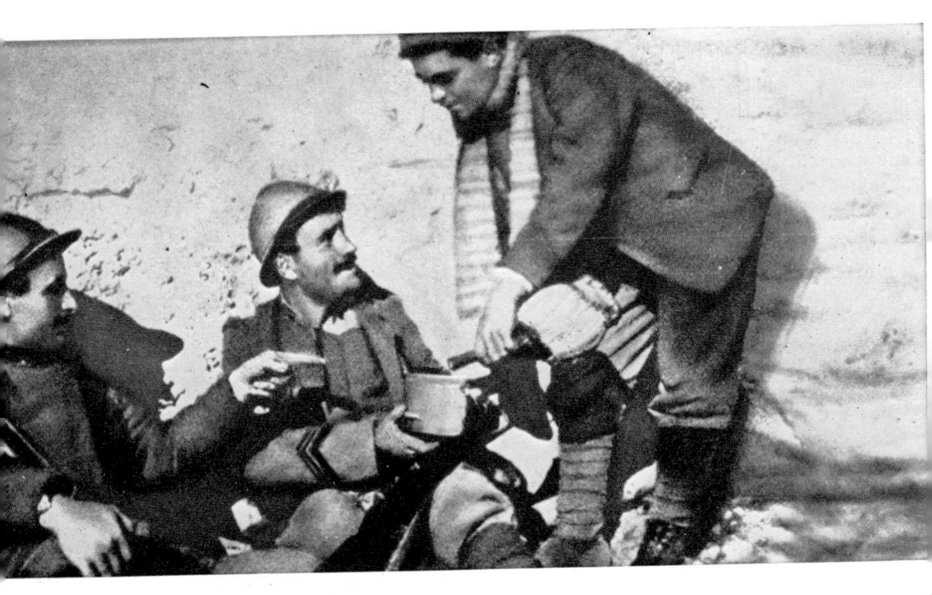

During World War One Mussolini served in the 11th Regiment of Bersaglieri and received wounds. The lower left picture was taken in 1917 with his wife and son Vittorio and daughter Edda.

The offices of *Il Popolo d'Italia.* A hand grenade on the editor's desk, barbed wire in the courtyard, the editor's pate aglow with professionalism.

The Red Flag *versus* the Black Shirt. Communists guard a factory they have occupied with posted notices.

October 1922: The March on Rome. From left to right in the front row: De Bono, Teruzzi, Balbo, Mussolini, De Vecchi, Giunta.

October 1922: Mussolini barricades the streets of Milan against the Socialists, who had sworn to burn down the offices of his paper.

The London Conference.
Poincaré, Bonar Law,
Mussolini and Theunis.

King George V visited Italy in 192
and conferred on Mussolini the Mos
Honourable Order of the Bath.

"I feel myself profoundly rural"—Mussolini.

The battle for wheat – Mussolini reaps.

1929: The Lateran Pacts. The reconciliation between Church and State. With Mussolini is Cardinal Gasparri.

1933: Mussolini with the Soviet delegate Litvinov to the "peace and trade" talks.

December 1931: Funeral of Mussolini's brother Arnaldo—Mussolini in bowler hat.

15th June 1934: Hitler is received at his own request "on the soil of the great Fascist Revolution".

Mussolini drained the Pontine Marshes, where even Caesar failed . . .
and solved his unemployment problem.

Mussolini's new towns.

Italian women give their jewe
and wedding rings to fight Eder
sanctions against the Ethiopi
War.

General Galbiati commends the Militia Saubada Legion.

Galbiati and Passerone recruiting in Casale Monferrato, near the author's home in Italy.

Il Duce petrified in the desert, 1936.

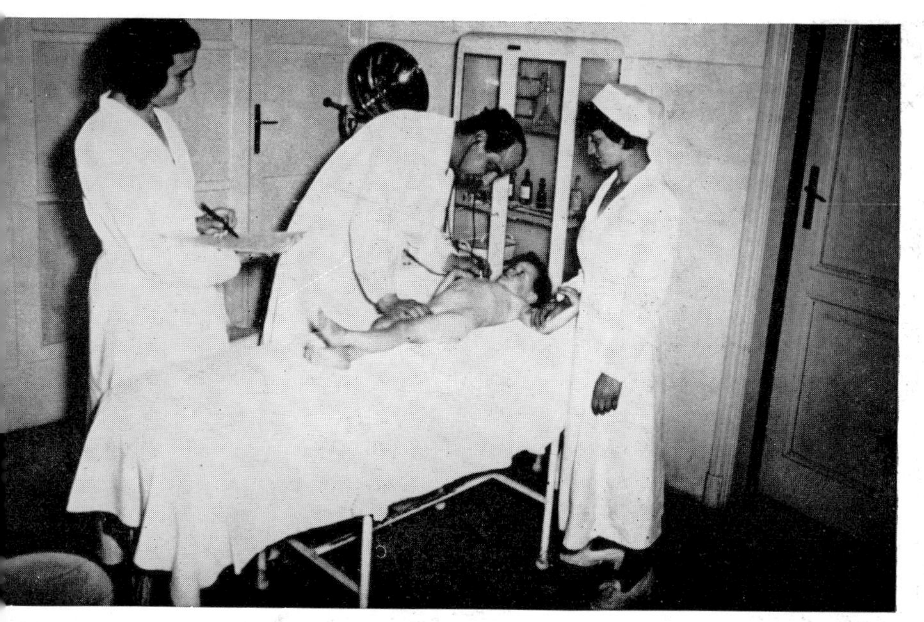

"Numbers mean strength." More babies and better mothers for the régime.

Mussolini—"idol of the young".

Avanti, crowds milled and cheered. An over-enthusiastic Fascist let off his gun several times, narrowly missing Mussolini's ear.

At three o'clock the Prefect of Milan asked Federzoni, by phone, for the latest news. Dissatisfied with Federzoni's answer, he rang the Prime Minister. He told Facta that Mussolini had already given him a list of ministers who were to be confirmed in their portfolios before Mussolini would leave for Rome. He was told by Facta that "it had nothing to do with him any more, he was trying hard to go home."

At 5 p.m. General Cittadini rang Mussolini to say that de Vecchi urged him to come to Rome immediately. Mussolini replied that he would not move until invited by the King himself to form a government.

At 11.20 Federzoni phoned again, told Mussolini that he was sitting in a room with Ciano, Grandi, de Vecchi and an aide of the King, and that they all "urged him to come to Rome . . . not a question of compromising the Revolution but of showing a sense of responsibility."

Mussolini rang off.

On October 29, 1921, *Popolo d'Italia* carried a leading article, in part censored, which ended with the words: "Fascism wants power and will have it."

The King, having tried every way of getting Mussolini to Rome without losing face, eventually gave in. His last hope—that of a Salandra Ministry plus Mussolini—had gone, as his mother had said it would. At four-thirty that afternoon he told Cittadini to wire Mussolini to come to Rome to form a government of his own. After a small party at the offices of *il Popolo d'Italia*, Mussolini left for Rome. He had refused the prefect's suggestion of a special train ("too expensive"), hurriedly packed some clothes in a suitcase, and said good-bye to his mistress at the station. His last act was to give the order to burn down the offices of *Avanti*. "Tomorrow it must not come out, or I'll have the whole country around my ears."

He arrived in Rome in the early hours of the 30th, just as the Fascist camps around the city were breaking up and the columns forming for the march on the city. The *ras* were white with fury. They had been "sold a government." But there was nothing to be done. They hurriedly changed the orders for invasion to one for celebration.

At 11.45 a.m. on October 30th, Mussolini, in a black shirt above unpressed trousers and unpolished shoes and with a growth of beard, presented himself to the King. "Your Majesty," he said. "I am sorry to come here in a black shirt, but I have come straight from the battlefield."

At twelve noon the march on Rome of 40,000 bedraggled Black Shirts began. It was no longer necessary. The chief had got there before them, unshaven but "within his rights." As Mussolini said himself: "I allowed them to share my triumph, without being indebted to them for it."

Farinacci and Bottai, both with colds (it had been raining for three days in their camps), entered the city sneezing. Federzoni told his friends that he was in office at last. General Badoglio told his wife that he had chosen the wrong side, but thought he could put it right. Grandi thought that he would soon be going on his travels. The King hoped he had done the right thing. Everybody set to work on aides and ushers, to get as early an appointment as possible with the new Prime Minister. Except his wife. In later years she told a newspaper reporter that she had not gone to Rome, because she "thought he might be busy and what could she have done, anyway, but light the stove?"

The Duce, said the slogans on the wall, was always right.

4

NORMALIZZAZIONE

NORMALIZATION

The man who was to be Italy's last constitutional Prime Minister for twenty years needed to think aloud to formulate his policy. Though he always believed himself to be a man of destiny, he believed, too, that there were malign forces conspiring continuously against those forces for good which were on his side. The procession of journalists which wound its way into the Hotel Savoia, and, by helping him to think aloud, crystallized his ideas, saw on his desk an agglomeration of good-luck charms—a rusty horseshoe, a cheap ring, several dried herbs and an unrecognizable miniature (popularly supposed to be of the Queen Mother).

The Italian and foreign journalists who interviewed Mussolini on his first day in power all described him as "informally dressed." His cuffs were stained with ink, his black jacket (borrowed) was too tight across the shoulders, his pin-striped trousers were like jeans and pleated horizontally below the knees, and he appeared to have lost his cuff-links. But, though informally dressed, there was no doubt about his determination to stay in power. Waggling his down-at-heel shoes, half concealed by worn, light spats, at Anacleto Francini of the *Gazzetta del Popolo*, he said: "I will seek no sort of compromise. If anybody tries to create difficulties, I will know how to deal with him."[1]

To Luigi Ambrosini of *La Stampa* he was even more precise, and Ambrosini found to his amazement that every politician of stature in Rome and Turin, including Giolitti, believed the "new order" (in Ambrosini's dispatch the phrase occurred for the first time) would, and must, survive.

But Mussolini's apparent intransigence only concealed a desire to "get things back to normal." It is true that Mussolini's idea of normality and those of other men differed in degree, but it is also true that everybody in Italy—with the possible exception of a few thugs on the Right and the Left—wanted an end to strikes, bloodshed in the streets and riots. The men and women in the street wanted a return to a half-remembered order. The shopkeeper wanted to be sure that when he opened in the morning, nobody would break his windows or walk off with the best of his stock. The lawyer who lived in the suburbs wanted to be sure the trams would run every morning. Women wanted to be able to walk unmolested through the streets and know that their children would be safe on their way to school. Peasants wanted to know, at least in general terms, what the price of wheat would be at the end of the farming year. Land and property owners wanted something done about rents, which were lagging behind incomes; and tenants wanted something done about their wages, which were lagging behind prices. A policy, a direction, the strong man with the steady hand—this is what the average Italian wanted. There was no alternative to Mussolini.

Mussolini honestly believed that he could absorb all men of goodwill into his government and administration, even if not into his party. He was encouraged in this by the attitude of the leaders of the other parties. The Liberal Party sent him a telegram on November 1st, which read:

> THE EXECUTIVE OF THE LIBERAL PARTY, MET TODAY, SENDS ITS FERVENT GOOD WISHES THAT THE COUNTRY HAS, THANKS TO THE WORK OF AND AGREEMENT BETWEEN YOUR EXCELLENCY AND THE NATIONAL PARTIES, FINALLY ASSURED INTERNAL PEACE, IN ORDER AND LIBERTY, AND WILL CONQUER IN THE WORLD THE PLACE TO WHICH SHE HAS A RIGHT BY HER VICTORY IN THE WAR AND THE INDOMITABLE VIRTUE OF OUR PEOPLE.

The Ministry of Agriculture, the "key ministry to the national reawakening" in Mussolini's first Cabinet, was given to the Liberal, Giuseppe de Capitani d'Arzago.

The Nationalists, who had actively helped Mussolini to power, though always maintaining that they were in some way superior by dint of their seniority and "legality," made it clear to him that they did not regard their separate existence as a party as essential—that a "merger" should soon be arranged.

In the first Mussolini government the Nationalists had Federzoni as Minister for the Colonies (later Interior), and Alfredo Rocco as Under-Secretary of the Treasury.

Mussolini tried in vain to persuade the Socialists and Socialist trade unions to join him. The Democrats and Social Democrats were not so reluctant. They had not blotted their copybooks by denouncing Mussolini's own trade-union movement (largely the work of Grandi), set up to rival the Socialist C.G.L. and the

Catholic C.I.L. Both the Demo-Social and Democratic groups were anxious for peace and prosperity. They were also anxious to make political capital out of the defeat of the extreme Left and to try to create something similar—and as potentially powerful—as the British Labour Party. They believed that Mussolini was the man—the only man—who could give them this opportunity.

They were rewarded with the Ministry of Public Works (Gabriello Carnazza, Demo-Social), the Ministry of Posts and Telegraph (Giovanni Colonna di Cesaro, Demo-Social), and the Ministry of Industry and Commerce (Teofilo Rossi, Democrat). They were also given three under-secretaryships: War (Carlo Bonardi, Demo-Social); Finance (Pietro Lissia, Demo-Social); and Posts and Telegraph (Michele Terzaghi).

The size of this representation did not represent so much the strength of these two groups in the country as their own estimate of their potential and Mussolini's estimate of their nuisance value if left out. At all costs, if he was to "normalize" life in the country, he had to have some representation of the Left.

The Popular Catholic Party had split over Mussolini's assumption of the government. He was anxious to placate organized Catholicism, just as he was anxious to placate any sort of organized opposition. He was also shrewd enough to know that in every Italian, no matter how vociferously anti-clerical, there was a desire to make peace with the Church; and for better or for worse, the Popular Party represented the Church in Parliament. Don Luigi Sturzo, however, would have nothing to do with Fascism. He still enjoyed the support of about half of the M.P.s of the party he had built up from nothing, and the indirect support of young men in the Vatican Civil Service. But the Right wing of his party, and the Curia Cardinals, felt that Mussolini represented the best hope for order and stability—the prerequisites for Church expansion and consolidation. They were willing to overlook his occasional blasphemy and his past history of priest-baiting. They advised several of their most loyal members to co-operate with Mussolini. They continued their removal of pro-Sturzo monsignori from the Vatican. From the pulpits, priests were instructed to follow the precept of civil obedience, and this meant obedience to Mussolini.

In his first ministry Mussolini gave Labour and Social Security to the Popular Party (the Minister was Stefano Cavazzoni), and under-secretaryships to Umberto Merlin (Freed Lands), Fulvio Milani (Justice), and Giovanni Gronchi, the future President of Italy (Industry and Commerce). Mussolini's "extra reason" for showing so much enthusiasm for the co-operation of the Church behind the scenes was, as he confessed to Buronzo, that he was "not yet ready to deal with the problems of agriculture, and the priests can keep the peasants quiet for a time."

The Premiership, Ministry of the Interior and Foreign Ministry, Mussolini kept for himself. This was in keeping with his belief that normalization at home and abroad were inseparable. Restore Italy's prestige abroad and opposition at home would evaporate. Restore order at home and the other powers would take Italy seriously again.

The other ministries and under-secretaryships were in Fascist hands, with the exception of Education, War and the Admiralty. Mussolini, anxious to placate—if possible, win over—the intellectuals, appointed Giovanni Gentile to be Minister of Education. He delighted the Army and Navy by appointing Armando Diaz to be Minister for War, and Admiral Thaon di Revel to the Admiralty. These two were the only service chiefs with unblemished records in the war.

Having stilled the gossip in the antechambers by submitting—and having approved—his list of ministers to the King, Mussolini set about literally restoring order. He ran through a list of prefects, scratching out the names of those who were either weak or known anti-Fascists, and replaced them. He raised the pay of the police. He ordered the demobilization of the militia (the Quadrumvirs, in a proclamation, "gave back its powers to the executive of the party"), and sent all his Black Shirts back to work. Some of the militia did not demobilize itself, and there were Black Shirts who had acquired a distaste for work, but they could be dealt with later.[2]

With many a spectacular gesture, Mussolini pumped blood back into the country's veins. At times there was no other way to restore the circulation. Some 35,000 civil servants were dismissed, assured of re-employment later, and the bureaucracy streamlined. When Balbo told him there had been some tardiness over the provision of special trains for the evacuation of the militia from the capital, Mussolini wired Ruffini Torre, a former colleague from his days of Socialist agitation in Romagna, and appointed him commissioner for railways. Torre took office in seventeen minutes; and walked down to his local station of San Salvatore to stop the train for Rome. The train was fourteen minutes late. Torre hauled the driver down from the cab, sacked him, recruited another from the drivers' rest-room, gave him a rise in pay and waved the green disc for the Off. From that day on, so Mussolini and Torre would boast, the trains in Italy always ran on time.[3]

Economic reorganization as such Mussolini left to Alberto de Stefani, who was undoubtedly Italy's greatest Finance Minister. For the first weeks of November the new Prime Minister devoted himself to public relations and preparations for a tour abroad.

The New York *Times* described him during this period as "relaxed." In the streets militiamen were burning the last of the opposition newspaper libraries. His usher, Quinto Navarra, commented that he was the fifth Excellency he had served and he seemed "all right." All over Italy local Fascists who had set out for Rome celebrated. The Rome correspondent of the *Daily Telegraph* wrote: "The place of the Red Shirt of Garibaldi has been taken by the Black Shirt of Mussolini."

On November 3rd Italian Embassy officials and ambassadors abroad wired Mussolini their congratulations that the lira had risen 8 points to the pound and almost 5 to the dollar. Only Count Sforza, Ambassador in Washington, did not join in the paeans of praise. The Queen Mother told de Vecchi that she had never liked the man anyway.[4]

On November 10th Mussolini kept the first part of his bargain with the Queen Mother. She had been working hard to assure him of the unanimous support of the Royal Family. She had even persuaded the King to declare that he had never had any intention of opposing the march on Rome. She sat reading poems about herself by Carducci and waited for Mussolini to make a gesture "within his limits." Mussolini, as good as his word, repealed the law (passed by Giolitti on September 24, 1920) which made shares non-transferable. The Queen Mother, like most European royalty and aristocracy, was pessimistic about the future of monarchy and was stockpiling bearer bonds, in case it should be necessary for her to live in exile. As she said to de Vecchi, she had no intention of living in discomfort, even as Mrs. Savoy. Mussolini's repeal pleased the whole of the stock market and made for brisk business.

Mussolini's speech-writing was interrupted by seventeen studio photographers, three assorted painters and the English sculptress Sheridan. General Badoglio also called to make his peace, and was allowed to take his place beside the Duce on November 4th at the Commemoration for the Fallen.

On November 16th Mussolini presented his government to Parliament. He said: "I have formed a coalition government—not just to have a parliamentary majority, which I could do without—but to gather together, to help the nation, all those, who over and above party interests, want to save the nation."[5]

The tone of his speech was almost friendly, but not conciliatory. The Queen Mother was amused by his aside: "I could have turned the whole of this Parliament building into an armed camp." The Opposition was not amused, but was powerless. A last-minute attempt to pry the Demo-Social and Popular M.P.s from Mussolini's grasp was made by the Socialist Party. The Communist Party refused to take part in any anti-Fascist alliance, "wanting to be free of any opportunistic position." Mussolini outlined his policy as one of solvency at home and peace with honour abroad. He reiterated his offer of November 2nd, that he would not "repel any offer of collaboration." When the Mussolini government was put up for approval, 422 M.P.s voted; 306 were for the "new order."

No sooner had the news of his success left Rome than Mussolini announced in his own newspaper (he had handed over the editorship to his brother Arnaldo, but dictated the editorials over the phone every evening at ten) that he intended to put Italy's prestige abroad to rights. He called in the correspondent of the *Daily Express* and told him that he expected to visit England shortly, when the British Government realized that "Italy wants to be treated like the sister of the other Great Powers, not like the maid." The London *Morning Post* wrote that he was: "the most powerful and interesting man in Italy, three years ago unknown abroad." He was soon to be a good source of copy for newspapers everywhere.

On November 18th, in the evening, Mussolini left for the Great Power meeting at Lausanne, at which the Middle East was to be "arranged." He stopped at Milan for an hour to see his family and give running interviews to the press. One journalist commented that Mussolini was courageous to leave Italy to his enemies so soon after upsetting them. The Prime Minister and Duce of Fascism commented: "They're still recovering from the shock."

At Lausanne Mussolini found himself received with great ceremony, but he was determined to enjoy himself. He told the government envoy at the station that it was not so long since he had been thrown out of Switzerland, reducing the man to tears of protocol. After dinner he went for a walk on the terrace of the Grand Hotel, accompanied by a Swiss detective. He pointed to a bridge with lights twinkling in the distance.

"See that bridge," he said. "Fifteen years ago your police arrested me for sleeping under it."

The detective shrugged his shoulders.

"*C'est la vie, Monsieur le Président.*"

Then, both laughing, they went off to a railway siding to wake up the French Prime Minister, who was dozing in his sleeping car.[6]

During his stay in Lausanne Mussolini found time to attend meetings of Italians in exile, grant innumerable interviews, and make a lasting impression on his French and British colleagues. Poincaré did not like him, but realized that he was an "undeniable phenomenon." Lord Curzon thought him "pompous and ridiculous." After two days Mussolini irritated them both by declaring that having got the conference under way and urged the solidarity of the West in the face of "Russo-German ambitions," he could go home and leave the rest to the professional diplomats.

On November 24th he was back in Parliament to give more details of his plans for "a reasonable settlement abroad" and peace at home. He repeated his intention to govern with all men of goodwill, denied Socialist allegations that his was an "anti-worker government," and threatened a sullen House with dictatorship, "but only if they failed the country." He was given the House's approval, with 275 votes for, 90 against.

On the first morning in December Mussolini transferred his private residence to the Grand Hotel. He did not stay in it for long. When he was not working at his various ministries, he was over in the Hotel Continental with Margherita Sarfatti. De Bono, the Director General of Public Security, and Bertini, Chief of Police of Rome, pleaded with him to be more discreet in his private life. On December 2nd he received the Socialist Zaniboni, and tried for the last time to convince his old party that he really would prefer a complete coalition to the coalition of Right and Centre he had formed. His friends on the Right, horrified, urged him to be more discreet in his public life. He shocked both categories of guardians of discretion by opening discussions with Krassin, a people's commissar, on a treaty of friendship which was to make Italy the first country to grant the infant Soviet Union official recognition. He opened these discussions in the bar of the Grand, with Margherita sitting on a stool near by. The publicity he gave to his meeting with Krassin immediately stopped talks between the parties of the Left which had restarted negotiations for an "anti-Fascist workers' alliance." If the Soviet Union was going to approve of Mussolini, the young Italian Communist Party did not want to find itself deviating from the international line.

The same evening, December 4th, Mussolini set off for London for talks on German reparations. Diplomatically, realizing that The Poet was feeling left out of the triumph, he sent a message to

D'Annunzio—leaked to the press—in which he acknowledged his debt to the "holy propaganda of The Poet and the light of Ronchi." Then he went to sleep, telling his aide-de-camp to read D'Annunzio's latest poems and see if he could detect any politics in them.

A large crowd met Mussolini at Victoria Station. Colonel Waterhouse brought him the official welcome on the part of the King, and a number of Italians gave him flowers. The London *Daily Mail* compared his chest to Caruso's and described his arrival as an exceptional event. The London *Times* commented on the brilliance of his eyes. The small son of the manager of Claridge's, where he stayed, called him the greatest man in the world. Mussolini commented that the English were undoubtedly the best brought-up hypocrites in the world. Neither Bonar Law nor the British Royal Family knew quite what to make of him. He was obviously well informed, and kept so by his *Popolo d'Italia* London correspondent, who, he said, was "always six days ahead of the Ministry of Foreign Affairs." He was dignified, his spats were white and his bearing correct, but he went around decorating Italian waiters. The British Royal Family had been assured by the Italian Queen Mother that he represented the "best guarantee for the permanence of all we hold dear"; and Bonar Law was secretly relieved that Italy had at last a determined Prime Minister.

Nothing was achieved by the London Conference. Neither Bonar Law nor Poincaré wanted to show their hand in its entirety to a man whose permanence in power might be limited, and Mussolini had no taste for the niceties of diplomatic chess. He preferred to make speeches in the open, and made a much-reported one to the local London *Fascio* as he handed them their colours.[7] He said: "The epoch of renunciation and abdication is over." A copy of the speech was sent to Bonar Law. Both Bonar Law and Poincaré decided that it would be better to postpone a settlement until 1923, when it would be clear whether or not this comical man in the white spats was going to last.

Mussolini left London on December 12th. On his return to Italy he found that his emergency measures for restoring order had had their effect, and that for the first time for many years his fellow countrymen could look forward to a quiet Christmas. On December 15th he called the first meeting of the Grand Council of Fascism in his hotel. The Grand Council was his own brain child. According to Buronzo, Mussolini at first intended it to be the beginning of a super-party—a body to which his allies in the Coalition could take their complaints and work out a common policy suggestion before submitting it for his final approval. He refused to call it the Fascist Council, the first name suggested by his brother, for this reason. All the leaders of parties willing to work with him were to be members of this council. In fact, the other party leaders refused to attend the December 15th meeting. It was not until January 12, 1923, that another party attended, and this was to celebrate its own disappearance. On that date the Nationalist Party officially merged with the Fascist Party, and Federzoni and his colleagues became National Fascists.

The year 1922 ended with the usual mixture of farce and tragedy, neither of which astonished the press. Mussolini received Eleonora Duse in his pyjamas and thanked her for her return to dedicate herself to her art in her native country. On December 17th there were riots in Turin, inspired by de Vecchi, who felt himself neglected. Mussolini sacked the prefect and chief of police of Turin, reproved de Vecchi, and told the press that he meant what he said when he promised order at all costs, even if it meant alienating the less civilized members of his own party. De Stefani asked Mussolini for the Treasury, as well as the Ministry of Finance. He could not see why there had to be two ministries, and Tangorra was getting in his way. At an official ceremony in Turin half a band played "The Royal March" while the other half played "Giovinezza." Italy beat Germany by three goals to one at football. The Queen Mother asked the Duce if he could arrange a marriage between Edward, Prince of Wales, and her too-gay grand-daughter Princess Jolanda.

The first event of importance in 1923 was the meeting of the Grand Council, at which the Nationalist Party committed suicide. This council meeting was an important one for other reasons. Continuing his policy of "normalization," and to placate the Regular Army, Mussolini agreed to put his Black Shirts under the control of the State's Armed Forces. He proposed the formation of a Voluntary Militia of National Security, and nobody could think of a better name for it. Major-General Galbiati, its last commander-in-chief, comments that the militia was not born without difficulty.[8] There had been talk since October of a "fusion" of the Fascist Militia with the Army, which young militia officers had taken to mean complete dissolution. Galbiati appointed himself their spokesman. These officers were in constant disharmony with the political leaders of the movement. The Fascist "Politburo" was composed in the main of men who had held executive command in the Army —of captains and majors. Militia officers were mostly ex-subalterns who had only taken orders. This gulf between subaltern and company commander acquired a political significance in Italy which it never lost. The rivalries it engendered had disconcerting consequences. Though the militia officers proper successfully opposed any "fusion," regular officers, especially officers in the reserve, did manage to transfer themselves to the militia and take the senior posts of command. After January 14, 1923, the original militia officers found themselves demoted, not promoted, in spite of their new-found legality and royal standard. They did not fail to point out that both de Bono and de Vecchi were Royalist regulars and deplored favouritism. The suspicion grew that the loyalty of the militia hard core was to Mussolini rather than to the King.

It would, of course, be wrong to describe either the new militia or the old as "Mussolini's bodyguard." As General Galbiati writes: "One does not stay in power for twenty years if one needs a bodyguard. And, above all, one does not deny material means of reinforcement to one's own bodyguard, as Mussolini always did when it came to any sort of concession to the militia. For five years after the formation of the militia, not so much as a pair of shoes was issued to the militia. Commanders of the various legions were forced to forge requisitions in order to clothe their men . . . and buy Army-surplus uniforms, embroider militia badges on them for their 'trousseaux' . . . protocol, prestige and no more."

Nevertheless, the militia was legally constituted and took its oath of allegiance to the King. The act hushed a good deal of criticism of "private armies" and "police states," even though this came from not strictly democratic quarters. It is interesting to note that Mussolini neither used the militia to suppress revolt or dissidence in the Armed Forces—as Lenin and Stalin used theirs—nor to eliminate his military rivals one by one—as Franco had done.

The Grand Council had nothing to do with Mussolini's next piece of pacification. Encouraged by those members of the Popular Party who voted with the Fascists in the House, Mussolini let it be known that he would not be averse to talks with the Vatican on some long-term truce between Church and State. He found it absurd that Church and State had co-existed in hostility for so many years, when most of the State's subjects were also faithful to the Church. Such hostility produced all sorts of by-products of disunity. Mussolini, though at that time not exactly clear about the innocuousness or scope of any possible long-term arrangement, was quite willing to listen to the other side's proposals. He was also flattered by the suggestion that he alone was capable of bringing about a conciliation. The Queen Mother, the source of the flattery, told one of her friends that it was not ignoble to hope for the sort of relationship which had existed between Queen Victoria and Disraeli, between herself and the Duce. She was the only member of the Royal Family who was not anti-clerical, and was still Mussolini's staunchest supporter and ambassador-at-large.

On January 20th Cardinal Gasparri and Mussolini met to discuss the "Roman question." Gasparri had come to the conclusion that Mussolini was capable of negotiating a conciliation, because he was the only man he had met who enjoyed the confidence of both the black, Papal aristocracy and a part at least of the white Piedmontese nobility at court. No record was kept of their conversations at this first meeting, but Mussolini himself confided in Buronzo at a later date that they had talked over "certain difficulties." The "difficulties" seemed to have ranged from the possibility of reintroducing the compulsory crucifix in all public buildings and schools, to the removal from the State of "organs whose existence and favour made Conciliation impossible." There were two "organs" which the Church found particularly distasteful, and neither seemed to be receiving the persecution it deserved. One was the Communist Party, which Mussolini at once set about emasculating. The other was Freemasonry.

Italian Freemasonry differs from its British counterpart in being anti-clerical, often anti-Christian, and in being—in a sense—less exclusive. The number of anti-clerical Masons in Italy in 1923 was not less than 500,000. Mussolini, though both anti-clerical and an atheist all his life (according to his family), disapproved of what he called "the cult." So did the Queen Mother, though the men in her family were nearly all Masons. All three—the Queen Mother, Mussolini and Cardinal Gasparri—believed that authority (monarchical, political or spiritual) was indivisible. Gasparri suggested that it would show goodwill if Mussolini publicly pronounced his hostility to Masonry. On February 12th he recalled the Grand Council to debate the matter. He was astonished, as he admitted later, to find how many of his intimates were either members of the Grand Orient or Scottish rite lodges. Dudan, Acerbo, Balbo and Rossi all refused to discuss his proposal for a declaration of "incompatibility between Fascism and Masonry," but the declaration was made on February 15th. Perrone, Tamburini, General Ceccherini and Curzio were all revealed as Masons, but hurried to resign and repledge their allegiance to the party. The Grand Orient, in an attempt to save itself, encouraged its members to default, urging them to meet where and when they could in secret to "keep the Rite alive."

Though Mussolini won himself an ally in Cardinal Gasparri by his prompt acceptance of the Church's suggestion that Masonry be, in effect, outlawed, he did not foresee the trouble it was to cause among his *ras*. Farinacci at Cremona, Balbo at Ferrara, Grandi at Bologna, Giunta at Trieste, Giampaoli at Milan had all "normalized" the victory of Fascism in their own ways, establishing themselves as viceroys. Mussolini, though he knew of this, knew, too, that until the whole police force had been reorganized he would have to depend on his *ras* to keep order. At the very least they could be persuaded not to provoke disorder. The stability of the régime, as policemen, depended on harmony between Mussolini and the *ras*, and the dispute over the compatibility of Masonry disrupted that harmony. It is true that, as in China, a new emperor always has trouble establishing his authority over his viceroys when that authority depends on those viceroys for its existence, but for a few weeks it looked as if the Freemasonry issue was going to provoke the crisis of central authority before its time. However, there was still no alternative to Mussolini, and the crisis slept on uneasily for a few more months.

When Gasparri saw that the danger had passed, he set about preparing, in his turn, a token of goodwill.

While Gasparri conspired and figured lists of "subversives" in the Vatican, Mussolini went to work on party unity. On February 26th he gave a banquet to celebrate the Nationalist-Fascist "merger," and another to celebrate his own acceptance of the rank of corporal of honour offered him by the *arditi*. He made his Minister for War "Duke of the Victory," and offered Admiral di Revel the title of Duke of the Sea. He made speeches. He gave parties, though he hated this. He even charmed Princess Vittoria Colonna, who noted in her memoirs that "he is a man who must have suffered much in his lifetime." He flattered the Queen and promised her a quiet life. Wherever he could make friends and tranquillize the opposition he did so. He seems to have been confident of his own permanency, but he took steps to assure it. Vincenzo Buronzo was told to organize a youth movement, "the next generation of Fascists." Michele Bianchi, the secretary of the party, was told to "plan for reorganization, for central direction." Mussolini had little time for the operations in Libya under Rodolfo Graziani, which were successfully reconquering "lost territories." The first he heard of these subimperial adventures was when he was asked to arbitrate between the Minister for the Colonies and the Minister for Freed Lands, as to who should assume responsibility for the freed colonies.

By the end of March, however, Mussolini felt free enough of crises to leave Rome in high spirits in his Alfa Romeo, followed by distraught policemen in slower cars, and open the first of his *autostrade*, from Milan to the lakes. He told the Mayor of Milan that he was glad to get away from Rome, not because of any threats by his opponents, but because they had opened a night club next door to his office and he could not work there any more.

On the same day, March 25th, Mussolini announced his first electoral reform. He said that he had every evidence to show that proportional representation produced only inefficient parliaments, and had decided to revert to single constituencies, with election by simple majority. To celebrate this "victory of common sense in democracy," he let Nenni out of the jail in Milan, where he had been taken for "editorial irresponsibility" in *Avanti*. On March 28th the first "pilgrimage" to the tomb of Mussolini's mother was made, and the "personality cult" was born. April opened with a triumph for the militia—one of its bright young men, Passerone, inveigled Mussolini into visiting its stronghold, Casale Monferrato. And a triumph, too, for the Church—Mussolini had his wife and his children baptized. Casale Monferrato had never known such a day of glory, and even its principal industry (a medium-sized cement works) forbade to strike. The Church had never had such a clip of illustrious ammunition.

Cardinal Gasparri had completed his plans for a preliminary entente. He first insisted that Mussolini act as principal witness at the wedding arranged between Princess Jolanda and Count Carlo Calvi (the Prince of Wales having proved unwilling). Then, on April 10th, he met Mussolini secretly to discuss "the stages to be completed to a satisfactory permanent settlement." The first of these came as something of a shock to Mussolini. He had always believed that the Popular Party enjoyed the confidence of a large part of the Catholic hierarchy, even if they disapproved of its methods. Gasparri, however, hinted that they would not take it amiss if the Popular Party were to become a thing of the past. If a conciliation were achieved, then a special party to protect Catholic interests would not be necessary. In any case, Pope Pius XI did not like Luigi Sturzo and would favour the removal from Mussolini's coalition of all "professional political Catholics."

Mussolini had removed Tangorra from office, but had had good reports of his three Catholic under-secretaries. He did not like the idea of losing good administrators, and above all did not like the idea of suddenly breaking with the Popular Party and laying himself open to charges of anti-clericalism, no matter how well founded. He was advised from all sides to placate organized Catholicism, not antagonize it. As it happened, the necessity for the making of a first move on his part was obviated by the behaviour of the Popular Party itself.[9]

On April 21, 1923, Italy celebrated its first Fascist Labour Day, decreeing it "undesirable" to observe on May 1st the traditional *festa del lavoro*. During the celebrations several *ras* got out of hand and made inflammatory speeches, urging "action," deploring the coalition, threatening the Mussolini government's allies with an assortment of fates, none of them constitutional.

On the following day the National Congress of the Popular Party, meeting in Turin, heard a heated debate on the desirability of continuing in the parliamentary alliance. Delegates came to blows. Pestalozza described Mussolini as "the man sent by Providence." Luigi Sturzo disagreed. However, he pointed out that as the Fascist Party had accepted the Popular Party's policy on the class struggle (that it was not inevitable) and on the political syntheses of economic forces, it was not possible to disagree violently, ideologically, with Mussolini. Farther to the Left of Sturzo, angry delegates urged the end of the "unholy marriage," with no extenuating circumstances. Gronchi, a more intelligent man than most of his contemporaries, realized that public debate of this sort did not help the cause of democracy or of his party. Italy had more to gain by broadening the base of Mussolini's support and not allowing events to drive him to dictatorship. Gronchi also knew of the attitude of the Curia Cardinals and Pope Pius XI. He suspected that the violence of the debate was not accidental. Mussolini's prompt telegram of protest to the congress confirmed his suspicion. Gronchi hurriedly rushed through a motion of "non-committal confidence" in the Coalition Government. It was non-committal in that it did not speak of political principles; of confidence, in that it stressed there was no alternative to the present government. But it was too late. Mussolini saw his chance of implementing Cardinal Gasparri's own suggested policy of excluding "special Catholics" from the government. He called the Popular Party ministers to Palazzo Chigi and accepted their resignations. On April 25th the Popular Party's support for Mussolini officially ended, though for some months many of its M.P.s voted with the government consistently.

Cardinal Gasparri was delighted. He marvelled at Mussolini's celerity, as Mussolini had hoped he would. He told his colleagues in the Vatican that Italy and the Church had been sent a man who changed whole circumstances at the stroke of a pen. From that moment on there was never any doubt that a conciliation between Church and State would be made, and made in such a way that public credit would be reflected on Mussolini.

On May 12, 1923, King George and Queen Mary arrived in Rome to start an unusually important state visit. It started well with demonstrations of humanity, even gallantry, on the part of King George. He had the British Consul in Milan send a large bunch of roses to Mussolini's wife. All Italy approved of this reproof to its Prime Minister, who did not keep up the required appearances of family unity. Then the King refused to have a suite to himself in the Quirinale, insisting on having Queen Mary with him. The press made much of the state visit, as showing that, since World War I there had been "misunderstandings which had apparently weakened the traditional friendship between Britain and Italy," but that these misunderstandings were now to be cleared up. Credit for this, of course, was due to Mussolini. On the first ceremony of the visit he was given the Order of the Bath, which the Italian press interpreted as a sign of Britain's admiration for their Duce. He had had a special prime minister's uniform designed for the visit, with sword and plumed hat, and this amused his royal guests. Foreign Office officials who accompanied them were not deceived by the finery, appreciated Mussolini's anxiety for "conclusive talks," and were not offended when the Prime Minister allowed the Italian Royal Family to entertain King George and Queen Mary.

The British government had watched Mussolini's progress with relief and admiration. The situation in Europe north of the Alps was not so reassuring. Germany seemed to be in a state of deepening chaos. The economy had ground to a halt under the weight of reparations. The mark had started to lose currency in 1922, and had now been so far inflated as to be valueless. The French had occupied the Ruhr to ensure that reparations would eventually be made, and this had still further depressed the German economy. The German political Right seemed at best to be undesirable, in the hands of lawless Army officers and infant parties like the Working Union of the Fatherland—fighting leagues led by a madman, Adolf Hitler. The political Left, the Social Democrats nominally in power, was incompetent, and only resentment at the French occupation of the Ruhr and the solidarity it engendered kept Germany intact. There were no signs of the collapse of the Soviet Union, on which many of its advisers had counted, and the West needed a wall to stop any further advance of Bolshevism toward London and Paris. Many Foreign Office experts held the opinion that France was too exhausted to stop anything more violent than a pillow fight. Somebody had to "stabilize the situation" across the Channel. There was only one man, Mussolini. He had shown "extraordinary foresight" about Bolshevism. He had signed a treaty with Lenin which "removed the threat, at least for the moment." He had brought order out of chaos in Italy, and more important, defeated the Left in Parliament and out. "One might disapprove of his methods, and of course they would never work in Britain, but there was no denying their effectiveness." What the Foreign Office hoped was that Mussolini would form some sort of alliance between Catholic Austria, Catholic South and West Germany, and Italy herself, even if the alliance was more cultural and commercial than political. Mussolini could declare himself the sentinel of Catholic Europe and would tolerate no encroachment.

When Mussolini heard all these analyses and proposals he was intrigued and not a little amused. He told Aldo Finzi that when he was running priests out of Forlì he had not thought he would one day hear himself proposed as Sentinel of Catholic Europe, especially by dull, hypocritical Protestants. But, as he said to Finzi, the situation had possibilities.

As always, Mussolini's considerations of public policy were mixed up with his private preoccupations. This did not always affect Italy adversely, as he was undoubtedly almost a caricature of the typical Italian. It merely made him seem inexplicable—almost Machiavellian—to the British. Mussolini realized that he was in a strong position vis-à-vis the British. They were influential in Yugoslavia, a state which was virtually of their own devising. Yugoslavia owned cities and lands which were "*italianissimi*." D'Annunzio had been worrying Mussolini with his demands for heroic titles, by consorting with known anti-Fascists and by disparaging his statesmanship. Mussolini realized that he could placate D'Annunzio at one stroke, strike a hard bargain with the British, and arm himself adequately as sentinel. He could ask for Fiume. The British had virtually admitted that their treatment of Italy at Versailles had been less than courteous. Now was their chance to make amends, in return for Mussolini's promise to work toward an anti-Bolshevik axis in Europe.

The British Ambassador and his Foreign Office colleagues had no alternative but to agree. The only concession they managed to wring out of Mussolini was that he would not insist on occupying Fiume before the New Year, which would give the British Government time to "make its arrangements" with Belgrade.

The state visit ended amicably. The King and Queen of England departed amid cheering crowds. The British Ambassador was told by an aide-de-camp: "Impossible, that feller Mussolini." And replied: "Only too probable, my dear man."

The Queen Mother told Mussolini, possibly untruthfully, that she had put in a good word for Fiume with King George. Mussolini, who had kept her informed of his conversations, sent her three dozen roses.

His visitors away, Mussolini turned to home affairs, consolidation and distraction. He went to the zoo. He received a delegation of suffragettes. He sent a telegram to Spalla, who had defeated Ven der Weer for the European boxing title, urging him on to world honours. He sent another telegram to Torre, his commissioner for railways, involved in a riot outside Alessandria Station, saying it was good to know that Torre was always on the job. He travelled himself, by land, sea and air, on the first of what were to become annual triumphal tours. In the first three weeks of June he covered some twenty towns and cities, including Venice itself. In Sardinia he set off demonstrations of enthusiasm which kept the police locked indoors. On June 21st and 22nd he toured Sicily to sympathize in person with the victims of the eruption of Etna. He was met everywhere by cheering crowds. Thousands of young boys and girls, members of Buronzo's Bálilla, cheered in line abreast. To Popular Party allegations that his Youth Movement was "thuggism," he replied that for the first time children in Italy now saw the crucifix on the walls of their classrooms.[10]

The triumphal tours, his passionate interest in everything from boxing to the Bálilla, his ready ripostes and epigrams infuriated the opposition. They also weakened it. Many Italians, bowing to what appeared to be the inevitable, moderated their criticism. There was trouble still from a few *ras*, disappointed at the passing of the need for violence. There was trouble from careerists in the party, who offended public taste. But it was June, and the middle class went away to the seaside happily, feeling that everything was under control at last. Only Mussolini was really miserable. Not because his party, the *ras* or the middle class upset him, but because he had a bad tooth and his Jewish dentist Piperno in attendance every morning. The press, as journalist to journalist, sympathized with his toothache.

There was a pause, even in the mass production of abuse by the *Corriere della Sera* and *La Stampa*. Missiroli of the *Corriere* wrote of the success of Mussolini's normalization programme: "Fascism represents the entry of the people into the Life of the State . . . the decisive stage of the Risorgimento." Luigi Barzini wired from New York: "IN TWENTY-FIVE YEARS OF JOURNALISM ABROAD I HAVE NEVER FELT MYSELF TO BE THE SON OF A COUNTRY SO MUCH RESPECTED AND APPRECIATED." King Boris of Bulgaria passed through Rome and admired Mussolini's seventeen-hour day. At the station he told the Duce: "I haven't even got time to make love any more. I wish I knew how you did it." Mussolini had a rapid succession of mistresses, whom he sandwiched in between dispatches. They came into his office, were hurled on to the cushioned window-seat, and then dismissed. Only his wife and Margherita Sarfatti held his affection, and they knew him too well. When a friend asked Margherita why she had never spent a night with Mussolini in all the years of their friendship, she said: "He wears a nightshirt. He would be afraid I'd laugh at him."

In and around the party, but not affecting Mussolini himself, a civil war was being waged among the intellectuals. Some of them were repelled by the absurdity and superficiality of many of the gestures which were becoming habitual among the *ras*. Many were bemused by the apparent lack of any sort of philosophical basis for the continued existence of the Fascist Party, a lack which made any discussion of Fascism at an intellectual level impossible. Some politically committed writers, like Gobetti, felt instinctively that Fascism was wrong, but admitted (he studied Marx, then fashionable) the apparent inevitability of it. His counsel to his friends was not to organize any anti-Fascism, because anti-Fascism would be anti-history. Fascism was essentially transitory, a pause for breath. A year or so and it would be gone for good and still the trains would run on time. Malaparte commented: "The unworthy world against which we [Fascists] fought had few defenders among the people, many among the intellectuals . . . but we intellectuals in the classical sense . . . ought to have inflicted harsh justice on the cowardly family of domestic intellectuals." More coherently, Giuseppe Bottai, in the first number of *Critica Fascista* (June 15, 1923), admitted the non-existence of a philosophy of Fascism and deplored it, insisting that anti-Fascism be met with thought for thought, word for word, and not—as Malaparte advised—with a club on the head. Otherwise, as Bottai foresaw, the Fascist Party would fall into the hands of the professional organizers, "arid like all specialists, knowing only numbers, crowds, the mob." Bottai recommended a "serene will to criticism which, starting from the undisputed premises of essential Fascism, tends toward a constant revaluation of men, functions and ideas."[11]

Mussolini took no part in this argument, reserving himself only the right to send telegrams to Bottai commending the quality of his magazine. In private discussions with Margherita Sarfatti ("she is like all intellectual women, she dyes her hair") he approved of the idea of intelligent "loyal criticism."

During the month of July he closeted himself, once the offending tooth had been removed, with his Finance Minister de Stefani. Though they quarrelled perpetually, he and de Stefani admired and respected each other. Mussolini had a great many public-works projects which he had declared to have "absolute priority in a civilized state." There were many communities still without light or water. There were whole rural districts without a single made-up road. There were areas the size of Rome without a telephone or any way of summoning medical assistance other than walking to a doctor's house. Drainage everywhere was rudimentary. Mussolini insisted that these works be started, and he also insisted that a network of fast motor roads be built, if the country's economy were not to stagnate. He added, in this last connection, that a social function of his road network was to bring the south more closely, and daily into contact with the north, help the flow of internal migrants, and remove regional rivalries. De Stefani, while conceding the essential nature of much of this work—and especially the importance to the economy of an adequate road network—sniffed and hacked away at estimates prepared for him by his civil servants, and kept on "revising" Mussolini's plans, cutting them down to his budget size. The two would often spend hours shouting at each other, then dissolve into helpless laughter as the usher, Quinto Navarra, would open the door of Mussolini's study cautiously, to see if murder had been done. Between them a start was made on the enormous backlog of public works. And between them, though this is largely to de Stefani's credit, the budget deficit was reduced to three thousand million lire from sixteen thousand millions, and unemployment was cut from 407,464 to 110,298.[12]

One of the major achievements of this first few months of the Mussolini government was the establishment of a reliable statistical service. It is undoubtedly true that in later years Mussolini, and more particularly his friends, played about with statistics as they came to hand, and even falsified them in their speeches, but nevertheless they did have *access* to the true figures, and no government had had that privilege before. The foundation of the present-day (1963) statistical service was laid in 1923 with the formation of a directorate general of statistics, part of and in close liaison with the Ministry of Industry and Commerce (later the Ministry of National Economy). A census had been taken in 1921, but the returns had never been analysed or even summarized, because nobody would accept the responsibility for the work or guarantee its outcome. It was not until 1923 that Italy had any idea of what changes had taken place in her population since the previous decade.

On July 12, 1923, the Fascist Party had over 800,000 paid-up members. The Grand Council was still working at the new electoral law and studying a draft by Acerbo. Proportional representation was to end, but what next? Mussolini wanted to ensure that whatever party won the most seats had a working majority in Parliament, without having necessarily to win an absolute majority of votes at the polls. The basis of the new law, as proposed, was a provision that the party which had 25 per cent of the total vote or more would take 66 per cent of the number of seats. The Opposition in Parliament called the law a swindle. This the Fascists took to be an admission that they did not feel confident of even winning a quarter of the votes. The leaders of all the Opposition parties spoke during the debate on the Bill and so did Mussolini. It was one of his most brilliant speeches. To the Popular Party, which offered its collaboration without restrictions on condition that he abandon the proposed "reform," he said: "You offer me again your collaboration with hidden reserves, like one of those marriages of convenience which do not last. . . . You haggle over percentages [Don Luigi Sturzo had suggested raising to 33 per cent the simple majority necessary to obtain the two-thirds of seats in the House] like small shopkeepers, rather than speak as political custodians of your country's spiritual life."

To the Socialists Mussolini said: "I deny your right to speak to me of liberty. You won a large number of communes, majorities in provincial governments in other institutions, without understanding that this was perfectly useless if, at a certain moment, you did not become masters of the brain and heart of the nation."

It was not a long speech, but it was so effective that many Socialists and Popularists voted for the government against their own party's instructions. Thereafter Mussolini never doubted but that he could master Parliament.

Throughout the rest of July, Mussolini busied himself with making friends abroad. He ordered his Ambassador in Ethiopia to be civil to the Emperor. Gabriele D'Annunzio, fast approaching his dotage, threatened to organize his own march on Rome if Mussolini weakened in his "attitude to the blacks." The Duce sent him a book of poems. Mollified, The Poet sent back a packet of silk ties he had chosen himself, three of which Mussolini passed on to the King at Christmas.[13]

On July 27th an admirer gave the Duce a lion cub, which he insisted on keeping in his drawing-room. He would sniff as he entered the room and say to his guests: "Ah! A smell of lion here!"

On July 29th the lion-taming Prime Minister was forty. He forbade the press to mention it. He received telegrams of congratulation from leaders of all parties. The Honourable Labriola said that he felt sure that Mussolini was a Democrat at heart. Mussolini's comment was: "To be a liberal in Italy is not a way of thinking, but a dignified way of waiting without hope." The Duke of Aosta sent him a granite column four yards high. It was removed to the cellar to join other cumbersome gifts. Mussolini remarked to his usher: "If I'm ever out of a job, I can always set up a stall in the Flea Market."

The first biography of Mussolini appeared, entitled *The New Man.* Mussolini did not read it. Luigi Sturzo resigned as secretary of the Popular Party, and many of his members joined the government on its back benches. The Popular Party, deserted now by the Vatican in its entirety, was fading. The new party line was that it was every Popular M.P.'s duty to join the Fascist Party, to Christianize it and prevent it from falling into anti-clerical hands. (Agostino Semeria.)

The London *Times* wrote: "Benito Mussolini can boast, with reason, of having saved Italy in a few months from terrible internal dangers."

On August 23rd Mussolini was fined for speeding in Corso Umberto.

On August 27th the Italian Military Mission, commanded by General Tellini, was measuring out the new Greek-Albanian frontier when they were attacked and killed by Greek irregulars. Mussolini was furious. He released two communiqués to the official news agency, emphasizing the extreme gravity with which the Italian government viewed the situation. On the evening of August 28th he sent a note, which was virtually an ultimatum, to the Greek government. Then he had no idea of what to do next. There was nobody in Rome. Everybody was on holiday, even his principal Foreign Affairs Secretary, Contarini. He consulted a journalist friend, an Anglophile, who told him that in the circumstances the English would send a small flotilla to lie threateningly off some Greek port. Mussolini rang his Admiralty and ordered Admiral Solari, on *Conte di Cavour,* to steam to Corfu with his destroyer squadron, bombard, then occupy the island.

In Geneva there was panic. The League of Nations awoke from its summer madness to find itself saddled with an international incident. The British delegate urged Greece to make a formal protest. Lord Robert Cecil was presiding and accepted the protest. The Italian delegate said that the capital of Greece seemed to have been moved to Geneva, and on Mussolini's instructions threatened Italy's withdrawal from the League.

Contarini, still on holiday, read about the incident in the London *Daily Mail.* To Ward Price, the *Mail's* special correspondent, Mussolini had given an interview during which he had said that if the Greeks did not pay an indemnity of fifty million lire he would occupy the island permanently.[14]

Contarini hurried back to Rome. He found Mussolini cheerful but undecided. He confessed that he was "in a mess," and urged Contarini to get him out of it. Contarini did his best. By hurrying, telegraphing and placating, he managed to find a formula. General Tellini was technically under the command of the Allied Foreign Ministers, who had ordered the demarcation of the frontier. Greece must, therefore, pay fifty million lire to the Foreign Ministers, who would use it for the benefit of the dependants of the men killed. Italy would pay Greece fifty million lire for the damage done during the bombardment, and withdraw her troops. In this way everybody would win. "Contarini is a marvel," said Mussolini to Margherita Sarfatti. "He has even persuaded me to give my lion to the zoo."

Throughout the late summer Mussolini recriminated with his British acquaintances on the "unfriendly attitude of the British at Geneva," and threatened to "rethink his policy in Europe." He was reassured. Fiume would be his, and there would be no further incidents. Lord Robert Cecil would be recalled as soon as decency permitted.

On October 12th Mussolini got rid of his most troublesome *ras,* de Vecchi, by making him governor of Somalia. When, on October 28th, he went to Turin to see for himself what damage de Vecchi had done during his time as "viceroy," he was received without enthusiasm. He commented that his worst enemies were his so-called friends, and hoped that de Vecchi would not lose them Somalia in his cups.

The American banker Otto Kahn said: "Founded on a spiritual base, the Mussolini phenomenon is not a passing one."[15]

The Swedish writer Werner von Heidenstam added: "Happy a people with a man like Mussolini."

The unhappy German people watched their country disintegrate still further. An attempt at a *coup d'état* by Hitler's Bavarian Nationalists failed miserably. This "Munich beerhouse *Putsch*" produced from Mussolini the comment: "Just silly boys." Then, hearing that Goering was being hunted by the police, he gave orders for the air ace to be issued with a visa. He was taking an advanced flying course himself: "We aviators must stick together." Goering, as he crossed the Italian frontier, said: "From November 8th we have learned that we must study the methods of the great reformer of Italy if we wish to achieve unity in the Fatherland with honour."

On November 18, 1923, King Alfonso XIII of Spain arrived in Rome to begin a state visit. It was a Sunday and raining, and Mussolini took this to be extremely unlucky. The visit might have passed off uneventfully. As it was, Mussolini scrutinized every moment of the programme for spells. King Alfonso did nothing to help reassure the Duce. He introduced General Primo de Rivera as his "own little Mussolini." Sensitive about his height and contemptuous of Primo de Rivera, an apoplectic bandit, Mussolini did not even acknowledge the introduction. The same evening, at a gala performance at the Constanzi, Mussolini confided in Aldo Finzi that the enormous glass chandelier over the royal box where they were sitting was likely to fall on their heads at any moment, and sent Finzi backstage to urge the cast not to sing too high or too loudly. The orchestra, after the national anthem, struck up the Fascist "Giovinezza." King Alfonso, anxious to retrieve himself for his *gaffe* about Primo de Rivera, started to stand up again, but King Victor Emmanuel pulled him down by his coat-tails. Mussolini, white with anger, asked the King's aide the meaning of this "gratuitous insult." General Cittadini replied that "Giovinezza" was not an official tune. "It will be tomorrow," Mussolini said to Finzi. "Remind me to make a decree." This was the first quarrel between the King and Mussolini. It came to nothing, because the Queen Mother took the Duce's part, but it was the beginning of what grew to be a rivalry between the little family-man King, proud if ineffective, and the hypersensitive public figure.

Ezio Maria Gray, one of the first Fascist M.P.s and an intimate of Mussolini's, told the Duce that he should use to his advantage the sense of inferiority which he engendered in kings, and especially in the visiting King of Spain. At this time Mussolini had no ideas of empire in his head; his aim was to make Italy solvent and admirable and, above all, be taken seriously abroad.[16] But this did not necessarily mean territorial aggrandizement. He said many times, and again to Primo de Rivera, that "Fascism is not exportable." The apoplectic general was anxious to know how the trick was worked—how a decaying country was so effectively revived and the Left stifled. When he heard that Primo de Rivera was anxious to make a pastiche of Fascism in Spain, Gray urged Mussolini not to take the idea too lightly. There could be no harm in having an ideologically indebted neighbour across the Bay of Genoa. It was not imperialistic to think of "artistic and intellectual supremacy in the Latin world" as Italy's due. She had had it—she could regain it. Mussolini had come to power to refurbish the flag: this was a modern, even Socialist way of asserting the right to be a "vanguard."

Gray was persuasive. Mussolini told him to go away and work out a plan which could not offend any nation which came to hear of it. It was not to involve occupation of Spain in any way. This would offend Britain at Gibraltar, and France. But he did not see why the Spaniards should not have the advantage of learning from Italy's experience, and not be subject to an idiot king, always bringing bad luck, and an apoplectic general.

Mussolini prepared for Christmas. He finally pushed through the Senate a Bill which had started on its journey through the Lower House on November 10th. It repealed another of Giolitti's acts, one which had increased death duties on land to the point of confiscation. The Queen Mother had urged Mussolini to do something about it. It was unfair to peasant sons succeeding their fathers. It was also unfair to royalty. The Duce made the gesture.

On November 30th he silenced "neglected" students by going in person to explain to them the educational reform prepared by Gentile. The next week he spread goodwill among civil servants by praising them publicly and raising the pay of those who had survived his purge. On December 13th he addressed another meeting of students and told them that he expected not only passive, but active, support from them. His old enemy Nitti had his villa sacked by some over-enthusiastic Fascists, and exiled himself to Paris. Mussolini's fellow journalists at *il Popolo d'Italia* had had his old rifle mounted and chased for him for Christmas. On Boxing Day one of his most virulent enemies, Amendola, editor of *Mondo*, was beaten up in the streets. Princess Jolanda told Donna Rachele that she was expecting a baby. *Pax Mussoliniana.*

It was a quiet, satisfactory Christmas. Thirty thousand greetings arrived at Mussolini's office. Winston Churchill's was amongst them; Mussolini described him as "the most powerful brain in England." Salvemini sent him a card—"An angry young man." Nenni—"Ignorant and ingenuous"; and Giolitti—"A venerated body who gets himself forgiven for his errors in the past by preserving silence in the present." Even the great Liberal philosopher Benedette Croce wrote: "I recall my words of October 29th to you. There no longer exists a question of choice between Liberalism and Fascism. Where now are the forces capable of accepting the succession to your government. I do not see them. I see instead an almost universal fear of a return to the anarchy of 1922. Nobody wants a change."

As the year drew to its close a Commission of Five (Rossi, Acerbo, Giunta, Bianchi and Finzi) was preparing the joint Nationalist-Fascist list of candidates for the coming elections. Mussolini pretended to have nothing to do with this work, but in reality he checked every name before it went on the list. Everybody took the coming elections seriously. The anti-Fascists were told by their more intelligent leaders (especially by Gobetti in *la Rivoluzione Liberale*) that it would be no use abstaining from the elections in the hope that the masses would interpret this as a protest. The time for abstention had passed. He, Gobetti, was as guilty as anyone for not having seen that some positive mass anti-Fascist action was necessary, but perhaps it was not too late? He urged the Socialists and the Left Wing of the Popular Party to combine in a campaign to unseat the Fascist Coalition.

Parliament was dissolved, and the election date fixed for April 6th. Mussolini was not going to lay himself open to charges that he had rushed such an important event.

On January 21st Lenin—Mussolini's old idol—died. The struggle for power between Trotsky and Stalin became fiercer. Mussolini was visibly moved by the death of Lenin, and not overheartened by Contarini's opinion that he would eventually be replaced by "that boorish fool Stalin." De Bono came to see Mussolini an hour after the news had reached him and said: "Ha! Well, we have one enemy less now." Mussolini replied: "That is not the point. The world has one more immortal." His courtesy to Jansen and Jordanski, the Soviet delegates to the Italo-Soviet trade talks, was exemplary.

On January 27, 1924, Mussolini signed a treaty with Yugoslavia which handed Fiume over to Italy, "once and for all." The British government had kept its promise.

On February 22, 1924, Fiume was formally annexed to Italy. The Queen Mother insisted that Mussolini receive the Collar of the Annunziata, Italy's highest decoration. She threatened to beard him in his den and hang it around his neck if he refused. Graciously, with flowers, the Duce accepted. Alarmed that maybe The Poet in the north would feel slighted, he asked the King to make D'Annunzio Prince of the Snowy Mountains. D'Annunzio was delighted.

For the rest of the spring Mussolini gave himself up to electioneering. It was not really necessary. On March 30th de Stefani announced that, for the first time since the reunification of Italy, the budget had been balanced. The news took the heart out of the Opposition. Only 63 per cent of the electorate voted on April 6th. Most of the abstentions were Socialists, Communists, disillusioned Liberals, and supporters of the Popular Party who had seen their leaders go over to Mussolini. Four million, three hundred thousand votes were cast for the government, 3,000,000 against. The new House was composed, according to the "majority law," of 356 National Fascists, 40 Popular, 25 official Socialists, and 22 other Socialists, 18 Communists, 7 Republicans, 5 of Giolitti's personal following (Liberals), and a small assortment of Democrats, Demo-Socials and peasants.

It was an overwhelming victory. It was a victory partially assured, once any sort of simple majority had been won, but nevertheless a vote of confidence.

As soon as he knew the results Mussolini made an approach to the leaders of each anti-Fascist group and offered them representation in a national government. He told them that he had tried to "normalize," eliminate fratricidal rivalry from, and "fuse together," the nation, ever since his days as editor of *Avanti*. If not strictly true, then it may well have been true in 1924. To the Rome correspondent of the London *Times* Mussolini repeated his offer, and added that nothing was further from his mind or the spirit of Fascism than reaction, or anti-democracy.

The anti-Fascist groups did not take kindly to his offer. They did not refuse it outright, as they ought to have done, but haggled. Through the political correspondent of the *Corriere della Sera* they counter-offered a Coalition based on the "three mass parties"—Fascist, Socialist and Popular. Mussolini rejected the counter-offer and withdrew his own. The Opposition was never to get another.

On April 26, 1924, the British *Statist* reported on the progress of the Italian economy since the Fascist victory in 1922. The report infuriated the anti-Fascist Opposition, which was finding itself abandoned on all sides, even by its former friends abroad. Giacomo Matteotti, the Socialist leader, replied to the *Statist*,[17] protesting that the reason for the reported improvement in the budget was that in the last pre-Fascist year there had still been war expenses to meet; that the reason for the increase of revenues on current account had been simply that the wrong figures had been written into the last pre-Fascist estimates (250 million lire for Customs instead of 1,208 million); that the explanation of the reduction in the size of the Civil Service was not one of economy but a simple political purge; that the only reason why the loss on the State-owned railways had been cut by 400 million lire was that the price of coal had gone down; and finally that, if things were getting better, it was due to the long-term planning of previous governments. This plea by Matteotti seems to have been a bit much, even for the Socialist press, which did not reproduce it when asked. All it achieved was a widening of the personal and political gap between Mussolini and Matteotti—the one intent on national unity and the other on factional supremacy. It is pointless to argue that Mussolini wanted national unity and allies because he would find it easier to control his own fractious *ras* if he had them. Nor is the argument valid that Matteotti preserved the purity of the Left by preserving his independence. Mussolini told lies to hold the country together; Matteotti told lies to split it again. And regardless of long-term political policy, Italy could not have afforded a further six months of disunity.

On May 30, 1924, as the new Parliament assembled, the Matteotti-Mussolini dispute flared up on the floor. Matteotti contested the validity of the elections. He maintained that there had been corruption, intimidation and a lack of democratic spirit. He was not impressed by interjections from the Right that, alas, these were the characteristics of elections in Italy and had been since the first. Matteotti's speech was frequently interrupted, little heard. Some of the interjections had a pleasant irony: one member asked the Left how it was that Gorki, recently arrived in Italy for a holiday, could quote Trotsky as saying that Mussolini was "our splendid pupil," if Mussolini were really so anti-Left. Most of the Fascist shouts lacked this subtlety. They ranged from Farinacci's "Kick him out!" to cries of "Traitor!" and Starace's "We've got the power—we keep it!" When Matteotti's motion was put to the vote, it was lost by 285 to 172. Not all the Fascist M.P.s present voted for the government.

Some voted, by mistake, for the Opposition, walking automatically through to the Yes lobby.

Mussolini was very angry, not with his inexperienced M.P.s so much as with himself for his apparent failure to unite the country behind him. He remained convinced all his life that the only reason for Socialist Opposition was the fact that he himself had left the Socialist Party executive and had succeeded in getting power where his former colleagues had failed. Nenni, in his memoirs, writes that Mussolini left the Chamber muttering that if he were not surrounded by cowards, such a speech as Matteotti's could not have been made.

As Matteotti left the Chamber he joked with his friends that now he could "go home and make his will." [18]

Giacomo Matteotti had many enemies in the Fascist Party, several in his own. He was the son of rich landowners, which made his Socialism suspect to some. He had been educated in England and Germany, and had taken a neutralist line in 1914, which made his patriotism suspect. During World War I he had repeatedly made speeches accusing his fellow countrymen of being assassins, which did not endear him to ex-servicemen. Roberto Farinacci detested Matteotti, because the Socialist M.P. was clever, if not loyal. Marinelli and Aldo Finzi detested Matteotti because they had grown up in the same town, Fratta, and thought that he brought disgrace on it.

On June 2nd *il Popolo* commented that the Honourable Matteotti's attitude was monstrously provocative.

On June 3rd five members of the Opposition were beaten up in the precincts of the House.

On June 4th, after a speech in the Forum, Mussolini called de Bono to him and told him that beating up insignificant M.P.s was no way to silence the Opposition. He told de Bono to use his head, to attack where the Opposition was vulnerable. He also told him that he must take care to act like a director-general of public security. He had been told that there existed a sort of Cheka in the Fascist Party, of which de Bono was a passive member, which organized punitive expeditions among the Opposition M.P.s. Mussolini commented that this did not distress him too much, but it was amateurish, and he was sure that the members of the Cheka were incompetent. Lastly, he ordered de Bono to find him a culprit for the assaults in the precincts of the House.

De Bono went away, as one paper put it, "visibly moved." The journalist in question put it down to the Duce's speech, "an interlude of poetry."

On June 7th Mussolini, commiserating with Amendola, pointed out that 18 Fascists had been killed and 147 wounded in the recent election campaign, and urged him to stop exchanging bruises in the House.

On the morning of June 10, 1924, Mussolini received a medal from the Dante Alighieri Society for his services to Italian culture.

At 4.30 in the afternoon Matteotti left his home at Via Pisanelli 40, to walk to the House. He was wearing a light grey suit, carried a briefcase, and was hatless. He walked toward the river, toward a long-bonneted Lancia which was waiting at the corner of the next street.

At 4.33, according to an old man who was smoking his pipe at a near-by window, three men leaped out of the Lancia, thumped Matteotti in the stomach, stopping his flight with a blow on the back of the neck. Then the three men pushed him into the car and drove off at high speed.

The old man rushed out of the house, waved his fist at the retreating car, then ran down to Matteotti's. The Socialist M.P.'s wife would not see him. Her maid said he was a well-known drunkard, certainly begging. But at 7.30, with no sign of her husband and a phone call from the House asking why he had not shown up, Matteotti's wife sent for the old man and listened to his story of the assault on her husband. She told a friend, M.P. Modigliani, who reported it to the police. At 9 p.m. Mussolini was told that the Honourable Matteotti had disappeared under "mysterious circumstances."

At this point the history of the disappearance divides. Socialist historians maintain that Mussolini was not surprised, having been told by Finzi that he and his friends were going to kidnap Matteotti and "teach him a lesson." Fascist historians maintain that, until two days later, Mussolini knew nothing of either kidnapping or worse. The truth lies somewhere in between. Finzi certainly told Mussolini that he would "teach Matteotti a lesson," but it was understood that the Duce would be kept in the dark about the time and place. He could not afford to be implicated personally, and de Bono was still smarting at Mussolini's rebuke for inefficiency. The whole affair was "put into the hands" of Marinelli: Giuseppe Marinelli was not even to tell the Duce what was going on. Cesare Rossi, his press secretary, was to do this after the event.

At 11 p.m. on June 10th Mussolini was told that there was still no news of Matteotti's whereabouts and that nobody could find Marinelli either. Mussolini received Umberto Poggi, a messenger from D'Annunzio, complaining about some imagined slight. Mussolini was in a bad temper. Poggi said later that the Duce cursed the Opposition for its intransigence, and that he had the impression that the Duce was worried about Matteotti, though he knew nothing at that point.

At midnight the Duce learned part of the truth. Filippo Filippelli phoned him and told him that four men—Dumini, Malacria, Volpi and Poveromo—had asked him for the loan of his car. He had guessed that it was to be used for some top-level punitive expedition, or for smuggling some woman into some leader's house, and he had handed over the keys to Dumini himself. Now, said Filippelli, Dumini had phoned him from somewhere outside Rome and told him that they had used the car to abduct Matteotti, had beaten him up and dumped him in a wood 15 miles outside Rome, and what should they do about the bloodstains on the upholstery of the car? Filippelli told Mussolini that Dumini was quite sure that Matteotti was still alive and would crawl to a near-by house before morning. The cold air would bring him to. A few minutes later Marinelli called to say that something seemed to have gone wrong.

Throughout the next day the whole of Rome gossiped in uncertainty. The papers, by agreement, carried no sensational disappearance story, for fear of alarming Matteotti's old mother, a rare instance of sentimentality. De Bono, who by that time had learned from Dumini that Matteotti had been taught too good a lesson—had died in the car, and been buried in a loose grave—tried hard to hold the news back until the four murderers had got away. The Duce was not told.

On June 12th, at five in the afternoon, Mussolini answered questions in Parliament about the disappearance of his Socialist rival. He said that if a crime had been committed, the culprits would be brought to justice. An hour later he received Matteotti's wife and told her the same thing.

At 8.30 de Bono went to see Mussolini and reconstructed the crime for him. It was a story of bungling from start to finish. So many precautions had been taken to assure secrecy that nobody knew quite what was going on, and had not known for days. False trails had been laid, even for those involved in the affair, who had all been told a different version of the story. De Bono confessed that Matteotti was now dead and asked Mussolini what he proposed to do about it.

Mussolini told him to sit down. Quinto Navarra, who was listening to the conversation through the open door, heard Mussolini give him the sort of dressing down a schoolmaster might give to an idiot boy. He was told to hand in his resignation immediately. Then Mussolini asked him how much danger there was that the details of the affair would leak out. His enemies were hinting at a "Fascist crime," but if the Fascist criminals could be got out of the way, then maybe the whole affair could be hushed up. After all, there had been a fair amount of blood spilt in the struggle for power since 1919. De Bono confessed that he did not know whether or not the criminals had escaped. He thought they had, but how was he to know? A thick mist of "security" had fallen over the enterprise from the start. Enraged, Mussolini phoned the chief of police and gave orders for the arrest of anybody concerned, excluding de Bono, but including Filippelli and his own press secretary, Rossi.

By the morning of June 13th the story was on the front pages. Dumini had been arrested at Rome terminus. Filippelli had been picked up at the offices of his paper, the *Corriere Italiano*. Cesare Rossi was arrested in the foreign ministry, and Marinelli, the administrative secretary, in the offices of the Fascist Party itself. Even the "flight" of the Cheka had been bungled, giving the maximum of aid to the enemies of the party and the maximum of undesirable publicity.

On the morning of the 13th Nenni and his Socialist colleagues met in Milan to discuss the murder. It was their considered opinion that Mussolini was finished, would resign. There was no need for further action. Protest in Parliament would be enough, and would show the world the "respectability" of Socialism. There were to be no reprisals. Not even Nenni would go so far as to accuse Mussolini of having given instructions for the murder. Knowing his old friend, he assumed correctly that some hot words had heated some empty heads. Mussolini was right to mutter, "They have thrown a body between my feet." [19] But it was without doubt a "disgusting affair." For the next few days Mussolini sat silent in Parliament, ranted and raved in his room. He was astonished, or not astonished, at the tender disloyalty of his friends. He saw Fascist M.P.s hard at work disclaiming responsibility, suggesting that they would be prepared to serve under another chief. Fascist buttonhole badges vanished from Fascist buttonholes. An attempt was made to mobilize the Rome Militia. It failed. Nobody wanted to appear on the streets in a black shirt.

Rossi escaped from custody. Like Finzi, he barricaded himself in a house, armed to the teeth, and wrote a memoir accusing Mussolini of everything except driving the murder car.

At 11 a.m. the Opposition met under the presidency of Bruno Buozzi in the Parliament building. Like the Socialists in Milan, they were "sure Mussolini had been brought at last to his knees."

Like the Socialists in Milan, they decided to do nothing about it except "withdraw from participation in the activity of Parliament until the government's reaction be known."

At midnight the Grand Council of Fascism met. It was a memorable occasion. For the first time the *ras*, the thugs and the less reputable but more forceful Fascists, found themselves at a disadvantage. The three Nationalists who attended the meeting found it no longer necessary to conceal distaste for some of the methods which had been used to achieve power and were apparently still being used to retain it. Confirmed was the decision to arrest and punish those responsible for the murder of Matteotti, with an especially severe punishment for those who were trying to shuffle all the blame off on to Mussolini. Mussolini himself did not escape unscathed. He was told by Federzoni that he must once and for all break with, and break the power of, the *ras*. The militia would have to be reorganized, its command changed at regular intervals, to break up "private armies." Lastly, he, Federzoni, was to become Minister of the Interior and supervize the next, non-Fascist, stage of pacification and normalization.

Telegrams of protest at the presumed murder (confessed, but no body as yet discovered) arrived by every courier. Ramsay MacDonald sent one, and Arthur Henderson. Mussolini's Conservative friends sympathized with him.

In Germany, Mussolini's admirers, unbeknown to him, admired his "energy and ruthlessness." Hitler's scattered following mused on how much better things might have gone at Munich if Mussolini had been in charge.

The corridors of Palazzo Chigi, Mussolini's office, were deserted. All the job hunters, favour seekers and admirers, seemed to have taken fright. Quinto Navarra says that, apart from himself and a female admirer, Matilde Serao, the Duce spent the night alone. When in the morning a few leaders arrived from the provinces to find out for themselves what was going on, Mussolini, unshaven, looked like a shopkeeper about to announce his bankruptcy. But he never reached the point of declaration. He found other friends, "just as the number of backs turned toward me seemed to grow to an innumerable wall of hostile bricks."

The Queen Mother, when she heard that Mussolini was thinking of resigning, sent him a note telling him "not to be ridiculous." She had "calmed the King." In fact, the only mention in the King's diary of the whole affair in June is the laconic entry on the 13th (he had been to Spain): "Came home, Disappearance of Matteotti."

On June 17th Grandi and Balbo, having conferred with the other *ras*, decided that there was no alternative to a continuance of the Mussolini government, and embarked on a programme of "personal appeals" to the mob to "stand firm." "Give me, O people," said Grandi, "a message that I may take to the Duce when I see him tonight, a giant alone in his greatness, at his post . . ." Ironically, Mussolini's rivals backed him up. His ornate intimates in the party in Rome put away their uniforms until better times came again.

The Vatican, full of new-found friends, stood firm behind Mussolini "in his hour of need." Cardinal Gasparri confided in the Belgian Ambassador, when he heard that the Opposition was about to appeal to the Holy See to remove Mussolini by moral persuasion: "I know nothing of the religious faith of these people, and frankly I do not see why they want to worry the Holy Father. The Pope is very sorry about the whole affair, but does not see how he can lend himself to a manoeuvre which would ally the Holy See with the Socialist Party against Fascism."

The King, the same evening, said to Bruno Gemelli: "I know that Mussolini is loyal to me and that he is not responsible for what has happened. He will remain the Government."

On June 18th the Regent of Ethiopia arrived on a state visit. The crowd was distracted. Thousands still went, efficiently marshalled by the Socialist Party, to gape at the spot where Matteotti had been bundled into the Lancia. But thousands went off to cheer the black prince, with his black beard, and cloak covered in signs of the zodiac.

On June 22nd Farinacci harangued 50,000 Black Shirts at Bologna: "Be always ready to march."

But Mussolini did not give the order to march. He did not need to. The masses may have melted away from him in Rome, and his entourage may have thinned out, but this did not disturb him. At least he now knew who his friends were. And there were powerful friends hovering solicitously in the background.

By the afternoon of the 24th Federzoni had managed to reinforce the government by adding three more Liberals—Casati, Sartrocchi and Nava. General di Giorgio took over the Ministry of War from Diaz, who had shown signs of wavering. Mussolini spoke again, a long speech to the Senate. He quoted Talleyrand at the Left, and the Italian Socialists who had been writing in *Pravda* at the Right. As always, he won over the majority by his eloquence. Federzoni's able horse-trading with the Liberal Party gave Mussolini's confidence an air of respectability. In the Senate, the economist Pantaleoni recalled the recently deceased economist Pareto's praise for the Fascist government and added: "The Prime Minister's entourage, of which I hear so much evil, does not consist of those criminals in jail but of Honourable Senators here in this Chamber. After all, who put the economy of the country in order again, Rossi or Alberto de Stefani?" In the end, only twenty-one voted for the vote of No Confidence proposed by Luigi Albertini.

On June 25th Mussolini called together his M.P.s and gave them a pep talk. His refound enthusiasm infected his friends. Farinacci urged that those comrades who had defected be shot. Mussolini called him a vegetarian tiger and told him to organize a tour of the provinces in a hurry.

On the 27th Mussolini set off on tour to speak to the people. Dressed in militia uniform, he was back in his element, on balconies with crowds beneath him. He told the crowd at Naples: "I'm still here, you see. The same as yesterday, the same tomorrow." At each town the duologue between the Duce and the crowd grew ever more emotional, enthusiasm and affection washing up and down and around the balconies, then ebbing back to the crowd itself.

Back in Rome, the Opposition refused to take part in the activities of the Lower House. But the Lower House was closed. The Opposition did nothing. The moment passed. The public forgot the "affaire Matteotti" in a welter of scandal about the private life of the discredited part of the Duce's entourage. Princesses were making love to old de Bono on black velvet divans. This was more interesting than inquests on the guilt of the assassins. Mussolini told his press supporters to fill the papers with gossip. He sent his own journalists to interview every grand old man of politics he could find, for quotable opinions on the stability of his government. They even followed Giolitti to Vichy and interviewed him as he took the waters. "Mussolini has no opposition," he said wisely. "The Opposition must go back into the House and work from there if they want to be called constitutional. A boycott is no answer. If Mussolini finds only his friends in the House, he may become convinced that he can do without Parliament. He may prefer to talk direct to the people."

On July 22nd the Grand Council met again. Blood was beginning to seep back into the veins of its members. "We cannot go back," Mussolini added. "We must learn to live dangerously." The era of the slogans had begun.

The summer grew hotter. The crowd at the seaside forgot the murder. On August 14th a policeman found Matteotti's body. It was too late for even the body to help the Opposition, most of whom were in the mountains or at the lakes. The King noted in his diary: "Very hot today. They found Matteotti's body."

D'Annunzio, who had been rumoured a member of a new anti-Fascist organization called the Lega Italica, denied his membership and swore eternal loyalty to the Duce. Piero Gobetti was beaten up by the crowd in anti-Fascist Turin for abusing the war hero Delacroix. The tide was turning again. On September 12th a Fascist M.P., Armando Casalini, was shot five times in a tram by the trade union leader, Corsi. His funeral was enormous, spectacular, vulgar, in the worst of taste and very effective. Mussolini went on tour again. His secret allies breathed sighs of relief. Cardinal Gasparri said, at a diplomatic reception: "To overturn the Mussolini government would put the whole country under fire and sword. We must be calm and patient . . ."

The British Under-Secretary of State for Foreign Affairs commented that: "Our information leads us to believe that the present government of Italy is firmly based."

The King refused three times to accept petitions for the removal of Mussolini. Cardinal Gasparri confided in Mussolini that he had forced Luigi Sturzo to resign as secretary of the Popular Party, that the Popular Party was at an end. The "mass of Christians hopes, from you, for stability and prosperity." [20]

But Mussolini had allowed himself to be lulled into a sense of false security. The Liberal Congress at Livorno in October revealed, at long last, an Opposition which realized that it must galvanize itself to activity if it were not to disappear. The principal leader of the Opposition, Amendola, directed the campaign. He decided that the only way to get rid of Mussolini was to get every venerated statesman and politician in Italy to declare himself publicly *against* the Duce. Throughout that autumn he worked to convince the waverers and the optimists that they were on the eve of a dictatorship. Eventually he managed to impress even Giolitti. The ranks, for the first time, were closing. For the first time the Opposition looked united.

The second prong of Amendola's attack was the press. There were still many widely read newspapers and magazines which had anti-Fascist editors. Mussolini, Amendola knew, was sensitive to press campaigns, as only an old journalist can be. The Opposition leader found the ideal centre-piece for a campaign, the memoirs of Rossi, Mussolini's press secretary, in which he accused Mussolini of having ordered, directed and approved of the Matteotti murder (it was the third draft of the memoirs). *Il Mondo* was chosen to publish the memoirs. The other Opposition newspapers, as each bold-typed short instalment came out, reprinted, dissected, and tut-tutted over it.

Day after day, week after week, as the memoirs dragged on in *il Mondo*, and as a wave of pamphlets, loyal addresses and printed speeches washed up at the King's feet, as the Opposition, imitating Mussolini, toured the country haranguing the mob, the position of the government weakened. Mussolini fought back in his own paper, but the odds were against him in the battle for readership. He fought back in Parliament, even going so far as to officially commemorate Matteotti's death. He was still obviously losing ground as Christmas approached. Former enemies, like the anti-clerical Liberals and Don Luigi Sturzo, teamed up to abuse him. Luigi Sturzo even managed to have de Bono summoned by the high court to answer charges of complicity in the murder, and there were rumours that Mussolini himself was to be impeached. The Senate refused to confirm eight new nominees sent up by the Duce, and sent back the list with a note urging "reconsideration." A warrant of impeachment was prepared which Giolitti himself promised to take to the King. As Christmas came Mussolini seemed to have lost his grip on the situation. He just laughed nervously when posters, appearing on the walls in Rome, showed his face splashed with blood.

In the provinces Mussolini's loyal militia officers, the junior officers with the ranks of consul and below, were worried.[21] They could not understand why he had not ordered them to react, even with symbolic violence, against the increasingly numerous anti-Fascist speechmakers and pamphleteers. Enzo Galbiati had the idea that the Duce's confidence was shaken, that he had been more affected than was realized by the defection in June of so many collaborators seen every day and trusted. He had seemed to be on top of the situation in September, and yet now he was undeniably slipping. Maybe, thought Galbiati, he believed that the militia was disloyal, that every militia was like that of Rome which had refused to mobilize in June. Galbiati knew that Mussolini did not entirely trust Grandi and the *ras* who had made so many loyal speeches in the early autumn. The price of this reaffirmation of loyalty would be high. Selfless devotion was only to be found among the junior officers, or so Galbiati reasoned.

Galbiati phoned or wired every consul he had ever met. He proposed a new pro-Mussolini march on Rome, but the practical difficulties were too great. And it was pointed out to him that Balbo, the organizer of the abortive march of October 1922, would not take kindly to the idea. So Galbiati, Tarabella and Passerone decided to form a deputation of consuls to go to see Mussolini on New Year's Eve (a holiday he detested) to "give him courage." One hundred and sixty-three consuls agreed to go. Thirty-five turned up outside the Duce's office. Tarabella, Passerone and Galbiati went in, telling Navarra they were going to wish the Duce a Happy New Year.

The effect on Mussolini of the arrival of the consuls cannot be exaggerated. They did not flatter him. They told him that he knew the "extent of their affection," but they were disappointed. They were ready to go to jail if he asked them to—to fight if he asked them to—but they were not ready to surrender to anybody at any time, nor were they prepared to do nothing while Mussolini's enemies and false friends betrayed him. The decisive hour for Fascism had come. He, Mussolini, must know this. The rank and file of the militia were behind him. He ought to ignore the Jeremiahs in Parliament and out. The old men who commanded the Army, who had been thrust on them as senior officers in the militia, did not, to them, seem to be bellicose or loyal. What was needed, said the consuls, was a sharp lesson to all concerned. Tarabella even thumped the Duce's table. Then they stalked out.

Nobody had ever spoken to Mussolini like that before. He was petrified. Then he realized that their violence was a loyal violence, as unexpected as it was welcome. He sent General Gandolfo to reprove them for leaving their posts. He made up his mind.

On January 3, 1925, Mussolini addressed what had dared to appear of his Parliament. He reviewed the events since he had taken power, "without a drop of bloodshed on the day." He stressed the "efforts I have made toward normalization and normality." He detailed the recent violence, verbal and physical, of the Opposition (the New Year had come in with a flurry of Socialist "punitive expeditions"). He quoted the Opposition leaders where they had given him credit for credit due. (His most constant adversary, Albertini, said: "The Fascist régime assured Italy of an order to which we all aspired: it ended the general strikes, continuous and intolerable, in the public services; it restored discipline to public and private firms; it has continued successfully the work of restoring the finances of the country begun by previous Governments, balancing the Budget; it has followed a sane and courageous foreign policy.")

Mussolini came to the point. He said: "Gentlemen, many of you have had illusions. You believed that Fascism was finished because I compromised it, that the party was dead because I punished it and had the cruelty to say so. . . . Italy wants peace, tranquillity, calm, work; we will give Italy these things, with love if possible, with force if not. You may be sure that in the forty-eight hours after my speech, the situation will be cleared up everywhere. And you all know that what I do is not just personal caprice, nor any lust for power, nor any ignoble passion, but is based on a possessive and limitless love for my country." The era of normalization was over. The dictatorship had begun.

5

UOMINI NUOVI

NEW MEN

Major-General Galbiati, in his history of the M.V.S.N.,* sums up the impact of Mussolini's speech of January 3, 1925:

> Rarely has a political speech had such an impact, or so much success. The Legions mobilized spontaneously. Fascist badges reflowered in the buttonholes of waverers' jackets. The local Fascist headquarters were suddenly crowded again. The timid became bold. The bold became lions. Anti-Fascists were to be found again in every economic, political and social organization created by Fascism itself, working hard. Office managers and departmental heads in every Civil Service branch once again boasted of having shaken Mussolini by the hand. The question of "morals" brought up by the killing of Matteotti, and transformed into a standard and even a battle-cry by the Opposition, seemed to disappear, sight and sound drowned in the accumulation of thousands and thousands of enthusiasts saying: "I told you so." [1]

Rarely has an Opposition failed so disastrously to delay or destroy a government's efforts to suppress it. Rarely, Fascist historians say, has an Opposition forced a government so clearly and decisively into the position from which it could only retreat to dictatorship. During Mussolini's speech itself he laid himself open to attack, had there been any sort of coherence of stamina in the Opposition's plans and leaders; quoting Article 47 of the Constitution, he urged any M.P. who believed him guilty of the Matteotti murder (which he was, if only morally) to avail himself of his right to cause him to be impeached. Anti-Fascist historians have said that no such move was made because "it was a well-known fact that the King would have been prevented or dissuaded from signing the impeachment, just as he had been prevented or dissuaded from signing the state of siege which could have stopped the march on Rome" (which never took place, as a decisive political act). But there was surely no reason why some member of the Opposition should not have tried. In the next three years many Opposition leaders made pointless gestures of

* Milizia Volontaria per la Sicurezza Nazionale.

defiance, "only to be imprisoned, then with the badge of imprisonment a guarantee of their anti-Fascism, to exile themselves abroad." This was especially true of those Opposition leaders who had flirted at one time or another with Fascism and needed the respectability of persecution to rehabilitate themselves (in this not unlike many ex-Communist refugees from Hungary in 1956).

By their almost puerile act in withdrawing from parliamentary life, the Opposition made it nearly inevitable, and certainly very easy, for Mussolini to destroy, emasculate, or change the nature of Parliament (according to the point of view of the parliamentary historian). Mussolini's direct challenge to impeachment was not taken up. Neither was the indirect challenge of the insolence with which he treated custodians of the Constitution while the old Albertian Constitution was still in part in existence. The Opposition contented itself with forming discussion groups.

Mussolini, however, did not hesitate once he had decided that he had been "too generous, perhaps even old-fashioned" in his treatment of Parliament and the old Constitution. On January 5th he published his first decrees severely curtailing the freedom of the press. Those newspapers which had been most outspoken during the autumn campaign against him were suspended for two weeks. When they reappeared—*Avanti*, *Giustizia*, *Lavoro*, *Mondo*, *La Voce*, *La Stampa*—they were frequently either suspended or confiscated again until in the end they were either "domesticated" or disappeared.

The anger of the Opposition at this first, indisputably dictatorial, act ought to have provoked it to do something, even if it were something illegal, to try to destroy the incipient dictatorship. The moment was all the more propitious because Mussolini was taken ill on January 7th, and confined to his bed for weeks. The Duce said himself: "Fit and well, I could understand their reluctance to face me. Confined to my bed with a painful stomach ulcer, it seemed to me I represented less of a threat. But, in fact, those who did not pray for my death as an easy way out of their difficulties, sent me flowers and messages hoping I would get well soon."

While Mussolini lay in bed and the *ras* rivalled each other in demonstrations of noisy loyalty, Parliament gave Mussolini an inevitable vote of confidence. Only a handful of Opposition M.P.s, led by Giolitti, even bothered to attend to vote against the motion. Even more ominously, eighteen "wise men" were chosen to begin "a work of revision of the Constitution in the light of changes made necessary by changing economic, social and political circumstances in the life of the Nation." On February 21st D'Annunzio gave his unqualified allegiance, once and for all, to the "régime" (as it was beginning to be called), and the last "idealistic" Opposition faded away. On February 23rd Roberto Farinacci was appointed Secretary-General of the Fascist Party and began the work of party organization which was to complete the organization of the militia begun by Balbo. With both the party and the militia incomparably disciplined, there was to be no more danger of defection.

On March 23rd Mussolini was well enough to get out of bed and go on to the balcony of Palazzo Chigi to speak to a cheering crowd. There was a storm of applause. "I'm in a good mood for speaking today," he began. And he was. For nearly ten years he never lost the knack of holding the attention of the huge and fascinated crowds which gathered beneath his balcony.[2] But after his speech had dissolved into inebriate cheers, Mussolini talked quietly to Federzoni (who had adopted the custom of wearing militia uniform) and denied that he had any intention of creating a permanent dictatorship or "disguised monarchy." He said: "The Opposition one day said—I think it was Amendola in a speech—there was a need to form a new Italian, that without a new Italian there could be no new Italy. He was right. I think of myself as a dictator ad interim, an educator. Italy will become a classroom. The militia will be my rod. One day the whole of Italy will belong to the Fascist Party, or form part of the Fascist movement. Then there will be no more party. The party will be the nation. There will be no more dictatorship, because the dictatorship will have become democracy."[3]

But this conversation was never reported, and it would have been ridiculed by the Opposition. Federzoni is, however, convinced that Mussolini at this point was sincere in his desire to make his dictatorship a means and not an end. There was still a "revolution" in the air. Mussolini used the word often. Soon there would be such a thing as Fascism, a *post hoc* ideology, and then this would slowly dissolve and disintegrate into Mussolinism, a religion with every one of the prophet's words elevated to a dogma. But for the moment Mussolini did not want to be an Italian Lenin. At the end of March 1925 he was weak after his illness, self-conscious about his age, and anxious to "die young after living dangerously," leaving behind him a reinvigorated and super-Socialist Italy.

It is quite certain that at this time no thought of "internationalist" Fascism had occurred to Mussolini. He had spoken several times during 1924 of the absurdity of the programme of the "world revolutionists" in the Soviet Union, and had commended, to members of the Soviet trade delegation, the last words of Lenin and the first words of Stalin, as his successor, on the subject. "For the moment, Bolshevism cannot be exported. In the same way, Fascism cannot be exported, ought not to be exported, is not exportable."

During his illness his wife had read to him (semi-literate, she was an ideal reader to the sick) an account of a debate in *Epoca* which began on January 24th with an article by the Italian Fascist leader in London, Camillo Pellizzi: "How long will it be before our chiefs in Rome realize that there can be a universal function for Fascism, that a whole world exists beyond the frontiers of Italy? Why is it a *gaffe* to cry in the papers of the world: 'Now we will set to work to unite all the Fascist currents in the world'?" Pellizzi's article called for an Internationale of "Fascist-type movements." Mussolini found the idea absurd. Too ill to reply himself, he asked Giuseppe Bottai to reply for him in *Epoca* (February 27, 1925).

After making quite clear that what Pellizzi called "Fascists" abroad were neither Fascist in name nor ideals, but nationalists, Bottai wrote: "Italian Fascism, an original creation which has yet to reveal itself in all its clear but complex nature, must not and cannot become the common denominator of the most diverse instincts of reaction which ferment in the world ... Recent history, a *pròposito* of the internationale of socialists, has shown us how the concept of an internationale broke down before the legitimate interests of different peoples ... Italy, through Fascism, will become once more a Nation, alive in the world . . . a Nation with a mission, with a function of her own."

Bottai's influence and that of the intellectuals seems to have been in the ascendant at this time. Mussolini, as soon as he was out and about again, asked Bottai to find out just how extensive his support was among the "great thinkers" of Italy. The failed elementary schoolteacher wanted to add the approbation of the professors to that of the mob and the militia. On March 28th the completed list, marked with the crosses of those who had agreed to sign a manifesto of support, was handed to Mussolini. Certainly the professors had done him proud. On the list were the names of the philosopher Gentile (Croce had changed his mind about Mussolini after a quarrel with Gentile), Volpe, del Vecchio, Soffici, Panzini, Ojetti, Ungaretti, Barzin, di Giacomo, Pirandello, Pizzetti, Pende, Coppola, Codignola, Pincherle, Ricci, and many others. Mussolini was not so pleased when Croce compiled an anti-manifesto, bearing the names of Salvemini, Salvatorelli and Einaudi, historians for whom Mussolini had an admiration which went beyond what he called their "political feebleness." But the majority of artists, writers and intellectuals in Italy in 1925 were not hostile to Mussolini.[4] Many believed him to be "a necessary evil who might even become a distinguished phenomenon" (Buronzo).

On April 21st (the Fascist May Day) leaders of organized workers added their names to the list of the "convinced intellectuals."[5] At the end of April those militia consuls who had hung about in and around Rome to see to it that Mussolini did not weaken, went home satisfied that the country was in good hands and that "a stable situation had been restored." Tarabella, who had registered as a patient at the University Hospital, Modena, to stay as near as he could to the Duce and account for his absence from his command, was nearly kept in the hospital for six months; the Duce had discovered the stratagem and had tried to persuade the doctors in charge to punish him. Galbiati and several other consuls were not as sanguine as Tarabella and his friends, not so sure of the "stability of the situation." Tarabella shrugged away their misgivings by telling them they knew nothing about politics. This the younger consuls were willing to admit: "We consuls of the militia . . . were young men who had never belonged to any political party, who had given themselves to Fascism not to make politics in the strict sense of the word nor to make factions, but because that movement was presented to us as the only logical development, social and civil, of the war fought and won." They may have known nothing of politics, but they knew enough about the local party leaders to be quite sure that Mussolini had better put his own house in order soon, or find himself—once the economy was well on its feet—overtaken by his ambitious subordinates, with the party organized against him in secret. "It seemed to us," wrote Galbiati, "that all the efforts of the régime to eliminate its adversaries would be better spent refurbishing and reinvigorating its own organs."

The militia consuls eventually convinced their self-appointed leader Tarabella to send a memorial to the Duce suggesting that the congress of the Fascist Party, scheduled for September, be brought forward three months and made an occasion for "distinguishing friends from other people's friends; distinguishing policies from other people's policies." Mussolini, acknowledging his debt to the young consuls, did as he was asked. He also promulgated a number of new party and national decrees against Freemasonry, a complex of sects which was anathema to the generation of Tarabella and Galbiati. These law decrees were sent to the King for approval on May 16th. Just how strongly the provincial consuls felt about Freemasonry may be seen from their second memorial, which begins: "If we isolate Freemasonry as our target, it is because in our documented and documentable opinion, this complex of sects is the principal instrument which disloyal elements in the Party executive use for their tortuous activity, and also the principal tool in the hands of the Opposition, which in its turn uses the Party executive for its own purposes." Galbiati and Tarabella founded an Order of Soldiers for Good Wars, an anti-Masonic order. The order had only paper and ink for weapons, but these it put to work. (On August 10th they were expelled from the Fascist Party for doing so.)

While the young militia colonels were putting their order to work, the party was planning a super-congress. It was to be held in Rome, and Mussolini gave instructions that all "provocations" which might result in bloodshed or rioting were to cease, the Opposition was to be lulled to sleep for a month, and the civil population kept calm. On June 6th the King and Mussolini exchanged patriotic, apolitical telegrams on the occasion of the Silver Jubilee of his reign. The "Aventino" M.P.s, still refusing to take part in parliamentary life, started to plan a commemoration of those "fallen in the fight against Fascism," to take place on June 10th, the first anniversary of the murder of Matteotti. Farinacci, who had agents even in the Aventino, got to hear of these plans and threatened them with a counter-commemoration of all the Fascists who had died in "the fight against Bolshevism and disorder." To make sure his threat was doubly effective, he suggested to Mussolini that the whole Parliament building at Montecitorio be closed for cleaning and repairs to the plumbing on June 10th. There were no commemorations.

The first "overseas delegates" to the party congress started to arrive in Rome. For the first time, they had their credentials checked. As Farinacci remarked: "There has been such a surprising rush to join the party . . ." Cesare Maria de Vecchi, fit and well but sure he had been missing something, returned from Somalia for the occasion. He spoke angrily about "mistaken ideas," and was almost sent back to the Italian colony by the next boat. Farinacci, as secretary of the party, was closing the ranks.

The party congress itself was a memorable one. It came as no surprise to hear Mussolini announce the abandonment of the policy of "normalization." Those who knew where to read Mussolini's thoughts in print had already seen an article by Bottai in *Crìtica Fascista* (June 1, 1925) which said: "It must be admitted that Benito Mussolini's attempt [at normalization, absorption of men of goodwill into the government] was premature, because it was not preceded by the impossible [in the circumstances] work of slow, day-by-day contact and discussion with the parties who contended with him for power." Mussolini's eighteen "wise men" had prepared a number of recommendations for the "improvement" of the Constitution, not all of which were discussed by the congress. Mussolini's speech at the Augusteo on June 23rd made it quite clear that the "wise men's" plans had been approved and would be put into effect, but that this was the work of the Duce. What was the task of the party? The first disturbing indication of the dictatorship to come was the proclamation of "devotion to the Leader." Bottai understood quite well what this meant, and said so in *Epoca* on June 24th. He hinted that though he approved, up to a certain point, of the suppression of "sterile" (i.e. anti-Fascist) criticism, he was hostile to the suppression of self-criticism in the party. Shrewdly locating the origin of this drive toward "unanimity" in Farinacci's brain, Bottai wrote: "Farinacci has an important task—that of ensuring that nobody tries to remove him."

Bottai himself stressed points in Mussolini's directive to the party which he found less disturbing, such as the abolition of honorary membership. By the end of the congress, however, he was convinced that somehow Farinacci had convinced Mussolini that he, Bottai, was dispensable. After years of close collaboration, of acting right up to the eve of the congress as Mussolini's spokesman, he was being "edged out." And as he knew, he represented the "thinking Fascist," the "Fascism as a mean to an end, the continuous revolution"; he was the intellectual who spoke for the inarticulate young officers of the militia who could not understand a half of what he said.

Bottai felt it his duty to warn the Duce that two sentences in his speech at the congress, certainly touched up by Farinacci after it had been edited by Bottai (Mussolini read his speech of policy declaration, one of the five times in his life when he did not make his speech up as he went along, from a skeleton on a sheet of paper), were capable of misinterpretation. "Violence is profoundly moral, more moral than compromise . . ." Bottai commented that: "All our critical work is permeated with the concept that while some violence may be called creative, or order and new life, sporadic aggression by the many against the few, without direction or an Ideal, is ignoble and ungenerous." Bottai had come a long way since his days as a futurist, storing bombs in Mussolini's stove. Another sentence which disturbed Bottai: "We must prefer the *squadrista* who acts, to the impotent professor." "Let us be frank," commented

Bottai, "we like to face up to difficulties. Many people have thought that these words, because of the name of our magazine, were directed at us." [6]

The congress consolidated Mussolini's position as leader of the party. Grandi, his rival at the first party congress, abandoned his attempt to prepare himself "for the succession." The congress also divorced Mussolini from the reality of the party, and left it in the hands of Farinacci, who, with his successors, slowly removed Mussolini from every contact with the rank and file. His leadership became something superhuman as the man himself was slowly built up by the party propagandists as a superhuman. Eventually it was the party secretary who was the link between Fascism's supporters and Fascism's creator. In a single-party state it is not enough to be Prime Minister—the office of Prime Minister, even if parliamentary institutions survive in name, is of no importance. The successful single-party statesman keeps control of the party. Such a control, added to the direct contact he has with the masses, not only makes Parliament a luxury and himself indestructible, it enables him to keep in touch with the movement of feeling when the cheers have died away. Stalin and Khrushchev learned this lesson from Lenin. Mussolini did not.

One of the first consequences of the "new order" created at the party congress was a drive to remove physically from the scene those parties and politicians who had made the dictatorship necessary. The public, which was usual in high summer, was only interested in getting away into the country or to the seaside and was prepared for the drive by Bottai. He started a campaign aimed first at ridiculing the Opposition leaders, then deducing that they were dangerous as well as ridiculous and ought to be jailed or exiled. He was helped by the absurdity of many of the articles and speeches made by Amendola, Salvemini, Salvatorelli and Gobetti, the principal objects of Bottai's attack. Salvatorelli, like many others before him, had a belief in Germany's future, in the rôle of the "new Germany" as saviour of Europe. He wrote that it had been a mistake to fight Germany in 1915—such an old ally of Italy. He and his friends quoted unread German commentators (Tilgher and others) on the crisis which the war had produced in Europe, and Salvatorelli had even gone so far as to write in *La Stampa* that: "Only reaction follows the victory of the Entente over Germany; that Germany which, under a thin crust of so-called Prussian Militarism, was working out the ideal world of the 20th century." [7] Bottai made great play with this Germanophilia, contrasting the Germany of 1925—bankrupt, disorderly, stricken by riots, humiliated by the French—with Italy as it had been restored to comparative prosperity. Salvemini was accused of "total disrespect for the State," and his trip abroad to lecture to London University (King's College) without a passport was instanced as an example of his "essential indiscipline, visible in his life, visible in his writings." Gobetti was denounced as an anti-patriot, guilty of continuing to deprecate the efforts of those who had died or been wounded in the war. Amendola, always nagging at the Duce, was accused of "having brought Parliament into disrepute."

The harsh words and often imbecile criticism were followed by direct action. Salvemini was arrested at the printers where he had composed his equally imbecile anti-Mussolini newspaper *Don't Weaken.* He was tried on July 13th; the court adjourned immediately because the prosecution had lost its main witness, and Salvemini was set free. On July 21st he was rearrested. On the same day Amendola was beaten up near Montecatini. Sundry *ras* were given orders to make speeches attacking both Salvemini and Amendola bitterly. Both men took the hint and exiled themselves, escaping dramatically if not really necessarily, at night, over the Little St. Bernard. Gobetti, who had a fair sense of drama, helped Salvemini over the frontier, and followed a few months later. Amendola and Gobetti died in exile the following year. Salvemini got a job with the *Manchester Guardian.*

Salvatorelli, the co-editor of *La Stampa*, was the fourth to be "neutralized." In constant fear of being beaten up, even in anti-Fascist Turin (a fear he never lost), he left *La Stampa* in 1925, and exiled himself. Mussolini, as he never tired of pointing out, got rid of his principal enemies, without cost to himself, without even the expense of maintaining them in jail. Only Giolitti and Croce lingered on, Giolitti with one foot in the grave and often the only non-Fascist M.P. present in the House, Croce as editor of an anti-Fascist magazine which few people read and which only helped Mussolini to deny accusations of "thought control."

There remained, in the fall of 1925, only those non-Fascists whose presences were in some ways useful to Mussolini—Socialists, Communists, the sort of enemies a man could boast of having on his trips abroad to emphatically capitalist and conservative countries.

On October 5th, at a meeting of the Grand Council of Fascism, "special measures" were discussed to be used against outlaws and self-exiles; they were to be regarded as deserters and their property confiscated. At the same meeting Mussolini had his first quarrel with almost the whole Grand Council over the appointment of Pietro Badoglio as Chief of the General Staff. It was, felt the council, unwise. He was not a man to be trusted—anti-Fascist one day, pro-Fascist the next. Even the King disliked him. But Mussolini insisted that at least Badoglio knew one end of a musket from the other (a jibe at Farinacci), and anyway could be kept in check by the militia, for which he would have special care. More to the Grand Council's liking was the draft of new laws for a "modernized local and central government," to be presented to Parliament in December. Mussolini left the draft with the Grand Council and went off to Locarno to a meeting with Austen Chamberlain, Briand, Stresemann, Luther and Beneš.

The Locarno Conference was to agree on new frontiers between Belgium, France and Germany; Britain and Italy were to act as impartial and disinterested guarantors. Mussolini, irritated by the Germanophilia of his enemies at home, told Chamberlain that he did not think the Germans were to be trusted, but would be more dangerous bankrupt than at least solvent. He urged Chamberlain to keep an eye on all the "lunatic nationalist elements"; said that he himself wanted peace on his northern frontiers. There was no more talk of Italo-German alliance, except as part of a general Western Alliance against Bolshevism. Mussolini disliked Chamberlain and thought him an oddly ineffective man. He teased him with having inspired a book, "a masterpiece of undigested nonsense," which had just come out, a book inspired by his namesake, the "philosopher." The book was called *Mein Kampf*, and the author Adolf Hitler was under threat of expulsion from his own Nazi Party. Mussolini returned to Italy after the Locarno Conference convinced that there was not another politician in Europe his equal. Not only did he understand events, he told Navarra, he was popular with the crowds now in almost permanent expectation beneath his balcony.

On November 4th, the day of Commemoration of the Fallen, the police arrested the Honourable Tito Zaniboni, a Socialist M.P., for attempted assassination. On the fifth floor of the Dragoni Hotel, at a window overlooking Mussolini's office, they found a sniper's rifle trained on the balcony. According to the police, the assassination attempt had been paid for by the Czech Masaryk, organized by Garibaldi's grandson, and betrayed by a starlet who was the mistress both of Zaniboni and of a police spy. The next day Nenni arrived in Rome to fight a duel with Malaparte. Mussolini commented that Rome was getting more like the second act of an operetta every day.

Farinacci decided that both the attempted assassination and the Nenni-Malaparte duel (which came to nothing) were the work of such Freemasons as were still loyal to their "sects." Federzoni agreed. There was good reason, they said, to wind up the drive on the Opposition with an order for the closure of the "Masonic" press. The *Corriere della Sera* fell out of the hands of Albertini into less "Masonic" hands. All Masonic lodges were closed down. The Socialist Party was declared illegal. *Unita*, *Avanti* and *Giustizia* were suspended indefinitely. The London *Times*, ignoring its Socialist counterparts, deplored the passing of the independence of the *Corriere*.

On November 7th the first of Mussolini's "show-the-world" flights came to a successful conclusion. After 34,375 miles over India, Australia, China and Japan, Francesco de Pinedo flew home to land on the Tiber in his seaplane "Gennariello."

On November 17th the Senate congratulated Mussolini, both on his miraculous escape and on the "epoch-making flight." Next day Mussolini started the debate on his "new provisions" for "safeguarding the stability of the State." The provisions involved the emasculation of both the Senate and the Lower House. Mussolini began by informing both Houses that in the Grand Council of Fascism they had debated the whole question, and though the Grand Council was "not yet legally an institution in the strict sense of the word, yet it was already respected as the soul of resurgent Italy." Trade unions, as they had been known, were to disappear, and in their stead there would be a new organization of workers, with wages guaranteed by the government. New measures were to be taken to make sure that the workers kept their representatives in touch with their needs, and these measures would make the government more sensitive to these needs. There would be a drive toward "complete social justice." There were to be no factions in local government, no party waste of time at council meetings. In rural areas first, then in towns, local government elections were to disappear. There were to be no more mayors. In their place there would be *podestà*, responsible to the provincial authorities, who would be responsible to the government. There were to be no more local executives, only advisory committees in each administrative district, without any power of veto. These measures, said Mussolini, would enable him to hear the beating heart of his people. Closer to home, he proposed a revision of the Constitution. There was as much vagueness about that, he suggested, as there had always been about the discussions at local council meetings. The office of

Prime Minister was not even specified in the old Constitution. The King had to appoint ministers and leave the ministers, responsible to Parliament, to appoint their chairmen. This was untidy. Under his new law (passed on Christmas Eve) the head of the government would no longer be responsible to Parliament, but only to the King, who would appoint him. Ministers would be appointed by the King on recommendation of the head of the government. These ministers, too, would not be responsible to Parliament, but only to the King, via the head of the government. And nothing was to be discussed in Parliament without the permission of the head of the government. All these provisions would save time, said Mussolini, and put an end to useless wrangling at all levels on unimportant topics.

The Opposition, few in numbers and weak in resolve, protested that Italy was returning to the shades of the Middle Ages. But the man in the street was not conscious of this, perhaps because he had few Opposition newspapers to read to enlighten him in his medieval shades. The man in the street noticed only the new roads, the new hospitals, the new aqueducts, the suppression of drug traffic, the closing of 25,000 of the worst drinking pits, trains arriving on time, smartly dressed policemen (75,000 of them) who made it safe to go out at night again.

Above all, the middle class and lower middle class were impressed by the steady rise in Italy's prestige abroad. In foreign newspapers, on sale everywhere, they read Mussolini's praises. The New York *Herald-Tribune*: "Mussolini is the modern Caesar, the Napoleon of 1926." *Le Figaro:* "Many people have got the habit, since three years ago, of taking one of those roads all of which lead to Rome. The incredulous have finally realized how great is the interest aroused by Benito Mussolini and his works." London *Daily Mail*: "It becomes more and more evident that, in our time, we are witnessing another revolution of the world's ideas, a revolution started by the tireless and fertile genius of Mussolini." London *Morning Post:* "Mussolini's works are little short of a miracle."

But, though the year 1926 was to be a year of triumph and began with a paean of praise for the "new Caesar," it also began sadly for him. The Queen Mother died, and Mussolini, at Bordighera on January 4th, to pay his last respects to his old friend and supporter, was visibly moved. She had shown confidence in him when the rest of the Royal Family had merely thought him amusing. She had helped him at the time of the march on Rome and at many moments of crisis since then. She had acted as his own personal spy in the royal palace, and after her death he was never well-informed of the

King's moods or his aides' attitude to the régime (a lack of information which was one day to prove politically fatal). The Queen Mother had even advised him on how to correct his extravagances in dress and look more at ease in the ritual uniforms of high office. Mussolini's wife adored her because she had told her she envied her her husband. The Queen Mother's last gesture shows the extent of her affection and admiration for Mussolini; she made him her executor. Mussolini gave her a state funeral in Rome, of which she would have approved, "the first Queen of Italy to love Fascism, who was loved by Fascism in return."

One of the more curious consequences of the intimacy between the Queen Mother and Mussolini was that for years after her death he treated the King like an idiot brother, even insisting as to when it was "high time" the royal children married. In February 1926 Mussolini, now Prime Minister, Foreign Minister, War Minister, Minister for the Navy and Minister for Air, spoke sharply to the King about his son Humbert whose "escapades with actresses were diminishing the dignity of the Royal House." And it says much for his influence that when Badoglio reported that some of his "agents" had discovered a plot to remove the King from his throne and substitute Mussolini, with Balbo as Prime Minister, the King told Badoglio "not to be so ridiculous, Mussolini and Fascism are both loyal to the Crown." Mussolini's father would not have been pleased.

On March 23, 1926, a minor crisis in the government distracted Mussolini from an exchange of abusive letters, much to his liking, with the Berlin government over the "nationalism" of the German-speaking part of Northern Italy. Luigi Federzoni, still Minister of the Interior, but more important as "liaison officer" with the old Nationalists, interrupted a conversation about the desirability of strengthening garrisons on Alto Adige with the remark that some of his Nationalist-Fascist colleagues were "somewhat irritated" by Farinacci and the less literate Fascist leaders. They felt they ought to be exempt from Farinacci's over-enthusiastic attempts to "re-educate them" to "pure Fascism." After all, said Federzoni, the Nationalist Party was considerably older than the Fascist Party and did still command the loyalty of the aristocracy, the upper middle class, and of many big businessmen. This loyalty, Federzoni said, was always at Mussolini's disposal. Anyway, said Federzoni, it was not a good thing to leave any man in the party secretaryship too long, where he might have ideas above his station. Mussolini took the hint, realizing that he still needed Federzoni and his Nationalist friends, if only to lessen his own dependence on his colleagues.[8] Farinacci was removed, and Augusto Turati, a leader from Brescia, hard working but unknown, took his place.

Part of the Nationalist Party's contribution was the efforts of its members to make Italy not only admired abroad for her achievements, but also respected by the world's black-and-white aristocracy. The ambassadors, embassy staffs and their friends (all Nationalists in sympathy and one day to be replaced by Fascists), did much to make Rome seem not just a "revolutionary museum," but an intellectual, scientific and technological centre. They made much of the flights around the world which Mussolini organized to show off his new aeroplanes. They also encouraged learned and scientific bodies to hold their international congresses in Rome, "Mother of Civilization."

On the morning of April 7, 1926, Mussolini proudly inaugurated a redecorated Capitol, and addressed the International Surgery Congress meeting there. He made a speech recalling his own debt to medicine and surgery in the war, and metaphorically flexed his wounds. At a minute past eleven Mussolini left the hall, to the cheers of the waiting crowd outside and the waiting surgeons inside. Walking past a haggard old woman at the exit, he noticed her plunge her hand into her handbag and bring out a pistol. Moving his head aside just in time, the shot only grazed him. But as Grandi, who rushed him back inside the hall, commented later: "He nearly bled to death with all these doctors standing about discussing the best way to stop the flow of blood." When he heard that the haggard assassin was an old Englishwoman, Violet Gibson, mentally deficient and out of sight of her nurse, he said: "Ha! Perfidious Albion. We must not alter the day's programme." Then he went off to inaugurate a new air service, open the new headquarters of the party in Palazzo Vidoni, and make a speech to his crowd beneath the balcony. Messages of congratulation and commiseration poured into his office. Among them were those from the King, the Duke of Aosta, the Pope, Cardinal Gasparri, even the old mad woman's brother (a peer of the realm). "We will all consider the incident closed," he said. "There must be no mistaken reprisals." There were no reprisals against Britons or British property. The local *squadristi* celebrated by wrecking the offices of *il Mondo* and beating up the staff.

On April 8th Mussolini set off in triumph to inspect the garrisons in North Africa. He opened new Fascist headquarters wherever he went. He received full military, naval and air honours. For five days he toured Libya, accompanied by de Bono (now governor of the colony), both of them wearing feathers in their hats. Hassan Pasha hoped it would not be long before "the Crown of the King of Italy be changed into the Crown of an Emperor."

On his return to Italy the Indian poet Rabindranath Tagore was waiting to hand over in person his collected works. Instead of being flattered, Mussolini crossed himself and fingered his good-luck charms for hours after the meeting. Navarra writes that day by day the Duce was becoming more superstitious and more lonely. Having lost his trust in most of his former friends and becoming slowly convinced of his own infallibility, he no longer tolerated visitors coming to beg favours. Reuters' correspondent in Rome described the approaches to and entrance hall of Palazzo Chigi as: "Striking, for the profound silence made the more noticeable by the noise in the street." For days Mussolini spoke civilly only to Navarra and his maid, Cesira Carrocci. When he travelled he preferred and usually insisted on driving his own Alfa Romeo, to the unnerving of Italo Balbo, who was his usual passenger. He tried to do everything himself. That summer as the reports of the harvest came in he found himself proved right in his belief that Italian farming was badly behind its competitors in Europe; in the areas where he had declared "a battle for wheat must begin," yields were up 10 per cent; in other areas there were stagnation and lack of enterprise. When he said, on August 10, 1926, that it was perfectly possible for Italy to become self-sufficient in wheat, nobody dared contradict him, though everybody privately thought him mad. In fact, in less than seven years (by the end of 1933) his "battle" had been won.

Nobody dared contradict him. Vincenzo Buronzo says that: "Mussolini used to boast that no man had ever slapped him on the back. Even before he came to power, he was reserved and aloof in this respect, discouraging informality even from his friends and relations." The King held him more and more in awe as the year wore on. He said to Donna Rachele: "You ought to be as proud of your husband as the House of Savoy is grateful to him for his work. I am a great admirer of your husband, an exceptional man. . . ."[9]

On September 11th Gino Lucetti, an anarchist, threw a bomb under Mussolini's car as he was being driven to work. For once, Quinto Navarra had persuaded him to take the heavy official car rather than his Alfa Romeo. His powers of persuasion saved the Duce's life.

This third attempt on his life made Mussolini even more solitary than ever. Some contemporary historians date his political isolation from this period, pointing out that from 1926 on his only contact with the world was through the newspapers and interviews with journalists (his input), and through his direct contact with the masses (his output). His speech after the bomb throwing (speeches slowly became duologues, then monologues broken by choruses, then a national litany) is typical:[10]

MUSSOLINI: In the great shout of welcome you have just given me on the occasion of the third—

CROWD: The last! The last!

MUSSOLINI: I can feel your faith in me, your devotion—

CROWD: YES!!

MUSSOLINI: I have little to say this time, but what I have to say is important. At the end of this demonstration, first of all, I insist that there must be no disturbance. A great people like ours knows how to keep its nerve.

CROWD: No! No! There is only one Duce!

MUSSOLINI: But we must put an end to that tolerance of assassins in their midst across our frontiers, if they want to keep our friendship. Episodes like this put a strain on friendship.

CROWD: Down with France! [Lucetti had been living in France, and was said to have been given his bombs by the anti-Fascist exiles in Paris.]

MUSSOLINI: I think certain steps will have to be taken here at home too. I don't ask it for myself—

CROWD: Yes, for you! For you! You are the Nation!

MUSSOLINI: Just as we have abolished strikes, we must put an end to these attempts at assassination . . . You know that when I speak direct to you, the people, I don't speak in vain. We must act—

CROWD: Act like Fascists!

MUSSOLINI: That's it—act like Fascists!

On October 31st, during a visit to Bologna to inaugurate a new Fascist stadium, a youth fired a shot at him as he rode through the city in an open car. The youth was beaten to death by bystanders.

This fourth attempt on Mussolini's life worked up a nationwide hysteria. Anybody and anything which could reasonably or unreasonably be described as "anti-Fascist" was doomed. Houses were ransacked (including Matteotti's). Men and women were beaten up or rushed on to trains into exile. Those anti-Fascists already in exile were deprived of their citizenships (the King signed the decrees, his hand shaking with anger). The chief of police lost his job, and his place was taken by the most genial of all the rumoured *éminences grise* of the régime, Arturo Bocchini. Chamberlain and his wife (with whom Mussolini had spent a day cruising in their yacht at the end of September) sent their regrets and told reporters: "What a tragedy it would be if Italy were to lose this man!" Even Senator Albertini, hiding from possible unjust retribution, cabled his deploration of the attempts on his arch-enemy's life.

On November 5th Mussolini presented his Cabinet with a list of decrees "for the Defence of the State." The death penalty was introduced for attempts on the life of the King or Regent, Prime Minister, Queen or Crown Prince. Federzoni, as Minister of the Interior, was made responsible for a whole series of laws which in effect created "the police state." Passport issue was now strictly controlled. A political police force was organized, and the border police reorganized to increase their efficiency. A special police tribunal was established in which political cases could be heard in camera and without the normal guarantees for the accused. (This tribunal became effective as of November 9th.) All freedom of the press vanished (effective November 25th). All Opposition M.P.s who had taken part in the Aventino secession and refused to participate in parliamentary life were deprived of their seats; Mussolini was livid to find out that though they had, from the very best motives, avoided the Council Chamber, they had been drawing their salaries the whole time. The few prominent anti-Fascists who were not either in exile or in jail were arrested on the night of November 8th—including Antonio Gramesi, the secretary of the Communist Party (the Communist Party of Italy, meeting at Lyons in France to deplore the régime, sent its regrets to his wife).

In Paris, headquarters for the anti-Fascist exiles, most of the second-class hotels run by Italians were occupied by the Opposition—Turati, Treves, Gobetti (who died shortly after arriving in Paris), Modigliani, Saragat, Zannerini, Buozzi, Nitti, Baldini. Their presence in the French capital was to be a constant source of irritation in Franco-Italian relations for the next ten years.

Only Croce, Mussolini's "official critic," Giolitti, too old to make trouble, and Malagodi were allowed to linger on in the "official twilight" of controlled anti-Fascism. They were all kept in Turin. There, said Mussolini, it was easy for them to take a train to Paris if they had a mind to, and they were out of his sight. It was in Turin, a few years later, encouraged by Crown Prince Humbert, that the first faint stirrings of a resistance were noticed and shrugged away by the local leaders. But for the moment there was nothing. Lights burned only in the offices of the Tribunal for the Defence of the State, where lawyers worked late to prepare cases against men who might one day be disloyal. The only plots hatched were those hatched by Fascists themselves, for their own advancement in the "Régime Which Must Last."

The world outside Italy took the conversion of a weakened democracy into a dictatorship quite calmly. The general opinion abroad was that it was a good thing, that the Italians needed a strong man, and Europe needed a strong Italy. The British government, with troubles of its own, secretly envied Mussolini his special powers. In England the general strike had confirmed the worst fears of those who believed that "Bolshevism was about to let blood again." The trade unions seemed to be out of control, to have "lost their understanding of the nation's needs." Opinion was that they were paid by Moscow. Only the incompetence of the Left prevented a minor coup: the situation was similar to that in Italy in 1920–21. How had Mussolini dealt with his noisier, more violent, Latin Left? The British Chancellor of the Exchequer, Winston Churchill, went to Rome to find out, on a "private visit."

On January 15th Churchill was received by Mussolini in Palazzo Chigi, and they talked for an hour. The next day Mussolini returned the visit and the talk lasted longer. Both men, said Navarra, seemed nervous, almost conspiratorial, though Churchill "hung on the Duce's every word." According to Navarra, they parted on the first occasion with a promise by Mussolini to prepare a lengthy memorandum for Churchill on the "means to combat the spread of godless Bolshevism," the memorandum to be sent through the normal diplomatic channels, but reserved for the Chancellor's eyes alone. After their meetings Churchill said: "If I were Italian, I am sure I would have been with you from beginning to end in your victorious struggle against the bestial appetites of Leninism. It is quite absurd to say that the Italian government does not rest on a popular base or that it is not kept in office by the active consent of the great mass of the population. . . ." And of Mussolini, the man: "I could not but be fascinated, as so many people have been, by his courteous and simple bearing, by his calm and serenity in spite of so many burdens and dangers. It is easy to see that his only thought is for the lasting welfare of the Italian people, as he sees it, and that other considerations of less weight do not have for him the slightest importance."[11]

The Belgian Cardinal Merry de Val added his New Year greetings: "I am grateful that such a man has in his hands the reins of government in Italy, and that with a clear vision of the reality of things, has desired that religion be respected, honoured and practised."

Behind the scenes, Mussolini's special counsellor was working hard with the future Pope's brother, Pacelli, on the "great project for a Conciliation." What was pleasing the Church especially at this moment was "Mussolini's work for the sacred institution of motherhood and for the welfare of our children." The O.N.B., or Bàlilla Yòuth Organization, had been given formal status in April 1926; it was reorganized, taken out of the hands of Vincenzo Buronzo, and put into the hands of Ricci on January 9, 1927. The O.N.B. started its life as an attempt to "create the Boy Scout spirit" in Italy. Under Ricci it gradually became para-military; "the work of strengthening the spine of our people, of perfecting the race." It embraced young people of all ages, from five to twenty-one, and is supposed to have been modelled in its later stages on the Communist Youth League. It prepared young boys (eventually girls) for membership of the adult party, just as the Young Pioneers and Young Communists do in the Soviet Union. Mussolini's work for motherhood was given legal form in the O.N.M.I. (for Maternity and Infancy) in several stages during 1926, and came into force in the first months of 1927. Just as all the young people in the O.N.B. (even the armed *avanguardisti*) were obliged to go to Church, so Italian women were practically encouraged to follow the Church's teaching on procreation. The churches filled and the birth rate went up by 9 per cent.

Mussolini suppressed an issue of *Crìtica Fascista* in which the less worthy, but rather more exact, aims of the two movements were outlined: "The organizations of the O.N.B. get young men and women used to the idea of thinking politically."

The year in which the "physical construction of the Fascist State" went into top gear was 1927. The new administrative apparatus was completed by the increase in the powers of the prefects, who became, in effect, local regents or viceroys. Orders were handed down to them directly from above (they acquired the title, Your Excellency), and they saw to it that they were carried out. There was no way for ideas to come up from below save through the ranks of the party, which, like the Communist Party, acquired a separate, almost constitutional function, or in the cries of the crowds below Mussolini's balcony.

Having created the bare administrative bones of the Fascist State, embarked on enormous public works, and encouraged an increase in the birth rate, Mussolini had to re-order the economy and readjust it to his needs. This was not done without some difficulty. The first stage was to "perfect" labour relations, keep the workers and peasants happy. Mussolini dealt first with the peasants. They had already been shown that it was possible to increase the production of wheat, and they were encouraged by a succession of competitions (with medals and trophies), exhibitions, tractor rides by Mussolini himself, and harangues, to consider themselves in the front line and "part of a united labour force." Peasants were in fact frozen to their land, and manpower mobility diminished. The drift to the towns was stopped. This had its positive side, as there had been a tendency to leave farming to those too stupid or too old to get jobs in near-by factories, and this had not been good for either quantity or quality of output. Production rose. Prices were held steady, or their fall was controlled. Real wages on the land increased. Mussolini's following among the peasants, from start to finish, was almost 100 per cent.[12]

He had less success with the workers. This was not entirely because they had Socialist pasts, as he had, and were still sentimentally attached to them, but rather because he turned upside down the whole structure of capital and labour as it was then known.

There are various claimants to the title of draughtsman of the Work Charter and architect of the Fascist corporations. D'Annunzio's friends insist that the idea of returning to medieval, closed economic communities—like the old Florentine guilds—was an idea of the soldier poet. This is not unlikely, for by 1927 D'Annunzio was already in his dotage, sitting in open fields on a gold throne, listening to people perform his verse plays. The man who really got down to a "New Order" for workers and employers alike was the man who thought up most of those ideas which later came to be known as "Fascism." There was no such thing as "Fascism" when Mussolini came to power in 1922. There were Fascists, men like Galbiati with no political affiliations, who found in Mussolini a spokesman for their frustration; and there were pro-Fascists like the lower middle class who wanted order restored; the Queen Mother who wanted death or glory; the cardinals who wanted a settlement for the Church; big businessmen who were afraid of Socialism. But there was no ideology, no *Mein Kampf*, no policy. There was only a programme, and an agglomeration of armed bands to implement it. There was something almost formal about Nazism, "National Socialism." The principal characteristic of Mussolini's rule was that he made his policies and his ideologies up as he went along. When, in 1923, he realized that the world would want to know his "philosophy" if he succeeded, he got young Bottai to work one out in the pages of *Crìtica Fascista.* When success was assured and the economy was recovering, he asked Bottai to prepare an ideological apology for de Stefani's successes as Finance Minister. These successes had to be proven to be "Fascist successes," not just the work of a brilliant administrator. That Bottai's "background" eventually suffocated de Stefani's brilliance was probably the fault of neither of them.

Bottai believed that it was necessary to change the whole character of the relationship between employer and employee as this relationship had developed under capitalism. Both Bottai and Mussolini accepted Marx's teaching that, as long as this relationship was allowed to develop unguided and according to the "laws of history," class struggle (leading to revolution, disorder, riot, bloodshed and the triumph of Communism) was inevitable. It had happened in the Soviet Union. In 1926 it looked like happening, even in Britain. Bottai concluded that what was necessary was to halt the development of "capitalist" socio-economic relationships in its tracks and put something in its place: "moral, political and economic unity." [13]

The Work Charter was Bottai's first draft of a system of economic relationships which would develop this "moral, political and economic unity." It was promulgated on April 23, 1927. The basic idea was to put an end to class struggle by uniting employers and employees in one enormous "trade union" divided into twenty-two sections which covered the different occupations of its members. Guarantor of this trade union—its referee, superviser and non-elective president—was the State. In the person of the head of the State, men and women would find symbolic leadership in their working lives, just as they found symbolic leadership in the same person (as head of the State—head of the single party) in their political lives. The head of State would be the "boss," the symbolic No. 1 worker, the symbolic No. 1 foreman, the symbolic No. 1 employer. By making economic associations vertical instead of horizontal, clashes would be avoided on a class level and would occur, if necessary, only at a trade level. There would be no competition between employer and employee for scarce resources such as consumer goods, but only between trade and trade for scarce resources, raw materials and investment capital.

The thirty articles of the Work Charter tried to give legal form to this idea. "Work is a social duty . . . and the complex of production is unitary." The charter made work a duty and a right. Conditions of work, from wages to sanitary fittings, were regulated by the State as referee between trade and trade. Ideally, each trade was to settle its own internal wage structure by itself, though the State would give advice when asked. Unity, for the good of the individual and the development of the nation's strength and economic potential, was the goal.

There were certainly no strikes in the days of the Work Charter. When the corporations came into existence some years later, it seemed as if the idea Bottai had transformed into institutions would really work. Certainly many economists came to Italy from the United States, Great Britain, Germany, Spain—from democracies and anti-democracies—to see it work. The "collective contract" was presented as a development of almost every idea of association based on obligation rather than conflict. Unkind critics of it in its early days suggested that Bottai had been given his head only to stop him making rude remarks about the party and its not too intelligent leaders in *Critica Fascista*, but they overlooked the fact that Mussolini's enthusiasm for the idea lasted at least until 1935—eight years was a long time for any idea to retain the Duce's interest and approval. Certainly when it became obligatory to make "collective contracts"—fix wages and even a scale of profits on a national, all-inclusive basis—the idea attracted even the workers. In the first six years of the new system 566 national agreements and 10,021 local variations of the national agreements had been made and were being observed in apparent harmony by both "sides." The national wages policy which the system made possible enabled Mussolini to fix prices to suit his trade policy—which was to keep out foreign goods, not by raising tariff barriers but by lowering prices at home. Mussolini knew that any attempt to set up tariff barriers on his part (notwithstanding his trade treaties with every sort of country from the Soviet Union to Great Britain) would bring about reprisals and block his earnings of foreign currency. On the other hand, "peaceful competition" hurt nobody. If he wanted to keep out English wrenches, then Mussolini just lowered the labour-and-profit element in the cost of production of Italian wrenches until Italian wrenches were so much cheaper. The inflow of English wrenches was stopped and an export trade in wrenches to England created overnight. Any "temporary hardship" in the wrench industry could be dealt with by State action on a massive scale through the wrench trade union of which it was president.

Throughout 1927 this new economic order was discussed. Its critics reserved their final judgment until it had been given a chance to work or not work. They were silenced, anyway, by Mussolini's announcement in May that he had succeeded in revaluing the lira with an improvement of nearly 30 per cent over what he had found in 1922. His methods of revaluing the lira astonished many economists. He reduced the national debt by the simple expedient of burning Treasury bonds. He managed to convince the masses of workers and peasants that they ought to offer to reduce their own wages: in May the peasants' union in Brescia cabled Mussolini an offer to cut their wages by 10 per cent, an offer which was immediately emulated by the local peasants' union in Pavia; this was followed in its turn by a similar voluntary cut in all wages and salaries in the province of Bologna, and by an offer of workers and employers in Genoa to cut five million lire a year off their wages bill and profits.[14] When the campaign to cut salaries and profits had reached its peak, Mussolini stabilized rents and ordered local authorities to fix prices so that every worker and peasant was above the subsistence level. As de Stefani commented: "I don't know how it will all work out in the end, with a depression in the air, but it is certainly astonishing."

Enthusiasm for the régime was not lacking. In the summer of 1927 Mussolini drafted the first plans for the draining of the Pontine Marshes and for the building of a whole chain of new "garden cities." The Pontine Marshes project was immense. For twenty-five centuries rulers in Rome had been trying to do something about the malaria-ridden 3,000,000 acres (Mussolini's plan, which became law on December 8, 1928, was the 146th recorded). Marcus Cornelius succeeded in reclaiming a little in 162 B.C. Julius Caesar had a plan, but was knifed before he could put it into practice, though it was part of his plan (for a system of canals and the diversion of tributaries of the Tiber) which Mussolini did bring up to date. Nero did, in fact, dig a canal 100 miles long, but he was more preoccupied with ensuring that "two quinqueremes could pass on the waterway," than with its drainage application. The Goths tried and failed to do anything with the marshes, and when they became part of the Papal States, they defeated even the ingenuity of successive Popes. It was left to Mussolini to pick all their brains, learn something from each, and successfully drain this immense area.

In the long term the draining of the marshes and the bringing into cultivation of some 3,000,000 acres has proved invaluable. In that short term it was useful to de Stefani and Mussolini. Wherever their "economic policy" broke down, and as the world-wide slump began to affect even the "planned economy" of the Fascist State, Mussolini would move the unemployed out of danger areas as far away as Venice and settle them on his "virgin lands."

In 1927 a whole sackful of public works was approved—even

such absurd testimonies to the idolatry to which Mussolini was subject as the Monolith and Obelisk and immense statues of the Duce.

On September 27th, obsessed like everyone else in Italy with her husband and his talk of the glory of the New Rome, Donna Rachele gave birth to another son. He was christened Romano.

Mussolini's foreign policy up to this time had been essentially one of the "normalization" he had abandoned at home.[15] His principal aim was to make friends with the Great Powers by first impressing them with concrete achievement, then lavishing their representatives with "Roman hospitality." He hoped the Great Powers, his former allies in World War I, and the Soviet Union, would "respect us for our efforts to stabilize the Mediterranean." He thought little of Germany and its odd National Socialist Party, other than that he did not like Hitler's looks, nor did he appreciate Hitler's admiration and imitation of his "methods." Goering had returned to Germany after his asylum in Italy, full of Mussolini, his Black Shirts, the militia, the trains running on time, and the enthusiasm of the crowds beneath the Duce's balcony. Hitler, at first cold, found Goering's enthusiasm infectious and sent messages to Mussolini on the anniversaries of the march on Rome. Mussolini did not take him seriously. He "did not want imitators, nor disciples." He was well aware of the potential instability of his own régime and wanted only stability among his neighbours.

The only area which absorbed Mussolini's attention at this time was the Adriatic. He had come to power on a promise to restore Fiume to Italy, and this he had done. He had been stalemated in the Ægean, and this had to be revenged. Yugoslavia was stable, but both Yugoslavia and Greece had to be kept that way. The Vatican Secretariat of State, with whom the Duce was in touch at least once a week via his envoy, Professor Barone, showed him its reports from its Apostolic visitor in Bulgaria, which indicated that the essential instability of the Bulgarian Balkans might well spread to Yugoslavia and Greece. The Apostolic visitor, Archbishop Roncalli, would not have been pleased to know that his reports were useful, or even read by the man responsible for his exile to Sofia. But Archbishop Roncalli and all the other priests who had helped the Popular Party and believed in it as an alternative to Fascism, were no longer consulted about anything, and their pleasure or displeasure did not count.

In the summer of 1927 relations between France and Italy became more and more strained as the French government refused to do anything about the anti-Fascist colony active in Paris, and was even suspected of subsidizing it. Mussolini even asked the British government, which professed its friendship once a week, to use its good offices to have his exiles expelled from France. But the British government of the day, while pro-Mussolini, was watching out for its own interests in the Mediterranean and was anxious that its rivals there—France and Italy—should not form any sort of alliance which might threaten her naval supremacy. Above all, the British government was suspicious of the talk of a "Latin alliance of Italy, France and Spain." Such a Latin alliance according to the Foreign Office's source of information, would hand over French Bizerta to Italy in return for hegemony in the Middle East. Spain would be given Gibraltar. This "plan" was being canvassed by some of Mussolini's friends, notably Ezio Maria Gray, but had as yet found no favour with the Duce himself. He did not like the Spanish King, who had insulted his Fascist anthem. He did not like Alfonso's "little Duce." And he did not like the French.

Far from concluding any sort of alliance with Italy or promoting a Latin association, France decided that Italy "must not be allowed to develop its ambitions in the Mediterranean." In late October 1927 talks between the French and Yugoslav governments on a treaty of peace and friendship were brought to a successful conclusion. By the terms of the treaty, signed in the first week of November, Italy was to be sandwiched between the two countries, who were to watch Mussolini closely for "plans of expansion." France would keep an eye on the western Mediterranean; Yugoslavia on the east.

When Mussolini heard of this treaty, he put aside his plans for new statues of himself and called in Contarini to discuss a counter-measure. Contarini's counter-measure was a simple one. Mussolini would have a talk with the King and find a Princess to marry King Boris of Bulgaria. That would tidy up that end of the Balkans. Rumania was already well on the way to becoming a pastiche of Fascist Italy, so that took care of another length of Yugoslavia's land frontier. Austria and Germany were still weak and not inclined to conclude treaties with France, so they could be written off as neutral. Greece seemed likely to "go Fascist." All Mussolini had to do, in addition to finding King Boris a wife, was to sign a treaty with Albania. Then he would have a beach-head on the Yugoslav Adriatic seaboard which could be put to use if ever Yugoslavia and France "acted rashly." Mussolini thought this a splendid suggestion. He told Contarini to get on with preparing a treaty with Albania (it was signed on September 23rd). He himself went to see the King and tell him what "Italy expected of the House of Savoy."

The situation in the Mediterranean became stable again.

Mussolini announced, in a message distributed by the Agenzia Stefani, that he intended to make the year 1928 one of stability at home and abroad. "A year of undeniable achievement." To increase the prestige of the régime both at home and abroad, Mussolini gave Italo Balbo, as head of the Air Force, carte blanche to "make a show." Balbo, a brilliant organizer, made the same sort of success of organizing the Air Force as he had of organizing the early party militia. In 1928 the pilot who had won the Schneider Trophy race for Italy in 1926, de Bernardi, beat the world air speed record. Donati took the world high flying record, and de Preto the distance record. Italo Balbo himself led his "Flying Circus" on a sweep of the Mediterranean which impressed everybody, especially the British and Russian observers, and first demonstrated the flexibility of the air arm as an instrument of mass movement, potentially of mass attack.

Mussolini made speeches to workers and peasants. The "battle for wheat" was fought again and won. Building was booming everywhere. In December he decided to "tidy up" what was left of the old Constitution. On the 9th he passed a law which projected the integration of the Grand Council of Fascism into his new Constitution, and put an end to "old-style elections." From now on the job of the Grand Council was to keep always on hand a list of ministers, including a prime minister, should the King feel that a change was necessary. There was no system of parties with an alternative government ready, so some substitute had to be devised. It was one day to bring about the fall of Mussolini, but such an event seemed not only unlikely but almost miraculous. In 1928 the new law seemed only to fill a gap and integrate the party into the life of the nation. From now on there was to be no difference between the two. Italy was a Fascist State. Everybody was a Fascist. There was no longer an "old-fashioned Opposition" (the last of the old guard, Giolitti, was dying as the law was drafted). There were only Italians united behind the Duce, so it was only proper that the party should be "open to all," and its Executive therefore "Italian" rather than factional. Bottai, in one of his last pamphlets before he became absorbed into the life of the corporations, explained that:

> The old conflicts have now disappeared. The Nation is the Party and the Party is the Nation. The Party's institutions are the Nation's and

> those of the Nation belong to the Party. Thus the old dilemma of democracy—what to do with the Revolution once it has succeeded—is resolved. The Fascist Corporate State is a new phenomenon. The Party, and the anti-Party, the old-style Opposition, have now fused to become the super-Party. Unity is its watchword. It is essential to remember that the super-Party is not a single Party which has suppressed the Opposition. Here there is no Opposition. There may be disagreement about the means, but there is unity and agreement on the end—a prosperous, glorious Italy.[16]

On one of his visits to the palace to look for suitable brides for Boris, Mussolini told the King of his project to "tidy up" the Constitution. He expected the King to be pleased. Now the King would be, in a sense, not only the constitutional symbol, but also the symbolic head of the party-nation. But the King was not pleased. For the next year (he managed to delay Mussolini's implementation of the law for almost a year) he wrangled with the Duce about the desirability of the law. He told the Duce that one day a Grand Council with constitutional powers would be the end of him. Why bother to constitutionalize it just to please a few Fascist theorists? Let the party die away into unity. Let it fade away into the nation. The new law would strengthen the party at Mussolini's expense—give it a double life.

But Mussolini would not be told. He told the King that, though he respected his opinion, "in some matters I have a greater flair." He said that he planned a plebiscite election, a Yes or No to Fascism, for the next year. "We shall see then whether the people are friends of mine or of the Grand Council." The King still grumbled. It was the beginning of the King's suspicion that Mussolini was about to do away with the monarchy. As long as the Queen Mother was alive, he knew that ties of sentiment and promises made before the march on Rome would suppress Mussolini's old republican instincts. But now? He wrote in his diary: "One day he will tidy me up too."

Mussolini had, in fact, more important things on his mind. Having "stabilized the economy," and made Italy "respected abroad" and "united at home," he was anxious to solve the outstanding problem left unresolved since the reunification of Italy. The tenth anniversary of the formation of the *Fasci* in Milan was in 1929.

Mussolini wanted to show that the movement, in ten years, had brought about a reconciliation with the Church which had defied the ingenuity of his predecessors for sixty years.

He had been working to this end for many years. Most of the negotiations were conducted in secret. Mussolini even went so far as to deny that negotiations were taking place, as late as December 1928, and most people, knowing his past, agreed that a *rapprochement* due to Mussolini was "unlikely." The gestures he made—baptizing his family, invoking the name of the diety with an air of piety—"deceived no one." The German Socialist newspaper *Vorwarts* published a cartoon which showed Mussolini gagging the Pope, above the caption: HOLY FATHER, YOUR WORDS ARE INFALLIBLE, BUT MY REMEDIES AGAINST WORDS ARE EVEN MORE SO.

Mussolini (see above, pp. 83, 108, 141) had had conversations with Church leaders since before he came to power, especially in 1921–1922. After the march on Rome he did his best to lead his party, many of whom were anti-clerical, toward a reconciliation with the Church not because he himself hoped to find personal salvation that way, but because he knew that—especially in a country like Italy—no régime survives indefinitely without at least the tacit approval of the Church. Mussolini's laws against Freemasonry may have been advertised as an attempt to placate the younger militia officers, but they were certainly part of his bargain with Cardinal Gasparri. Similarly, his repeal of a vaguely anti-Vatican decree of April 5, 1923, which was described by *Civiltà Cattolica* as "a very noble act which reveals the good intentions of the Government." In his triumphal tour in the autumn of 1923, Mussolini even recommended religion to the hierarchy of the party (speech at Vicenza, September 23, 1923). In 1924–1925 Mussolini placed at the disposal of the Vatican many of the facilities offered by the State Diplomatic Service to help the Pope in his preparations for the Holy Year.[17]

However, Mussolini's pro-clerical behaviour before 1926 was almost certainly part of a simple, unambitious bargain with Gasparri which limited itself to promising the Vatican's help in destroying by emasculation Mussolini's rival Popular Party, in return for minor concessions like the restitution of the crucifix to school classroom walls. Both men certainly hoped that better things would grow out of this "collaboration in the interests of peace, harmony and prosperity in the nation," but until some proof of good faith had been shown on both sides neither would trust the other. Gasparri knew all about Mussolini's past, his atheism, his civil marriage, his priest-baiting. Mussolini had been brought up to mistrust anything which even remotely resembled a priest. Neither side, strictly speaking, approved of the other, but both sides were convinced that they needed each other. The Vatican believed that the Fascist Party represented the only viable alternative to Bolshevism. Mussolini knew that the power of the Church, especially in the countryside, was enormous, and preferred to have it harnessed in his interests rather than pulling the other way.

But after 1926 both Gasparri and Mussolini seem to have come to like and trust each other and to want to do more than strike electoral bargains or swap concessions for favourable sermons. Mussolini had no further need of Gasparri electorally—the Popular Party had been destroyed and its leaders exiled. Gasparri had no further need of Mussolini—the Communist Party had been exiled, its secretary jailed. Both men were, however, convinced that, having got thus far, they might as well go on and see if they could not achieve, once and for all, an equitable settlement of long-outstanding differences between Church and State. On May 4, 1926, in a letter to the Keeper of the Seals, Rocco, Mussolini commented that the régime had given "a whole new direction to the religious policy of the State." On December 9, 1928, closing Parliament after having announced the date of the first plebiscitary elections (March 24, 1929), Mussolini looked up to the ceiling with an air of sanctity and said: "When I think of all the extraordinary things which have happened to me in my life, I raise a prayer to the Almighty . . ." The pose was captured by a hostile cartoonist, who reproduced it in a "drawing for a stained-glass window to celebrate the canonization of St. Benito" (*Whare Jacob*, Berlin).

On February 7, 1929, a hostile newspaper in England revealed that there had been 150 exchanges of visits between Professor Pacelli, the future Pope's brother, and Professor Barone, Mussolini's plenipotentiary, and conjectured that "something is up." On the same day Cardinal Gasparri entertained all the diplomats accredited to the Holy See and announced that: "Less than twelve hours ago the finishing touches were put to the final text of an agreement which will put an end to discord between Church and State."

This "happy news" irritated Mussolini for the way it was given out, more especially because he had kept from the King the fact that the conciliation was imminent. The King, like all the living members of his family, was anti-clerical and did not like the idea of a reconciliation, anyway. And their quarrel over the constitutionalization of the Grand Council had strained their relations to the point of courtesy. However, an apology had to be made to the King, and Mussolini made it with a good grace in a series of handwritten notes (next day he sent a letter to the King asking for copies of them, as he was "documenting the affair"). He informed the King that the foreign press had been notified of the imminence, and the Italian press would be told to release the story the next day. To amuse the

King and to reduce the "weight and significance" of the whole event, Mussolini added that he was still fighting the Vatican over some land outside the Holy Office which they wanted for a gateway—apart from this, the boundaries of the new Vatican State would be identical to those of the old Vatican. The King replied, "Thank you for the interesting news. I am happy that you managed to have your own way over the gateposts."

At noon on February 11, 1929, the plenipotentiaries of the Vatican and the State, Cardinal Gasparri and Mussolini, met in the Apostolic Palace of St. John to sign the three Lateran treaties, known as the Lateran Pact. Mussolini's immediate comment was that he was "happy and proud to have obtained this victory over a problem tackled in vain by statesmen of the calibre of Cavour and saints like Don Bosco."

Cardinal Gasparri's comments to his friend were: "We have made a good bargain, above all because we have reached an understanding with a régime (the word was to be used from now on almost exclusively instead of the word government) which in its principles agrees intimately and profoundly with the Catholic ethic. If the same conditions had been proposed to us by a Liberal democratic government we would not have accepted them, as their doctrines are substantially opposed to ours."

The bells rang for days. The King, realizing that Mussolini really had brought off something of a coup, made it up with his "old friend and affectionate cousin." The country as a whole felt relieved, rather than hysterically delighted, that "at last it's settled."

The Opposition to Mussolini turned the three treaties upside down to find flaws in them. Some of the pact's critics commented that: "It contains many provisions, so vague and equivocal in form as to mean little or nothing." Others were "worried about the extension of the Church's power." They pointed to the clause by which the government took upon itself to "prevent any sort of demonstration in Rome which could be considered in contrast with the sacred character of the Holy City," and suggested that this could be interpreted as an instruction to the government to prevent the building of Protestant churches. Some silly critics wrote that the clause guaranteeing "protection to ecclesiastics wherever this is necessary to the discharge of their duties," meant that the State police would now have to help carry out sentences of the Inquisition. The only serious criticisms of the pact pointed out that, under the clauses specifying certain privileges of the clergy, priests would be exempt from many taxes, military services, the jurisdiction of State courts in certain cases, and would enjoy interference by ecclesiastical courts in others. The anti-clericals and atheists also criticized the clause specifying that: "The foundation and the aim of education in primary and secondary schools must be the teaching of Christianity according to the Catholic tradition," and the clause admitting the new Vatican State and Holy See as a joint authority in the validification of marriage.

These criticisms, however, did not worry Mussolini or Italians in general. They certainly did not upset the Holy See. What did upset the Holy See was Mussolini's speech to his new "Parliament" on May 13, 1929. He said that he wanted to emphasize the real nature of the treaty signing and of the Fascist-Catholic State. There would be no monopolies granted to the Church, he said, in spite of uninformed comment, mostly abroad. Mussolini added:

> Some people have said that by emphasizing the sacred character of Rome we are denying freedom to worship to those who are not Catholic. But this is ridiculous. It has even been suggested that we must now close down all the synagogues in Rome, and this is even more ridiculous. There have been Jews in Rome since time immemorial, and I have no doubt they supplied new clothes to everybody after the rape of the Sabine women. They will not be disturbed . . . I must add that some Catholics, active in politics, have recently revealed that they have not cut themselves off yet from the mistaken ideology of the dead Popular Party. I have confiscated more Catholic newspapers in the past three months than in the past three years. We shall not permit the resurrection of organizations we have destroyed . . . The Régime, when it fights a battle, leaves only a desert behind.

A month later he forbade his daughter Edda to marry a young Roman Jew.

On July 14th Cesare Rossi, Mussolini's press secretary in 1924—heavily implicated in the Matteotti murder—was sentenced to thirty years' imprisonment for treason. He had fled Italy and spent three years selling his memoirs, supposed letters written to Mussolini implicating the Duce in the murder, and accounts of the Duce's love affairs. Captured at the Swiss frontier, he had been "interrogated thoroughly."

The trial and the sentence passed on Rossi raised a certain amount of speculation about the nature of the political police, the O.V.R.A. The rumour went about that Rossi had been kidnapped and brought back to Italy by force, and that this sort of thing happened all the time. It was certainly true that the secret police force was well supplied with men and materials. The funds allocated openly to "public security" rose from 134 million lire in 1924 to 1,106 million in 1929, and one of the chiefs of police in later years revealed that he had another 500 million in "reserved funds" at his disposition.[18]

It was a standing joke in Italy that all police were stupid, and the O.V.R.A. could not even keep their stupidity secret, but the fact remains that the O.V.R.A. *was* efficient. The quality of its rank and file was not exceptional, but its officers were well led. Bocchini, the best of Mussolini's police chiefs, always assessed a man's intelligence (usually low in the case of O.V.R.A. rank-and-file agents) then gave him a permanent job to suit it. There were men in "the sewer division" whose only job was to explore the sewers and cellars of Rome and other cities visited by the Duce to prevent a sort of Italian Gunpowder Plot. Other agents were told to specialize in "isolating non-Fascist symbols," like red ties, and their lives were never complicated by other instructions. When a man was given the job of issuing identity cards and travel documents, he was not asked to use his common sense as well—it is well known that residence permits were issued to prisoners serving life sentences, for example. Nevertheless, stupid or not stupid, O.V.R.A. did what it was supposed to do, and because it was so large and built up by its own propaganda to even larger proportions, and sinister, it stifled plots and Opposition plans. Liberal anti-Fascist newspapers abroad helped to make O.V.R.A. impressive with their reports of torture and bestiality. "No doubt," as Leto, a former secret policeman, has written, "there were instances of bestial treatment of prisoners, but it seems significant to me that not all the researches of the anti-Fascist organizations can prove that in the 17 years of existence of the Tribunal for the Defence of the State, with which O.V.R.A. worked closely, only 25 people were executed for crimes against the State. This is a record which can compare favourably with records of hangings, lynchings and execution in democracies and also with the record of other non-democracies, including the Soviet Union."[19]

Mussolini kept his promise to "establish immediately" the corporations, twenty-two vertical trade unions which were, under Bottai, to "relegate the class struggle to the textbooks of subversives." His new government, formally constituted on September 12th, had Bottai as first Minister of Corporations, with Joza to help him. Michele Bianchi (Minister of Public Works), Italo Balbo (Minister for Air), Dino Grandi (Minister for Foreign Affairs), General de Bono (Minister for the Colonies), were the only survivors of Mussolini's intimates of 1924. On September 27th Mussolini inaugurated the first session of the Italian Academy, to which most of his other former colleagues were relegated (including Federzoni, later president of the academy, and Marinetti, the old Futurist, now bombless).

Mussolini, who had moved into Palazzo Venezia, ended the year with a tour of public works in progress. He also decided, having rid himself of most of his old colleagues, to tighten up on the informality with which the survivors treated him. On his grand tours they were no longer permitted to lounge about on balconies, but had to stand to attention throughout his speeches. At meetings of the Grand Council in Palazzo Venezia it was suddenly forbidden to smoke, though de Bono, de Vecchi, Bianchi, Balbo and he, had been, as Balbo said, "blowing smoke at each other for years." Shortly afterward Mussolini gave up smoking, to show his fellow councillors that his will was "strong in the small things as well as in the big." Then, one day, though he knew every grand councillor by name (there were usually twenty present), he insisted on having a roll-call to which everyone had to answer *presente* as if they were at school. The sittings of the council normally went on right through the night, Mussolini sipping orange juice and getting more and more aloof as the night wore on. He was "in charge." He made sure everybody, at home and abroad, knew it.

The years 1930–1933 were the first to which Mussolini devoted his whole attention as a foreign policy-maker. It occurred to him, as the slump grew worse and worse in the "democracies," that he had really discovered something extraordinary stable in Fascism. He was still not bitten by the bug of empire, but that day was not far off. He was bemused with success. He was still open to advice, but only to the wrong advice. The first piece he got in 1930 was one which was to ruin his career. Ezio Maria Gray went to see him and reminded him of their talks about "Latin Primacy." Mussolini was still impressed by the logic of Gray's argument. Nobody could accuse a government, which wanted to give a "moral lead," of imperialism. Italy's academy should become the academy to which the French, Spanish, Portuguese and Rumanian academies would look for leadership. Mussolini said as much to Camille Mallarmé, when she came to see him. He added: "Intellectually, even physically, France and Italy ought to be always on the same side of the barricades." But the Duce still did not see how Italy could establish herself, take her rightful place at the head of the Latin bloc, without hammering some senses into the head of his potential following.

Rumania, like Hungary (with its Latin-Rumanian minority),

had an imitation Fascist dictatorship. But France? And Spain and Portugal? They would not take kindly to hammering and they had powerful friends. Perhaps, suggested Gray, it would be a good idea to try diplomacy. Gray's plan was to have a series of secret talks with, first, Spanish and Portuguese leaders of the Latin bloc in Europe. He himself would go to Spain and Portugal. The talks should be both general and particular. He would discuss a proposal for a Latin mutual defence agreement. If they could get Spain and Portugal to agree to the proposal, then Rumania and France would, with varying degrees of enthusiasm, follow suit. One way of bringing pressure to bear on France to join such a defence alliance would be to arrange for Italian troops and ships to occupy the Balearic Islands.

Gray was sent off to Spain and Portugal for "explanatory talks." While there he was also to sound out political leaders on their feelings of admiration or otherwise for Mussolini and Italian Fascism.[20]

With Gray out of the way, Mussolini decided to carry on as if Gray would fail, while never forgetting the possibility that he might succeed. Mussolini told his friends that he was not pessimistic about eventually winning over every Latin nation except France, but France, he feared, would be "difficult." The French would never willingly submit to rule from Rome. It was with some reluctance that French Catholics did so. This being the case, it was essential to bring a subtler sort of pressure to bear on France than that suggested by Gray, with his ideas of taking over Majorca and Minorca. France and England enjoyed a love-hate relationship which was worth exploiting. He decided to do everything he could to impress the English with his (genuine) admiration for some of their qualities, and wait for the French to approach him with bigger and better bouquets than the English would offer. He was much impressed by this as a policy. He said to Nicolò Maraini: "The leaders of the white races must stick close to the English. We must not forget that the British Empire is probably the last white one. It is quite indispensable that for at least fifty years the sons of Albion should continue to be the world's policemen."[21]

Mussolini was given a chance to warm his amiability and admiration for the English into friendship on New Year's Day. Two of the British Embassy staff were arrested in the ruins of the Coliseum, where with a proper sense of time and place they were making love to their Roman girl friends. Mussolini had them let out of jail with a flourish, sending a message stressing his own recognition of Rome's peculiar responsibility as an international city. Unfortunately, his good work was brought to nothing by the incompetence of a protocol official a few days later. On January 8, 1930, Prince Humbert was married off to Maria José of Saxe-Coburg-Gotha. As a relative of the bride and representative of the most firmly seated monarchy, the Duke of York ought to have been treated with great respect. The more especially since Mussolini, who had given the marriage the State's blessing, provided most of the food and drink and expected diplomatic results. But by some oversight the Duke of York was seated next to the ex-King of Afghanistan, deposed with British connivance, and felt so slighted that he ate nothing and left Rome without saying good-bye to his hosts.

"So much," said Mussolini, "for my hopes of becoming a Knight of the British Empire."

Mussolini's meeting later in the month, at the London Naval Conference, still further removed him from his knighthood. The conference was held to fix the size of the world's navies, on the assumption that if they were all kept small there would be no war. Great Britain and the United States were allotted the greatest tonnage, followed in second place by Japan, then France and Italy. Mussolini and Grandi set out to increase Italy's allotted tonnage, but without success. Their diplomatic failure did not upset them too much, as Mussolini pointed out that he intended to arm as he pleased, anyway, if and when the time came. In later years he commented that the London conference of 1930 had had a decisive affect on the future pattern of the world's navies, because, limited in total tonnage, the world's potential aggressors set to work to build small, efficient submarines and fast cruisers. Or "stopped getting their feet wet and started to build up naval air forces." The conference also struck Mussolini as being "one of those occasions when you realise that world diplomacy, as conceived by the British, consists of telling half-truths, never believing a word of what the other party says, yet acting as if every word was the literal truth." [22] Grandi became a great admirer of Britain at this time, and set to work to learn English in preparation for his posting to London as Italian Ambassador.

Back in Rome again and more marriages in the air. Mussolini's daughter Edda was finally saved from a Lebanese jeweller and married off to Count Galeazzo Ciano.

The King told Mussolini that he had now found a suitable wife for King Boris, his daughter Princess Giovanna. This marriage would be "most convenient" for the royal family, because the Princess had fallen in love with one of Mussolini's air aces, de

Pinedo, and had to be got out of the way. Mussolini was delighted and said he was now sure, "not only of the sympathy of the Belgians, but also of the Bulgars, and this would check any attempts by the French in the future to counter his prestige in Northern Europe or the Balkans."

Mussolini was secretly delighted when the marriage of Boris to Princess Giovanna turned into a diplomatic defeat for the Church. Archbishop Roncalli, the Apostolic delegate in Bulgaria, had wrung a promise from King Boris that his children would be brought up as Catholics, that the wedding itself, indeed, would be held in a Catholic Church. Boris came over to Italy, married the Princess in Assisi, then promptly went back to Sofia with his bride and forced her to go through a second wedding ceremony at the Orthodox Cathedral. Orthodox Patriarch Stephen told the Princess that she could not be recognized as married when only "witnessed" in a Catholic Church. He also told her that any children she might have would certainly be baptized into the Orthodox Church. So the Catholic Church, instead of gaining a King, lost a royal princess and several royal infants to come. The Pope was furious with Roncalli, and even with Mussolini, who took it all as a good joke which even further cemented the Italo-Bulgar alliance, because Boris now owed him an obligation.

According to Mussolini's wife: "A good crop of weddings also produces a good crop of funerals." That same year saw the extinction by death of those few of Mussolini's rivals whose power and authority had not been diminished by giving them sinecures. Michele Bianchi was the first to die, on February 3rd. Mussolini acknowledged his great debt to the party's first organiser: "I see him again at the offices of *il Popolo d'Italia*, at meetings, on the platform, indefatigable. After the march on Rome, which he did so much to prepare politically, he accepted without a murmur a place in the background, where he continued to serve the Régime . . . ." To his intimates he added: "His brain was worn out and his ideas threadbare." In August his nephew Sandro died of leukaemia, and he was genuinely moved to see his brother almost stricken with grief; by the end of the year his brother was literally dying of a broken heart. Dying, too, were the Duke of Aosta—after the Queen Mother, Mussolini's best friend in the old royal family—and Tomasso Tittoni, first president of the academy and one of Mussolini's intellectual supporters. Antonio Salandra was also dying. He had been the first Liberal friend, and then the last surviving Liberal enemy, of the régime. And Enrico Corradini, the war hero who had helped Federzoni to bring about the marriage between Fascism and Nationalism through the union of the two parties, was dying.

The old order was changing. The Council of Corporations came into active operation, and the last trade unions disappeared from the Italian scene. The old laws disappeared, too, their place being taken by the new civil and penal codes. The last opposition among Italian scientists disappeared when Marconi accepted the presidency of the academy. The party was given a new secretary in Giovanni Giurati (October 8, 1930), who declared his intention to "perfect our organization, integrate the Party into the life of the Nation via the Corporations, organize above all new Youth Movements which will prepare moral, economic and political unity from the ages of five to twenty-one."

There was not much left of the old order for the Opposition to cling to. And there was little or no opposition left in Italy. It was all in France or the United States, and so remote from Italian reality that it was surprised when a leaflet-dropping plane over Rome was laughed at (July 8, 1930), and the leaflets provoked hilarity instead of an uprising. Italians at home knew that, for the moment at least, their world-wide "air sweeps" by Balbo and his "circuses" had "given the Duce the skies." They were no longer interested in leaflets. The mob, the masses—even the formerly loyal Socialist workers—knew that their function in the nation's political life had been reduced to cheering and duets with the Duce from a balcony. And why not? they said. Everything was under control, and they could think of other things.

But though Socialism as an effective antidote or opposition was now a thing of the past, Mussolini's enemies inside his liberated Vatican did not give up. Patient men, heirs and successors to patient men, they knew that, given time, Mussolini would give them an excuse for righteous anger. The mild-mannered but fanatical new party secretary, with his all-embracing plans for youth, gave them such an excuse. With the creation of *Juvenile fasci di combattimento*, with a membership aged from eighteen to twenty-one to supplement the various categories of young people from five to eighteen which formed the "*Òpera bàlilla*," the Fascist Party had control over the formation of future generations in a way which had previously been the prerogative of the Church. This irritated those former members of the Popular Party who were trying to keep some sort of an organisation intact so that, if and when Mussolini and Fascism disappeared from the scene, they could re-form. More particularly it irritated priests and laymen who belonged to Catholic Action. They had not approved of the Pope's enthusiasm for the Lateran Pact, and they did not like the idea of being supplanted by Mussolini and his Bàlilla lieutenant, Ricci.

Hostility between the party, its new secretary, Ricci, and Catholic Action, smouldered all through the winter of 1930–31. There was not much the leaders of Catholic Action could do, and no way in which they could state their case—the *Osservatore Romano*, with leaders praising the Òpera Bàlilla, had effectively silenced their propaganda outlets. It was the ill-advised deputy secretary of the Fascist Party, Carlo Scorza, who sparked off a flaming public row. In the magazine *Gioventù Fascista* (April 12, 1931) the case of Monsignor Galosi, found guilty of sexual assault on an eighteen-year-old young man and banished, was discussed with a notable lack of Christian charity. The *Osservatore Romano* commented in these terms, and urged the Fascist Party to observe the "rules of piety." The leaders of Catholic Action, thinking the Vatican "General Staff" was now ready to speak sharply to Mussolini—perhaps even insist on the dissolution or modification of his monopoly of youth—immediately launched a campaign of criticism of the government unlike anything which had been heard or seen for years. Unfortunately for them, the Vatican had no intention of alienating Mussolini. In his encyclical of June 29, 1931, Pius XI reproved Mussolini for allowing some of his lieutenants to "move toward a pagan ideology and monopolize youth," but in private Pius told his friends to silence Catholic Action and not "upset his arrangements." In return for muting this pseudo-Christian opposition, the Pope via Pacelli told Mussolini he would have to ask that both the secretary and assistant secretary of the Fascist Party be removed from office. Mussolini, who had been as disturbed as Pius by the evidence of "dissension" on the eve of the tenth anniversary of his call to power, ordered the removal of Giurati and Scorza. On November 8, 1931, Achille Starace became the new—and longest lasting—of the secretaries of the party, and the breach with the Vatican was repaired.

Three months later Mussolini paid a state visit to the Vatican and was received by Pius XI on the third anniversary of the signing of the Lateran Pact. For the rest of Pius XI's life there was no further talk of rivalry between Church and State.

The year 1931 brought personal tragedy to Mussolini with the death of his brother Arnaldo, who had never recovered from the death of his son. It brought the deaths of all the men who had been dying during the winter of 1930–31—Tittoni, Salandra—but the nation had never seen Mussolini as stricken as he was on December 21st, when he was told that Arnaldo had "given up the struggle." Mussolini wrote: "A politician may doubt the loyalty of his most faithful colleague, see himself denied even by his son, but of his brother he is sure. Arnaldo was the soul to which from time to time I could anchor mine. . . ." The dictator, against whom the Soviet press had started an ideological campaign of "anti-tyranny," put aside the cares of State and wrote *The Life of Arnaldo*.[23] It remains Mussolini's own political testament, and it is by any standards a moving book, the more surprising because it was written in three weeks by the head of a police state in the middle of a world economic crisis.

But if Mussolini grieved and Catholic Action was peeved, most of Italy was preparing for a celebration on a scale to rival those of Nero's. The year 1932 saw the tenth anniversary of the march on Rome and the end of the first ten years of Fascist power. The man in the street did not know that Mussolini had failed to complete the pattern of alliances he had hoped to celebrate. France was still obdurate. Bulgaria, Rumania, Hungary, Albania, were all lost in admiration, but Greece had become hostile, fearing Italian expansion on the Western Mediterranean, and Venizelos, though he had signed a treaty of friendship with Mussolini, had assured his fellow dictator that Greece's friendship was "not elastic." Greece was a disappointment; an even greater disappointment was Spain. Gray had had long talks with King Alfonso and had returned with assurances that at the right moment a "Latin Pact" could be concluded with the active and enthusiastic participation of Spain. Gray and Mussolini had discussed this at length and had agreed to launch the "Latin bloc" during the celebrations of the First Fascist Decade. Gray had returned to Spain to discuss the "charter of the bloc, only to escape assassination by a Communist by about three inches and "see the monarchy disappear before my eyes into a cauldron of bubbling Bolshevism."[24]

Without Spain, who would be not only a dignified member, but could contribute the Balearic Islands (to intimidate France), Cadiz (to keep the English in Gibraltar up to the mark), and the Canary Islands, there was not much point in going on with the plans for a "bloc." Portugal, said Gray, was not yet "ready," though there were hopes of a pro-Fascist coup there. Without the Iberian peninsula, without France, Italy would do better to look north and south, to Africa (the colonies now well policed and pacified by General Graziani) or to an alliance with Catholic Austria and Bavaria.

Mussolini suggested that all thought of foreign affairs should be put aside to "treat seriously at home the anniversary of the march on Rome and examine its significance." Gray agreed that, if not desirable, at least the delay was necessary. All Rome would be celebrating. In October 1931 Mahatma Gandhi had a preview of the celebrations, and said of Mussolini: "He is a worthy man."

The year in which all the world's eyes and sympathy were turned on Mussolini was 1932. When that year's two assassination attempts (they had become almost a feature of the régime) were publicized, the telegrams of commiseration and congratulation almost filled the study of the Duce, grown twice his size with pride and achievement. "Dictatorship is contagious, as in the old days liberty was," commented the French poet, Paul Valéry. In the streets of Paris members of the *Croix de Feu* marched up and down, their arms raised in the Fascist salute. In Holland the Dutch N.B.S. did the same, singing the "Wilhelmus." Silver Shirts in America, led by Major Powell, and Blue Shirts in Ireland led by General O'Duffy—the number of imitators multiplied the flattery. A former Labour Cabinet Minister in Britain stayed even closer to the original, planning a march on London with well-drilled legions in shirts of an impeccable shiny black satin. Oswald Mosley, Léon Degrelle, Mussert, Admiral Miklós Horthy. Even Chiang Kai-shek sent a messenger, pleading with the Duce to loan him an adviser. Visitors—among them Anthony Eden—flocked from abroad to the Great Exhibition of Ten Years of Fascism, in Rome, and to see all the other marvels of the régime. On July 9, 1932, Mussolini brought to a conclusion the apparently interminable Conference on Reparations, and earned the undying gratitude of his German neighbours. In spite of the fact that Europe's middle classes had been hit by three years of slump, Italy—alone among the nations of Europe—managed to keep its figures of tourism up to 60 per cent of peak. All roads led to Rome.

Alberto de Stefani, the financial genius responsible for the invisible foundations of the régime, was asked to make a detailed report on the condition of the economy. The lira, he reported, was stable, and its purchasing power, in relation to other European currencies, was increasing. More especially, its purchasing power, relative to the dollar and the pound sterling, had increased by 13 per cent since 1926. The Budget had remained balanced, in spite of a vast programme of public works, often planned on the spur of the moment—at a banquet—by the Duce himself. The industrial sector of the economy had suffered, inevitably, from the world slump conditions then prevailing, though the worst of the slack had been taken up by a programme of factory building and the public-works programme in general (9 milliards a year). Taking 1929 as a base year (General Confederation of Industry figures), production in the industrial sector had fallen to 72.4 per cent in 1932, to rise again quickly thereafter, reaching 100 per cent again in 1936. But this decline was less than that experienced in any modern state in Europe or Asia, and was less by 23 per cent than the decline calculated in the United States. Even the worst-hit of all Italian industries—and that in competition with the worst-hit capitalist countries—the textile industry, showed a drop in production of only 32 per cent compared with 58 per cent in Great Britain. Perhaps the most significant figures are those furnished by the Institute of Statistics, which confirmed a total growth in industrial production, 1922–32 of 82 per cent. Communications were in excellent order, and electrification of railways was second only to Switzerland. The reserves of power available to industry and for domestic use alike had increased by 62 per cent. Many factories and homes had electric light, where this had been unknown before 1922.

Perhaps the most interesting figure is that for the unemployed, which, even at its worst, was less than a third of that recorded in Great Britain (813,000 compared to 2,652,181, April 1931). This figure is all the more creditable because, in 1921, the United States put a quota on Italian immigrants, which dropped the expatriation of the unemployed from 600,000 a year to 70,000; to have absorbed these frustrated emigrants was nothing less than a triumph of "population engineering."

But perhaps the most eagerly awaited report was the one the Duce himself gave to the Permanent Wheat Committee on September 24, 1932:

> I communicate to you that the harvest of wheat this year has risen to 75,150,000 quintals. This year's production is the highest ever recorded in Italy, greater even than a result considered extraordinary in 1929, 70,795,000 and last year's 66,619,000. During the six years before the war, 1909–1914, the average annual production stood at 49,273,000 . . . And the increases in harvest are not due to an increase in the amount of land under seed, as these figures show—1909–1914—4,756,000 hectares, 1932—4,952,107 hectares. It is the production per hectare which has increased. The rural population now works with the rhythm imposed on it by the Fascist Régime.[25]

Within a year from the date of Mussolini's speech it was announced that Italy was now self-supporting in wheat and in most other basic foodstuffs (1933 was an exceptional year, 81,000,000 quintals, but the level was almost maintained in succeeding years). This meant that the world's hardest currencies, which Italy would need to spend to buy wheat, were no longer necessary for this purpose. Italy could spend her dollars on other things—perhaps even more important, she had no need to fear the United States, should good relations between Italy and "the granary of the West" deteriorate at any time.

Not surprisingly, membership of the Fascist Party had risen to 2,411,133. That year Mussolini became almost untouchable. Even Quinto Navarra felt the weight of the Duce's success and the gulf widening between Mussolini and "ordinary men." Starace, the able secretary of the party, was encouraging the widening of the gulf for his own reasons. The party's propaganda machine began to set aside a part of the effort previously devoted to pure politics, to the pre-funeral canonization of their leader. Babies began to be born with the sign of the *Fascio* on their foreheads. Peasants dug up record potatoes in the shape of Mussolini's head. One man was reported to have refused to wash again for as long as he lived, because Mussolini had kissed him when awarding him a medal. The duets between Mussolini and the crowd beneath his balcony grew more frenzied. Mussolini himself, without friends or confidants, began to need the crowd almost as much as they deluded themselves that they needed him. He began to be solicitous for his audience. He insisted on music in the square to entertain them while they waited for him and police to help them away to buses and trains. Nurses and doctors were ordered to stand by to succour those "overcome by emotion." After a speech Mussolini—instead of celebrating with his intimates—retired alone to his study to sit staring at his collection of lucky charms.

Sometimes, of course, Mussolini was not alone—not physically alone. A constant stream of women passed through the door and ended up on the floor or among the cushions on the window seat. Attractive, even beautiful, women came from all over Europe and America just to be hurriedly dealt with, between dispatches, by the Duce. Margherita Sarfatti had long since gone. Her successor as Mussolini's mistress was still too young. The Duce did his duty by his distinguished female guests, then went home late in the evening to his wife.

Mussolini was not yet blind, however, to the gaps in Italy's economy or in the every-day life of the State. As he said: "Twenty thousand leaders, teachers, engineers, bankers, businessmen; five thousand officers; three thousand magistrates; ten thousand Civil Servants—all of the very first quality. This is what Italy needs if the clockwork of the State is to function without stopping or losing time. My function is to train these men."

But with all the shouting and the cheering as the Ten Years of Fascism were celebrated, it was difficult for Mussolini to concentrate on the gaps. It was easier to march with the crowd—at the head of it, of course—and cheer as loud as anyone. He could not cheer himself, so he cheered Rome. "In this dark world, tortured and wavering, solution can only come from Rome."

On October 23rd, in Turin, Mussolini said: "We do not want hegemony in Europe. . . . We will remain members of the League of Nations. It needs us, especially now, when it is very ill, we must not abandon it. . . . We are against any sort of hegemony, especially if this seeks to make permanent a great injustice."

On the same day Hermann Goering, reading a new translation of *Dottrina Fascista* (each edition dated its composition earlier, this one to 1921) and a letter to Michele Bianchi, commented to Goebbels that what they did not have was the all-around approval of the "men of property and education." Mussolini had it. Mussolini also had money, and the National Socialist Party was bankrupt. Goebbels and Goering knew that, if they were to get over their crisis and into power, they would need three parts luck and one part infamy. There were no thoughts of hegemony in their minds.

On October 28th Mussolini opened the Via dell'Impero. The day before, he had said, apropos of the opening: "Inside ten years all Europe will be Fascist, or Fascisticized."

On January 30, 1933, his crisis overcome, Adolf Hitler became Chancellor of Germany. Mussolini made no comment. Italy did not notice.

6

UN POSTO AL SOLE

A PLACE IN THE SUN

If Mussolini failed to realize the full significance of the seizure of power by Hitler in Germany, he was not alone in this. His enemies in Britain were delighted to see "a pupil who might well outshine the master" come to restore order in Germany, more especially since this pupil was, like the master, an avowed anti-Bolshevik. Mussolini's enemies elsewhere in Europe were occupied with their own domestic problems and saw Hitler's nomination to the Chancellery through those same chauvinistic lenses which had served them so well in the past. But of all the political leaders of Europe, probably Mussolini attached the least importance to events in Berlin in 1933.

Why did the man who had "a gift" for politics remain blind for some eighteen months until the dramatic, physical revelation of Hitler's territorial ambitions? One reason is that Mussolini no longer had the slightest idea of what went on outside his own immediate sphere of influence, and based his policies and programmes on assumptions which had been valid in the twenties. Italian journalists abroad were, for the most part, engaged in making daily anthologies of tributes to the Duce's genius and had given up politics as a bad and dangerous job. A glance at any Fascist-censored newspaper dated after Starace came to the secretaryship of the party is enough to confirm this suspicion.

But even if Mussolini had known that a potentially strong Germany was in the making—a Germany as united, hardworking and self-consciously virtuous as his own country—the news would not have affected him deeply. He thought of a friendly Germany as a sort of windshield beyond the Alps and Dolomites—a useful potential ally in case of trouble with the French or British. Alternatively, a hostile Germany could be the source of a renewal of friendship with France and a reinforcement of friendship with Britain—the re-creation of the 1914–1918 Entente. Either way, Germany represented, in political terms, something positive from which only benefit could accrue to Italy. As soon as the shouting had died down after the celebration of the First Decade of Fascism, Mussolini and Ezio Maria Gray went back to their discussions of a Latin alliance, at the head of which would stand Italy, on the shores of "our sea." The project had suffered a setback in Spain, where the pro-Fascist monarchy had been overthrown by "Bolsheviks." It had lost Mussolini's attention while there were triumphal speeches to be made. But it was basically a sound idea, and as a lot of hard work had gone into it already and Mussolini was loth to waste this effort, he and Gray discussed its potentialities again. Bulgaria was now tied, though scandalously, to Italy by marriage. Greece was treaty-bound to friendship, and similarly Albania. Yugoslavia was weak, and its anti-Italian treaty with France could be disregarded. Rumania was pro-Fascist and manifestly pro-Italian. The rest of the Mediterranean was either busily neutral (Turkey) or idle and apathetic. The only hostile neutral of importance was France. France was still, therefore, the country to be coaxed or bullied into joining some confederation. As Mussolini, with some foresight, said to the French Foreign Minister early in 1933: "There will come a time when the Europeans on the shores of the Mediterranean will be wise to have close ties of friendship. Arab nationalism is a fact, only rendered harmless by a lack of leadership or moral fibre."

A strong Germany could be used to either force France to join the Latin alliance in self-defence (she could not turn to Britain, who was jealous of any plans to consolidate alternative power in the Mediterranean), or to coax her to join by stressing the distance to be gained by swimming with the tide. Whether Germany became hostile or friendly, her renaissance was only to be welcomed, according to the Duce and his advisers. It may well be, also, that Mussolini under-estimated not only *Germany's* potential but also Hitler's.

During the Decade of Fascism celebrations, Mussolini had been deluged with telegrams and presents from imitation Fascist leaders abroad, and must have received the impression that, at least from 1932–33, the whole of Europe considered him a prophet. He certainly despised Hitler, largely for his unbecoming appearance and his Austrian origin. Mussolini was also convinced that National Socialism in Germany, being nothing more or less than a Teutonic imitation of Fascism, could never enjoy the strength or success of the original. To the normal practised eye and informed ear, it seemed as if Mussolini was right. Hitler himself was under the influence of Goering, who not only went about saying that Mussolini and his air force were "a revelation," but urged Hitler at every opportunity to "study the Italian pattern." Goebbels was enormously impressed by the efficiency of the Italian propaganda machine and by the fact that the régime apparently enjoyed the support of every social stratum and every shade of opinion, including that of the Pope. Goebbels did not hesitate to add to Goering's own opinion that they should "study Mussolini." It is not surprising that in his public pronouncements Hitler should echo this admiration, nor that Mussolini should draw the wrong conclusions.

Everything Hitler did during 1933 seemed to show him no more than an apt pupil of Mussolini. He proclaimed a National Labour Day to win over the trade unions. He brought to an end "old-style" collective bargaining, and substituted "regular labour contracts," after the pattern of Mussolini's corporation contracts. He dissolved trade unions and arrested "old-style" trade-union leaders. Dr. Gottfried Feder, Hitler's first tutor in economics and a firm believer in Bottai's diagnoses and remedies for economic ills, was made a junior minister. Hitler even emasculated the storm troopers (formed by Ernst Roehm on the model of Balbo's militia), just as Mussolini had done, by transferring supreme command to the Army and diluting the militia with former regular Army officers. It seemed as if a Teutonic corporate state—from public works to talk of "discipline"—was in the making, and that its leader would automatically run it by consultation with the master in Rome.

The truth was somewhat less flattering to Mussolini, who would not have welcomed idly the National Socialist State if he had known it. Hitler did admire Mussolini, largely for his intuitive grasp of the trend of events and mastery of them. He admired the way Mussolini, an ex-Socialist, had been swept to power by a wave of anti-Bolshevism and had been the first man to sign a treaty of friendship with the infant Soviet Union. This was the sort of politics worthy of a place in *Mein Kampf* and worth emulating. Hitler also admired Mussolini's "trappings," that is to say not only the super-organization of every citizen, from the cradle to the grave, in the service of the régime, but also the aesthetically satisfying way this was done—the uniforms, the parades, the martial music, the trans-atlantic flights, the ships, the smart, punctual trains—in short the stage management of a complete state.

Goebbels never ceased to impress on Hitler that Mussolini's major contribution to modern politics was the use of the new science of psychology to make success predictable. The Russians, vice Marx and Lenin, had glimpsed something of this potential, but had reduced it to something pedantic and applied their conclusions with indifferent efficiency. Mussolini, though not in Lenin's class as a thinker (and by implication, not in Hitler's, either), had subordinated everything to a day-by-day diagnosis of the wants and needs of the newly enfranchised mob. It was not for nothing that Hitler revered the Rome of bread and circuses. He was to take Mussolini's discovery and apply it with such success to his own people that the rape of half the world was made possible. The only other scientific hypotheses which have had their veracity confirmed so dramatically have been those of the nuclear physicists.

What Hitler needed in 1933–34 was a friendly neutral Italy. If he had to feed the press eulogies of the Duce as the price for this friendly neutrality, he was prepared to do so. If Mussolini read more into this flattery than was really there, then this was Mussolini's fault and not his.

In the spring of 1933 it seemed that Mussolini's estimate of the potential political usefulness of Germany as an unconscious promoter of the Latin confederation or alliance was as accurate as ever. France was horrified by the way in which Hitler had achieved power; more especially horrified by Hitler's anti-Semitism. Polish Jewry reacted similarly and had fears, shared by the rest of Poland, for Poland's territorial safety. Anti-German demonstrations were held in Paris and Danzig. General Pilsudski, the Polish "strong man," even suggested a joint Franco-Polish punitive expedition, "just to discourage the Junkers."

Mussolini was horrified when he heard from Bastianini, his ambassador in Warsaw, that partial mobilization had been announced as a "precautionary measure" and that Polish youths were chanting about fighting for freedom. A war in Northern Europe would upset all Mussolini's plans. He could not consolidate the Latin—and by implication, Italian—hold on the Mediterranean, with all the risks of "difficulties" with Great Britain this entailed, if Northern Europe was not "stable." Mussolini reacted immediately. He sent Bastianini to gate-crash the Franco-Polish talks being held (April 1933) in Warsaw. Bastianini was authorized to say that Mussolini personally guaranteed the "unchangeability" of the situation in Europe; that any attempt by any power—Germany or Franco-Poland—to change that situation would be met by force; that if France wanted added reassurance she should seek it in a closer alliance with Italy. Bastianini pointed out that neither France nor Poland was ready for even punitive expeditions. Germany, he added, was certainly not ready for any sort of "aggression," and Hitler's anti-Semitism might well abate if "Jews would only collaborate with the new régime, realizing that it has an anti-Bolshevik potential."

The danger of war passed. The Western world sighed with relief, and the eulogies of Mussolini multiplied. Hitler let his gratitude be known, and the British Ambassador passed on His Majesty's Government's compliments. On June 7, 1933, Mussolini put his guarantees into the form of a Four-Power Pact, signed in Rome (all roads led to Rome in 1933). Interpreting Hitler's speech of May 17, 1933, as a sincere avowal of peaceful intentions, Mussolini persuaded France that it would do no harm and would be more realistic to abandon attempts to restrict German rearmament. As Mussolini said, Germany was rearming and would go on rearming. Nobody except Italy had the war potential to stop her, and this war potential she did not intend to use. A partially rearmed Germany would, in any case, make Germany less dangerous. It would stop the generals' grumbling. And Mussolini, he assured the British and French ambassadors, would see to it that Hitler did not over-reach himself. The Four-Power Pact delighted everybody. It seemed to offer guarantees of stability, without costing Britain and France a penny. Hitler knew it guaranteed nothing of the sort, but it did give him a breathing space. Not believing in anybody's peaceful intentions, he assumed that Mussolini, too, needed a breathing space for some reason, and hastened to assure the Duce that whatever it was he was up to he could count on Germany's support.

Mussolini's relations with France improved overnight, and he told Gray that "some future action together in the Mediterranean is not impossible." In talks with a secret envoy of Laval, Mussolini noted that the situation in Portugal was improving and that it seemed likely that "young Salazar" would establish a philo-Fascist régime there. This would be "most interesting," because Portugal—as Great Britain's oldest ally—could be used to assure the Latin alliance of sympathetic British neutrality in the event of any "disturbance" in the Mediterranean. Mussolini did not tell Laval that he had been having "friendly talks" with the opposition to the Republican Spanish Government. He had not offered to help in any restoration of the monarchy (Mussolini was having a quarrel with the King of Italy about the question of precedence and was temporarily anti-monarchy), but he was interested in establishing yet another philo-Fascist régime. Mussolini knew that France regarded Spain as her "sphere of influence" and would be suspicious of any other power interfering where her own interference was proving unsatisfactory. It seemed to him that there were hopes of neutralizing—at least—and possibly "ideologically colonizing," the whole of the Iberian peninsula. But with France in a new mood of friendliness, it might be as well to put off any aid to the Spanish opposition for a time, and first get France's agreement to an extension of Italian influence in North Africa. This Mussolini discussed, too, with Laval and his envoys. He was told that there was no question of Italy's being active any farther west than Ethiopia, because this would affect France in Algeria, Tunis and the Sahara. But Ethiopia itself? Laval said he could not see why France and Italy had quarrelled about it in the past. It seemed to be a natural extension of the already existing Italian colonies in Somalia.

Hitler, grateful for the silencing of Pilsudski and the legalization of his rearmament, sent a midsummer message to Mussolini to the effect that North Africa awaited the civilizing genius of Rome.

Mussolini read the message and put it aside. He did not care whether Hitler approved of his plans or not. Hitler's duty was to put Germany to rights and leave well enough alone in Europe. Mussolini said as much to Laval in the fall of 1933, as the talks about the Latin Mediterranean alliance dragged on, and the French began to haggle about guarantees for Algeria. The French negotiating team also digressed to urge Mussolini to help France to reinforce "the walls of Europe," to keep Germany sandwiched between friends. The French knew, they said, that Mussolini's commercial relations with the Soviet Union were good. A pact already existed which could have the effect of limiting German expansion to the west—why not another pact, with the Soviet Union, to limit any possible German expansion to the east? Once an Italo-Soviet treaty of friendship and non-aggression was signed, France could subscribe to it and turn her attention to Italy's "difficulties" in the Mediterranean with a clear conscience and an easy mind.

Mussolini, realizing that the French did not believe him capable of signing such a pact, got in touch with Litvinov, the Soviet Commissar for Foreign Affairs, and suggested it to him. Both Stalin and Litvinov were delighted with the idea, especially with the idea of "containing Nazism." Stalin's opinion of National Socialism was sulphuric: "It is said that in some countries in the west Marxism has already been destroyed by the bourgeois nationalist trend known as National Socialism. This is nonsense. Only people who are ignorant of history can say such things."[1] On September 2, 1933, Mussolini and the Soviet Ambassador to Rome, Potemkin, signed the non-aggression pact, with added trade protocols to a value of almost 300 million lire. The French were open-mouthed with admiration. Litvinov himself, it was said, would visit Rome in January 1934, and perhaps would even call on the Pope.

Hitler was furious when he heard of the pact. He ranted and raved at Goebbels and accused the absent Duce of "betrayal." On October 14th he announced that Germany would withdraw from the League of Nations. He would hold a plebiscite to get the final approval of "his people." In vain Mussolini assured Hitler that the pact had only peaceful aims and that the League of Nations was a valuable sounding board for any dictator with a grievance, not to speak of its more noble aims. On November 12, 1933, Hitler's plebiscite was held. He was given the vote of confidence he asked for. He went further. Anxious to discharge or rub out any political debt he might owe to Mussolini, he ordered his ambassador to Poland to start talks for a ten-year non-aggression pact between Germany and Poland. Marshal Pilsudski "would learn that the Germans made better friends than Latin peoples." On January 26, 1934, the Polish-German pact was signed.

This time it was Mussolini's turn to be astonished. Hitler had turned an enemy into a friend overnight. Pilsudski and Poland had, in effect, been detached from France, which had protected Poland since she regained her independence at Versailles. Perhaps Hitler was hoping to march east with Poland against the Soviet Union? If he did so, he would steal Mussolini's crown as the principal (if double-dealing) champion of anti-Bolshevism. Mussolini advised Litvinov, when he came to Rome, that there were only two possible steps to be taken. The Italo-Soviet Non-aggression Pact had to be extended to France and, if possible, Great Britain (France signed, in fact, in December 1934). And the Soviet Union had to be brought into the League of Nations to fill the gap left by Germany. Litvinov left it in Mussolini's hands to see that these two steps were taken, assuring him of the Soviet Union's undying admiration.

Mussolini tried once more (February 1934) to persuade Hitler that the Italo-Soviet Pact was "only a formality" and that Hitler should have more sense than to think that he, Mussolini, had any interests outside the Mediterranean. Mussolini even suggested that Hitler reapply for membership of the League of Nations where they could "work together." Hitler dismissed the suggestion. He could not, however—on sober reflection—afford to offend Mussolini for the moment. At least Mussolini was a man with ideas similar to his own, and a man who had put these ideas into practice for twelve years with conspicuous success. As Goebbels said, there was something to learn from Mussolini, and a friendship to be cultivated.

Hitler decided to concentrate first of all on persuading Great Britain not to join the Italo-Soviet alliance, or sign any sort of addendum to the Italo-Soviet Pact. On February 21, 1934, he assured Anthony Eden that if only Britain would see the situation as "essentially stable" and "not assume new commitments in Europe," then he, Hitler, would, on his honour, assure Eden of a steady run-down in the numbers of men under arms in his militia, the S.A. In this he was successful. Great Britain did not subscribe to the pact. In May 1934 Sir John Simon even proposed that Germany should be given time to disband her para-military forces (all of which were strictly illegal) and then given parity of armaments with Britain, France and Italy. This idea was promptly sat on by the French, who instinctively moved even closer to Mussolini.[2]

Having convinced the British Government that Germany was going to be the thickest shield the West would ever need against Bolshevism, potentially more reliable and better placed than Italy, Hitler decided that Mussolini had to be placated. Unfortunately, Hitler had nothing to offer Mussolini, except a reiteration that he would support any Italian move in the Mediterranean. He had, in fact, stalemated Mussolini's plans for an Italo-Soviet Franco-British alliance and given nothing in return. He was also, as Mussolini put it, "giving himself airs." There was only one thing to do and that was to go to see Mussolini and make friends again over the dinner table. Perhaps flattery would work where diplomacy had sown only discord. On June 10th, in a letter nauseating in its fulsomeness, Hitler asked to be received by Mussolini "on the soil of the great Italian Revolution."

Mussolini could not understand why Hitler wanted to see him. He did not want to see Hitler. He had a full programme of speeches and galas in Venice—the only interest he took in domestic affairs now was that of a ribbon-cutter, opening things. But he could not ignore the letter, and perhaps it would be interesting to see what this awkward barbarian looked like. Mussolini suspected that the meeting would not be pleasant for either of them. At this time most politically alive Austrians were either philo-Fascists or philo-Nazis. Austrian Chancellor Dollfuss leaned perceptibly toward the philo-Fascists, and the Austrian aristocracy enrolled in the ranks of the Heimwehren to a man. There were, of course, some Austrians who saw in Hitler the man who would lead them to Pan-German federation, starting with an *Anschluss* of Germany and Austria, but both Dollfuss and Mussolini had made it plain to the Austrian Nazis that Austria's independence and pro-Italianism were sacrosanct.

Nevertheless, there had been troop movements on the Austro-German border, and Mussolini resolved to ask Hitler what he was up to. He replied to Hitler's letter coolly but courteously, and told him he would be available for talks at any time during his tour of Venice, from June 13th to 18th.

Hitler arrived in Italy on the 15th. He was not pleased to learn that Mussolini had dissolved all the Italian National Socialist societies the day before. It was raining. Hitler, squeezed into a light-coloured raincoat over a badly cut dark suit, was indistinguishable from the scores of plain-clothes policemen sent by Chief of Police Bocchini to guard the Duce from his demonstrative followers. The Duce himself felt well that morning. He had spent the night with a blonde Venetian countess and the early hours of the morning with his wife. He felt not only satiated but virtuous. He was wearing his best uniform, that of the Corporal of Honour in the *arditi*, and surrounded by party officials and officers of his militia. Side by side, the two men looked like a boarding-school headmaster condescending to take tea with a promising new boy.

The first Hitler-Mussolini talks were held in a villa at Stra. They were not conspicuously successful. Mussolini tried to get assurances from Hitler about his intentions in Austria, but "all that man did was recite *Mein Kampf* from memory. I never could stand that book." The Duce told some journalist friends of his that Hitler was "certainly mad, probably a liar." To his wife he said: "He is an aggressive little man with no self-control." To Gray he added: "I am not flattered to think that Adolf Hitler made a revolution after the pattern of my own. The Germans will end up by ruining our idea. They are still the barbarians of Tacitus and the Reformation, in a constant struggle with Rome."[3]

The aggressive little man went home after two days. On June 30th Hitler vented his spite on every man he could think of who had ever shown any sort of admiration for Mussolini, or in other ways represented a threat to his "supremacy." Roehm, the man who modelled the S.A. on Mussolini's militia was dragged from his bed and shot in a bloodbath at Munich. General Kurt von Schleicher and his young wife were shot on their doorstep. Schleicher, in 1932, had advocated a grand alliance of Italy and Germany, "a curtain for Europe." Every S.A. leader or Army officer suspected of disloyalty was shot. In a speech in the Reichstag on July 13th Hitler accused them of "conspiring with a foreign power" (he did not name Mussolini) to alter the direction in which the Reich was moving.

To show his further contempt for Mussolini and anybody else

who made him feel small, Hitler mobilized his "Austrian Legion" on the frontier with Austria, and publicly ordered it to be "ready to march." Inside Austria orders were given to pro-Nazi groups to disrupt daily life as much as they could by blowing up bridges, tearing down telegraph wires and flooding public buildings.

On July 15, 1934, Mussolini's ambassador to Vienna was called by Dollfuss and asked to warn the Duce that there was a "suspicion that an attempt might be made to stage an annexation of Austria, under the camouflage of civil war." On July 17th the ambassador was given a note for Mussolini in which Dollfuss was more explicit about the threat. From information he had received, he wrote, he was to be murdered and a puppet chancellor installed in his place. One Alfred Frauenfeld, who had been broadcasting from Munich regularly, alleging that he had been exiled by Dollfuss, was the rightful leader of the Austrian people, who should murder Dollfuss as soon as possible. It was not clear how or when the murder was to take place, but immediately afterward Germany was to be invited to "restore order" in Austria, and presumably would never leave.

Dollfuss, according to Mussolini, was almost cynical about the threat, though it appeared to be a very real one. In response to several telegrams from the Duce, he agreed to send his wife to join the Mussolinis at the seaside, and Frau Dollfuss arrived on July 22nd. Her husband would follow, she said.

At midday on July 25, 1934, a posse of imported S.S. men in Austrian Army uniforms forced their way into Dollfuss's office and shot him in the throat. Simultaneously, the radio station was taken over and a news item put out that "Chancellor Dollfuss has resigned."

Dollfuss died at six that evening. By that time Mussolini had heard the news. He acted immediately. Two divisions already on the Brenner Pass were called to the alert; two more divisions were mobilized and moved on to the Austrian frontier, ready to cross it at a moment's notice. Mussolini himself cabled the Austrian Vice-Chancellor, assuring him that Italy would be faithful to the provisions of the Austro-Hungarian-Italian Pact of August 1933, which guaranteed Austria's independence. Cables were sent to Paris and London, urging them to take the same attitude.

During that afternoon, while Dollfuss's wife was being comforted by Donna Rachele, Italy alone stood in the way of the *Anschluss*. The first replies from London and Paris were vague and unsatisfactory. The Foreign Office "did not intend to assume new commitments." The Quai d'Orsay let it be known that no action would be taken without England. But, by the morning of the next day, it was clear that the attempted coup had failed. Hitler was too frightened to move, and von Schuschnigg soon restored order in Austria itself. The quality of the Austrian Nazi was not exceptional, and their leaders, Frauenfeld and Theodor Habicht, were indifferent. Britain and France added their congratulations to the many others which arrived on the desk of "Mussolini, the Keeper of the Peace."

The Dollfuss incident convinced the permanent officials at the Foreign Office that Italy, under Mussolini, had stopped the onrush of Bolshevism in the Mediterranean, "dealt with problems of chronic disorder and poverty," and was now a powerful state in her own right. Mussolini had stopped Hitler, alone. This was impressive. The pro-Mussolini faction, which had transferred its affections to Hitler after 1933, retransferred them to Mussolini. Sir Samuel Hoare, Sir John Simon, Churchill, all "marvelled." Even Anthony Eden, who disliked Italians and was unpopular in Rome, did not criticize.

Berlin was as impressed as London. Moscow, though not liking to overdo the praise, was enthusiastic. The Duce was "a statesman."

The Duce himself, who had been frightened that the Dollfuss incident would lead to war, soon recovered from his stunned relief. He had just enough troops and supplies for a few short campaigns up and down the Mediterranean, none for a European war. Now it seemed that he had averted war in Europe and made so many friends and admirers that he might be able to make a move in the Mediterranean without firing a shot.

On August 14, 1934, Mussolini declared: "It is not a question of being prepared for war tomorrow, but today. Armed forces, I remind you, represent the essential element in the hierarchy of nations."[4]

In September the nations who had stood by while Mussolini saved Austria from extinction voted with him to admit the Soviet Union to the League of Nations. The British "boycott of Bolshevism" had failed. The Duce's "containment of Bolshevism" had taken its place, and was to remain the policy of the non-Communist West for decades after his death.

In October Mussolini said: "The Order of the Day is Believe, Obey, Fight!"

On November 5, 1934, a group of Abyssinians attacked the Italian consulate at Gondar. A month later Captain Cimmatura, garrison commander at Ual, had to fight to prevent the massacre of himself and his men by Abyssinian regular troops.

Mussolini, not without a sense of humour, appealed to the League of Nations for "redress in consideration of this outrage."

At this moment Mussolini showed himself to have acquired considerable self-control. He could have marched straight into Ethiopia, to avenge the perfectly genuine assaults on Italian nationals who had every right to be where they were. Nobody could have accused him of "nursing a long-standing hatred of Haile Selassie," since he himself had sponsored Haile Selassie's application for membership in the League. As the climate of world opinion was at that time, not a finger would have been raised to stop an Italian invasion and destitution of the "Lion of Judah." But Mussolini made no move. Instead, he continued to play the rôle of peacemaker, of the "Saviour of Austria." He had negotiations under way with the British and French governments, the Soviet Union assenting, for the eventual signing of a four-power pact which would improve on the pact of 1933 and furnish real guarantees to Austria, as well as reassuring every other European power. At the same time he was solicitous for the welfare of France in her dispute with Germany over the Saar (which voted on January 13, 1935, to return to Germany). On January 7, 1935—before the Saar plebiscite was taken—Mussolini signed a treaty with Laval, which offered "unlimited guarantees" to France. In the January 7th treaty mention was made of "Italy's natural interests in Libya," but almost casually. A secret protocol, giving Italy the right to do what she pleased in Abyssinia in return for guarantees of the *status quo* in French North Africa, was not published. Mussolini promised to make no move in Africa until Laval had consulted his British colleagues and until "the peace of Europe was settled."

Laval did not find much enthusiasm for Mussolini's proposals in London. For one thing, neither Simon nor Eden liked the idea of a growing power (and the Dollfuss affair had given them a perhaps exaggerated idea of the strength and war potential of a country which they had previously under-rated) expanding in Africa. Kenya was too close to Ethiopia for Britain to see the latter change hands gladly. And again, Eden, especially, was ambitious, anxious to see Britain "make her mark and keep up her position." The idea of losing the hegemony of Europe to Italy was distasteful to Eden, many of whose fellowcountrymen believed the Jungle began at Calais.

Eden's reaction to Laval's suggestion that, as Mussolini was obviously at the top of his form, they follow Italy into some new system of guarantees of European security, was one of horror and contempt. Eden's counter-suggestion was that they keep Mussolini quiet by letting him think they were falling in with his plans, but instead make their own peace with Hitler on their own terms. It might well be necessary, Eden opined, to be generous with Hitler. For the moment it did not seem as if Europe needed Italy as a bulwark against either Germany or Russia. Something was needed as a bulwark against Italy. Eden's proposals, presented jointly by Britain and France in February 1935, were that Germany should be granted the right to rearm "on the same basis" as the other European powers, and in return should sign some sort of treaty which would guarantee the European *status quo*. The treaty would be between Britain, France and Germany. Italy would not be consulted. Hitler, quick to smell deceit when it was thrust anywhere near his nose, immediately notified Mussolini that he had better "take serious considerations of our common interests." When, shortly afterward, Sir John Simon offered to double-cross even France—with whom he had been double-crossing Italy—and sign some sort of two-power treaty with Hitler, the Fuehrer must have thought himself one of the few honest men in Europe. Hitler did not go through with the projected talks with Sir John Simon, planned for March 6th, but instead announced to the world on March 10th that Germany had already begun to rearm, and what were the Versailles Treaty Powers going to do about it? Hitler continued his unilateral abrogation of the Treaty of Versailles by decreeing, on March 16th, compulsory military service to provide an army of some 500,000 men. On Sunday, March 17th, the whole of Germany celebrated, not the rebirth of militarism (which had never died), but its affiliation.

Caught in the toils of their own half-cleverness, there was nothing for Eden, Simon and Laval to do but to climb out of the net as best they could and go looking for Peacemaker Mussolini. On April 11, 1935, at Stresa, feeling rather like a lonely paragon of virtue among rogues of the deepest synthetic dye, Mussolini held court. He drafted a treaty which "guaranteed the national sovereignty of Austria, and recognized the situation in a Europe in which Germany's increasing might and prosperity must not be allowed to overbalance existing values." As it turned out, it was a singularly worthless treaty in everything other than that it gave Mussolini his first taste of diplomatic victory over Britain, a not common experience for any statesman.[5]

At Stresa Mussolini "confided" in Sir John Simon his "difficulties" in Africa, where the Emperor of Ethiopia was "committing daily outrages against Italian nationals." He assured Sir John that he had no designs on any British territory in Africa. He reminded the unfortunate man of the exchange of notes between himself and the British Ambassador in Rome, which, as early as 1923, had recognized Italy's interests in the "Abyssinian region." He also told him that three Italian Regular Army divisions, "Peloritana," "Gavinana" and "Sabauda," had been mobilized, together with two divisions of Black Shirts, "March 23rd" and "October 28th."

Thoroughly frightened, trusting neither Hitler nor Mussolini, the British diplomats at Stresa went home undecided what to do about either Europe or Africa. Public opinion in England was hostile to the idea of "selling Haile Selassie." It was also hostile to Hitler and his anti-Semitism, and Sir Oswald Mosley's home-grown Black Shirts did nothing to endear the British public to either Nazism or Fascism. The only "decent" allies for Britain were France and the Soviet Union, and France was weak and the middle classes hostile to a *rapprochement* with Stalin. The policy decided upon was one of appeasement—appeasement of Germany in the faint hope that she could be used as a brake on Italy, or at best be "contained."

To this end the British government invited Hitler and von Ribbentrop to London in June 1935, to discuss "friendship." There was much quoting of Hitler's speech of May 21st—"The German government recognizes the overpowering vital importance . . . of a dominating protection for the British Empire on the sea . . . [and] has the straightforward intention to find and maintain a relationship with the British people and State which will prevent for all time a repetition of the only struggle there has been between the two nations." One people, one blood; an Anglo-German alliance which would "hallow ancient ties of friendship and kinship." In return for this "friendship," Germany would ask for approval of a fleet 35 per cent the size of Britain's in total tonnage. Hitler, remembering his talks with Mussolini on the subject of the future pattern of wars on sea and in the air, insisted that he be allowed parity of numbers in submarines, though this would not affect the total tonnage ratio. There was more talk of peace and friendship, kinship and blood. The British government refrained from informing her fellow signatories of the Stresa treaty of what she was doing. Simon even refused to admit that he had been going behind France's back when taxed with this by Laval.

The British government, convinced that its duplicity had "settled

Europe for at least a decade," sent Eden to Rome to see if Mussolini, too, could be bought, bribed or placated. Showing an almost incomparable misunderstanding of the situation and of the temper of the Italian people, Eden, on June 24th, offered Mussolini a small piece of desert—Ogaden—if Italy would renounce her claims on Ethiopia. Mussolini explained patiently to Eden ("a young, ambitious, effeminate snob") that Italy, for the moment, had the largest Army and Air Force in Europe and a more than adequate Navy. Italy did not need to bargain. Italy's diplomatic activity had been undertaken to keep the peace in Europe because, as the Dollfuss affair had shown, Italy alone could make and keep the peace. If Mr. Eden cared to speak to the Emperor of Ethiopia and advise him to make reparations for damage done to Italian property —pay compensation for Italian lives lost, and hand over a sufficient acreage of Ethiopian land to guarantee the future security of Italy's possessions in Africa—then he, Mussolini, would do his best to hold the Italian people in check. This would be difficult, he said, because, unlike the British people, they were well fed, fully employed, healthy, and united behind their government. The Italian birth rate was 15 per cent higher than that in Britain, the death rate from disease 24 per cent lower. The figures spoke for themselves. There was both energy and unity in Italy.

Eden went home even more anti-Italian than before. Rome had shown him scant respect. The "nattiness" of his dress was considered effeminate and his elegance unhealthy. Side by side with some of the cream of the militia on guard at Palazzo Chigi, he looked like a bank clerk watching the changing of the guard at Buckingham Palace. His professional disappointment and personal pique are understandable. What was scarcely believable when it happened was that the British government should be induced to react by sending the fleet steaming up and down the Mediterranean, as if Italy were a backward feudal state in Asia, susceptible to gunboats. The gesture only made everybody laugh. The Royal Navy even accorded naval honours to Italian warships it met escorting troopships to Eritrea, so presumably the Naval Staff saw the joke too. The only man who seems to have been frightened by the Royal Navy's "waste of paraffin" was Marshal Badoglio, who wrote Mussolini that: "Your Excellency ought to avoid at all costs a clash with England."

Mussolini's interpretation of the gesture was to conclude that Britain was not taking the Mediterranean seriously. He told Nino d'Arona that he was afraid of neither the Mediterranean Fleet nor of

British public opinion. By the time the "great newspapers" had got correspondents out to Ethiopia, his war would be over. Even the League of Nations, debating the "Italian threat to Ethiopia" throughout September 1935, could not agree on measures to be taken to prevent any action by Mussolini; when possible "sanctions" were mentioned, it was difficult to find a delegate prepared to explain exactly what these would be or how they would be applied. Mussolini was further encouraged by the knowledge that a faction inside the British Conservative Party, slowly gaining strength, was convinced that Eden had made a fool of himself and was continuing to do so at the League of Nations in an unworthy cause and for personal reasons. After all, the Emperor of Ethiopia had a well-trained, well-equipped army, so any invasion would be no push-over. An Italo-Ethiopian war would last a long time, and in the process Italy would be gratifyingly weakened. If by any chance Italy won a secret committee of enquiry recommended that, in return for Britain's "friendship," the victorious Duce should be asked to "adjust" the frontiers of Kenya, the Sudan and British Somaliland, and ask for control of Tana. Britain, if given these "compensations," ought then to support any request by Mussolini for Ethiopia's expulsion from the League of Nations under Article 16.

On September 10, 1935, Starace, in an Order of the Day, announced that the Duce had ordered "the general mobilisation of all the forces of the régime."

"With the League, without the League, against the League, the problem has only one solution," added Mussolini in a speech to students gathered beneath his balcony. "We will shoot straight." To peasants gathered to see their sons and brothers off from Naples, the Duce added again: "The plough makes the furrow, but the sword defends it."

On the afternoon of October 2, 1935, church bells and loud-speakers sounded the call for everybody to go out into the squares and wait for the word of the Duce. His speech gives a good idea of the state of emotion of the whole Italian nation, united at this moment as seldom before.

> Black Shirts of the Revolution! Men and Women of all Italy! Italians scattered throughout the world, over the hills and beyond the seas: Hear me!
>
> A solemn hour is about to strike in the history of our country. Twenty million people fill, at this moment, all the squares of Italy. The history of man has never known such a sight. Twenty million people, with one heart, one will, one decision alone. This manifestation ought

to show the world that Italy and Fascism are a single entity, perfect, absolute, unalterable. Only crass idiots, ignorant of Italy in 1935, the thirteenth year of the Fascist Era, could believe otherwise.

For many months the wheel of destiny, under the impulse of our calm determination, has been moving towards its goal; now its rhythm is faster and can no longer be stopped. Here is not just an army marching towards a military objective, but a whole people, forty-four million souls, against whom the blackest of all injustices has been committed—that of denying them a place in the sun. When in 1915 Italy mixed her fate with that of the Allies—how much praise there was from them, how many promises! But after a common victory, which cost Italy six hundred and seventy thousand dead, four hundred thousand mutilated, and a million wounded, at the peace table these same Allies withheld from Italy all but a few crumbs of the rich colonial loot. We have waited for thirteen years, during which time the egoism of these Allies has only increased and suffocated our vitality. We have waited patiently for redress in Ethiopia for forty years. Now—enough!

At the League of Nations, instead of recognizing this, there is talk of sanctions. Until I am proved wrong, I refuse to believe that France . . . or the people of Great Britain, with whom we have never quarrelled, would risk throwing Europe into catastrophe to defend a country in Africa, well known to be without the least shade of civilization. To economic sanctions we will reply with our discipline, our sobriety, our spirit of sacrifice!

To military sanctions we shall reply with military measures! To acts of war we shall reply with acts of war!

But let it be said at the start, in the most categorical way, that we will do everything possible to avoid this colonial conflict flaring up into a European war. But never, as in this historic epoch, has the Italian people shown so well the quality of its spirit and the strength of its character. And it is against this people, people of poets, of saints, navigators, that they dare to speak of sanctions. Proletarian and Fascist Italy . . . on your feet! [6]

Throughout Italy the speech was greeted with deafening applause, and recorded—with the applause—for the party's record library.

At dawn on October 3, 1935, under the command of de Bono, Italian armies crossed the Ethiopian frontier at Mareb. Within a week, Adua and Axum had been taken and the advance guard of the northern army was 45 miles into "enemy" country. To the south, General Graziani shot out of Somalia, and by the end of the week was 65 miles into Ethiopia and came to a halt only to let his supply trains catch up.

The terrain over which de Bono and Graziani fought was not easy. After the war was over, some of Mussolini's professional detractors tried to say that his armies met with no opposition and drove to the capital of the Lion of Judah without incident, stopping only to refuel.

Major-General Galbiati, who commanded a legion in the fighting, had this to say of the terrain and the enemy:

> On the one hand, the distances involved—3,750 miles from the mother country—and the number of ships needed, the readying of ports, the accumulation of food, arms and ammunition; on the other side, the traps waiting in unexplored mountains, deserts, scrub and forests, and the warlike and fanatical character of the Abyssinians themselves . . . the war machine of the King of Kings (Haile Selassie) went into action as its duty required at the right time and place. But Italy, unprepared for a campaign of this size, found herself capable of reacting in a way she had not thought possible, improvising a perfect organization which stretched from the mother country to the Red Sea and the Indian Ocean . . . the Italian workers and peasants astonished themselves. At impossible temperatures, when the natives ran for shade and water, they went on unloading supplies, making roads with pick and shovel, ploughing through the unknown without losing heart, making railways over shifting sands, and creating whole villages of workers and soldiers where formerly there were only patches of barren ground barely dented by the short stopovers of nomads.[7]

As Galbiati commented later: "To fight such a campaign needed an extraordinary psychological stimulus—not just the stimulus of an appeal to history (which is effective only to the generation which made it, it being a fact that the man in the street is indifferent to reminders that Tessaglia and Numidia were once Roman provinces, or that Gaul was a tributary of Caesar Augustus) . . ."

The extraordinary stimulus was to come from outside Italy, to reinforce the general belief that the Duce was always right, and did everything for the best. Since 1933 the man in the street had had little chance to make his pride or prejudice felt. The Duce had been swept into the international arena, and the press reported that he was settling the fate of Europe. Not that the man in the street believed all he read in the newspapers—only pro-régime newspapers existed, and, after the creation of the Ministry of Popular Culture in 1935, most of these were written in Rome by the Duce himself. The only time the man in the street saw Mussolini he was cutting tapes or making a ceremonial hit with a pick, or celebrating one or both in a speech from fifty feet up above the crowd.

Italy, in general, was anti-war in 1935, and when the first enthusiasm whipped up by Mussolini's speech of October 2nd and the swift successes of the first weeks of the campaign had died down, this anti-war feeling might well have made itself dangerous. It could have manifested itself in "go slow," in sabotage, in a steady lowering of morale at home and abroad, with fatal consequences for a régime which needed prestige as a car needs petrol or a balloon needs air. But, fortunately, the League of Nations gave that outside stimulus Mussolini needed. At Geneva, Anthony Eden, whose personal hatred for Mussolini seemed to have no limits, made speeches advocating the severest sanctions, a complete economic boycott, and "moral isolation" of the "aggressors trampling down this ancient Christian kingdom." The debate at the League lasted for nearly three weeks. Many of the delegates were not convinced about the Christianity or Christian charity of Haile Selassie. Others noted that on October 20th 200 Coptic churches made their own peace with Mussolini, and the Coptic archpriest stated that he was sure they would enjoy more freedom and spiritual purity "in league with the Holy sepulchres of Rome." On the same day de Bono issued a decree abolishing slavery in territory already liberated by the Italian Army, and promising to do the same all the way to Addis Ababa. But the pressure brought to bear by Britain was so strong (it consisted not so much of an appeal to moral solidarity as a threat to withdraw credits) that the League voted for Eden's sanctions, which were to come into force on November 2nd.

This was all Italy and Mussolini needed. Instead of a colonial war, the campaign in Abyssinia became overnight a war of self-defence against the might of the British Empire and her allies. Who could object to this? Only Germany (which was outside the League) and the Soviet Union ignored the economic sanctions completely. The first weeks of November were lived in the atmosphere of a beleaguered garrison. All criticism of Mussolini came to an end. As he himself wrote: "Italy lived through one of the most dramatic periods of her history . . . never was a war felt (from the date of the sanctions) so completely, never an enthusiasm more sincere . . ."

At home Mussolini proclaimed that within the shortest possible time Italy must become self-sufficient, to minimise the effect of the sanctions. He did not know how effective or ineffective they would be, and in any case a tightening of the belt would do the country no harm. Synthetic fibres were perfected, like the "lanital" made from skimmed milk. "Carcadè," a synthetic tea made from brown coal, was the fashionable afternoon drink. Foreign labels were removed from bottles, and foreign words (wrote the *Corriere della Sera*) were frowned on. For flirt, read *amoretto*. The personal columns of newspapers announced changes of name to "Roman" names—from Adam to Adamus. Advertisements showed how patriotic traders had become, renaming their goods to suit the hour (EAT OTTOGALLI'S CAKE MADE WITH VICTORY BUTTER). The editorial columns were full of stories, gathered by Starace, of men walking 300 miles, barefoot, to volunteer. The sanctions, said *il Messagero*, "are doomed to fail." Ugo Ojetti, in the *Corriere della Sera*, wrote: "Mr. Anthony Eden has, behind his famous long eyelashes, two eyes which are expert in the Greek and Latin past—but in the present, things close to him, he cannot see clearly. He can read Homer in the original, but he does not understand Mussolini, even in translation."

In Africa de Bono went on with his good works, receiving priests, building roads, perfecting plumbing. Mussolini was furious. He knew that the war must end as quickly as possible, while enthusiasm at home (and anger at the sanctions) was still white hot. There were other reasons for haste. A general election had been announced for Britain, and Mussolini knew that Britain would not take any large-scale military action, or complete any economic boycott, before the election. If victory was in sight by the time the elections were over, then the sanctions would never be applied. Ezio Maria Gray was in Athens, where Metaxas had told him that, although he had voted for sanctions against Italy, he "admired Mussolini and wanted to help him." He had suggested to Gray that, since—by the terms of the sanctions—Italian ships could not unload in Greek ports, and vice versa, they could get over this by unloading offshore into small boats. If the war dragged on, then Britain—after the elections—would stiffen up waverers like Metaxas and make the sanctions really effective. This would be disastrous.

Marshal Badoglio was despatched by Mussolini on a tour of inspection of the front line to see what was holding up de Bono. He sent back a report, agreeing with de Bono's opinion that "some consolidation of the position was necessary." [8] Mussolini was furious again. He ordered a new advance along the front toward Macalle-Tacazze. De Bono obeyed, came within sight of the main force of the Abyssinian Army, then stopped. Behind him the main supply line stretched for nearly 100 miles to ports still confused by the inflow of war material. In spite of a rush of telegrams from Mussolini, de Bono refused to go any farther until he was sure of his rear. On November 14th Mussolini relieved him of his command and appointed Badoglio to the Supreme Command in East Africa, with Graziani his deputy. He commented to Starace: "What does that old man de Bono mean by 'security'? This is a revolution."

On November 17th the League ordered its members to apply the agreed sanctions "fully." The decision, reported in the Fascist press together with a message from the Grand Council, stirred up both anger and enthusiasm again. Starace ordered his party officials to gather stories of men walking even 500 miles barefoot to volunteer, and promptly joined the Army himself. Marshal Badoglio advanced, then came to a halt to build air hangars. Mussolini made a speech to the Italian Academy and promised to bring the light of civilization to the oppressed tribes.

Behind the international scenes, Anthony Eden worked hard to get the League's sanctions applied with ferocity. But he found that the enthusiasm he had whipped up among the delegates at Geneva did not extend to their governments, and more particularly to the businessmen behind the governments. The French government, in particular, showed its doubts by buying a portrait of Mussolini by Breyer, with state funds which should have been devoted to subsidizing the boycott.

The American government, learning that supplies of Russian wheat were on the way to Italy, renewed its contention that Mussolini was a "human wall against Bolshevism," and wondered itself about the wisdom of the sanctions. Even Eden's colleagues at home were divided. There was a strong Mussolini faction which did not approve of Eden's action in any particular; there was a moderate faction which did not like Italians, or the idea of Italy's power in Africa increasing, but felt it wiser to humour the Duce. Behind Eden's back, negotiations by Sir Samuel Hoare, begun in October, resulted in the signing of the Hoare-Laval Treaty of December 6, 1935, which virtually—though secretly—handed over Ethiopia to Mussolini and abrogated the sanctions. Eden's principal ally, the press, fortunately or unfortunately, found out about the Hoare-Laval Treaty and forced Hoare's resignation. Britain, France and America, embarrassed in the extreme, drowned the noise of the scandal in shouts for even more sanctions, even more help for the Christian Emperor of Ethiopia whose slaves Badoglio was freeing.

The political front against Mussolini reunited. The business front continued "flexible". The need for a quick victory again impressed itself on Mussolini and his advisers. The Bucci Restaurant in Piazza delle Cappelle was serving Sanction Soup. Mussolini ordered Badoglio to prepare for a general advance in January, and set to work to find ways to carry the nation with the war into the New Year.

What Mussolini needed was a well-publicised act of sacrifice on the part of the entire nation. Shortages of foodstuffs and clothing, never very acute, affected the least well-off. There were suspicions among the middle class that other social groups were sending up fewer volunteers. Skilled workers were in reserved occupations; peasants were tied to the land. Though public restaurants advertised austerity meals, there was still the "back-room menu." Mussolini needed the complete sacrifice which would involve every social group and at the same time bring the nation at war some benefit. He hit on the idea of calling up the nation's wedding rings. The Queen was the first to offer hers, and that of the King. The rest of the country followed. December 18, 1935, was Day of the Offer of the Pledges. In Rome, in front of the Tomb of the Unknown Soldier—and in every other town in front of the monuments to the fallen of 1915–18—women stepped forward and placed their wedding rings in hot crucibles, where, blessed by priests, they were to be recast to buy munitions of war. In return, women and men were given metal rings, also blessed by priests (in Rome by Monsignor Bartolomasi; in Milan by Archbishop Schuster). The gesture was imitated by anybody who had gold ornaments about his person. It became a shameful thing to wear anything in gold, when the gold could be "better used" by the nation. A bishop, Margaria, personally gave Mussolini his golden crucifix and chain, with the words: "Duce, permit me, as a member of the Episcopate, to bring you the solidarity of the Italian clergy to be joined to that of the masses, which, under your glorious leadership, have fought and won the battle against the sanctions. I thank God that I have lived to see this day." [9]

It was half true that the battle against the sanctions had been won. The League called for more and more, but nobody cared to be the first to apply them. There was a great display of verbal humanity at Geneva, but little in the city of London or on Wall Street. Nevertheless, some sort of blockade did exist, and Mussolini was determined to see that it never became universal. What he needed was dramatic action—the sort of dramatic action which would convince the fifty-two nations that they had backed the wrong horse and "abused me, who for four years has kept the League of Nations alive." And the home front had to be kept aware of danger—alive to a glorious future.

Mussolini, realizing that Badoglio was not really much better as a "political general" than de Bono and was proceeding very cautiously through what was admittedly difficult country, consulted Starace, just back in Rome on leave. As 1935 drew to a close the two men discussed the political needs of the campaign. Starace's opinion was that Graziani, a tough ambitious general, should be urged to launch an offensive on his own. Badoglio would not be told until later, but, seeing Graziani advance, would realise that his personal prestige was threatened, and in his turn would risk a politically useful offensive. Starace promised to act as a go-between with Badoglio on the northern front and Graziani in the south.

On January 12th Graziani advanced, excusing himself for not consulting Badoglio by saying that he "saw an unforeseen tactical advantage to be gained." He moved rapidly through High Giuba, along the Doria Canal, until he came to the main enemy fortifications at Galgallo. He attacked at Galgallo at night, sending his three companies of native troops to cause confusion inside the enemy lines and approaching, himself, from the front on a white horse, waving a sword. He took no prisoners. He pushed on from Galgallo, fought off a strong counter-attack at Ddei Ddei, and entered Neghelli on January 20th. This incredible forced march—just over a week, averaging twenty miles a day, in spite of hard fighting—destroyed the Abyssinian forces on the southern front and scattered the army of Ras Desta (which Haile Selassie had hoped to use to invade Italian Somaliland). A large quantity of Swiss and Swedish arms and ammunitions was captured and made Graziani temporarily independent of his own supply lines. The rapidity of the advance to Neghelli also emasculated the army command of Ras Nasibu and cut it off in a triangle between British and French Somaliland, where it was unable to play any further part in the war.

As Starace had predicted, Graziani's success woke up Badoglio and the Regular Army in the north to the possibility of Graziani's reaching the capital first. On January 21st Badoglio gave the order for a general advance to meet the armies commanded by Ras Cassa Darjie, Sejm Mangascia and Mulugheita, who had been digging in during the month of inactivity. During the several battles of Tembien all three armies were defeated, though the depth of their positions made any follow-through impossible until the end of February. On February 23rd the fort at Amba Alagi was taken and the remnants of Mulugheita's army annihilated. Between February 27th and March 1st the remaining troops under Sejm and Cassa were surrounded by the I and II Italian Army Corps. Farther to the west, an army under Ras Immiru was destroyed. At this point there remained only the Abyssinian strategic reserves, commanded by the Emperor himself, between the Italian armies and the capital.

This success astonished the League of Nations. Its members realized that the sincerity of their majority was not exceptional. It was alleged that even Switzerland, the host nation, had continued to supply arms to Mussolini during the winter campaign. The Palais des Nations rang with recriminations. The press of every country in Europe reported denunciations of the League and of the Fascist victory. One interested reader of the news was Adolf Hitler. In spite of his quarrel with Mussolini, he had done as he had promised and supported, in his press, the Ethiopian campaign by "this great, the greatest political genius of our time, Benito Mussolini." At first he had been (on the advice of his generals) cynical about the military prowess of this political genius. They and he were confounded. Those who had hoped that Mussolini would either lose the war or be stalemated in Ethiopia—thus giving Hitler a chance to take over Austria without opposition—were forced to rethink. One thing, however, Hitler did realize, and this was that without Mussolini the League of Nations was impotent. On March 1st he gave orders to prepare for the occupation of the Rhineland, then demilitarised but under French protection. For a week his generals argued that they could not deal with even the mildest opposition, should the French decide to risk what was virtually annexation. But Hitler was not afraid of the French, nor (after the fiasco of the sanctions against Italy) of any intervention by the League of Nations. He was afraid of Mussolini and took the trouble to consult him about "measures he should take should the German subjects of the Rhineland be persecuted." He received assurance from Mussolini that he could take the Rhineland—in return for a promise to stop agitating for autonomy for, or an *Anschluss* of, the German-speaking provinces of Northern Italy. On March 7th Hitler marched into the Rhineland, and, as he had predicted, his entry was unopposed.

According to Gray, Mussolini at this moment was unsure of the future direction of his foreign policy.[10] In spite of his gratitude to Hitler for taking his part over Ethiopia and his pleasure at being consulted over the occupation of the Rhineland, he was by no means sure that Hitler was an ally either to be trusted or desired. Ideally, says Gray, he would have liked a world in which everybody but himself was at peace—friendly neutrals—with himself free to expand Italy's "civilizing influence" as the country's resources permitted it. If such a state of affairs was impossible, then he still favoured a Latin alliance dominating a Mediterranean confederation.

France was now so overawed by Mussolini's successes that she was raising no objections to a "consolidation" of the Mediterranean. Portugal was in the hands of a friendly dictator. Envoys of the Spanish court in exile (who were not received) and of the Spanish Army in Morocco (who were) came and went at Palazzo Venezia to beg him to help them purge the rest of the Iberian peninsula of Bolshevism. But if Mussolini invaded Spain, would not Britain object, with her base at Gibraltar at stake? Even if the Spanish Nationalists staged a successful uprising, would he be wise to commit Italy to a war of intervention? How would the Italian people in general take the idea? For all his speeches, he had no illusions about their stamina.

British Ambassador Sir Eric Drummond, who got to hear of the discussions about intervention in Spain, let it be known that His Majesty's Government would take a very serious view of the situation. The leak of the Hoare-Laval Pact had made a conciliation of Italy difficult in the face of a largely hostile British public opinion.

Mussolini's alternative to a Latin alliance, should intervention in Spain turn out to be highly undesirable, was an Italo-German-Soviet bloc. Bastianini, called home from the embassy at Warsaw to become Under-Secretary at the Foreign Ministry, suggested this one to the Duce. Here were three dictatorships, said Bastianini, ideologically divided, but the only countries—other than perfidious Albion—who were really physically capable of keeping the peace. Bastianini and Mussolini's other advisers all agreed that Germany would welcome such an alliance, and the Soviet Union was rumoured to be receptive to the idea, provided she was given some "frontier adjustments." These would be at the expense of Poland (and, to a lesser extent, Rumania). The fact that all three potential members of the suggested bloc had treaties of friendship of one sort or another with Poland did not disturb Mussolini, and he did not think that it would distress Stalin or Hitler either.

In the end Gray records that Mussolini decided to wait and see just how quickly the Ethiopian campaign could be brought to an end, and if any reprisals were forthcoming from Britain.

Mussolini wired all his commanders in Ethiopia to accelerate their advances. The first man to respond was Achille Starace, who, after a fighting forced march on the Graziani model, led a column into Gondar on April 1st. Badoglio, up against the bulk of the Emperor's reserves, moved forward more slowly. Graziani asked his permission to make a lightning dash for Addis Ababa, take it, and catch the Emperor in the rear, but Badoglio ordered him to march north instead, to mop up the troops still entrenched near the frontier with British Somaliland. The main army pushed forward to Gobbo (April 10th), and Dessie (April 15th). Here Badoglio fought a pitched battle and sent forward two Eritrean divisions to reconnoitre the road to Addis Ababa. On April 26th the Emperor left the battlefield and returned to the capital to make preparations for its defence. He was fired on by his own troops just outside the city—they mistook his American armoured limousine for an Italian armoured car. On May 2nd Haile Selassie abandoned Addis Ababa for Djibouti and a British ship to take him into exile. Three days later Badoglio wired the Duce that he was entering the capital. The war was over.

Mussolini, who, whatever else he was, was certainly the newspaperman of the century, spent the next two days reading the press of the entire influential world. He called most of the European ambassadors still in Rome to see him, and ordered his own chargé d'affaires to call on foreign ministries abroad. His summing up of the situation on May 7th, according to Gray, was that not one finger would be raised to evict Italy from Ethiopia; that his prestige had never stood higher; that the world, in fact, was waiting to see what he would do next.

Mussolini's next gesture was a gilding of the lily. He had filled his speeches with references to the Rome of Cacsar—why not proclaim the rebirth of the Roman Empire? It cost nothing. It would be popular with the crowd beneath his balcony. It would gratify the King and set the seal on an incomparably successful adventure.

On May 9th the Grand Council of Fascism met. In the evening Mussolini spoke from the balcony and proclaimed "the reappearance of the Empire on the hills of Rome."

Italy went mad. For hundreds of years she had been divided. For seventy years and more she had been humiliated by the Great Powers, almost squeezed out of Africa by Britain and France, snubbed at Versailles. Now, after Mussolini the great peacemaker—acclaimed throughout the world—came Mussolini the new Caesar. The man and woman in the street cheered until the morning came. At least 5,000 people camped beneath Mussolini's window, cheering every movement of the door to his balcony.

It seemed as if every problem had been solved. There were no unemployed. The few hundred thousand peasants who were seasonally unoccupied, or hoping to leave the land for the city, found themselves offered cheap land, freehold, in Ethiopia, a country with immense natural resources as yet unexploited. The best in food and clothes came back into the shops from the storerooms as, one by one, the members of the useless League of Nations started up trade again. If anybody complained, it was only of what were called the "inanities" of the party, for which they did not hold Mussolini responsible. There would be a relaxation of censorship; a greater variety of books and newspapers to read. The worst of the régime's magazines had been suppressed, anyway, as an economy measure during the war. No doubt, people said, now Mussolini would restore some of the freedoms which he had abolished during the "crucial days." He might even let Antonio Gramasci, dying in prison after nine years, rejoin his family. The intelligentsia comforted themselves with the thought that Mussolini, for all his "idiocies," had not descended to the bestialities of the sister régime in Germany where anti-clericalism and anti-Judaism had reached fever pitch. Visitors to the Berlin Olympics were revolted by discrimination against Jews, but Mussolini was on record as saying that he was against persecution of the Jews and disgusted with the racism which seemed to have appeared in Europe. The opinion current among most former Liberals and members of the Popular Party was that they had certainly paid a price for the régime, but maybe it was worth it for the prestige abroad and the security and prosperity at home.

If the people as a whole were happy with the régime, the party was delighted. Its own secretary was a war hero who had played an important part in the campaign. There were medals for all, and free trips to Germany, Rumania and Albania. Several party officials left for China, where they stayed for many years as advisers to Chiang Kai-shek, following de Stefani, the man responsible for the Italian economic miracle (de Stefani saved himself from trial as a war criminal in 1943 by seeking, and being granted, political asylum in Chiang Kai-shek's embassy in Rome). Local party secretaries were overwhelmed with applications to join, and looked with favour on Mussolini's suggestion that the whole nation should be offered membership, thus "inaugurating the new era of politics, that of the super, national Party," Jobs were in the offing everywhere.

The King was delighted to be an Emperor. His wife had taken the lead in sacrificing her wedding ring for an emergency which had fortunately never materialised. His son had never left the wharf at Naples and had worn his arm thin waving good-bye to the troops, but then he had never been much of a son. His daughters had enrolled in the nursing corps. Mussolini, though his ego was inflated, remained respectful and refused a title. The only man who worried him at all was Marshal Badoglio, who spent the whole of the week of celebrations of the Empire asking for a dukedom (and got it), but Mussolini assured him that at the first possible opportunity he would be sent away, possibly to China. And the Queen—the Empress—was delighted with it all, and this made family life much more agreeable than it had been for some time. The King—the Emperor—was essentially a family man and liked to live in peace and not bother his head too much about politics. He had a Prime Minister, a Duce, who was more than competent.

The Church was as pleased with Mussolini as every other Italian institution was. It had made its gestures of approval during the war, had even refused to allow Monsignor Roncalli home for the funeral of his father, because it was well known that Roncalli reminded Mussolini of Don Luigi Sturzo, whom nobody liked. Bishops and archbishops had given their rings and chains, and prayers had been offered up in all the churches. Monsignor Margaria summed up the Church's satisfaction, in an article in *Italia e Fede*, in the first summer of the Empire: "For we believers, the victory of Italy in the difficult circumstances in which she found herself is a tangible sign of Divine Intervention; it is the Seal of the Conciliation, the fruit of the new atmosphere in Church-State relations. Italy won because in the chaos of today, in a sea of Communism, atheism, immorality, Italy has remained faithful to her Catholic traditions, a bulwark of order, Christianity and civilisation. After God, our thoughts, our gratitude go out to . . . His Majesty the King of Italy, Emperor of Ethiopia, and to the Duce, whose genius compelled this arduous enterprise."

The subworld of business commerce and industry made no official pronouncements about the proclamation of the Empire, or the victory which had made it possible, but it did not conceal its satisfaction. There had been some doubts about Mussolini when he embarked on his programme of reorganisation of the structure of the economy, with his corporations, and the abolition of the old-style collective bargaining at which employers had always been more astute than their employees. But these doubts had vanished. Nothing sensational had happened, and what had seemed to be a revolutionary idea had turned out to be just a reshuffling of well-worn cards. They were better off than before, if anything, even though taxes were high. There was stability and there were no strikes. The ordinary share index moved steadily upward. In 1933, when Mussolini had first worried big business by venturing largely into international politics, the average earnings of 100 units of share capital were estimated at 4.10 per cent per year. In 1935 this percentage rose to 5.74 per cent, and in 1936 it had already reached 7.50 per cent for the first six months of the year. A record harvest was forecast, and a good market, heavy with demand. The sanctions had been a failure; overseas trade had passed the 1934 figure and seemed likely to reach almost double that figure.

There was, in fact, no opposition to Mussolini at that moment. Whenever the perennial exiles in Paris, London and New York complained about the régime, they were looked upon as madmen. "If only we had a Mussolini," was the usual reaction to any mention of Italy.

Abroad, Mussolini's prestige grew daily, so fast that it was vastly inflated. Having under-estimated Italy and the Italians for years, the world was now inclined to over-estimate them. As the *Popolo d'Italia* put it: "Italy is like a young and beautiful girl ready for marriage, with a rich dowry and even greater expectations. She can pick and choose her suitors."

Mussolini, on Italy's behalf, was blandly confident. He sounded out the British government on a future *rapprochement*, and found the idea enthusiastically received—when would the Duce or his Foreign Minister care to visit Britain? The reaction in Berlin was the same. Anfuso, Ciano's principal secretary, went to Germany to see if the "Anglo-German love affair was making any headway," and found that any British hopes of setting off Germany against Italy were frail, to say the least. Where Mussolini did not find admirers, he found friendly neutrality. Those who would not commit themselves to open friendship immediately told him that, "as soon as the fuss about the sanctions has died down, then we can show our hand."

It was this attitude of adulation and fearful admiration which convinced Mussolini that, without caring a dime for anybody else, he could proceed, after all, with his venerable plan for a Latin alliance, a Mediterranean confederation. He was even offered the leadership of part of the Arab world, and a Sword of Islam was fashioned for him. But the first step, it seemed to Mussolini, was to liberate Spain. The Church was enthusiastic about this as an idea—talk of Islam could come later. This time, however, Mussolini determined not to move until he had been guaranteed some reward for services rendered. He called to mind the talks Gray had had with King Alfonso and Primo de Rivera. He sent Gray off to see de Rivera and put it to him that the time for a Nationalist uprising in Spain had come. The Soviet Union was pouring arms into the country. There was a Marxist president in office. Spain's enemies were getting stronger every moment. On the other hand, Spain's friend, Italy, would never be better placed to help de Rivera and his friends. In return for their help, it would be only generous to keep the promise the King and he had made, and concede to Italy the Balearic Islands. It would be useful to Mussolini to have his Navy stationed there, if the new Popular Front government in Paris was going to last.

Primo de Rivera, consulting his friends, agreed to Mussolini's terms. On July 13, 1936, a Communist assassinated Calvo Sotelo, the leader of the Right Opposition in the Spanish Parliament. Immediately the Italian press and radio accused the Soviet Union of plotting to set up a puppet State in the Iberian peninsula and recalled Lenin's prophecy that "Spain will be the first Bolshevik State in Europe." The Soviet ships *Neva* and *Yevek* were already unloading arms and ammunition for a *coup d'état* at Jerez and Algeciras, said Mussolini's staff writers in *Milano.* The date of the coup, originally fixed for May Day, was now to be August 1st. Quoted extensively in the Italian press, too, was the report of the 7th Congress of the Communist International: "The workers in Spain have finally realised that the scope of their struggle can only be the seizure of power, and only the Soviets can achieve that power." The editorials implied that there was no time to lose.

The British Ambassador called on Mussolini and almost begged him not to intervene. He pointed out that the League of Nations sanctions had been called off nine days previously "with Britain's blessing." And only three days previously, on July 11th, an Austro-German Treaty had been signed "guaranteeing peace in that sector, no small credit for which must go to Signor Mussolini himself." Mussolini's destiny, said the ambassador, was surely that of a peacemaker, a referee, and as such he would be remembered with gratitude by history.

Mussolini was not impressed. A week later he announced that his rôle was, and always had been, that of a container of Communism, and he intended to see that Italy's interests in the Mediterranean were safeguarded. To save the Mediterranean from Communism, he despatched a large force of ground and air troops to the Spanish mainland. To safeguard Italy's interests in the Balearic Islands, he sent Count Bonacorsi to annex them, payment in advance. Mussolini confided in Ciano that he trusted nobody, not even Primo de Rivera. He lived only in the pious hope of being proved pessimistic.

The scale of Italy's intervention in the Spanish Civil War (General

Franco was already fighting full-scale battles) stopped Western Europe short in its diplomatic tracks. Even Hitler was alarmed. There was no halting this Italian, "the greatest political manager of our time." Hitler's reaction was delayed but determined. He wanted a share of the loot. He spent a week discussing the situation with Baron von Neurath and Ribbentrop. Ribbentrop did not like the idea of German intervention in Spain, believing that an Anglo-German alliance was still a possibility and would be more beneficial than any alliance with Latins. Neurath advised Hitler to do two things: send troops to Spain immediately; and get Ciano or Mussolini to come to Germany as soon as possible to "cement this natural friendship which has been growing since your first meeting." Ribbentrop's star was falling and his usefulness to Hitler diminishing. Neurath had his way. By the end of the month German troops and planes were fighting side by side with Italian troops on the mainland and in Morocco. Ulrich von Hassell, the German Ambassador in Rome, was calling on the Duce daily. General Franco was effusive in his gratitude. The coming and going of ambassadors did not abate. Most of them brought presents with them. The Grand Marshal of the Court of King Boris of Bulgaria hung the Order of St. Cyril around Mussolini's neck. Colonel Ekrem Bey, the Albanian Royal Ambassador, handed over the Collar of Skypuija. The Swedish Minister brought along the Order of Seraphims, in a suitable box. Even Monsignor Borgoncini Duca, representing the Vatican State, came with the insignia of the Golden Spur and the appropriate uniform—a double-breasted red tunic with black collar and cuffs embroidered in gold, a gold belt and golden dagger, gold epaulets.

But, for almost a year after the outbreak of the Spanish Civil War, it was impossible to get a major decision out of Mussolini. It was rumoured that he was tired, after fourteen years as "a single ox in double harness." It was for this reason, they said, that Mussolini had handed over the Foreign Ministry to his son-in-law, Count Ciano. Others denied that the Duce could be tired; were insulted by the idea that the Duce could lose interest in anything he had once put his mind to. Their explanation was that the Duce considered the world to be shaping up well under his direction, and if the other powers wanted advice, they had only to telephone Rome to get it. Ciano knew what to do. Donna Rachele Mussolini, in her memoirs, says that it was she who persuaded her husband to hand over the reins to Ciano and concentrate on being Duce and family man for the first and longest period in their marriage.

Whatever the reason for the sudden relinquishing of absolute power and homogeneous direction, Mussolini certainly did devote most of the year 1936–1937 to enjoying his family, and enjoying being the most talked-about statesman in the world.

The Mussolini family spent most of its time at Villa Torlonia, away from the captains and the kings. The house was too large for them, and too pretentious for Donna Rachele, who was happier when they went back to Romagna, to the Rocca overlooking the low hills on which they had played as children. She never quite got used to being the wife of a famous man, and it was not until after his death that she realised just how important he had been during the years of his rise to power, and at its zenith. She found her husband faintly ridiculous, with his talk of advising other statesmen, and found it difficult to believe that they really did telephone to her house and ask to speak to the man she had met as an impoverished schoolteacher, his head full of bombs.

The children of the family occupied as much of the Duce's time as he could give them. If he had been growing away from his wife, he had certainly been brought back to an awareness of her and of his responsibilities during the Ethiopian campaign, when his little daughter Anna Maria was stricken with polio. Young Romano was not yet of school age either, and he often phoned them from his office and had them brought into the city to see him for a few minutes. His older children, Vittorio and Bruno, caused him no anxiety. Bruno had already left for Spain, after distinguishing himself in Ethiopia, and Vittorio had gone into the film business. By the end of 1936 they were both engaged, Vittorio to a girl from Milan, Orsola Buvoli, and Bruno to a Roman, Gina Ruberti. Both the Mussolinis were delighted that neither of their sons had taken a wife from the aristocracy, which was always urging its daughters to "get a Mussolini while the going was good."

In the grounds of Villa Torlonia, when he could find the time, Mussolini liked to ride one of the dozen horses he kept in his stables, all of them gifts. His favourite was an Arab mare, a present from Tripoli, called Fru-Fru. Obsessed as always by age and fitness, he would go from the ride to a workout with his fencing master, or play a set of tennis on his own court, with one of his leaders always in attendance.

The Paramount film company of America, hearing that a home life of the Mussolinis did exist, asked permission and was granted the right to make a documentary about it. A director and camera crew invaded the house and grounds and shot hundreds of feet of film, even in the stables. They bullied the Duce into jumping on his horse, playing games, kissing his children. In the end he lost his temper and said: "Well, you must make the film you think best, but it seems to be my fate never to be shown as I really am. What does all this sentimentality mean? Is America afraid of me? If there is such a person as Mussolini, he does not exist only as a paterfamilias who loves his children or who can make a horse jump in the air like a mounted policeman. You have come here to make a myth." [11]

But nobody helped to make myths more assiduously than the Founder of the Empire. There was no more talk of Fascism as a "development of politics, a new theory of the State." The State existed by the Grace of God and Mussolini, and not always in that order. Mussolini-ism had taken the place of the old compromise between politics and expediency. The theoreticians, the Bottais and the Buronzos, had all been sidetracked and given routine jobs to do, looking after arts and crafts or making short lists of men to be nominated Academician. Even Bottai, who to the last hoped that one day it would be possible to make some political progress, became almost a figure of fun. He hawked his new "Charter for Education" around the receptions, hoping to catch the Duce in a moment of weakness and get an enabling decree signed. The Duce was not interested. He had time to spare only for the mythmakers, however much he affected to despise them. He always laughed at Starace, inevitably uniformed and bemedalled, but never failed to dress in uniform himself, even consulting Starace about the medals to wear with changes.

Mussolini read every press release before it was passed for publication, and often sat for hours drafting minutes on the proper treatment of some story or other which would be dead in a day. Time did not mean anything to him any more. As far as he was concerned, the closer the story was to his own person, the more important it became. He had his own pictures taken to accompany releases, once one of himself ski-ing semi-nude ("This is to serve as an example to the sedentary"). Every day he gave instructions in detail on the "treatment of the Duce's movements this day." "Speaking of Mussolini, it is not correct to speak of the Chief, but only of the Duce." "No photographs of the Duce are to be published showing him with the monks of Monte-Vergine." "No paper, including the illustrateds, is to publish pictures of the Duce at yesterday's show at Terme di Caracalla." "It must be noted that the Duce was recalled ten times to the balcony by the crowd." "All services from Sicily must be checked and references to the Duce dancing removed." "No reference must be made to the Duce dancing at Belluno." "It should be noted that the Duce was not tired after working the combine harvester for four hours." "As is well known, the Duce does not like the press to remark on his birthday. No reference will be made to it, therefore, not even in releases for abroad."

Whenever he made a speech, the whole of the resources of the Ministry of Popular Culture was mobilized to make sure that it went down to posterity in the proper form. Mussolini even laid out the front pages of several newspapers, specifying typefaces, choosing the accompanying pictures, and writing the headlines himself. He added instructions on whom to interview: "In reporting that the Duce's speech has been heard by millions of people at home and abroad, even if stories are sent half an hour before the speech is made, underline first reactions. Interview men and women of all ages and classes and get their reactions to the speech, with pictures. The main points of the speech must be the principal topic for all editorials on the following day. Suggest isolating the most important parts of the speech, boxing them or putting them in bold type."

When Mussolini wanted his docile press [12] to really soup-up a speech—one of his historic speeches—he would order them to "*sensibilizzare*" the accounts of it. "*Sensibilizzare*" meant remove everything from the front page in which posterity would not be interested, tidy up grammar, polish style, and even insert into the true text local references which would please the regional readership of the papers concerned.

Whenever he tired of the bureaucracy of his myth, Mussolini would call up Starace and Bocchini and announce that he was off on another tour. They were to make the necessary arrangements. He would set off in high spirits, his arms full of the books he had just finished reading. These he would hand out to his entourage with titbits of advice and potted reviews. To Starace one day he gave Essad Bey's *Life of Stalin*, with the comment: "Just read that and see what a real dictator's like. If the Italians had a month under Stalin they'd pledge themselves to Mussolini for life." He gave Bocchini a copy of the telephone directory and told him to read it, because "all good Romans spend hours fluttering the pages inventing gossip. Gossip is the firm base of all good police work." To Quinto Navarra he gave the collected works of Nietzsche and Baudelaire (which he promptly took down to the cellar full of Mussoliniana), saying: "These two had the right idea. Dictators are the servants of the people." Again to Starace he said: "Take this. It's an atlas. In Italy, too few people buy atlases. I bet you don't even know where Madagascar is." Starace did not know, and the Duce made him pay. Like Khrushchev in a later day, Mussolini entertained his entourage by talking to each of its members about his own speciality: to engineers about bridges; to aristocratic hangers-on about horses and heraldry; to one secretary about philately; to another about patent clocks.

He plotted his tours himself, on one of the atlases so few Italians read. He was convinced that he owed it to the people to show himself in each region as often as possible and not discriminate between them. He told Navarra that he had solved "all the problems which had baffled Cavour—the problems of Church and State, State and Empire, and of the economy at home and abroad—now there remains only the elimination, the elimination by fusion, of the rivalries between North and South." Looking at his atlas, Mussolini would suddenly notice that a particular province had not seen him for a year or so. In twenty-four hours he would be off.

According to Navarra,[13] his most hectic day was July 24, 1937. The day began with breakfast at 6 a.m. He had his entourage in attendance, sitting bolt upright while he offered them advice and résumés of his most recent reading. By 6.30 they were all on the road to the airport. At 7.30 they landed at Peretola (the Duce himself piloting the plane). From the airport at Peretola, after an exchange of gossip with a handful of flight mechanics, Mussolini drove to Florence, where he visited the Air Academy and watched a demonstration by cadets at the Carabinieri School. This done, he took off again and flew to Pisa, where he saw the test flight of a new bomber and inspected it when it landed. With great difficulty dissuaded from trying out the bomber himself, he loaded his entourage into a fleet of cars and set off for Viareggio. Halfway there, he stopped his convoy and dashed into a field where some peasants were threshing. He stripped off his tunic and shirt and stayed chatting with them for twenty minutes. It was now 11.30 a.m. He got back into his car and drove off again, arriving at Viareggio in time to hire a bathing costume and go for a swim, surrounded by an admiring crowd in the water and cruising nearby in boats. Back on the beach again, he towelled himself, dressed, and went off to have lunch with his daughter Edda and his grandchild. After lunch he reassembled the convoy and drove to Tirrenia, where he had a long talk with Giovacchino Forzano and watched a run-through of some films being cut for a coming festival. After an impromptu discussion on the films, he took off for Rome, arriving at 7 p.m. He worked for an hour at Palazzo Venezia, reading the foreign press summary and annotating it for Ciano, then went home for supper with his family at eight. At nine he was at a concert. By midnight he was fast asleep, and his weary followers dragged their feet to their homes.

This was an exceptional day, but it was characteristic of Mussolini to "get the whole world moving faster." Unkind critics said that the fuller his day, the less he was required to think. Hesitant when it came to making decisions about subjects of which he knew little, he preferred to immolate himself in familiar routine. And this particular routine was essential for the preservation of the dictatorship, a part of his recommended "living dangerously." Certainly Mussolini knew that the best way to keep interest in himself alive was to expose himself to risk and fatigue, Italians being conditioned by many centuries to the vicarious thrill of the circus.

It is almost surprising that the Duce had time for any sort of sentimental distraction other than that provided by his own family, but his well-known (and much exaggerated) weakness for women was a part of the myth of eternal youth, itself a part of the myth of the super-Duce which Mussolini felt obliged to cultivate. And, as he said to a bishop, "Would you like to eat the same dish every day?" Quinto Navarra writes that the Duce at this time preferred to receive his casual acquaintances in the Sala Mappamondo. Timid girls who came only to be made love to by the most famous man in Europe, egged on by their mothers, found themselves pushed back on to the cushions on the window seat. Older, more experienced women generally ended up on the thick carpet on the floor where the Duce could roll and be gymnastic to their hearts' content. Mussolini was not a lover who wasted too much time with preliminary tenderness. He was busy. There was, perhaps, a quarter of an hour available, and his inflamed visitors had to make the best of that.[14] But there was a streak of sentimentality in Mussolini's make-up, even when it came to dealing with his "kennel." He had a weakness for love letters, and always read them attentively, marking especially well-written passages, and passing them over to Navarra to read and then file away.

It was during this period of abstraction from international affairs, of intense preoccupation with his own myth, that Mussolini fell in love with Clara Petacci, who was to be his mistress until his death, and indeed die with him. Other than his wife, Donna Rachele, and Margherita Sarfatti, it is doubtful whether Mussolini ever loved any other woman. And neither Donna Rachele nor Margherita Sarfatti (the first intelligent, mature woman to treat him seriously and pay him attention) had the patience, the undemanding devotion which was characteristic of Petacci. This girl, daughter of a Roman doctor who held a semi-hereditary appointment in the Vatican, had been infatuated with Mussolini since her girlhood. She had a large collection of photographs of him which she kept in her bedroom, and she had lived from day to day on the glimpses of the Duce she caught as she moved about Rome or saw him on his tours of the country. She intrigued him because she belonged to the "first generation of Fascist women" trained by his Youth Movement, a girl whose earliest memory of Rome was of the arrival of the Fascist columns come to liberate it from the past. Her devotion was, for Mussolini, a sort of confirmation of his success both as a mythmaker and (because Clara was an intelligent girl) as a politician, even statesman. If she loved him, then the rest of the youth of Italy must love him, and it was with youth that he was concerned, if not obsessed.

Galeazzo Ciano watched the comings and goings of his father-in-law with affectionate amusement. The old man had done his duty and was entitled to his distractions. Like Clara Petacci, the young Ciano scarcely remembered what pre-Mussolini Italy had been like, and did not want to know. The régime had come to stay. None of the old man's sons showed the slightest interest in politics. His son-in-law would be in a strong position when the inevitable day came for death or disappearance. Ciano had no doubts about the future, which would be Fascist, nor about his own as the heir apparent to the creator and prophet of "the Movement."

Unfortunately for Ciano, he was neither as intelligent nor as shrewd as his father-in-law. Both Hitler and the British government were relieved when he was appointed to the Foreign Ministry. He could be dealt with, almost certainly, by flattery. Goebbels gave instructions to the German press to make Ciano sound important whenever his name was mentioned, "not because he is a great man but because he must think we think he is." The British Ambassador to Rome told an Italian friend (who promptly told Ciano) that it would be much easier now to re-establish good relations with Italy because they had a snob at the Italian Foreign Ministry, and, after all, Great Britain was the earthly paradise for snobs. A presentation to the King of England, and a treaty was as good as signed. This diplomatic gossip of the summer of 1936 produced in Ciano a mild form of xenophobia, and for a few weeks after taking office he told his friends that his father-in-law was quite right to stay uncommitted, except to the anti-Communism he had always led. There were no good or valid reasons why Italy should sign any more treaties, since she was their only possible guarantor. He told his principal secretary that his general policy, in consultation with his father-in-law, would be one of enlightened neutrality. This would take the form of the speedy conclusion of the "affair in Spain," to be followed by a "consolidation of interests" in the Eastern Mediterranean. And nobody was to worry his father-in-law with questions affecting the foreign policy of the state. From now on, he—Ciano—would attend to "such things."

Ciano's enlightened neutrality was, however, disturbed by off-the-cuff remarks made by his father-in-law during his tours, and especially during the interviews he continued to grant to foreign journalists.

In August 1936 Mussolini made a speech in which he reiterated his gratitude to Hitler for his non-participation in the "game of sanctions played by the decadent democracies," and expressed his pleasure at the assistance German troops were giving to his good friends in Spain. Ciano did not know quite what this speech implied. A week later Mussolini once again commented that there existed "an identity of interests in certain questions between Fascist Italy and those countries which have followed our example." What did this mean? Was he, Ciano, supposed to go off and sign a treaty with Germany? He did not like to ask his father-in-law what he was supposed to do, so he welcomed a suggestion by the German Ambassador to Rome (under great pressure from Hitler to get Mussolini to Berlin) that he go to Germany to discuss, in general terms, future relationships and the "avoidance of misunderstandings." When Ciano told Mussolini what he proposed doing, he was told to "go if you like, but don't expect me to leave Italy at the moment." On October 19th, the day before Ciano left for Berlin, Mussolini said, at a private dinner: "It is not in the interests of heirs of Rome to show respect or friendship to a horde of barbarians."

Ciano, bemused, went to Berlin not knowing whether it would be correct to accept all the overtures of friendship made to him, or whether his father-in-law really wanted to try to achieve some sort of permanent neutrality. What made matters worse, he knew that Mussolini would not hesitate to dismiss him if he made a wrong move, but was always likely to make an important and contradictory policy statement on the spur of the moment—after a good lunch in some remote province on an unplanned tour. Ciano found

Berlin impressive, in spite of his mental reservations and diplomatic caution. He found his hosts well informed about Italy and anxious to "avoid misunderstandings," but he was naturally reluctant to make any firm commitment about the precise nature of the future relationship between the two dictatorships. He contented himself with coining the now famous word "Axis," to describe the identity of domestic and external interests—and similarity in aims—of two countries which were not bound by any formal alliance.[15]

It was as well for Ciano that he found this formula. He got home to find his father-in-law in what he called "a mood of strong neutrality." What had brought it on was a quarrel with Bottai, then Governor of Rome (he ceased to be Governor of Rome after the quarrel). Bottai, in a moment of courageous criticism, had accused him of "throwing Italy into Germany's pot to boil with the rest of the boots." Like most of Bottai's criticisms, it infuriated Mussolini, causing him to react violently against the critic, but at the same time induced him to react in the desired direction.

On the day of his return to Rome, Ciano heard Mussolini reject all suggestions of a close alliance with Germany and speak instead of a "necessary *rapprochement* with England." England, for the moment, had ceased to be a decadent democracy. The fleet had stopped steaming up and down the Mediterranean under his nose. On November 9th, in an interview with the London *Daily Mail*, Mussolini said: "Anglo-Italian interests in the Mediterranean are not antagonistic but complementary." He went further. He told Ciano to investigate closely the possibility of "drafting a treaty which would specify and enumerate these common interests," and offered to speak to the British Ambassador himself about it. Ciano's first reaction was to give a conspicuously anti-German press conference. He said, in answer to questions by his father's staff: "I found the Germans malleable. Neurath thinks himself a fox, but I soon had him in my pocket. Goering is just an ox. He is the best disposed towards us of all the Nazi hierarchy, and has an unlimited admiration for the Duce. Goebbels is the sharp one. He is worth watching. Hitler—well, it is just incredible to me how such a man has been able to drag the whole German people after him. The Duce has sized up the situation correctly: Germany is in the hands of men of modest intelligence who can be used if necessary to further Italy's purposes."

On November 25, 1936, Germany and Japan signed the Anti-Comintern Pact. Ciano found the British government only too anxious to come to some sort of understanding. The British reaction to the Anti-Comintern Pact was to suspect it as a smoke screen to hide an expansion of Japanese interests in the Pacific, at the expense of Britain. Talks between Ciano and Sir Eric Drummond "proceeded in an atmosphere of the utmost cordiality."

On January 2, 1937, Britain and Italy signed a "Gentleman's Agreement," which committed both sides to preserve the *status quo* in the Mediterranean. It also committed Mussolini's side, by secret protocol, to help counter any Japanese move against British possessions in Asia.

Throughout the remainder of the winter and the spring of 1937 Mussolini prodded Ciano into "action which would demonstrate to England that we intend to maintain our commitments." Cardinal Schuster, always good for a quote, was induced to describe the atmosphere of Italy as "essentially one of religious peace," and Mussolini as the "man who gave Italy back to God." Ciano, knowing that the British government held that of Yugoslavia in high regard, opened negotiations for the Italo-Yugoslav Treaty of Friendship, which was signed on March 26th. He made statements to reassure France. Chamberlain commented that "all seems to be well again." In the same month of March Mussolini set off on a tour of Libya, which had been reorganized and brought to a peak of colonial efficiency by Italo Balbo. In answer to alarmed inquiries by the British Ambassador, as to whether this was "a prelude to further African adventures which might cause Italo-British relations to deteriorate again," Ciano replied, more hopefully than knowledgeably, that his father-in-law had only gone there to see an old friend, Balbo, and to make the same sort of routine tour of rural and urban settlements that he made regularly on the Italian mainland. Sir Eric Drummond was amused when reports came back from Libya of Mussolini riding at the head of a cavalcade of white Arab horses and wearing a new imperial uniform. He was relieved to be able to transmit to London the full text of an extensive speech at Tripoli in which Mussolini deplored "the neurotic alarmism shown in some countries by this visit of mine, which is simply that of a father visiting his children. We have no aggressive designs on anyone or anything. Inside and outside the Mediterranean we want to live in peace, and we offer our collaboration to all who wish to do the same. We have work to do here in Libya. Our people need peace, tranquillity, for themselves and their children."[16]

But that day marked the high-water mark in Italo-British relations. No sooner had Ciano geared himself to the pro-British diplomatic machine than his father-in-law, on the eve of his departure from

Libya, declared himself to be "the protector of Islam, the liberator of centuries of Muslim slaves." Eden reminded Chamberlain that the Middle East and the Arab world were British "spheres of interest." Here was Mussolini, claiming to be a new Lawrence.

By the middle of April Ciano found himself again listening to the blandishments of Ulrich von Hassell, the German Ambassador, instructed by his father-in-law to "work out a *modus vivendi* with our neighbours." He got to know that Britain, disenchanted, was "seeking accommodation" with Hitler, that the Neurath faction had been temporarily discomfited, and the pro-British Ribbentrop restored to favour. Luckily or unluckily, Ribbentrop soon made himself unpopular again. By the first week in May talks between von Hassell and Ciano had been resumed, and there were even speeches by Mussolini, to quote in the German press, which spoke of a visit to Berlin by the Duce as a "likely eventuality in view of the necessity to draw together." Austria was out of favour again—"The Austrians hate us, their hate is implacable, tenacious, profound, historical." Italy would not "move to protect those who seek alliances elsewhere." The German press noted that the Austrian Chancellor was placing himself in a difficult position, and wondered if the independence of Austria was viable, in view of the strong pressure by its population for a union with the greater Germany. France, according to Mussolini, was "in a grave state of crisis, which does not permit her to have a foreign policy." Czechoslovakia was "the aircraft carrier for Bolshevik Russia." British foreign policy documents were "like detective stories, and only the British Prime Minister reads detective stories."

Giuseppe Bottai, in his diary, noted: "I have made no entry in this diary for some time—why? Is it a fear of the birth of a new policy? There is too much talk in the Grand Council about the military machine . . . subalterns are heroic but unprofessional . . . talk of 'doctrinal wars' and the difficulty of forming a military conscience for such conflicts of ideas."

On May 15, 1937, in a speech to the Third General Assembly of Corporations (in whose activities he had long lost interest), Mussolini defended the idea of "Autarchy": "In a world like that of today, armed to the teeth, to lay down the arm of Autarchy means to put ourselves in the hands of those who have the material already to hand for a long and bitter war."[17] Autarchy, as Bottai noted, means "the attempt, doomed to failure, to become self-sufficient; rich in raw materials in a country devoid of raw materials. Even worse, it means that the idea of social justice through a development of the

Corporate State is dead, and that the Corporations now are no more than one of a number of institutions preparing us for war. Fascism is dead. A dictatorship is looking for a window from which to jump to oblivion."

In June 1937, by "common agreement," Italy and Germany withdrew from the International Committee of Non-Intervention and the Control Commission for the Spanish War. British envoys, hurrying in and out of Palazzo Chigi, tried hard to secure assurances that Mussolini did not intend to establish permanent bases in the Balearic Islands when the Spanish "affair" was over. Commenting on their withdrawal from the committees and on the Spanish "affair" in general, Mussolini said to Bottai: "Germany and Italy are the only countries sincere in this struggle. It is in our interests to restore the national sanity to Spain inside a Latin association, and the Balearic Islands, and so we fight hard and well. But the Soviet Union is not yet ready for a Bolshevik state in the Iberian peninsula, and so does not give the aid she has promised to the Republicans. It is in her interests to keep the war going for as long as possible, to destroy the Republican bourgeoisie. Britain encourages volunteers on both sides, being only interested in keeping Gibraltar and weakening an old enemy."

Bottai was inclined to be suspicious of German sincerity, and suspected that Germany was not giving as much help to the Nationalists as she could, in order to prolong the war and weaken her "sister" Italy. There seemed to be an unusually large amount of hypocrisy on all sides, and Bottai was struck "by the transparent honesty of the Duce, who speaks so frankly that nobody will ever believe what he says."

In August 1937 the Royal Navy, having refuelled, started to steam up and down the Mediterranean again. The Foreign Office made threatening noises through its embassy officials at parties, warning Italy off the Middle East. Mussolini, who had forgotten all about his new title of Protector of Islam (the Sword of Islam was in the cellar), was half amused, half angry.

On September 4th Mussolini went on a tour of Sicily and saw the Royal Navy steaming past the coast. He was more angry than amused. To a casual meeting of pressmen, he said: "Is Great Britain determined to destroy the pattern of alliances which was victorious in the last war?" Then he let fall the remark that he intended to visit Berlin. When, during the tour, he was told of the reinforcement of British military installations in Suez and of the strengthening of the Mediterranean Fleet, he commented:

> Our colonial and maritime frontiers we hold in common with Great Britain. They meet. When you translate this word [turning to a group of British journalists], be careful to translate meet and not clash. When I look back over the history of Italo-British relations, over the past two years, I am struck more than anything by the lack of comprehension, by the depth of misunderstanding in London. British public opinion is years out of date. Many people still have a mistaken idea of Italy as superficial and picturesque, with the special sort of picturesqueness which I detest. They do not know this new, young, strong, resolute Italy . . . Italy will co-operate with anybody to resolve the dilemmas which confuse European politics. But we must take into consideration the realities of the situation . . . the reality of the Empire . . . of the decadence of the League of Nations. . . . This League of Nations, it has been dead for sixteen years. . . . It is a stinking corpse. . . . If you will not bury it for reasons of political seriousness, then we must help to bury it for the sake of public health.[18]

The Mussolini state visit to the Reich on September 24th was a triumph of stage management. If Hitler had hired a public-relations team to create the image of the desirable ally, he could not have been more satisfied. When Mussolini spoke (in German, halting but intelligible) hundreds of thousands of people stood motionless in the pouring rain to hear him, then cheered him to the echo. Not the happy, hysterical cheers of an Italian crowd, the crowd which cheered him as it exchanged jokes about his leaders, his uniforms, the absurdities which co-existed with the strong points of his régime. The cheering in Germany was of a cold hysteria, of a transparent discipline. Mussolini was stunned. He saw torchlight processions and parades. He saw prototypes of fighters and bombers, and a vertical take-off plane. Guns rolled past the saluting bases on which he stood. The uniforms around him owed nothing to the theatrical costumier, they were the working clothes of an entire people transformed into an army. Goering gave his Italian guests a banquet the like of which Lucullus had never seen. He paid Mussolini extravagant compliments, reminding him that he owed his "life and career to Italy which had given him shelter after the Jewish plot at Munich." Hitler and Goebbels competed with each other to sit motionless at dinner, listening to the words of Mussolini, as if they were the First Fishermen.

Mussolini and his entourage returned from Germany rigid with admiration for what they had seen. There was no more talk of "barbarians." The talk now was of "steel" and "warriors." Mussolini behaved as if a full orchestra was playing Wagner in his left ear. He was unapproachable, except at meetings of the hierarchy to discuss "Autarchy." He would offer no suggestions other than "Ethiopia—I want an all-black army which will enable us to sweep clean the plains of Africa. . . . Libya: they will send us a hundred thousand men. . . . Spain: to forge a warrior people there is only one way, to have masses always around who have made war, and to have masses always in reserve to want to make war. . . ."[19]

Ciano, though it was obvious that for months his father-in-law could not be expected to recover from the tour, set to work to cement the Anglo-German alliance. To Bottai he said: "The Duce speaks of nothing but strengthening our bonds of friendship with Germany. I agree, for the moment, but we must avoid being too rigid. This Axis must be thought of as a long-term project, if it has any military connotations. . . . We must make reservations. . . . The Duce once said to me: 'It would be ideal if we could handle the politics and they the fighting.' This is an ideal formula. . . ."

Ciano, not wanting to see Italy with only one ally, Germany, should the worst come to the worst, drafted an Italo-German treaty with the one hand and with the other made notes for a "horizontal Axis to counterweight the vertical, Rome-Berlin Axis." He urged his ambassadors in Bucharest, Budapest, Tirana, to seek some formula for a "line of sympathy and common interest along the Danube to the Black Sea, where Italy's voice is heard first." Ciano himself entertained Yugoslav Minister Stojadinovitch at the golf club.

On November 6, 1937, Italy adhered to the Anti-Comintern Pact, bringing into being the Italo-German-Japanese Alliance and the war one day closer.

On November 25, 1937, Ciano sent Ambassador Chigi to Vienna for "talks about the future" with the Austrian Chancellor. He said, before Chigi left: "You are like a doctor sent to give oxygen to a dying man without letting his heirs know. But don't forget that we are more interested in the heirs."

On December 11, 1937, Mussolini (according to Bottai "a man walking in his sleep") called a meeting of the Grand Council of Fascism. Starace, well briefed, proposed the withdrawal of Italy from the League of Nations. There was no discussion. The noise of Wagner in Mussolini's left ear shut out every other sound. After nine minutes of bureaucracy the meeting of the council was declared closed. Mussolini stalked out on to the balcony in his new, Teutonic manner, his boots striking the marble floor of the Council Chamber to the beat of "The Ring." After the ritual exchange of compliments with the crowd, he said: "For many years now we have offered the world a spectacle of patience, which has gone unseen. We have not forgotten and we will not forget the attempt to strangle us economically at Geneva. But some of us hoped, believed, that at a certain moment the League of Nations would have offered us an apology or made some gesture of reparation. This has not happened. In these circumstances our presence at Geneva has become intolerable." [20]

A fortnight later, in the Piazza di Spagna, there were Christmas carols in the open, in German.

7

MEGLIO UN GIORNO DA LEONE

BETTER A DAY AS A LION

The people of Rome have an interesting if untidy New Year custom. They throw out of their windows, into the street, anything old they find in their flats and houses—empty bottles, broken chairs, pictures, pots and pans. The custom symbolizes a rebirth, a renewal of good intentions, a parting of the ways between Good and Evil.

In 1938 there was no more enthusiastic Roman than Benito Mussolini. It seemed that he was determined to destroy everything Roman, Italian—even exaggeratedly Italian—which he had been at such pains to create and re-create during the preceding years.[1] He did not hear the sound of bells ringing in the New Year. His head was still full of martial music, German bands and the crunch of jack boots. He did not hesitate to put into effect new ideas he had had to "stiffen up" his people. He ordered his Under-Secretaries of State for War, Air and the Navy to "make their men grow." He told his son-in-law Ciano that the King, being a small man, had tried to make the whole Army shrink to size. This must be stopped. In future, photographs of Italian infantry must be taken so as to show height and breadth—a question of camera angles, or even of photographing only troops in lorries. There had to be some re-designing of uniforms (Starace was given this task). Even the way the Army, Navy and Air Force marched was decadent, and had to be changed. Impressed by the sinister thump of the goose step, Mussolini ordered the introduction of the "Roman step," which was something between the goose step of the S.S. and the slow march of the British Brigade of Guards. When there were protests at this last piece of Germanophile eccentricity, Mussolini denied that the *passo romano* was an imitation of anything—it was invented in Florence in the fifteenth century, he said. And he suggested that anybody who objected to it on aesthetic grounds did so because it required effort—"men who cannot see over their stomachs are always left behind." Even more sinister than the campaign to toughen the muscles of mind and body, came a belated recognition of "the need for a racial policy" for Italy, "if Fascist Italy was to preserve its purity."

Absurdity succeeded absurdity in quick time. The immediate cause of the first absurdity was the isolation both of Mussolini himself and of Fascist Italy. The Duce, built into a myth by Starace, and unable and unwilling to resist further myth-making ("If there were no Starace, I would have to invent one"), lost touch, not only with his own people, but also with the world around him. He did not lose interest in events at home and abroad as much as he lost all sense of proportion, seeing himself as the only real innovator of a century which would only survive by innovation.

He was intensely jealous of advice and reputation at home. He refused to see Bottai on many occasions, because he felt instinctively that Bottai was about to point out to him some defect in his "masterly incoherent logic," thus depriving himself of the "brains" of Fascism (Bottai retired to the Ministry of Education where he vainly tried to reform the whole antiquated system). The Duce even refused to listen to old friends from the "big-stick" days. Italo Balbo told him he was making a laughing-stock of Italy with all his new, neo-Nazi decrees, and firmly refused to march "in the new Roman way." Mussolini said of him one day, after he had described the *passo romano* as "like the shameful waddle of a drunken duck," "There goes a man whose future I would not guarantee."

Bottai says of Mussolini's isolation at home:

> There were two periods in his life. During the first, while he lacked confidence and his indecision was marked, he would hear advice, even if he did not listen to it. During this period, from 1915 to 1935, he ignored nearly all of our advice and we were subsequently proved to be wrong, or at least proved to his satisfaction to be wrong. Italy's triumph over the League of Nations finally convinced him that when Longanesi said "Mussolini is always right," he was not wrong. The second period in the Duce's life was one during which advice never reached him. The Church, the King, the mob, Starace and the party, were as convinced as he was that he could make no mistakes. My friends and I, who were his only real friends, offered him advice still, and we were subsequently proved to be right. But by then it was too late. Advice bounced off him and came back at us like a boomerang, in the form of epigrams and mottoes.[2]

But if adulation at home and the sheer survival of the régime for so many years isolated the man who had once boasted of "making a new policy every day, appropriate to the realities of the situation," then the attitude of other nations and other politicians abroad certainly helped to solidify the isolation.

The little nations of the world seemed to be lost in admiration for brute force. Why, then, should Mussolini bother to theorize or encourage his own theoreticians any more? All along the Mediterranean coastline little men at the head of little nations shouted their intimidation to the winds. To the west, Spain was slowly being "neutralized" as Franco, with Italian aid and advice, was driving the Red Republicans into the sea. Portugal echoed the fulsome praise which Mussolini's own newspapers injected into him each morning. The Arab world had become tractable since the conquest of Ethiopia, and was anxious to make its peace. The Italian ambassadors in Greece and Turkey reported a mixture of parochial dictatorship at home and tremulous neutrality abroad. Yugoslavia had been detached from France, was uncertain of its future relations with Britain, and (as events of 1939 were to show) thought more of placating Mussolini than of containing him. Even the Jews, in spite of his new declaration of racial discrimination, continued to plead with him to help them to their Zion. Dr. Chaim Weizmann, as early as 1934, had asked him for "moral support," and for three years the Fascist press had abused the British in Palestine in the belief that once the British were gone a pro-Fascist Jewish state could be created in its place.[3]

The only Mediterranean nation to show truculence was France. This was unfortunate, because no nation is less popular than France in Italy. Successive governments in Paris (and they came and went with great speed and indistinction) criticized the lack of "democracy" in Italy, though France was ruled, in effect, only by a non-elective Civil Service. Successive French governments refused to pay their war debts to Italy, and reminded Mussolini of their hostility at the Peace Conference of Versailles. A general dissatisfaction with Versailles had been one of the early sources of support for the *Fasci*. The French kept this dissatisfaction alive. Another sore point was Tunis, of which most Italians felt they had been "robbed" (i.e., beaten to the colonial finishing post). They felt that the French government had maltreated 180,000 Italians in Tunis. In general, France was believed to be a decadent, bankrupt, jealous nation which inflated her shrinking ego by sneering at Fascism and persecuting Italian nationals under her administration. Throughout 1938 and 1939 the continued hostility and intractability of France was to be one of the major factors in Mussolini's rake's progress from admirer of Hitler's Germany to inseparable military twin and ally of the Reich.

If France blocked most of Italy's and Mussolini's diplomatic moves out of sheer spite and chauvinism, convincing him that perhaps war was easier than peace, Great Britain was not far behind in political myopia. At times it seemed to Mussolini as if the British Empire and the British "family of alliances" in Europe were disintegrating. In April 1937 Belgium had left the "family" and declared itself "neutral." The Duce's new ally, Japan, sent him reports of disaffection in Australia, New Zealand, India and Burma, and hinted that it might be necessary for Japanese troops to go there to restore order. Great Britain and the Empire did not seem to be strong enough to make war, and yet had given little or no practical support to Mussolini's past attempts to make peace (the Four-Power Pact, the Pact of Stresa). There seemed to be an element of indecision, as he put it. Eden had inspired the "sanctions" at the League of Nations. Well, this was understandable, in a way, because Britain had interests in North Africa, and it had been possible to pose as "Guardian of Small Nations' Integrity," even if a small nation was a slave state. But having decided to oppose his campaign in Ethiopia, why not do it emphatically, by either sending troops or enforcing the sanctions? Instead, Eden had been forced to climb down, and the sanctions had come to nothing. More indecision. The only European statesman who had acted with decision recently, to save a small nation, was Mussolini himself, in Austria. He would not make that mistake again. He had been deserted at the last minute by Britain and France, Austria's other "friends," and left out in the political cold.

The little nations intimidated, France consumed by hate, and Britain eroded by indecision, the rest of Europe seemed to Mussolini to be either impotent or friendly. The Soviet Union's relations with Italy were distant and disinterested. Italy was a long way away and represented no threat to the Soviet Union, and the most recent Communist attempt to set up a Red state in opposition to Mussolini in the Mediterranean had failed miserably. Mussolini's reports told him that the Soviet Union had effectively abandoned the Republic of Spain and had returned to the *status quo* of ideological conflict and commercial friendship with Fascism. Hungary and Rumania were Fascist or near-Fascist, and Poland the same. No opposition or enmity there, even though none of the three was to be trusted. Germany—well, Mussolini had had recent proof, not only of German's admiration, but also of her increasing war potential. He remembered the condition of Germany in 1933, and compared it in his mind with what he had just seen on his tour. Marvellous. This was a country to watch, and Hitler the man to befriend. There might even be something to learn from Hitler, in spite of his protestations that he owed everything to the Duce, "the master of post-war Europe."

Mussolini had not lost sight of his project for a Mediterranean confederation, dominated by a Latin alliance, dominated in its turn by Rome. Nor had he lost sight of peace, even if this peace was to be a *Pax Italica*. Perhaps the only *real Politik* was a division of Europe into two—Latin and Teuton, with Slavs as serfs? His foreign policy for the year, he told Ciano, would be based on this assumption. Points to watch were: *British hypocrisy*—Great Britain would try to drive a wedge between Italy and Germany, might even try to make an ally out of Hitler and so put an end to *Pax Italica* and Italia; *French chauvinism*—the French would oppose any attempt by Britain to make her peace with Italy, if Germany should rebuff her; and the old enemy, *Bolshevism*—which meant finishing off the war in Spain as quickly as possible and reinforcing the moral fibre of the West.[4]

It is sometimes said that Hitler took no notice of Mussolini, that his protestations of admiration were false and hypocritical, that he did what he liked without taking into consideration the wishes of his "friend and master." The evidence disproves this. Certainly once the Italian war machine had shown itself to be rusty, without fuel and occasionally without a qualified driver, Hitler treated Mussolini with contempt, but this was surely the reaction of a lover who finds his mistress has a wooden leg, false teeth and a wig. Until 1940 Hitler never made a move without fully assuring himself of the Duce's support in principle—even if, on several occasions, he went further than he had told his "friend and master" he would do. The French Ambassador to Berlin (and later Rome) told Sir Nevile Henderson that: "Without doubt, Mussolini is the key to Hitler, who is very subject to the influence of the Duce."[5]

On November 5, 1937, when Hitler had announced his plans for war to his general staff, he stressed that any plans involving the appropriation of Austria were subject to the favour of the Duce and the attitude of Italy: "Which in itself depends on whether the Duce is still alive." A fortnight later Lord Halifax had a long talk with Hitler at Berchtesgaden during which (according to a German Foreign Ministry memorandum) it was made "quite clear that Britain is prepared to make concessions to Hitler as regards colonies, Eastern Europe and some other questions, in return for a general European settlement." British foreign policy at the time was to prevent a closer union of Italy with Germany, and to give Germany, in particular, "an opening to the East" (i.e., if she wanted to expand, she must expand at the expense of Soviet Russia and the Soviet Ukraine).

It is interesting to note that Hitler said he was not interested in any Anglo-German treaty, not even if this guaranteed him Great Britain's neutrality in Eastern Europe. He was certainly not interested in the implied anti-Italian protocol. Britain was unarmed, the Empire divided. Italy was, Hitler believed, strong, united, virile, armed to the teeth—a nation drilled by fifteen years of para-military thought into a condition of perpetual readiness for war. Hitler was even sure that Italy, helped in the supply of certain raw materials scarce at home, would be able to take on and at least stalemate both Britain and France. There was a time, in January 1938, when he discussed the "promotion" of a war between Italy and France, just in case Mussolini persisted in his penchant for a weak but independent Austria.

Throughout January 1938 Hitler sent emissary after emissary to Mussolini. They offered advice on economic organization and accepted advice in return. There were talks about the future, and an exchange of gossip and salacious scandal. The Germans were amused by stories of Clara Petacci, who was rumoured to be an effective Minister of Foreign Affairs. One of the Petacci stories described her and Mussolini as "Europe's horizontal Axis." Mussolini's entourage affected as much amusement at the news that General-Field Marshal Werner von Blomberg had married a prostitute (Erna Gruhn, whose mother ran a brothel in Berlin). This was a joke against the High Command which the Italian militia shared with their S.A. colleagues, both delighted that the Regular Army had been proved fallible, at least in bed. One of the things which distinguished Fascism from Nazism was that it was always possible to laugh at either in Italy, whereas in Germany it was frequently, literally, fatal to take the name of either the Duce or Hitler in vain.

But the more serious part of German missions to Italy in the first weeks of 1938 was concerned with peace in Europe, or what passed for peace in Europe at that time. Hitler had decided to implement his plans for a greater Reich, starting with the annexation of Austria, but these plans still depended, in Hitler's estimation, on the Duce's assent. Hitler first asked Mussolini for a Yes or No on January 31, 1938, the day before the *passo romano* was demonstrated to an unenthusiastic Italian public. The Duce tried to temporize, repeating what he had said during his visit to Berlin, that: "The Austrian problem must one day be solved," and urging Hitler to have patience. The same conversation was repeated on the following day. In the interval Mussolini had asked for a full report on the situation in Austria, and had been told that Schuschnigg, the Austrian Chancellor, had discovered a plot by Austrian Nazis, with Hess's approval, aimed at staging an uprising which would give Hitler an excuse to march into Austria to "restore order." Mussolini was also told by the Austrian Ambassador that Schuschnigg was very "disturbed" by this discovery, because he had promised two years previously (July 11, 1936, Austro-German Treaty) to do everything in his power to improve relations between the two countries, to the point of seeing if there was a basis for an eventual "voluntary *Anschluss*." Mussolini found that his ground as peacemaker had been cut away from under his feet. If the Austrians were deliberately steering their country toward a union with Germany, there was not much point in his restraining Hitler from accelerating this process by annexation. To Hitler, on February 1st, he said that, though he was still convinced that "patience is always repaid," he would not intervene in any military sense unless it seemed to him that a European war was about to break out. In such a case he would have to "consider very carefully" the position of Italy.

By this time Hitler had committed himself in his own mind, and in front of his generals and party colleagues, to an invasion of Austria before the spring was over. He repeated his determination on February 4th, when he (as he said in a letter to Mussolini) "completed my Revolution in the spirit of your final solution to the problems of lukewarm collaboration in 1925." In Hitler's case this meant the destitution of most of the survivors of the non-Nazi Right, and, as the *Popolo d'Italia* put it, the "strongest concentration of powers in the Fuehrer's hands." The old generals went, and left the High Command dependent on the Nazi Party and the Fuehrer. The older generation of professional diplomats went (von Papen, Neurath, Mussolini's admirer, Herbert von Dirksen in Tokyo, and Ulrich von Hassell—to Mussolini's delight—in Rome) and were replaced by "new men." Dr. Hjalmar Schacht, like de Stefani the architect of the solvency of a new order, was—like de Stefani—moved on. As in Italy in 1925, neither the spirit nor the flesh capable of overthrowing the dictator now remained intact. It was, in a sense, only a matter of time before the beginning of the end. Mussolini was not entirely pleased with the dedication of such a purge to him. He was glad to see von Hassell go from Rome, and told him so, but he had disquieting reports from his ambassador in

Berlin that Hitler was already talking of "restoring order in Austria," and mentioning, as an aside, that he had Mussolini's complete approval. Ciano was instructed to find out how Britain and France would react in such a case and to inform Hitler (via the new German Foreign Minister, Ribbentrop) that he was doing so.

On February 5, 1938, after a quick sounding of Paris and London by phone, Ciano spoke to Ribbentrop and repeated Mussolini's counsel of "patience and caution." It was not yet clear, he said, whether Britain and France would remain inactive, as they had done at the time of the last attempted *Anschluss*, and their activity or inactivity "must affect Italy's attitude." Ribbentrop replied in such vague terms that Ciano got in touch with von Papen, via the Papal Nuncio at Munich (Pacelli, the future Pope Pius XII), and repeated the implied warning and the "peaceful" admonition. This action of Ciano's had two repercussions. Hitler, when he heard of it from the dismissed but very hopeful von Papen, hesitated. At von Papen's suggestion he agreed to invite the Austrian Chancellor to come to see him at Berchtesgaden, to discuss a "peaceful annexation"—the rest of the world would be told that the talks were to "consolidate the good relations which have always existed between the two German nations." If Schuschnigg was obstinate, then at least it would seem as if Hitler had made an effort to avoid a clash of wills. If Schuschnigg agreed to betray his country, acquiescing to the inevitable, then bloodshed might be spared and the occupation of Austria could be treated as a "manœuvre." In each case, there would be ample justification for approval by Mussolini.

The second reaction to the Ciano warning came from the British government. Rebuffed by Hitler, Halifax and Chamberlain decided that the time had come to apply themselves more seriously to a *rapprochement* with Italy. Talks were to be started immediately, with a view to concluding an Anglo-Italian agreement, by the terms of which Great Britain would recognize the *fait accompli* in Ethiopia in return for Italy's services as peacemaker in Europe, especially in Spain. Eden immediately announced his resignation.

Ciano reported to his father-in-law that any delay in the annexation of Austria now must be to Italy's advantage. The longer Hitler could be held off, the better terms they could expect from Britain. Diplomacy might be coming into its own again.

The Austrian Chancellor went to Berchtesgaden on February 12th. There was, in fact, no discussion. Hitler told him that within one week he expected to see a number of Austrian Nazis take Cabinet offices in the Austrian government, German officers accepted as "technical advisers," and "a closer economic union which could be facilitated by appointing the Austrian Nazi, Doctor Fischboeck, as Minister of Finance." After three hours of hectoring and harangue, with melodramatic comings and goings of generals to impress Schuschnigg with the "gravity of the situation," the Austrian Chancellor capitulated. Austria was to be "absorbed" and war would be avoided.

On February 20th Hitler made a speech in which he announced that Schuschnigg had shown "great understanding." Ribbentrop told Ciano that "the Duce could be tranquil in the thought that by keeping the peace between Germany and Austria on a previous occasion he had greatly contributed to what would now be a peaceful settlement." Chamberlain expressed the same views. But neither Ciano nor Mussolini really liked the idea of a precipitate settlement, even if it was peaceful.

The talks with the British government were proceeding very slowly, and the Italian government needed time, if she were to gain the maximum advantage. Mussolini commented that "there is no stopping it now, and we cannot intervene again." Ciano gave instructions to Grandi, Ambassador in London and a lion in society, to "try to accelerate the speed at which the Foreign Office is working toward recognition of the Empire." At the same time he sent a message to Ribbentrop, expressing Mussolini's pleasure at the thought of peace being preserved, but commenting that: "It would be unfortunate if too much haste caused the wrong impression in foreign chancelleries." In order to slow down the "peaceful *Anschluss*," Ciano also contacted Schuschnigg, and repeated his message to Ribbentrop. This, he added, was as far as Italy would go in support of what appeared to be a secret betrayal of her interests, but the Austrian Chancellor might like to know that her sister Catholic nation had not forgotten her responsibilities, even though she seemed to have been forgotten.

By the evening of February 21st every newspaper in Europe was convinced that an annexation of Austria by Germany was imminent and that the Austrian government would be forced to capitulate to avoid a massacre of the civil population. What were their governments going to do about it? Most of the governments of Europe, according to Ciano's experts, were going to do nothing about it. The British government had left the matter in Mussolini's hands, to "do the best he could." In the House of Commons, on February 22, 1938, Chamberlain hinted at as much during discussions of the proposed Anglo-Italian treaty. The French government, afraid that any Anglo-Italian alliance would weaken the Anglo-French entente, and as hostile as ever to Italy, was willing to sacrifice Austria to prevent it. The Soviet Union professed disinterest. The smaller nations had no viable interest, anyway. The whole of Europe seemed to realize that if anything were to be done to stop the disappearance of Austria, it would have to be done by Mussolini's Fascist Italy, unpleasant though the thought might be.

On February 23rd Ciano instructed the Italian Ambassador to Vienna to inform Schuschnigg that he was expected to make some gesture of gratitude to Italy for salvation in the past and her continued interest in the present. On the 24th, in a speech to the Austrian Bendestag, Schuschnigg did as he was told, interpreting Ciano's message as an instruction to be firm and "go no further with concessions to any friend or neighbour which might impede Austria's freedom of action."

Schuschnigg's speech infuriated Hitler. He had thought the Austrian Chancellor had given up any sort of resistance. It was with the greatest difficulty that he was restrained from giving the order to invade Austria immediately, and only the fact that Mussolini was "not available" on the phone prevented him from "taking the risk."

Throughout the last week of February there were violent pro-Nazi demonstrations all over Austria, especially in Graz, Linz and Vienna. But the government and Austria survived. Mussolini, contacted at last, counselled "patience." To Schuschnigg he telegraphed that: "The situation is critical, though every attempt will be made to prevent an unreasonable settlement. It is essential, however, that you make no movement without consulting me."

During the first few days of March the tension in Europe seemed to have been blown away by an immense sigh of relief. The news of Mussolini's advice to Hitler and to Schuschnigg leaked out, or was leaked deliberately. Once again the Duce had preserved the peace and saved a nation.

Had the British government, between February 24th and March 4th, concluded the Anglo-Italian agreement, over-riding the objections of France (a weak and not very reliable ally in any event, and militarily impotent as it turned out), then Mussolini might have felt strong enough to continue to restrain his hysterical pupil in Berlin. Had Schuschnigg done as he was bidden and consulted Mussolini before he made another move, he might not have made the two disastrous moves which cost him his country.

But the *entente cordiale* was still strong. And Schuschnigg, like all weak men saved by a stronger, acquired a recklessness born of his salvation. On March 3rd he invited the Austrian Left to join his government, and in agreement with the leaders of the Left, announced that he would hold a plebiscite to see if the Austrian people wanted a "free, independent, social and Christian-united Austria."

Schuschnigg could not have done two more foolish things, knowing, as he did, that his survival depended on Mussolini's goodwill. Mussolini was perfectly willing to hold off an *Anschluss*, even at the risk of annoying Hitler, and had come to believe that this could be done indefinitely—provided the clerical-Fascist government of Austria remained in power. But Mussolini was not going to have a hostile Social-Democrat Austria on his doorstep, a home away from home for anti-Fascist Italians (like France), and a constant source of embarrassment. Such an Austria was unthinkable. It would destroy the northern half of Mussolini's defences against interference with his Mediterranean plans, and reinforce the anti-Mussolini opposition in Yugoslavia, a country he had only just won over. What was worse, Mussolini had no doubt that a plebiscite would result in a triumph for the Left. He was furious to think that Schuschnigg had made these two moves without consulting him.

On March 7, 1938, the Austrian military attaché presented his compliments to Mussolini and informed him officially of the plans for the Left coalition leading to a national plebiscite. The military attaché said he had come instead of his ambassador because: "It will cause less talk." Mussolini looked at him, speechless. He said: "Tell the Austrian Chancellor that he has made a mistake. You may also tell him that it was his last mistake."

On March 8th Mussolini told Ciano to inform Ribbentrop that "in view of the changed situation in Austria, he no longer considered himself responsible for the integrity of that country." He urged Hitler, however, to wait until after the plebiscite (announced for March 13th) had taken place. In this way—the result being certainly a victory for the Left—any move Hitler cared to make could be made in the cause of containing Bolshevism, a cause dear to both their hearts.

Hitler could scarcely believe his ears when Ribbentrop passed on the message. There was no time to lose. He called for Goering and General von Reichenau and for General von Schobert, commanding on the Austrian frontier. Austria had to be occupied immediately, before Mussolini changed his mind. The order was given for March 12th at noon. There would be no waiting for the plebiscite. There would be no need to march to "contain Bolshevism"—the excuse of "restoring order" would do just as well. On March 11th Hitler sent Prince Philip of Hesse off to Rome to explain in detail his proposals for a "Union of Austria with Germany," together with a letter for publication should the Western Powers accuse Hitler of having acted at the last instant without consulting his Axis partner. At 7.50 p.m. that day it was announced that the Nazi puppet, Dr. Arthur Seyss-Inquart, had been appointed Chancellor of Austria. The plebiscite was off. But there was no stopping the German war machine now that it was in top gear. The first German troops were already over the border, the first Austrian Nazis "at their posts" in the Viennese post office and state bank.

The reaction to the news of the actual invasion was much as might have been expected. France was without a government (it resigned on March 10th) and was without one until the fighting had stopped on March 13th. The British government was "excited" when it heard the news on March 11th (Ribbentrop was dining at 10 Downing Street when the news came through), and immediately asked what Mussolini was doing about it. When the reply came—"Nothing"—the British government went back to its cigars.

It is quite clear that Hitler's only worry after he received the "go ahead" from the Duce was that his "friend and master" would change his mind. Field Marshal von Manstein, testifying (August 9, 1946) at the war crimes trial at Nuremberg, said as much: "His chief worry was not so much that there might be interference on the part of the Western Powers, but his only worry was as to how Italy would behave. . . ." Italy behaved well. Hitler did not hesitate to express his relief and gratitude. He ordered Prince Philip of Hesse in Rome to "tell Mussolini I will never forget him for this . . . never, never, no matter what happens . . . if he should ever need any help or be in any danger, he can be convinced that I shall stick to him whatever may happen, even if the world gangs up on him. . . ."

Hitler's gratitude to Prince Philip of Hesse was somewhat less. In 1944 his wife, Princess Mafalda, was beaten to death by the S.S. in Buchenwald as a reprisal for the King of Italy's desertion of the "common cause." Prince Philip himself also joined Schuschnigg in a Nazi concentration camp later and escaped death "by good fortune and prayer."

The only nation to show any signs of alarm at the *Anschluss* was the Soviet Union. On March 17th the Soviet government proposed a meeting of members and non-members of the League of Nations, "to see how far steps may be taken to limit further aggression in Europe." This suggestion was dismissed as "pointless and interfering," by the British government on March 24th, and frowned upon by Britain's allies.

On April 10th a "plebiscite" confirmed the "desire of the Austrian people to form part of the German Reich." On April 12th Hitler summoned Keitel to his map room to discuss the "political aspects, and military conclusions" of a plan for the annexation of Czechoslovakia.

Bottai noted in his diary: "There is nothing to be done. Nazi Germany seems to have become here a paragon of virtue. Instead of the old friendship in which differences were acknowledged inside a responsible collaboration, there seems to be now nothing but a 'philia. . . .'"[6]

Bottai, however, was unduly pessimistic. Ciano and Mussolini, though slightly annoyed that Hitler had anticipated by two days the date of the *Anschluss* agreed upon, realized that Hitler's success had reinforced their position abroad instead of weakening it. Indeed, the only adverse comments they heard were from Bottai and his friends, who were convinced that the man in the street was becoming anti-German. These comments were brushed aside as being "irrelevant—as irrelevant as comments in the French press, for which we are always '*sales macaronis.*'"

Both Ciano and Mussolini realized that Britain, France, Germany and the Soviet Union had been taught the lesson that where and whenever the map of Europe was to be redrawn, they would find Mussolini's Fascist Italy holding the pencil. This state of affairs might not last for long, but it was a fact at the moment. The maximum of advantage should be derived from it.

On April 16th the British government stopped haggling and hurried to sign the Anglo-Italian agreement, "the prelude to the recognition of the Empire." France had a new government which was "settling in"—every one of its predecessors had been committed to the losing Republican side in Spain, so it came into office at a foreign policy disadvantage vis-à-vis the Duce. The Soviet Union, having digested Stalin's new constitution with some difficulty, was now shaken by a quake of treason trials. Hitler knew just how much he owed Mussolini for favours past and how much he would be in his debt in the immediate future.

Mussolini told Ciano that the Italian people would have to learn that the Axis was a fact. Hitler Germany was in his debt, politically and ideologically, and could be managed, at least for the moment. But this did not mean that an effort should not be made to neutralize France, detaching her from Great Britain by means of a peace-and-friendship campaign, nor did it mean that Italy's relations with the Soviet Union must deteriorate, Bolshevism or no Bolshevism. As far as possible, Ciano should develop a horizontal Axis[7] along the Danube, a treaty-bound alliance of the Danube states (which would act as a check on Hitler, now himself astride the Danube at Vienna). Simultaneously, he should press for real signs of "understanding" in Britain. With Eden gone, this should not be difficult. If an extensive understanding were achieved, this would, directly and indirectly, "stabilize" the Northern European situation, and Mussolini could get on with his plans for "taking over" the Mediterranean.

April 1938 was a month of manifestation of friendship with Great Britain. The Duce, reported the British Ambassador, was ready to implement his part of the bargain struck in the agreement of the 16th. He had already given orders for the evacuation of troops from Libya and the run-down of the concentration of men and material which seemed to threaten British interests in Libya. Anti-British propaganda, which had been continuous since the time of the sanctions, virtually ceased. Mussolini even abandoned, for the time being, his campaign to subvert the British interest in Palestine—which he had begun after his withdrawal from the League of Nations, partly just to annoy, and partly in the hope that Britain would withdraw and enable him either to found a friendly Arab state, or fulfil his vague promises to Chaim Weizmann and found an Israel. Ciano reported this disengagement, step by step, and asked British Ambassador Sir Eric Drummond (Lord Perth) when the British were going to implement their part of the bargain and recognize the Ethiopian Empire.[8]

Unfortunately for Mussolini's plans for a multiplicity of Axes, all passing through Rome, the Anglo-Italian Agreement caused some consternation among his prospective and existing allies. The new French government, anxious to make its mark, had committed itself to an early settlement in Spain, a victory for the Republicans, if possible. It was equally anxious to get the Italian Navy out of Majorca. Pressure was brought to bear on Lord Halifax and Chamberlain to postpone the implementation of the Anglo-Italian Agreement until Mussolini withdrew from Spain—an impossible condition which effectively avoided the agreement. Neither Halifax nor Chamberlain, constitutionally averse to offend, would say Yes or No to either France or Italy, and the treaty blanks gathered dust on the shelves in the Foreign Office and in the Italian Ministry of Foreign Affairs.[9]

There was nothing passive, however, about Hitler's reaction to the signing of the agreement. He knew that Mussolini, for all his talk of Empire, would prefer to keep the peace, and in the last analysis, if he had Britain as an ally, might resort to hostile neutrality (at best) in any chance war between Germany and the Entente. Chamberlain had already offered Hitler the prospect of colonies without bloodshed—might he not offer at least the same to Mussolini? And might not the British government make a peace between Italy and France by a judicious mixture of cajolery, flattery, bribery and concession, still further isolating Germany?

Notes flew back and forth between Berlin and Rome. Hitler told Ribbentrop that it was essential that he pay an official visit to Rome before the British woke up to the fact that Mussolini could be satisfied with less than he himself would take for peacemaking. Mussolini had to appear even more committed. The Axis, fragile though it might be and pointing in no particular direction, had to seem to be a permanent feature of European diplomacy. Mussolini hedged, then—afraid to be thought discourteous—fixed the date for a Hitler visit from the 3rd to the 9th of May. Hitler started to collect medals and orders for presentation, like a young man accumulating baubles for a lukewarm fiancée.

Lord Perth, in Rome, realized what was going on, that an engagement of convenience was being transformed into a marriage of true minds, and urged the Foreign Secretary to make some gesture—if possible to overcome French objections and implement the Anglo-Italian Agreement on the day Hitler arrived. A proclamation of the Italian Empire by Britain would still impress more people than protestations of friendship by Nazi Germany. But the Foreign Secretary urged caution, advocated diplomacy, temporized, and the opportunity was lost.

The Hitler visit to Rome was a study in frustration. Hitler was desperately anxious to fawn and flatter, and just as anxious to get the Duce on one side for a heart-to-heart talk about his attitude to a possible German annexation of all, or part, of Czechoslovakia. Unfortunately it had not occurred to him that, whereas he was both head of State and head of the government, his "friend and master" was only head of the government—protocol demanded that he be shown around by the King of Italy, Victor Emmanuel. He was made aware of this as soon as he left the station and walked to the line of cars. Mussolini walked away and left him with the little King, a man who had described Hitler as a "physical and moral degenerate." At every sort of public function Hitler found himself standing or sitting side by side with the King. He was furious. Mussolini sent him a message urging patience, adding that he had been patient for sixteen years. Any sort of private discussion between Hitler and the Duce was made the more difficult by Mussolini's anxiety to put on a good show. He was determined to equal the spectacle devised by Hitler the previous autumn. Starace, "looking every inch a theatrical producer" (Bottai), had organized a sequence of pageants and demonstrations which left little time for talk—even meals were stage-managed, interrupted by little girls with flowers for the Fuehrer, and at best stupefying.

It was not until the last day of the visit that Hitler found an opportunity for a serious talk with the "peacemaker." Hitler was so impatient that he plunged into negotiations without the necessary preliminary courtesies. Bottai says that this made it unlikely that he would get a good hearing, "though it was understandable, fearing as he did that either Starace or the King would burst in on them at any moment."

Hitler proposed, first, that he and Mussolini convert their vague, verbal expressions of sympathy into a written military pact which would provide for mutual defence as well as for a concerted world policy. This was the last thing Mussolini wanted. He had not yet given up hope of a multiplicity of Axes; of a special, unique rôle for himself as Holy Roman Emperor. Above all, he did not want to lose his political freedom to move, if Germany suddenly started to decline or the Entente became truculent. Mussolini knew what a "concerted world policy" meant—expansion for Germany. He did not want to find himself, one morning, committed to a war he had had no part in shaping. Last but not least, he knew how precarious the political position of the Axis was and how much it depended on the neutrality, albeit a hostile neutrality, of the Soviet Union. One might abuse Bolsheviks in public, but they were fair to trade with and they kept their promises. As long as he, Mussolini, limited himself to exchanges of official visits with Hitler—even proclamations of sympathy—the Soviet Union would stay out of the European arena. But as soon as any military alliance of the size and scope of Hitler's proposed Italo-German alliance was signed, Mussolini could see Soviet ambassadors flying off to London, Paris and all corners of the globe, bullying, embarrassing the democracies into some sort of action against the Fascist and Nazi dictators. Mussolini was no fool. Politely, with protestations that the "time was not yet ripe," he turned down Hitler's proposal.

Hitler was shocked, as he later told Ribbentrop. Nobody had

ever turned him down before. His respect and admiration for Mussolini grew like yeast. He even sat quietly while Mussolini lectured him on Czechoslovakia. Mussolini told his guest that he had good reason to believe that Hitler was about to provoke some sort of trouble in Czechoslovakia, probably to espouse the cause of the Sudeten Germans and demand their "return" to the Reich.

Mussolini did not like Czechoslovakia, an artificial creation of the Versailles Conference, at which Italy, like Germany, had been "grievously wronged." It was, he said, "a sausage state," and did not deserve to exist. He could also see Hitler's point about recruiting the Sudeten Germans to the Reich—they were hard working and no doubt anxious to share in the Reich's new prestige, as the Italians in Fiume had done in 1924. But he would have to be very careful. Precipitate action would not do. Britain, France—even the Soviet Union—were smarting from their defeat in Austria, and the accusations of infidelity had started to heap up on their Foreign Ministers' desks. If Hitler humbled the democracies still further too soon, they might snap out of their chronic lethargy and do something. The Northern democracies, according to Mussolini, were dangerous to attack in the spring, when they were full of hope and energy after the long winter hibernation. For many reasons Hitler would be well advised to forget all about "further adventures" until the fall. By that time the British and French should have forgotten all about Austria—the British would be shooting grouse, anyway, the French changing governments, and the Soviet Union bedding down beneath the snow for the winter.[10]

Hitler, disappointed but impressed by Mussolini's firmness, said good-bye to his host and went back home to brood. But, instead of taking Mussolini's advice, he determined to ignore the suggested timetable and strike almost immediately. A provocation could be made in a day. A military campaign should be possible which would be over in four days, too short a time for the Entente or the Soviet Union to react. Complete success would add still further to Hitler's prestige at home and abroad, and most important of all, would show Mussolini how wrong he was to delay signing a Pact of Steel.

On May 12th Konrad Henlein, the pro-Nazi leader of the Sudeten Germans, was briefed by Ribbentrop on his way to state the "Sudeten case" in London. The British Foreign Secretary and his advisers would be told that "the political structure of Czechoslovakia was disintegrating, and that intervention on behalf of such a state would be foolish and ill-advised. Better would be a policy which recognized the mistake of the Versailles Treaty Powers and voluntarily dismembered their artificial creation." Henlein did as he was told. The Foreign Secretary's chief diplomatic adviser, Sir Robert Vansittart, told Henlein that he much appreciated the frankness with which he, Henlein, had stated the case for Sudeten detachment from Czechoslovakia; that it was true that the Czechoslovak state was artificial, and such states were always unstable; that His Majesty's government, nevertheless, would regret any change in the *status quo* which might seem to have been "provoked or contrived."

This was precisely what Mussolini had predicted would be the British attitude, and infuriated Hitler even more when he received Henlein's report. Ribbentrop was told that "Mussolini must be wrong in this case," and was urged to start a "diplomatic offensive" aimed at isolating Czechoslovakia. Ribbentrop began the campaign on May 14th, when the American Ambassador called on him. He said that the Fuehrer was "greatly disturbed" by Czech provocations and felt that the Czech government "would be happy to see a full-scale European crisis develop rather than face the fact that their state was disintegrating under the pressure of national minorities of various sorts." The other ambassadors to Berlin were given the same story. All received it with varying degrees of scepticism.

Impatient and angry, Hitler got in touch with "war staff," O.K.W., and asked for a complete run-down on German and Czech strength and fortifications, with an estimate of the "difficulties." On May 17th he was told that a short war was unlikely, that the Czech fortifications were in good shape and their Regular Army in good heart. Still undeterred, on May 20th Hitler issued a directive on "the smashing of Czechoslovakia by military action," based on a report by Field Marshal Wilhelm Keitel. The report was cautious, the directive optimistic. Both were in the hands of the Italian Secret Service (and of the British, Czech and French) by 10 a.m. the same day—the two documents were generally known to be the "least secret" in Europe. The Czech government, as soon as it read the dispositions for an undated, but apparently imminent, attack, wired its ambassador in Berlin to make a formal protest at "reports of concentrations of German troops in Saxony." The German Ambassador in Prague was also told, by the Czech Foreign Minister, that "there was some perturbation at rumours that German aggression against Czechoslovakia was planned." There were, in fact, twelve divisions ready to march within twelve hours, and three divisions at the alert.

Both the German Foreign Minister and the German Ambassador

gave "firm assurances that no unfriendly act was intended," though it seems certain that neither of them knew what Hitler was up to (the German Ambassador to Prague wired later the same afternoon and asked what *was* going on). The Czech government took the assurances at their face value, nil. An emergency meeting of the Cabinet was called and it was decided to mobilize a part of the reserves immediately—calling up one whole year to the colours and mobilizing all essential technicians.

Hitler was furious, but still not dismayed. It was not until after two days of incessant coming and going by the British and French Ambassadors that Ribbentrop was able to convince him that both Britain and France—and possibly the Soviet Union, which was making uneasy noises—would in fact intervene in any German-Czech war. Ribbentrop offered, as one of his reasons for his conviction, that British Ambassador Sir Nevile Henderson had called twice to see him on Sunday, the 22nd. That same evening two more events occurred which put an end, for the time being, to the Czech crisis and to Hitler's plans for annexation—the Czech Ambassador called and informed Ribbentrop that full mobilization of the Czechoslovakian Armed Forces was being discussed; and Bernardo Attolico, the Italian Ambassador, called to say that the Duce would be phoning at eleven o'clock.

When Mussolini phoned, Hitler sent Ribbentrop and his secretary out of the room. Mussolini spoke in German (afterward Hitler remarked on his pedantic style) and told him that from all accounts he had ignored the advice he had been given in Rome. Well, this was bad. The French were deciding to fight, and he, Mussolini, knew that Hitler had insufficient forces in the West to resist even a moderate French offensive. There was no possibility of an Italian intervention to stalemate the French, as he, Mussolini, had expressed his views quite clearly on the way the Czech matter should be handled. The British Ambassador had told him that Britain would almost certainly join France against Germany, and there were rumours that Poland and Hungary would maintain, at best, a hostile neutrality. He, Mussolini, had considerable influence with the Fascist government of Horthy in Budapest and with the government of Colonel Józef Beck in Warsaw, but he would be reluctant to use it. Lastly, he had a copy of Hitler's directive against Czechoslovakia, and he had been advised that it was militarily unsound. Hitler, though almost speechless with fury and frustration, could only answer: "Yes, Duce." After a sleepless night he called off his plans and told Ribbentrop to inform the Czech Ambassador that reports of German troop concentrations and aggression w'ere "libellous and completely without foundation in fact."

The May Crisis, as it was called, still further reinforced Mussolini's prestige and influence with Hitler. The British, French and Czech secret services (which all had a sort of clearing house for information in Switzerland) made it known to their governments that it was the completeness of the Italian knowledge of Hitler's plans which had enabled Mussolini to put an end to the crisis. It was also hinted that the first warning to the Czechs had actually come from the Italian Ambassador in Prague, and that the Czech President was "affectionately grateful."

The British government, realizing that an Italo-Czech alliance—in abrogation of the Franco-Czech alliance—would strengthen Mussolini's Danube Axis too much for comfort, determined to "take action." Further friendly overtures would be made to Mussolini, talks about the precise date of the initialling of the Anglo-Italian agreement restarted, and it would be seen how the situation developed. The British Ambassador made it quite plain that nothing but good could come of a closer tie between Britain and Italy. Anything which helped to detach Mussolini from Hitler and prevent the conversion of the diplomatic Axis—in which Italy was the senior and more experienced partner—into a military alliance, in which she would be the weaker and less influential, was done.

It has been said that a really decisive effort by Britain in June and July 1938 might well have succeeded in detaching Mussolini from Hitler altogether. Giuseppe Bottai, back in favour again, was sent to the centenary celebrations of the University of Cologne, as an excuse to have a good look beforehand for the "holes in the German economy." Anti-German feeling around Mussolini increased daily. The King, whose dislike of Hitler had been reinforced during the state visit, and who had a suspicion that Hitler was advocating the conversion of the monarchy into a republic, sent for Mussolini at the beginning of June and had a long talk about "friendship" with him. Bottai says that the King even went so far as to beg Mussolini to "avoid Germany" and to apologize for any "strain which might have appeared in our always good relationships due to jealousy by members of Court of your incomparable success and even of your appointment to be a Field Marshal of the Empire."

Mussolini was certainly impressed, and on June 7th asked Ciano to approach Lord Perth and "speak to him very earnestly about the early coming into force of the Anglo-Italian Agreement of April 16th."[11] Lord Perth passed the message on, with a note to the effect that Mussolini appeared to be sincere, and had certainly done what he had promised to do in Libya and Palestine, "where the grave situation of revolt might have been much worse if Italian activity there had not ceased." Unfortunately, in the meantime, the French government—jealous and intransigent as ever—had got wind of "certain rumours of an undesirable close *rapprochement* between Britain and Fascist Italy," and advised "extreme caution in the cementing of such unlikely friendships." The French government did not openly advocate hostility to Italy, but preferred to suggest "terms" which it knew Mussolini would reject, and so prevent the coming into force of the Anglo-Italian Agreement, much as Hitler liked to have his patience exhausted in other countries. The "terms" the French proposed were all to do with Spain. Mussolini had, in fact, agreed to do his best to bring the war in Spain to a speedy conclusion, but nobody had any doubt that by this he meant a victory for General Franco. Now the French persuaded the British Foreign Office (through Sir Eric Phipps, the anti-Italian, Francophile Ambassador to Paris) that it would be a good idea to "get tough" with Mussolini over Spain.

On June 17th the Foreign Office sent out instructions to Lord Perth. On the 20th he went to see Ciano and reminded him of a statement made at the time of the signing of the agreement, that:

> His Majesty's Government regards the settlement of the Spanish question as a prerequisite of the entry into force of the Agreement between our two countries. . . . The difficulty remains of defining what constitutes a settlement of the Spanish question. British public opinion cannot be ignored. As Count Ciano will be aware, the Agreement was not universally popular at the moment of signature. . . . What we had in mind was that settlement, in the sense of meeting the pledges given, must be something which could be shown to have eliminated or be in process of eliminating the Spanish question as a source of international friction. This might be achieved in one of three ways: (a) by the execution of the Non-Intervention Committee's plan [for a cease fire, withdrawal of foreign volunteers]; (b) by the Italian government at once making a unilateral withdrawal from Spain; (c) bringing about an armistice.

When Mussolini heard Lord Perth read through the proposals drafted by Lord Halifax and inspired by the French, he just laughed. He said he had thought his son-in-law Count Ciano was joking when he told him of these new conditions for the coming into effect of the Anglo-Italian Agreement. He pointed out that this agreement, and the subsequent agreements to which it could lead, was the only guarantee of the elimination of sources of international friction, with Great Britain participating. If, as seemed to be the case, Britain did not want to join with Italy in promoting peace, and preferred her partnership with a decadent and bankrupt France, then this was Britain's right, but it seemed incomprehensible. When Lord Perth demurred and said that the British government was not being difficult, Mussolini commented that: (a) General Franco and the Republicans had both ignored the Non-intervention Committee so far, and seemed likely to go on doing so; (b) the very idea of a unilateral withdrawal from the war by Italy was laughable; and (c) the only people who might welcome an armistice were the Communists bottled up in north-east Spain. Lord Perth ought to take his instructions back to the Foreign Secretary and have them made both realistic and less amusing.

Throughout the rest of June and the first weeks of July Lord Perth had the unenviable task of trying to persuade the Foreign Office to be realistic, or alternatively to persuade Mussolini to be unrealistic. At every move the French government, and sometimes the British Ambassador in Paris, on his own, urged "caution." It is difficult to see what the British government thought it could gain, other than a continuity of tradition, by an alliance with France at the expense of one with Italy. Italy was strong, still solvent, united, respected, and under the direction of a man with a considerable aptitude for both domestic and international politics. Even men who hated Nazi Germany—like Winston Churchill—remained faithful to their early admiration for Fascism and gave credit to Mussolini where credit was due as the only man for whose opinion Hitler cared a straw.

Back on to the shelves in the Foreign Office and the Ministry of Foreign Affairs went the famous agreement.

Ciano and Mussolini decided to make contact with Hitler again and see if Mussolini could find out what his pupil was doing to disturb the peace. A few exchanges of notes between Rome and Berlin and London might bring him to his senses. On July 10th Bottai went to see Mussolini and told him that he had heard in Cologne—where there were still anti-Nazis—that Hitler had fixed the date of October 1st for an invasion of Czechoslovakia. There were hundreds of thousands of Italian workers in Germany, and some 6,500 were in the pay of the Italian Secret Service, most of them in the guise of "correspondents" of their local newspapers. One of them had contacted Bottai and told him that he had heard his employer, an arms manufacturer working on air rifles, say that

Hitler would ruin them all if he went to war before 1939. His German workers were spending their holidays compulsorily reinforcing the defences in the Rhineland, and this could only mean that Hitler was sealing off the West preparatory to a move to the East.

Ciano got in touch with the Italian Ambassador in Berlin and asked him to make discreet inquiries. Attolico came back a week later with a confirmation of both the plan and the date, and an even more interesting piece of news: that while Hitler had been sulking all summer in Berchtesgaden a group of senior army officers, led by General Beck, the Chief of the General Staff, had been preparing a plot against the Nazi Party to go into effect forty-eight hours before the actual advance into Czechoslovakia. The generals were convinced that it was the S.S. and party bosses who were "imprisoning the Fuehrer in crazy schemes."

Mussolini, once he had double confirmation of both the projected invasion and the plot, got in touch with Hitler and told him that he "knew all about Plan Green" (the code name for the Czechoslovakian adventure). Hitler was lost in admiration for the Duce's perspicacity and nearly sacked his own Secret Service Chief, Wilhelm Canaris, on the spot. But Hitler's being lost in admiration, and saying as much, did not stop Mussolini from giving him a long lecture on foreign policy as it should be made. How many more people must know about the plan? Did Hitler know for sure that Britain and France had not already taken counter-precautions? In his recent talks with the British Ambassador he had noticed a hardening of the British attitude . . . had Hitler seen Sir Nevile Henderson lately? What precautions had Hitler taken to avoid a repetition of the May crisis? Had he personally inspected his Western defences, which, according to his information, were being grudgingly repaired by unwilling conscripts? What about Hungary and Poland . . . had Hitler assured himself of their neutrality, or better, collaboration? Lastly, was he sure that the Army, Navy and Luftwaffe was enthusiastic about the venture, especially since there was a possibility that it could lead to a full-scale European war?

Hitler listened patiently. He said he did not think Britain would do much about any invasion, as she was only too anxious to keep the peace at any price. There was "an old fool, Runciman, messing about in the Sudetenland now, who seems to be begging the Czech government to give me all the territory to which we have made claims." And Chamberlain had said repeatedly that, as long as appearances were kept up and a plebiscite taken, he could not see any objection to the separation of the Sudetenland and Czechoslovakia proper. He was not sure about France, but thought it unlikely she would have stable government capable of mobilizing an efficient army. For the rest, Hitler confessed that he had not done much to "eliminate any possibility of interference." He would attend to it. And what did the Duce think of the idea of a "gesture of defiance at the democracies" that autumn?

The Duce said that in principle he would not move a yard to save Czechoslovakia—except in a case in which he felt war was threatened and might involve Italy. In the last analysis, said the Duce, Italy would fight side by side with her German sister, but there must be no last analysis. He urged Hitler to make great efforts to find out the state of opinion in Hungary and Poland and see closely to his war machine.

Hitler did as Mussolini suggested. He opened negotiations with the Polish and Hungarian governments and found them both anxious to share in any future dismembering of Czechoslovakia, though hostile to the idea of Hitler grabbing it all. Hitler conferred with Admiral Horthy on August 23rd, and Attolico—also a guest on board the *Patria* in Kiel Harbour—reported to Mussolini that Hungary was "safe." Colonel Beck, the Polish Foreign Minister, told the Italian Ambassador that Poland would be satisfied with the "return to Poland of her brothers in Teschen," and would on no account allow Soviet troops to pass through Poland to come to the aid of Czechoslovakia. Mussolini passed on the good news.

On August 26th Hitler went off to tour his Western fortifications and found that the Duce had been right to doubt their strength. He ordered Dr. Todt and General Adam, the engineer and general in command, to "make this Western Wall into a real Wall, and let the men know that who does not hold the wall is a *hundsfott*."

Hitler forgot about the Duce's hint that there were plots afoot, and ordered his generals to make ready readier.

On September 1st Hitler phoned Mussolini and said that the Duce could put his mind at rest, as "all the arrangements had been made." Mussolini and Ciano, confident that at least the most essential diplomatic steps had been taken to avoid a war, put aside the "Czech dossier" for the moment. About the generals' plot they said nothing. Attolico had reported that on August 18th General Beck, the leader of the plotters, had resigned as Chief of the General Staff. This probably meant that all had been discovered, and the fact that Beck's resignation had not been made public probably meant that he had not long to live.

While Hitler had been plugging the gaps in his master plan Green, Mussolini had been making a further effort to awaken Lord Perth and the British Foreign Office to the "realities." He now had the Czech business in reserve, as a bargaining counter—he was sure the British government did not have the detailed knowledge of the plan which had come into his possession (he was wrong, every secret service seems to have had copies of master plan Green, but not to have acted on it). The day after Hitler's phone call, on September 2nd, Ciano called in Lord Perth again and said that the Duce was prepared to make another gesture of goodwill to show the British government, and especially this British public opinion he was so worried about, that Italy meant what she said when she promised to solve the problems of today and forget the misunderstandings of yesterday. What was the thing which worried British public opinion most? The treatment of the Jews by Hitler. Well, now, the Duce was prepared to help here. As the British government knew, he had been in touch with Zionist leaders for some time, and had at one time thought of forcing the British out of Palestine to accommodate them.[12] But, with the possibility of a new era of Anglo-Italian relations ahead, he had abandoned this plan, as the British government had conceded, and had ceased to make trouble in the Near East. On November 2, 1937, said Count Ciano, "the Duce had asked the Honourable Vincenzo Tecchio to make further inquiries about the possibility of a home for the Jews, and Tecchio had discussed with him a most interesting idea—that of establishing the Jews in the empty spaces of Ethiopia and Italian East Africa. The Duce had conferred with officials of the German Racial Affairs Office (June 2, 1938) and the Honourable Farinacci had had long talks with them too. The Fuehrer was not yet convinced that this was not too humane a treatment for Jews, for whom he seemed to have a particular aversion, but the Duce felt he could persuade him. As Lord Perth must know, he had (August 3, 1938) brought his racial policies into line with the Fuehrer's, not because he intended to persecute Jews, but so that he could better arrange for their removal from places where they caused friction."

The British government was horrified. It had always made noises of extreme disapproval about Hitler's persecution of the Jews, even though many of its members shared the feeling of mild, passive anti-Semitism, characteristic of the British ruling class. In principle, it was anxious to help the Jews. It was not willing to hand over Palestine to them, and thereby upset all its friendly relations with the Arabs. And this idea of Mussolini's was unthinkable. It was bad enough being forced to recognise what he pleased to call his Empire, and to have an Italian colony on the frontier with Kenya. To have the colony strengthened beyond all belief and measure by the immigration of millions of Jews was the most dangerous idea it had heard of for a long time. Jews worked hard. They would obviously-be prepared to work twice as hard in Ethiopia to escape from European persecution. Mussolini would find himself as prosperous and powerful as England had become in the days when she granted asylum to Huguenot and other Protestant refugees.

Silvio Maurano accused Anthony Eden of having been the man to reject this solution of the Jewish "problem." He writes: "A great deal of glory would have accrued to Fascism for having carried across the Red Sea, even if in the opposite direction, the Chosen People Moses once led away from a similar persecution. But the policies of Eden unfortunately had a disastrous effect and pushed Italy in the direction . . . of the insane German racial policy in all its aspects." [13]

Whoever was responsible for the rejection of Mussolini's goodwill offer condemned Italian Jews, at least to discrimination, though not to active persecution. There were no gas ovens or mass-murder camps in Fascist Italy. It was in fact Fascist Italy which suffered by its race laws, impoverishing its universities (to Bottai's anger) of the physicists Fermi, Rossi, Racah, Pincherle, Pontecorvo and Debenedetti; the surgeon Donati; the mathematicians Volterra, Levi-Cibita, Enriquez, Castelnuovo, Fubini, Fano and the physiologists Ascolo and Herlitska.

Even more unfortunate was the effect the race laws had on men like Farinacci, who became more bestially German with every imitation of Hitler's excesses, even though their anti-Jewishness was confined mostly to words.

Having had his solution to the Jewish problem rejected, Mussolini restarted anti-British propaganda from Bari, and ordered his agents to restart the routine dynamiting of public works that he had promised the Zionists. When King Boris of Bulgaria passed through Rome on his way to London, Mussolini made another gesture of "immense goodwill," handing Boris a letter for Lord Halifax (which he lost) and giving him a message for Chamberlain (which he delivered). [14]

Neither Chamberlain nor Halifax paid much attention to King Boris when he passed on the message, probably because the occasion was after a good dinner, on September 6, 1938. The following morning, however, Chamberlain phoned Halifax and suggested that he get Sir Alexander Cadogan to go around and see King Boris and ask him if he would mind repeating the message. King Boris, a little startled by this super-Balkan way of conducting foreign relationships, agreed. On September 7th Sir Alexander Cadogan deposited a memorandum at the Foreign Office which was, as Mussolini had said, a message of something approaching goodwill, certainly an offer not to be treated in cavalier fashion as an after-dinner joke. King Boris told Cadogan that Mussolini was very anxious to secure the friendship of Great Britain. He was, however, afraid that a continuance of the present state of affairs (unreasonable delay in signing the agreement's protocols, submission to French pressure) might be dangerous; long engagements sometimes did not result in marriage. Signor Mussolini had done everything in his power . . . he had withdrawn troops from Libya, he had checked the Bari broadcasts, he had stopped propaganda in the Near and Middle East. He was now in the process of arranging for the withdrawal of Italian infantry from Spain.

This goodwill offer of Mussolini's ought to have convinced the Foreign Office that he really meant what he said when he offered Great Britain a closer alliance, an alliance which might have saved the peace. He was prepared to overlook the "sanctions" affair, because Eden had been driven out of office and the British Government could not be held responsible for all its ex-Foreign Ministers. He was even prepared to gloss over Britain's humiliation when the "sanctions" were found to be ineffective (as years later Eden's "sanctions" and punitive expedition against Nasser in Egypt were to be ineffective). Either Britain really wanted a stable Europe, or she did not. The most disturbing element in Europe was Hitler, and both the French and British ambassadors in Berlin must have told the Foreign Office that Mussolini—Italian friendship—was the only possible check on Hitler.

But the Foreign Office was still not willing to make the necessary move. Chamberlain and Halifax still cherished a belief that they could find a *modus vivendi* with Hitler by themselves. They were sensible to French anti-Italian hysteria, and they had all the Englishman's suspicion and contempt for Italians, "a people picturesque but spineless." In all the diaries published after 1945—and nearly everybody in Europe seems to have kept a diary at the time, though it is odd that none of them fell into the hands of the various intelligence services—blind faith in the past seems to have blotted out any ability to appraise the present. If Hitler, in his dealings with every other politician in Europe but Mussolini and Churchill, acquired the reputation of a genius, this was almost certainly because the competition was something less than mediocre. As Mussolini said: "The great weakness of the democracies is that in time of peace they are stagnant, and like stagnant ponds, the political scum rises to the top. Only war restores their dynamic and carries the scum away to retirement."

Rebuffed, Mussolini decided to "let the democracies stew in the pot" for a while. He told Ciano that he was convinced that before the year's end they would come crawling to Rome for help and advice. On September 7th the Germans in Sudetenland had broken off all relations and discussions with the Czech government—Attolico, from Berlin, told Ciano that this meant that Hitler intended to annex the whole of Czechoslovakia; that the pretext of "saving the Sudeten Germans from Czech persecution" had been abandoned. On September 10th Goering made a speech at a Nazi party Nuremberg rally in which he referred to the Czechs as a "miserable pygmy race oppressing a cultured people," and added that "behind it is Moscow and the eternal Mask of the Jew devil." [15]

On September 11th Attolico phoned to say that he had more confirmation that Hitler intended to invade Czechoslovakia on October 1st, with or without a pretext, with or without a belt of neutrals around him. Ciano was all for getting in touch with Hitler and telling him to "exercise caution and bear in mind the Duce's warning that another May Crisis might be fatal," but Mussolini believed that there was no immediate hurry. If Hitler had fixed October 1st as the date for invasion, he felt that nothing would make him change the date. "The Germans have a weakness in their lack of flexibility which is most apparent in their diplomacy. This is often the reason why they abandon diplomacy for war." As far as Mussolini was concerned, it would do Britain and France a world of good to sweat for a week or two. Then there was, according to Attolico, another plot in the offing ("Galeazzo, is Attolico still sound in the head?"), and this might make both diplomacy and war unnecessary. Mussolini set to work to compose an article, "Letter to Runciman," for publication in *il Popolo d'Italia* on the day after Hitler's speech on September 12th.

Hitler's speech was much as might have been expected. He was violent, abusive, eloquent and occasionally hysterical. His violence and hysteria were matched by that of his audience. He cursed the Czechs and the Czech President Beneš, and all their friends and allies. He demanded "justice" for the Sudeten Germans and said that it seemed as if Germany would have to see to it that justice was done.

There was a violent reaction in Sudetenland, where the local Nazis set out on an orgy of plunder and riot. There was a sharp reaction in Prague, where the government declared martial law. In Paris an emergency meeting of the Cabinet was called, and lasted all day. In London, Moscow and Washington, there was "some alarm." It was eventually French Prime Minister Daladier who woke the democracies out of their quiet alarm. He brought the Cabinet meeting to an end and sent for the British Ambassador, Sir Eric Phipps. For a time Sir Eric was not available, then was traced to the Opéra-Comique. Once found, he was urged by Daladier, in the strongest terms, to try to make a deal with Hitler and prevent the war in which France, as Czechoslovakia's ally and guarantor, would be committed.

At 11 p.m. on the evening of the 13th Chamberlain sent a message to Hitler almost begging to be received: "I propose to come across by air [he had never flown before] and am ready to start tomorrow."

Mussolini phoned the editorial offices of *il Popolo d'Italia* and told them to hold over his peacemaking article until they knew what Hitler's reply would be. Ribbentrop called Ciano and told him, unnecessarily, that Chamberlain wanted to come to see Hitler and that he believed the British Prime Minister was willing to make any concession to avoid going to war. He told Ciano that Hitler wanted very much to show a "united front" to the democracies and wanted to "destroy any illusions that the Fuehrer has not been in close consultation with the Duce in this matter." Ciano told him that he would consult Mussolini, who would issue no statement, but would publish a leader in *il Popolo d'Italia* which could be taken as a summary of his views. Hitler would find it identical to views the Duce had already expressed.

On the 14th Ciano and Mussolini considered their policy. It was quite obvious to them that Hitler had long since decided not to be content with the annexation of Sudetenland, but was determined to destroy Czechoslovakia. The Nazi Party newspapers were full of talk about the Fuehrer in the full flower of his manhood, leading the Reich to great victories. Mussolini had never held any brief for Czechoslovakia and was not prepared to guarantee its survival, especially as it persisted in its useless alliance with an emasculated France. But he was determined to avoid war. Italy was not prepared for a European war, had just enough in the way of men and war materials to finish off the war in Spain and cope with "incidental events" in the Mediterranean (i.e., expand as far as she could along the Mediterranean coast, north and south, without becoming involved in a major war).

Mussolini told Ciano that he was going to insist that Hitler preserve the diplomatic niceties. There must be a plebiscite in Sudetenland, which would result in a victory for the pro-Nazis. There must be no invasions. This must be the Reich's public policy. Hitler could go on rattling swords as loud as he liked, and there was a chance that Britain and France would capitulate and give him all he wanted without a fight. What Hitler should aim for was the end of the viability of Czechoslovakia as a state, then it would disappear by attrition. On the morning of September 15th the *Popolo d'Italia* came out with Mussolini's article revised, minus his signature, stating "Italy's Views" along these lines.

When Hitler read a translation of the leader, he was not pleased. In his own mind he had gone far beyond plebiscites. Czechoslovakia had already disappeared, and he was tentatively stepping out in Polish territory. But he realized that if this was Mussolini's limit then he would have to conform. He appreciated the hint in the article that sharp words and sabre rattling might produce a capitulation which would make a military campaign unnecessary. His generals would be pleased to hear this.

While Chamberlain was airborne on his way to Munich for Berchtesgaden, telegrams were on their way to German embassies abroad outlining Hitler's policy in full for the first time. Runciman in Czechoslovakia had already been informed by the Italian Ambassador that he was wasting his time "testing public opinion" in Sudetenland, that an *Anschluss* with Germany was inevitable. By the time Chamberlain left his plane and boarded the train for Berchtesgaden everybody but he knew exactly what the position was and what Hitler's minimum terms would be. All that was left for the British Prime Minister to do was to have tea, listen to a monologue from Hitler, then go home.

That evening the German Foreign Office wired all embassies that everything had gone according to plan, Chamberlain had agreed to the cession of Sudetenland, and was consulting his Cabinet about the best way to break the news. Ribbentrop told Ciano that Hitler had done as Mussolini wished, but still felt that Czechoslovakia was an anomaly. Having reached agreement thus far, would Mussolini object to a dismemberment of Czechoslovakia if it was done peacefully? Mussolini, who doubted the Fuehrer's ability to handle negotiations when they reached the stage of extreme delicacy, said, when consulted, that he had no objections whatsoever, but the Fuehrer was to keep him well informed. As he had said, attrition was better than invasion in the case of the "sausage state." Mussolini's ambassadors in Warsaw and Budapest reported that apparently Ribbentrop was taking the Duce's advice and making a serious attempt to guarantee Polish and Hungarian neutrality. He was offering them bits of Czechoslovakia as a bribe, and they seemed likely to accept. There was a general agreement that on September 20th the Poles, Hungarians and various other Czech minorities (principally the Slovaks) should make demands on the Czech government.

On the 20th, as the Czech Foreign Minister said, "a queue of false creditors presented themselves to the Czech State demanding its winding up as a going concern and sale by auction." The Poles were the most diplomatic—they presented an informal demand for the Teschen area, which they followed up with an "account rendered" next day. The British and French were neither diplomatic nor tactful. They stated bluntly that all the various demands, Slovak, Sudeten, German, Polish and Hungarian, must be met, and added insult to injury by warning Czech President Beneš against "aggression!"

Throughout September 21st Europe worked happily toward Czechoslovakia's demise. The Czech press launched an all-out attack on Mussolini as the author of her crisis, which he was not, and so robbed themselves of any possibility of salvation. The Poles and Hungarians were "firm." The Slovaks and Sudetens were noisy. The French double-crossed everybody, refusing to stand by their treaty, threatening isolation, then joining in the abuse of Mussolini and avowing every sort of alliance with the Czechs, finally exhausting themselves with an endorsement of the British note. The British note said quite simply that the Czechs had no alternative but to capitulate.

On September 22nd the Czech government both capitulated and resigned.

It seems that Ribbentrop phoned Ciano late on the 22nd to tell him that Chamberlain had arrived back in Germany and was talking to the Fuehrer at Godesberg. Ciano was told that the Fuehrer was going to get all he wanted without a fight, and was "immensely grateful" to the Duce for his constant advice. Having delivered himself of this lie, Ribbentrop hung up. For the next few days, incredible though it seems in retrospect, Mussolini forgot about the world and busied himself with writing past history. Pini, his editor at *il Popolo d'Italia*, was kept hard at work preparing the copy for a special edition to commemorate—on October 28th—the anniversary of the march on Rome. There were to be some changes made in the "generally accepted story." There had to be a sharp revision of the list of those present on October 16, 1922, in Milan when the march was discussed, and an even sharper revision of the attendance list for Naples a few days later. Marshals de Bono and Balbo were quarrelling about this (Pini was eventually forced to publish what was virtually disclaimed by de Bono, on the front page, with the implication that de Bono knew history was being rewritten and did not like it). Most important of all, Mussolini had now decided that he had wanted the march on Rome from the beginning, had not tried to do it without force—for fear of his colleagues' ascendancy over the movement—and had been the moving spirit of the whole adventure. Pini was to do his best to show the whole business in this light. And he was to be sure to phone the Duce and let him know how sales were going and whether they managed to get their special editions on sale before the *Corriere della Sera*.

As newspaper proprietor Mussolini fussed about his special editions, circulation figures, and image for posterity (Pini at one stage was ordered to write a full-length "official biography" for March 1939), the world went happily on along the road to war. Chamberlain's talks with Hitler on September 23rd went unnoticed. Hitler's ultimatum to Chamberlain—that by October 1st all the German-speaking and other mixed areas of Czechoslovakia must be ceded to Germany and her allies—lay without comment under the revolver Mussolini was using as a paperweight.

The Duce was brought sharply back to Europe by two documents delivered in person by Ciano. The first was a lengthy telegram from the Italian Embassy in Prague, to the effect that, incredibly, the Czech government had rejected Hitler's ultimatum, showing the first spark of independence since May. It must mean, said Ciano, that the Czechs had found last-minute allies, that perhaps Poland had agreed to allow Soviet troops to come to her aid. Whatever the reason, the Godesberg proposals, agreed by France, Britain and all the other undertakers, had been rejected by the corpse. This was, Mussolini commented, "a very sad state of affairs." Ciano's second document was a letter from Churchill. To all intents and purposes it was the same in content as the one Attolico had reported sent to the "conspirators against the Nazi Party," in whom Mussolini had been reluctant to believe. It was brief and to the point: "Should the frontiers of Czechoslovakia be crossed by German armies or planes in force, then I am sure that this will bring about a renewal of the World War. Britain will march side by side with France, and Europe may perish in the holocaust. Do not, I beg you, be misled on this point by the words or deeds of men who in the last analysis do not speak for their fellow countrymen." [16]

Churchill's letter had what Navarra describes as "an electric effect" on Mussolini. Hitler had deceived him. The democracies were arming. Poland and Hungary had betrayed them. Soon the vicious French would be pouring over the Alps and the tide of Bolshevism would flow up the Adriatic. Disaster. On the evening of the 25th Mussolini called Pini and told him to hold the paper until he had confirmation of the gravity of the situation. The confirmation was soon forthcoming. From London came the news that the French and British cabinets were meeting in the British capital.

On September 26th Mussolini issued a secret mobilization order. This produced consternation in the General Staff of both the militia and the regular forces, who were well aware of the difficulties Italy would find in sustaining a long European war. It caused even greater consternation among those like Bottai and the Under-Secretary for Corporations, Del Giudice, who saw in such a war a destruction of all that was positive in the régime: the roads, railways, aqueducts, flats and houses, seaside homes for children, hospitals and schools, the drained marshes and the dry but warm friendship of the Vatican. It was not possible to approach the Duce directly and tell him he was making a fool of himself with his talk of a new, glorious Europe rising from the ashes of the old (his speech in Venice). But it was made clear to him by the obviously pacifist crowds which greeted him on his whistle-stop tour of the North-East. Italy and the Italians wanted peace. Mussolini had built a new Italy, largely by giving Italy and the Italians what they wanted, either consciously or subconsciously. He hesitated, then decided to act.

Before he made a single diplomatic move, Mussolini called together his General Staff, most of whom were on tour with him, and cancelled the general mobilization order. Ten thousand troops were to be concentrated at Catalayud, in Spain, ready for trans-shipment to Italy, and as soon as they could be brought to the peninsula they were to be rushed to the north. Five divisions were to be mobilized, in the interim, and moved quietly up to the Brenner Pass. Then the Duce called Ciano to him and told him that he was going to repeat his "salvation of Austria," but with modifications. He had no intention of alienating Hitler's sympathies for good, by fighting to save a state whose existence was not viable. But he did intend to show Hitler that he would not tolerate action by the Reich without consulting its Axis partner. There had to be no doubt in the mind of the world who was master and who was pupil.

In Britain and France, meanwhile, tension had grown almost to breaking point. The Royal Navy had been mobilized, and the French had rushed thousands of young men to arms. In the opinion of the German Army and Navy chiefs, there would be 65 French divisions on the Western front within a week (to face 12 German divisions), and a complete blockade of the North Sea by the British Fleet (with reserve units steaming up the Channel). Chamberlain and Daladier were still anxious for peace at almost any price, but they were afraid there was no alternative to war. Sir Horace Wilson, the Prime Minister's special envoy, had reported on the evening of the 26th that Hitler was determined to go ahead with an invasion of Czechoslovakia unless the Czechs capitulated. Even the open-handed Runciman had been forced to admit that the Czechs would not do this—would not sharpen the knife that Britain and France were hoping to use to cut her throat.

But Mussolini and his generals had been working hard. By midnight on the 26th the divisions were in position along the Brenner. The Italian ambassadors in Bucharest and Belgrade had consulted the Rumanian and Yugoslav governments and urged them to make it clear to Hitler that they would not tolerate any aggrandizement of their neighbour Hungary. Italy would support them, they were told. In Stockholm the Italian Ambassador talked peace in such terms that the King of Sweden was impressed with his sincerity.

By the morning of September 27, 1938, when Hitler was supposed to receive Sir Horace Wilson and French Ambassador François-Poncet, to receive their "final answer" to his ultimatum (and, he hoped vainly, bring him more concessions), Mussolini had the Reich surrounded. Hitler first learned of this when the reports began to arrive of frenzied activity on his frontiers. The military attaché in Paris confirmed the French mobilization and said that not only had the Duce not "seized the nature of the situation"[17] and strengthened his garrisons on the French frontier (to prevent any French flanking movement through Northern Italy to the Brenner), he had weakened his garrisons on the Alps and blocked the Brenner himself. The British Fleet had steam up, and the ambassador in London reported a "hardening of public opinion." The ambassadors in Bucharest and Belgrade reported the "strange attitude" of their governments, and the ambassador in Budapest reported that the

Hungarians could not now be relied on. At 10 a.m., according to Goering, Hitler had to be forcibly restrained from jumping up and down on the table with fury at the perfidy of his "friend and master." But there was nothing to be done. At 11.30 Hitler decided to have one last try to get all he wanted by bullying Britain and France. He sent for the French Ambassador, François-Poncet, who told Sir Eric Phipps, the British Ambassador in Paris, exactly what happened at the interview. Phipps wrote to Lord Halifax:

> On arrival at the *Reichskanzlei*, he [François-Poncet] did not find a hostile atmosphere. Goering and Neurath issued from Hitler's room as François-Poncet entered; their greeting was friendly. . . . Only Ribbentrop was present, more offensive and odious than ever. Hitler began by shouting and ranting. Ribbentrop, far from seeking to calm him down, seemed to wish to egg him on. François-Poncet brought with him a map, showing in vivid colours the enormous concessions that were being made to the Germans. He in his turn loudly proclaimed that Hitler would go down in history as a monster if he started a general war in order to take by force in a day 100 per cent when peace would give him 90 per cent in ten days. He reasoned with Hitler, cajoled him and pleaded with him; but he made only little impression. Then, suddenly, Hitler was summoned to the telephone in another room. . . . In less than a quarter of an hour Hitler returned in a chastened mood, said he had been rung up by Mussolini . . . On his way, François-Poncet saw a table laid for about 40 people . . . the officers the Fuehrer was going to entertain before they left for the Czech Front . . .

Throughout the rest of the 27th Hitler sulked. He was rude to Sir Horace Wilson, but the violence was gone. The King of Sweden, Germany's old admirer, and President Roosevelt ("the old fool") sent messages to him urging moderation—messages which he believed, were inspired by Mussolini. He tried to talk to his "friend and master", but the Duce was not available. He was speechmaking, peacemaking, "troublemaking." By dinnertime Hitler realised that he was beaten. At 10.30 p.m. he sent a letter, by wire, to Chamberlain, hinting that a further conversation *à deux* might yet save the peace. To this Chamberlain replied immediately: "I am ready to come to Berlin at once . . ."

When Mussolini heard, on the morning of September 28th, that Hitler and Chamberlain planned to meet again, he was dumbfounded. When Attolico phoned from Berlin to say he was disappointed to hear of the meeting, because the conspirators against Hitler, led by General Halder, planned to make a Putsch that day, the Duce was livid. He shouted at Ciano: "That old fool Chamberlain is going to spoil everything. Hitler is going to spoil everything. They think they can do without me!" He added that Attolico was obviously off his head and ought to be brought home for a rest. Then Mussolini called back Attolico and told him to go to see Hitler immediately. He was to tell him that Lord Perth, the British Ambassador to Rome, had asked him, on behalf of the British government, to mediate in the Sudeten question. He had decided that the only way to settle the business was to hold a four-power conference (the first summit meeting?) under his, Mussolini's, chairmanship. It could be held at Munich, the nearest suitable place to Italy. France, Britain and Germany, under his chairmanship, would reach agreement. There was to be no tête-à-tête between Hitler and Chamberlain, or he—the Duce—would consider himself betrayed, abrogate both the Anglo-Italian Agreement (not yet brought into being) and the Axis agreement (unwritten), and make his own policies for Europe in concert with his allies and dependants.

There was nothing Hitler could do, again. He had been looking forward to bullying Chamberlain, but it was not to be. The Duce had won. He would get his Sudetenland and more, this he did not doubt, but the supreme pleasure of a triumphal drive to Prague—or, even better, a successful military adventure—would be denied him. After lunch Hitler sent a message to Chamberlain, outlining the Duce's proposals, saving his own face in the text as far as he could. Chamberlain had been speaking to a crowded House for over an hour when the message arrived. He had been speaking of the horrors of war, of the precipice on the edge of which the world stood, repeating his stupefaction that British lives could be lost in defence of Czech acres. He had noted with satisfaction Mussolini's intervention of the 27th, which had postponed German mobilization—the situation was grave, uncertain, but could be worse. When he unfolded Hitler's message and said: "I have now been informed by Herr Hitler that he invites me to meet him at Munich tomorrow morning . . ." the House of Commons was a cameo of the world's relief. M.P.s went mad with the sudden relaxing of tension. One man even said: "Thank God for the Prime Minister." [18]

In Berlin they were cursing Mussolini. In Paris there were sighs of relief and talks of some action in the near future to conclude an alliance with Germany which would deprive Mussolini of these conceited pleasures as peacemaker. In most of the other government headquarters of Europe and America the relief, if not as hysterical at that in the House of Commons, manifested itself in shouts of "Good old Mussolini!"

For Mussolini it was his greatest triumph amid a day of triumphs. The embassies all congratulated him. General Franco sent him a message of gratitude; told him that the war in Spain, thanks to him, was nearly over, and he could take away his troops who had "fought so valiantly"—thus enabling Mussolini to carry out his plan of reinforcing home garrisons without seeming to withdraw from a theatre of war. Crowds in all the big cities of Italy thanked God for the Duce, and the Vatican offered up prayers for his continued prosperity. Perhaps just as important to Mussolini was the date of this latest triumph, September 28th—a month from the official anniversary of the march on Rome. He had saved Italy from chaos and Bolshevism, without firing too many shots in anger. He had saved Europe from war and Bolshevism by a flick of a telephone switch and a flutter of inexpensive telegrams. Perhaps he was, as he had said himself, "one of the most intelligent animals to appear on the surface of the earth."

The only fly in the Duce's ointment was Attolico, who kept phoning about plots.

On the afternoon of the 28th Mussolini boarded the train which was to take him to Munich. Filippo Anfuso, Ciano's private secretary, writes that: "In the eyes of the authorities who had come to see him off there was an eloquent emotion . . . (which seemed to say) Courage! Bring us back peace and we'll all be with you. Don't let that madman work on you!" [19]

In Nazi Germany the discomfited Fuehrer was telling his intimates that he had better go at least as far as the Italian frontier to meet the Duce, that he must try to win his friendship again before this "stupid conference" started. But he was afraid that the Duce would have his way. It only remained to see what that way would be.

The Fuehrer, with Ribbentrop, Keitel and Himmler, was waiting at Rosenheim on the frontier, with his own private train warmed to welcome the Duce. According to Anfuso, who was with them, Czechoslovakia was not mentioned on the journey to Munich. The Fuehrer, desperately anxious to reassure Mussolini of his "cold intelligence," talked of other countries, of the countries over which one day might be fought the inevitable war with the democracies. He tried to impress Mussolini with his strength (his first words were "I have finished the Siegfried Line"). But Mussolini made no comments. He sat, silent, magisterial as a Buddha, and said nothing. Anfuso believed that this was because he had not come with a bulging brief-case to the Munich conference, and disliked impromptu discussions at this level when his reputation was at stake. Mussolini was silent, even morose, when they were joined by Chamberlain and Daladier and the conference opened. Chamberlain reported that he had tried to make polite conversation (literally, "Do you like fishing?"), but the Duce refused to gossip.

Nobody at the Munich conference took any notice of Daladier, who was plotting away in his own small head, looking for a way to make a private peace with Hitler. The Fuehrer made a short speech. Chamberlain mumbled. Then Mussolini, for whom they had all been waiting, outlined the "compromise" he had sketched in his *Popolo d'Italia* article two weeks before.[20] It was, in fact, the only solution he would accept. Hitler knew all about the "compromise" —he had read it in a press digest, and it had been discussed at length with Attolico, who had verified the accuracy of the translation and made some comments on the Duce's general attitude to the Czechs. Years later, survivors of the Reich claimed that this "compromise" was their own, that it represented merely a modification of the Godesberg proposals made by Hitler himself, and that Goering, Neurath and Baron Ernst von Weizsaeker had drafted it in Berlin before leaving for Munich. Hitler's interpreter was, in particular, guilty of a deliberate falsification of fact here, as was Theoder Kordt before a Nuremberg tribunal (the Fourth tribunal in 1948, at which Germans were being encouraged to stand up for their rights and become allies against the Soviet Union). Even Shirer (*Rise and Fall of the Third Reich*), whose whole Munich analysis is violently discriminatory against Mussolini, follows the Germans, instead of that of the text, forgetting that the Godesberg proposals, which the "compromise" resembled in part, were themselves based on the Duce's article in *il Popolo d'Italia.* The Germans, of course, were not alone in claiming credit for the "solution to the Czech problem." Chamberlain claimed it was along the lines of a proposal of his own; Sir Nevile Henderson thought it was a combination of the Anglo-French and Hitler proposals; François-Poncet opined that it was based on a memorandum by Sir Horace Wilson. In fact, Mussolini, who could follow the talk in English and French, led the discussion from the start and took agreement for granted.

At 1 a.m. the Munich Agreement was signed (September 30th), and half an hour later the Czechs were informed that the Germans would begin the occupation of Sudetenland by October 1st and complete it by October 10th. After examining the joint declaration to be made by Chamberlain and Hitler, the Duce took the Fuehrer off for a private talk, like an industrial peacemaker berating an incompetent plant manager who had nearly precipitated a strike.

To Chamberlain, Munich was: "Peace with honour . . . peace in our time."

For Churchill it was: "A total, unmitigated defeat."

The Czech Premier, in a broadcast, said: "We were abandoned, we stand alone."

The French government was already drafting a joint Franco-German declaration for submission to the Fuehrer.

Hitler was subdued.

The Poles and Hungarians swooped down on the now defenceless Czechoslovakia (the cession of Sudetenland had deprived the country of both its natural and artificial defences), and took their share of the plunder.

Mussolini was tired. If 1936 had marked the zenith of his popularity at home, then October 1, 1938, certainly marked its zenith abroad, but the "ever-youthful Duce" was ageing. Everything that was happening in his life after Munich, was, in a sense, an anti-climax. He no longer trusted anybody, perhaps not even his own judgment, which was all he had ever had to rely on. He told Ciano that before the year was over Italy's destiny would be decided.

Ciano knew very well what that meant. Either they had to conclude some sort of definite alliance with Britain and France, or throw in their lot once and for all with Germany, and no longer play the rôle of peacemaker in Europe.

The month of October was spent trying to save Italy from the Axis she had invented. As French Ambassador François-Poncet said: "I do not believe that any secret military convention yet binds Italy to Germany, but if we let more than about three months elapse without a general settlement, one may materialize. I believe that Mussolini would welcome an understanding with Britain and France which would render him less dependent, in the long run, on the only alternative—Hitler." [21] This was a precise and accurate estimate of Mussolini's intentions. Though François-Poncet was transferred from Berlin to Rome at the end of October, presumably to try to make such an understanding possible, his government and the British government sabotaged his work from the start—more by incompetence than by bad faith—and in the end Mussolini was driven into Hitler's arms, into an embrace from which he never freed himself.

A glance at British Foreign Policy documents for October 1938 shows the extent to which stupidity and bureaucracy triumphed over reason. The British government knew very well how much it owed the peace to Mussolini. On October 1st both the British and French governments were cabling him not to abandon the field, but to intervene on the Polish-Czech frontier where the land-grab was assuming alarming proportions.[22] In spite of his dislike of the Czechs, Mussolini was prepared to go to the length of guaranteeing the rump state, in return for an alliance with Britain and France; and Frantisek Chvalkovsky, the Czech Minister for Foreign Affairs, said as much to Lord Perth on October 5th. The French poured cold water on this question. They had done nothing to save Czechoslovakia, but they were not going to have Mussolini filling their gap. Chamberlain said, in the House of Commons, that in his opinion: "Europe and the world ought to be grateful to the head of the Italian government for his work—certainly notable and perhaps decisive—in contributing to a peaceful solution." But nothing was done to implement immediately the Anglo-Italian Agreement of April 16th. The progress of this agreement is an interesting lesson in bureaucracy.

The Anglo-Italian Agreement, which, had it been brought into operation, might really have contributed to a lasting peace in Europe, was in the same condition on October 3rd as it had been on the day of signing, five and a half months previously. In a cable to Lord Halifax on October 3rd, Lord Perth said that Ciano had been to see him to say as much. All the conditions had been fulfilled on the Italian side—10,000 Italian troops were even on their way home from Spain, as a special concession. Lord Perth repeated Ciano's warning that, if the British government did not make a move soon, at least to show goodwill—the agreement would lapse. The Grand Council was to meet on October 6th–9th; could Ciano have an answer by then? Twice on October 4th Lord Perth repeated this warning, adding on his own account that he believed that, once implemented, Mussolini would work for a relaxing of European tensions and general pacification.

On October 5th Ciano added that Mussolini was prepared to give an additional guarantee that no further troops would be sent to Spain to replace those now withdrawing. On the same day an almost incredible reply arrived from Lord Halifax, that, though he and Chamberlain were personally favourable to early action, "Parliament is now entirely occupied with discussion of the Munich agreement and adjourns tomorrow until November 1st." The peace of the world must wait until Members had had their holiday. Lord Perth went off to see Ciano on the 6th, and did his best to soften the blow. Ciano—and this is an indication of the anxiety which he and Mussolini felt—said that he hoped he could assume, then, that at least on November 2nd (a month later) they could spare the time to discuss friendship and alliance with the man who had made Munich possible. On the 8th the French urged Lord Halifax to temporize and be difficult over Spain. On the 11th the Soviet Ambassador to London saw Lord Halifax and was suspicious in his turn. On October 12th Lord Halifax cabled Rome to the effect that he could not guarantee any sort of action on the implementation of the agreement until well into November: "The House . . . will not reassemble until November 8th when the first business must be the debate on the address which will certainly last several days." On the same day Sir Nevile Henderson in Berlin sent Lord Halifax a memorandum on Italo-German relations in which he stressed that Mussolini was not only respected by Hitler, who was talking of a close Italo-German alliance, but also becoming popular with the German people. "At public meetings the name Mussolini is greeted with loud applause . . . even Italian delegations which now regularly appear at most German functions are made the object of more or less spontaneous demonstrations."

Lord Halifax was in a dilemma. Here were two of his best ambassadors, in Rome and Berlin, urging a close alliance with Italy to avoid any possibility of converting the Axis into something more substantial. Even enlightened Frenchmen like François-Poncet said the same thing. And yet the French government was as jealous as it could be, and the Soviet government, though it disapproved of the Axis, disapproved of an Anglo-Italian or Anglo-German alliance even more. And there was always Churchill, ranting about the necessity of drawing the Soviet Union into any alliance made to contain Germany. Halifax was not helped by the modest intelligence of Lord Perth's military attaché, who opined that both his German and Yugoslav colleagues, on whom he had eavesdropped, believed that Italy would fight alongside Britain no matter what happened. On the other hand, the military attaché, Colonel Burrows, said that he was forced to add (the same day, October 12th) that a friend of his, Major Viscaffe (who seems to have been in charge of a car pool in Rome), had said there had been no mobilization during the Munich crisis. On the 13th Lord Halifax did nothing.

On October 14th Lord Perth cabled that Mussolini was in a "stiff frame of mind," that it was no use appealing to him to appeal in his turn to General Franco about an armistice in Spain, that the Duce would do nothing until the British government moved sharper and brought this long-delayed agreement into operation, recognizing thereby not only the existence of the Italian Empire (which was a fact) but also Britain's debt to Italy at Munich (another fact). He added: "I feel it is of the first importance to avoid, if possible, keeping Signor Mussolini guessing for another three weeks."

On October 15th Lord Perth was asked to inform Mussolini that now there could be no question of discussing the Anglo-Italian agreement in the British Parliament until November 10th.

Mussolini, understandably, was furious. His natural reaction was to speak to Attolico in Berlin and tell the Fuehrer that he felt the time had come to discuss, in all seriousness, a more binding Italo-German alliance. He, Mussolini, had done his best, as the Fuehrer must know, to bring about a general relaxation and avoid the formation of blocs, but he was meeting with no response. Ribbentrop and Hitler responded immediately. On the evening of October 25th the news was given out that the German Foreign Minister was going to Rome on October 27th. No one had any doubts about what this meant—in London, Paris, Moscow or Rome. Lord Halifax immediately cabled Lord Perth that he could inform Signor Mussolini that the decision to bring the Anglo-Italian Agreement into force had been taken that very day, October 26th, by the full Cabinet and that new credentials would be issued to Lord Perth, recognizing the King of Italy as Emperor of Ethiopia, during the first week in November.

Mussolini was placated. With the anniversary of the march on Rome (October 28th) almost upon him, he did not want to be reminded of his pupil in Berlin or conclude an alliance with him which might reduce the pioneer to the status of camp follower. He told Lord Perth he was delighted that the British and French governments had finally made up their minds and now there could be serious talks.

On October 31st Lord Halifax cabled to Lord Perth that he and the Prime Minister thought it "might be helpful if he and I came to Rome." During the first week of November, in a friendly atmosphere, the Anglo-Italian Agreement was discussed in the House of Commons, approved, and brought into effect. Mussolini, delighted, said he would welcome both Lord Halifax and Mr. Chamberlain in Rome, and the date for their visit was fixed as "some time in the second week of January." [23]

Unfortunately, during the two months which remained of 1938, and due in great part to the chauvinism, political myopia and plain incompetence of the French, Mussolini was driven so far away from the Entente that, even before Chamberlain arrived in Italy, he and Hitler had taken the last steps on the road to an indissoluble military alliance. There was nobody in Paris or London able enough to convince their governments that Mussolini's rejection of the proposals for such an alliance, made for the second time by Ribbentrop on October 28th, did in fact represent a major policy decision.

The French government prepared World War II in a number of differing ways. It tried to double-cross the other Munich Powers by signing a declaration with Germany, which implied that it would, in future, be up to France and Germany to safeguard the peace of the world, not that "*sale macaroni*, Mussolini." Unfortunately, Ribbentrop told Mussolini all about the French negotiations, and even gave him, on October 31st, the text of the declaration itself, which was not made until December 6th. Nevertheless, the idea of an alliance between his old enemy France and his "pupil" in Berlin was not pleasant. Whether or not it was dangerous depended on whether or not Britain would break with France and move closer to Italy. It soon became obvious that Britain would not "betray an old friendship." Throughout November, when it was not trying to double-cross its Munich partners, the French government was sending memoranda to and fro, accusing Mussolini of "aggressive intentions" in the Mediterranean. He was supposed to be about to annex Tunis. He was supposed to be contemplating an invasion of Corsica. And, having won the Civil War for Franco in Spain, he was now going to hop over to Algeria and annex that, taking in Gibraltar on the way. The only evidence the French government had for these allegations was that, from time to time (and more especially during a November speech by Ciano in the Fascist Parliament), young Fascists (mobilized by Starace) shouted: "Tunis! Djibouti! Corsica!" It was pointed out to the French government that successive Italian governments had been agitating for some sort of rights in Tunis, where there was a large Italian population, ever since the French had diplomatically outwitted (some said cheated) them out of a colony there. The idea of an Italian invasion of Corsica was absurd, when she had Sardinia and the prospect of a permanent base in the Balearic Islands. Djibouti was a case for negotiation—it was a bridgehead for an Italian railway, and the Italians ought, in a way, to have some say in the town's administration. The British government dismissed as laughable (as indeed it was) the idea of an Italian appropriation of Gibraltar. For one thing, France would not allow it, though she might one day try to grab it. In vain did the British government, too, argue with its French opposite number about the desirability of Italian representation on the Suez Canal board—many Italian ships passed through the canal, paying their dues, and there were Italian colonies all around it.

Basically, the French attitude was that Italy, having been united and made viable by Mussolini, had gone far enough for French peace of mind. It was not comforting to have to regard Italians as diplomatic equals, after centuries of neighbourly contempt.

On December 17, 1938, Italy formally notified the French government that its government did not consider the Hoare-Laval Treaty in force, and that there remained no firm basis for Italo-French friendship. The British government, ineffective, urged "restraint on both sides." Mussolini told Ciano that it was too late to cancel the invitation to Chamberlain, but unless the "old fool" made some gesture which showed that he appreciated the "changed circumstances" of Italy and France, and showed disapproval of France's foreign policy in general, he would once and for all commit Italy to the Axis.

On December 27, 1938, Lord Perth wrote a long memorandum to Lord Halifax on "the existing situation in Italy." [24]

Lord Perth dismissed the dangerous French hints that Mussolini was "finished," that an alliance with Italy would be a betrayal of principle, without any compensating reinforcement of war potential. Lord Perth pointed out that there was, of course, criticism of Mussolini—"the tendency to criticise is in the Italian nature"—but "Signor Mussolini's authority remains absolutely unquestioned and he still commands the personal loyalty of the vast majority of Italians, who would follow him as they would follow no one else." "Mussolini has shown himself particularly skilful in retaining the confidence of the peasantry and the manual worker (taxes falling on the rich, and middle class) . . . the peasants have come to regard the Duce as their father and protector, and the industrial workers are content to see him moving steadily leftwards while their own institutions within the Fascist régime are becoming stronger and more effective." Lord Perth added that there were minorities who disapproved of Mussolini's foreign policy, of his económic policy, of his relations with the King, but ". . . He also made it quite clear that there was a strong current of opinion, shared by Mussolini to a certain extent (and to a greater extent after the dilly-dallying over the implementation of the Anglo-Italian Agreement), that alliance with England and France was useless because "they would prove in the event of victory even less grateful than the last time." On the other hand, by an alliance with Germany, Italy could hope to "succeed to a part of the French North African Empire and perhaps to our position in North Africa and the Middle East."

On December 31, 1938, Lord Perth followed up this appraisal with a polite quarrel with his colleague in Paris over Franco-Italian relations, by cable. Perth stressed that French excuses for their attitude, which was steadily forging an anti-French, Italo-German military alliance, were lame and based on inaccuracy and prejudice. He pointed out that Italy felt very strongly about the French attitude and had ever since Versailles (France had never paid her war debt), and that this was the basis of discord between the two countries. Perth also corrected Sir Eric Phipps, quoting the French government, on the "illegal occupation of the Balearic Islands," and pointed out that it had been done by arrangement with one of the belligerent parties in Spain. The French had chosen to help the losing side, that was all, but Mussolini could scarcely be blamed for that. Perth also stressed that Mussolini, the journalist, and Mussolini, the dictator, were both sensitive to the stream of abuse which poured from the French press—not only the gutter press and *l'Humanité*. In short, the French were making European politics as difficult as possible, if peace was desirable; as inevitable as possible, if war was the ultimate aim.

Right up to the moment of departure of Halifax and Chamberlain from London to Rome, the French government did its best to render the visit ineffective. The German Ambassador, worried at the prospect of Hitler's losing his "master and friend," a revivified Entente, called at the Foreign Office every day for news. He need not have worried. By the time Chamberlain arrived in Rome, on January 11, 1939, Mussolini had already decided that he was "*stufo*" (sick) of France, and "*stufo*" of Britain for encouraging her in her truculence. If they wanted him to unite the Pax Italica to a Pax Germanica, then this is what they would get—though no one knew the risks better than he.

The Chamberlain-Halifax visit to Rome was an indifferent success. The Romans, who had not been given a special holiday for the occasion, found time to cheer, just as they had cheered Hitler, but the spectacle was not as brilliant. For three days Chamberlain and Halifax doddered about, making polite speeches and mouthing polite platitudes in private. In their private conversations with Mussolini they found him polite, but not cordial. What the Duce did was to summarize all the steps he had taken for the past five years to safeguard peace, including his attempt to settle the "Jewish question." He added that at every stage he had been hindered rather than helped by the democracies, who persisted in regarding Italy as a country of ice-cream pedlars. As Mussolini said to Ciano:

"The British are no longer made of the same stuff as Francis Drake . . . they are tired children of a long series of rich generations . . . they will lose their Empire." As Chamberlain and Halifax left Rome on the 14th, by train, the British colony in Rome struck up, "For He's a Jolly Good Fellow."

"What is that stupid little song?" asked the Duce.

Forty-eight hours later, with the paint still wet on the protocol, Ciano sent for Lord Perth and curtly informed him that if the French intervened on the side of the beleaguered Reds in Barcelona, then the Italian government would attack Valencia, and had thirty battalions of infantry ready to leave at a moment's notice.

From then on no one doubted that the days of peacemaking were over and World War II just a matter of time.

On January 30, 1939, secret negotiations were opened in Berlin which ended as the famous Pact of Steel, three months later. Some historians have suggested that the Pact of Steel was "a brainstorm" (Shirer), a last-minute thought of the Duce's, but, though it was not impossible that the Duce would take far-reaching decisions in his bath or over a cup of coffee, this particular one had been his dream and nightmare for nearly two years. The evening of February 3, 1939, the Grand Council first heard Mussolini's plans for the alliance, which were to reinforce his old ideas of Mediterranean primacy—Hitler was to take care of the democracies in the north, the Duce himself would take care of the south from Gibraltar to Cairo. Bottai reported that this "March on the Ocean" provoked little discussion. What provoked more discussion in private, among the members of the Grand Council, was Starace's latest uniform, in which he went, booted and spurred, bicycling through the streets of Rome. If the Duce was to be the prisoner of a myth, then this myth ought to be intelligent. Starace, felt many of the Grand Councillors, must go. Perhaps then the party would become less like a circus and more the business-like affair its sister party was in Berlin.

On February 10, 1939, Pope Pius XI died—the "Pope of the Conciliation." Ciano, Federzoni and Balbo, who recognized just how much they owed to Pius XI for the Church's steady support of the régime, paid their respects to him as he lay in state.[25] Mussolini, Starace and Farinacci refused, and sowed the seeds of their own damnation, making the first breach in the wall of Church-State solidarity which had endeared the régime to many devout people who found Fascism appalling and Mussolini-ism ridiculous.

Much was to happen between the death of Pius XI and the coronation of his successor, just over a month later. On February 12th Hitler received the leaders of the Slovak separatist movement, who addressed him as their "Fuehrer" and urged him to help them gain their independence. Their Fuehrer, who was looking for an excuse to destroy what was left of Czechoslovakia, said he understood and sympathised with their aims, but until the Czech government acted in "extreme provocation," he himself could not take other than diplomatic steps, and he feared these would be ineffective. Hitler had learned his lesson from the Duce. He would never attack again without a "historical excuse."

Fortunately for Hitler, who, while negotiations for the military pact were under way, did not want to offend the Duce, the Czech government made a foolish move. Perhaps encouraged by a quiet winter, during which they had not actually lost anything, the Czech government decided to "consolidate" itself and put an end to the very separatist movements which were trafficking with Hitler. On March 6th it dismissed the Ruthenian (pro-Hungarian) government, and three days later the Slovak government, headed by Monsignor Tiso. On March 10th, in Rome, Ribbentrop outlined the gravity of the situation to Ciano and Mussolini. He pointed out that they would never again have such an opportunity to "avenge insults." The Slovak and Ruthenian governments had appealed to Germany for help, and she could certainly hear these appeals. It was fortunate that the new Pope, Pacelli, "understood" the situation, and perhaps a stroke of luck that Monsignor Tiso, the head of the Slovak government, had been placed under arrest by the Czechs. There was a good "religious angle." On March 12th Pacelli was crowned as Pope Pius XII. Ribbentrop was unimpressed by the coronation ceremonies and did not see the importance of sounding out the new pontificate. There was a monsignor on "our side"—the Slovak Premier—this ought to be enough for solidarity. Mussolini was more subtle. Pacelli, he knew, was a borderline case. The former Papal Nuncio in Germany, he had helped to bring into existence the concordat which Hitler and Pius XI had signed, and he had hoped to go down in Church history as the man who had done as much for the Church in Germany as Gasparri had done in Italy. But Hitler had virtually disowned the concordat, and the Catholic Church in Germany was now persecuted on only a slightly smaller scale than its Protestant rival. The Vatican had been assured that no persecution was intended, that there were only "individual excesses," but Pacelli's enthusiasm for the Nazi régime had waned considerably. However, the Duce was pro-German and he had, after all, reconciled the Church with the Italian State, its host.

On March 13th the Vatican Secretariat of State notified Ciano that no public protest would be raised against an occupation of Czechoslovakia to liberate Catholic Slovakia. Ciano passed on the message. On March 14, 1939, the Czech President, Dr. Emil Hácha, went to Berlin to make one last plea for the survival of his country. On March 15th, while Hácha was being bullied into a faint by Hitler and Goering, German troops crossed the frontiers and Bohemia and Moravia were "incorporated into the Reich."

Once more the Western democracies had shown themselves impotent. On March 18th the Soviet government again proposed some sort of alliance which could contain Germany. Once more, the proposal was rejected. Fear of "rampant Bolshevism" was a weapon the Duce had used for nearly twenty years, Hitler for five. On March 23rd Hitler annexed Memel in Lithuania. There was no comment. When, on March 31st, Chamberlain told the House of Commons that: "In the event of any action which clearly threatened Polish independence . . . His Majesty's government would feel themselves bound at once to lend the Polish government all support in their power," Hitler and Mussolini laughed.

Mussolini realised that Poland would be the next country to "interest" the Fuehrer. This did not distress him. Anything which kept Hitler busy in Northern Europe would serve his purposes. There was a separatist movement in Croatia which he, the Duce, had his eyes on. A good Catholic State persecuted by the Orthodox, Serb, Federal Yugoslav government. He knew that if he did not take steps toward an eventual annexation, Hitler would. The first step would be the annexation of a bridgehead, Albania.

Italy's occupation of Albania, which began on Good Friday, April 5, 1939, was an interesting exercise for his new amphibious troops. It did not represent much more than that. The Albanians did not fight, and most of them welcomed the Italian "invader," who had, in any case, built their roads, railways, and what industries there were in the shepherd state. The Albanian King, Zog, who fled at the first shots, was a nephew of the Turkish Minister of War, who had learned his political trade in Istanbul and had clawed his way to the premiership, then the throne, by a judicious blend of corruption, assassination and intrigue. He was not considered to be any great loss by his subjects.[26]

The British government knew nothing about the situation in

Albania until they sent the military attaché in Rome to Albania, after the Italian occupation, to see what the score really was. The British Minister in Durazzo, Albania, was a delayed Edwardian diplomat who attached great importance to the opinions of his German colleague because "he happens to be a gentleman." Sir Andrew Ryan, the Minister, also described the fleeing King Zog as "an oriental diplomatist of the old school," which further confused the Foreign Office, by then being asked by the Greek government what to do with Zog, a refugee on Greek soil, who was as likely to cut somebody's throat as not.

In the end the British government and its allies decided to accept the Albanian annexation as a *fait accompli* The Yugoslav government, which knew what Zog was, was not worried—why should London care?

The only Western government which reacted to the invasions of Albania and Czechoslovakia was that of the United States, and here Roosevelt displayed a naïveté comparable to that of Sir Andrew Ryan's. He sent an appeal to the Duce and Hitler, asking the question: "Are you willing to give assurance that your armed forces will not attack or invade the territory of the following countries?" Then followed a list of thirty-one including all the states of Europe. The Duce, when he read this telegram, turned to Goering (on an official visit) and Ciano, and said: "Chamberlain doddering. This old fool off his head. One with his mind crippled by age and the other by infantile paralysis—they have a nerve to ask me to join their alliances!"

The Roosevelt telegram gave Hitler an excuse for making one of his rare funny speeches (April 28th, in the Sportpalast). Mussolini ignored it. He and Goering had other things to talk about.

Mussolini was interested in two things: the military alliance with Germany, which was almost ready for signature; and the pacification of Eastern Europe. He told Goering that he now had in his hands the Danube Basin, vice his victory in Albania, and "unwritten agreements" with the government of Yugoslavia. He emphasized to Goering that Hitler should take steps to neutralize the area North of the Danube, and by neutralize he did not mean invade headlong. Italy would not be ready for a major war until 1942, and in the meantime diplomacy, as Hitler must surely see, was the order of the day. War with the democracies was inevitable, but it should be where and when the Axis Powers chose to fight it. Goering, Mussolini's first German admirer and his sometime debtor, agreed in principle. The difficulty, he said, would be to convince the Fuehrer that they were not being over-cautious. Meanwhile, said Goering, both of them should work out in detail their military strengths and requirements, so as to have facts and figures to put in front of the Fuehrer.

On April 29, 1939, Mussolini presided over a council of ministers to study the reports of the Under-Secretaries for the Navy, Army and Air Force. They were horrifying. That evening Bottai wrote in his diary that the Army was in a terrible condition; that the War Ministry confessed that they were almost without medium and heavy artillery. Bottai recalled that at one stage Mussolini had refused to believe that the situation was as bad as it was described, and commented that figures handed to him for his information were never exact. The situation, stripped of exaggeration and pessimism, seemed to be that the most modern part of the Armed Forces—the Air Force, the armoured corps, the parachute brigades, the "guards regiments"—were in good condition, and the Fleet in an exceptionally alert and proven condition. For the rest, too much enthusiasm for the new had left the traditional artillery, supply and transport services depleted. What misplaced enthusiasm had not done, pilfering, dishonest contractors and a general light-fingeredness, which had been Italian for centuries, had completed. More than ever, if Italy was to be in any state of readiness comparable to Germany by 1942, there had to be an interval of peaceful hypocrisy secured by skilful diplomacy.

There was not much to be hoped for from diplomacy in the West. The French government, satisfied by its success in estranging Britain and Italy, went on nagging the Foreign Office that "Italy is the danger." Throughout April Sir Eric Phipps transmitted extraordinary messages to the Foreign Office, many of them obviously based on French lies (as for instance the report that fresh Italian troops had landed in Spain in early April, and the British government should stand by for an attack on Gibraltar—this at a time when Italian troops were coming home as fast as ships could take them). When the Foreign Office was not being worried by false reports of activity in the Western Mediterranean, Lord Halifax was upsetting people by offering to Greece, Yugoslavia, and Turkey guarantees for which they had not asked and which caused them extreme embarrassment in their relations with Mussolini and his "pupil."

The Cardinal Secretary of State in the Vatican tried to restrain the French and ensure that accurate information about Mussolini's intentions reached London, but he had limited success. When Sir

Eric Phipps quoted the Cardinal as saying: "There is still time to prevent Signor Mussolini entirely throwing in his lot with Hitler," this was received with some scepticism.

It is not clear whether an intelligent appeal to reason on the part of Britain and France could have stopped the negotiations, at a very advanced stage, for the Italo-German military alliance. Probably not. It was too late. The approach should have been made when it was first recommended by Lord Perth.[27] As it was, Mussolini's general impression was of Frenchmen and Britishers breathing friendship in one ear, while other Frenchmen and Britishers breathed enmity in the other; and while both Britain and France conspired to isolate him in the Mediterranean. The Earl of Perth, on the eve of his departure from Rome (to be replaced by Sir Percy Loraine), was told by Buti, one of Ciano's aides, that war was closer today than it was yesterday and that the fault lay with the French. One of the most revealing reports ever made by Lord Perth (April 21st) showed that the French had even been double-crossing their British allies, that while urging Britain to be "unmoving" with Mussolini, they had actually sent an envoy, M. Baudouin, to Rome as long ago as February. This envoy had made far-reaching proposals, which Mussolini had accepted, then the proposals had been archived without further action from Paris. On April 22nd Sir Eric Phipps reported that he had had a long interview with the French Prime Minister, emphasizing the importance a Franco-Italian understanding could have, even at this late stage, but added that he feared he had failed to shake him—he was afraid that "Italian gangsters would destroy the wonderful feelings of loyalty that now exist all over North Africa and in Syria towards France," if negotiations with Mussolini opened to show France in a reasonable mood. At this point, though Mussolini seems to have decided to go ahead with his military alliance with Germany regardless, Ciano made (April 27th) a last effort to make the French less truculent, telling the French Ambassador to Rome that Italy had no territorial claims to make on France, but would like a seat on the Suez Canal board and a guarantee of the security of the Italian railhead at Djibouti. A report by Sir Noel Charles from Rome on April 29th suggests that this effort had been in vain, though it perceived, very acutely, that Italy wanted to get what she could diplomatically; "can put the curb on Hitler and still use the Axis for pushing Italy's ambition"; might well choose neutrality if a war broke out; and would be better off, anyway, if some way could be found to settle her grievances with France.

There was, however, at no time a danger that either London or Paris would move with the necessary dispatch to stop the Axis reinforcing its position. Natural hesitancy, acute perceptivity swamped by misinformation (Sir Andrew Ryan was predicting an attack on Greece), and a lack of diplomatic aptitude, made progress too slow for events.

On May 3rd Mussolini had a bright idea. Writing off the West as a field for diplomatic manœuvre, he had been studying the possibilities for treaty-making in the East. There was, of course, only one major power in the East—the Soviet Union. No country in the world had enjoyed better relations with the Soviet Union than Fascist Italy. Why not an alliance between Rome, Berlin and Moscow? He had mentioned this to Goering in a vague form, and had had it pooh-poohed politely. One of Goering's objections had been that Soviet Foreign Minister Litvinov was a Jew, and he could not see how the Fuehrer could possibly entertain Bolshevik Jews in Berlin while so many Jews of various political complexions were behind barbed wire in concentration camps. But May 3rd brought some welcome news. Litvinov had been dismissed and replaced by Molotov—a hard man, but, by stretching the definition, an Aryan. Mussolini put the idea to Ribbentrop and repeated it to Goering by phone. It was greeted as yet another master stroke. Goering left the same day for San Remo, where he could be pretending to holiday while Ciano's messengers informed him of further progress. Telephone lines were safer, anyway, than cable calls which could be intercepted. Ribbentrop told Mussolini that he would leave for the Italian Lakes in a day or two and could meet Ciano there to talk over plans for a Soviet-Axis pact in similar privacy.

Sir Nevile Henderson, who was well-informed, learned of Goering's departure and of Ribbentrop's imminent departure, but was told there was nothing sinister afoot. He seemed to accept the explanation.

On May 5th Georgi Astakhov, the Soviet chargé d'affaires in Berlin, discussed the Duce's idea with Dr. Julius Schnurre, the German Foreign Ministry expert on Soviet Affairs. They agreed to resume negotiations for a trade agreement which had been broken off some months previously, and see "on what basis further agreements could be reached."

On May 6th Mussolini was told the good news, that there seemed to be every likelihood of successful negotiations. The Duce did not hesitate. He did not want to appear lacking in belligerence, now that war seemed to have been postponed by the prospect of an agreement more binding than the Fuehrer's word. He instructed Ciano to make the final arrangements for the signature of the Pact of Steel. Ribbentrop, who had feared that the pact would take many more months to negotiate, pinned down Ciano to a communiqué to the press, and the news released, noted that "the future seems assured." Ribbentrop realized that the Duce's continuing enthusiasm was dependent on the signing of a Soviet-German treaty, to supplement the treaty already existing between Italy and the Soviet Union, and on May 20th instructed his ambassador in Moscow to approach Molotov in person to confirm the fact that the Soviet Union really did want a political alliance.

In all fairness to the Soviet Union, it should be noted that on May 8th Britain had rejected a proposal for an Anglo-Soviet alliance. To Molotov and Stalin there seemed to be only one alternative.

On May 22nd the Pact of Steel was signed by Ciano and Ribbentrop in Berlin with the maximum of pomp and circumstance. It committed Italy to every sort of alliance with Germany, including, under Article III, the commitment to go to war if Germany found herself in conflict. It was a sort of suicide pact. Sir Nevile Henderson noted sadly that "there had been . . . no intention of entering on a military alliance," that British diplomatic bungling had in effect forced the Duce to take this step with great reluctance. A week later, when Hitler's intention to make trouble over Danzig and eventually invade Poland became clear, he added an even sadder postscript: "Who can act as an intermediary between Poles and Germans? Personally I am convinced that nobody but Mussolini can, and am consequently the more perturbed over the apparent blind unwillingness of the French to settle quickly their really comparatively small differences with Italy."

Now Mussolini was committed to war. He had no illusions about Hitler, and he was as well aware as most observers that the German economy, under Nazi direction, in time of peace was not viable. It had been created as a war potential, and Italy would now be dragged down or up with it. Mussolini's only concern was to postpone the day as long as possible, so that when it came he could be strong enough to either conquer, or remain a friendly neutral, well-armed enough to be able to resist Hitler's threats. He was to be unlucky.

Throughout the last summer of peace Mussolini worked to get the nation on a war footing and to fill in the gaps in his "impregnable imperial wall." He sent innumerable memoranda to Hitler urging caution. Ribbentrop's replies were always vaguely reassuring, telling the Duce that he was busy signing pacts of friendship and taking the German-Soviet negotiations toward the successful end he was sure they would have.

Mussolini may have been reassured by Ribbentrop. Ciano was not. Both the British and French ambassadors and the Anglophile Italian society in which he moved, dropped hints that Italy would be double-crossed and find herself at war by late autumn at the very latest. It was not long before Ciano himself began to doubt Hitler's good faith. There had been an explicit protocol to the Pact of Steel which said, "No war until 1942," but would Hitler, in the last analysis, take any more notice of this protocol than he had of a hundred other agreements, written or verbal, to which he had pledged himself?

By the early part of August, Ciano could not keep from confiding his doubts to his father-in-law. Mussolini had been approached, too, by Sir Percy Loraine and others, and had received the impression that, though the British government had given up hope of concluding an Anglo-Italian alliance of any strength (the French were still too "difficult"), Lord Halifax had not given up hope of assuring Mussolini's neutrality. There was nothing Mussolini wanted more than a long period of neutrality. If Hitler was threatening war, then he could honourably abrogate the Pact of Steel. It was not popular in Italy, and maybe he had been rash to sign it. After all, where was this treaty with Moscow which Berlin was always saying they were on the point of signing?

On August 10th Mussolini sent Ciano to Germany to talk with Hitler and Ribbentrop. For three days, from the 11th to the 13th, they were scarcely out of each other's company. Ciano did not like what he saw or heard. His worst suspicions were confirmed. Generals wandered in and out of the Fuehrer's presence, talking glibly of war as if it were only a month or so hence. When Ciano left Berchtesgaden on the 13th to return home, he was convinced that Italy was being "dragged into an adventure."

Ciano reported to his father-in-law. At first the Duce was gloomily determined to "honour his obligations." Then it occurred to him that the word honour was scarcely appropriate when applied to Hitler. On August 15th, after a six-hour talk with Ciano, he had decided that "we must not march blindly with the Germans . . . we cannot engage in war because our condition does not permit us to do so. . . ." On August 18th he was ready to break the Pact of Steel, but afraid that if he did so Hitler would postpone his invasion of Poland and attack him instead, and the democracies would not come to his aid. On August 20th, with Attolico back from Berlin for consultation, this fear was uppermost. On August 21st he had a row with Ciano, who threatened to resign, and then reluctantly agreed to allow his son-in-law to see Ribbentrop to arrange for a meeting either between himself and Hitler, or between the Duce and Hitler.

On August 22nd the atmosphere became less tense. Ribbentrop phoned Ciano and told him that he was leaving for Moscow to sign the promised pact with the Soviet Union. The news at least relieved Mussolini of the fear that negotiations had been abandoned and that Hitler was recklessly gambling on Western inertia forever. Nevertheless, he was not convinced that an attack on Poland was not imminent, and this would be the ruination of Italy, left to bear the whole brunt of war in the West while the Reich liquidated the affair in the East. On August 25th the German Ambassador to Rome delivered a message from the Fuehrer which confirmed his fear—the attack on Poland had been fixed for the next day, August 26th! Mussolini was overwhelmed with despair, and sent off telegrams—even to Bottai, his Minister for Education—recalling all his friends to the colours. He was barely restrained from ordering a general mobilization.

Then Ciano told him that this was, in fact, the excuse he had been looking for to avoid going to war at all; to enjoy years of armed neutrality; to keep his own flag flying on the flagpole. The same evening Mussolini wrote a letter to Hitler, which he phoned to Attolico for delivery, in which he regretted Hitler's action, the more since he had been assured that, whatever their hesitancy in the past, the British would march. He wrote: "If Germany attacks Poland and the conflict remains localized, Italy will afford Germany every form of political and economic assistance which is requested of her. If Germany attacks Poland and the latter's allies open a counter-attack . . . it will be wiser for me not to take the initiative in military operations, in view of the present state of Italian war preparations . . . at our meetings, war was envisaged by 1942." The only condition on which he would go to war, wrote the Duce, was that Germany supplied him with a list (an impossibly long list) of material of which he had urgent need.

Hitler was furious, but this time he would not be stopped. The Duce had put the brake on the German war machine once too often. He extended the time limit for the invasion of Poland from August 26th to September 1st, but there was no going back.

On August 28th the King of the Belgians and the Queen of the Netherlands broadcast appeals for peace. On August 31st the Pope sent notes to all the governments of the West and Poland, beseeching them, in the name of God, to avoid incidents. The notes met with the same fate as the public appeal for moderation he had made shortly after his coronation.

Hitler sent a short note to the Duce, acknowledging his list of war material needed, and telling him he would: "go on because I must."

At the last minute the Duce attempted another Munich. This time he did not succeed. Hitler cabled back to him:

> I THANK YOU, DUCE, FOR ALL YOUR EFFORTS . . . IN PARTICULAR FOR YOUR OFFERS OF MEDIATION . . . BUT FROM THE START I WAS SCEPTICAL . . . BECAUSE THE POLISH GOVERNMENT, IF THEY HAD HAD THE SLIGHTEST INTENTION OF SOLVING THE MATTER AMICABLY, COULD HAVE DONE SO AT ANY TIME. . . .

By midday on September 1, 1939, German troops were well over the border into Poland. The British government delivered an ultimatum, to expire on September 3rd. It was rejected; Ciano's only cause for satisfaction on September 3rd was, as he noted in his diary: "During the night I was awakened because Bonnet had asked our Ambassador in Paris if we could at least obtain the symbolic withdrawal of German forces from Poland . . . I threw the proposal in the wastepaper basket without informing the Duce . . . this shows that France is moving toward the great test without enthusiasm and full of uncertainty." It was, Ciano believed, poetic justice. A France with a stable, intelligent government might have made an effective contribution toward the peace of Europe. As it was, she had antagonized the only man who was capable of halting Hitler in his tracks, and had forfeited all sympathy.

For the next eight months Italy lived in a state of suspended fear. It was, most people believed, inevitable that Italy should be dragged into the war. The Duce was a political genius, but not even he, though he had secured a temporary and honourable neutrality, could avoid being entangled. It remained the hope that the evil day would be postponed for as long as possible.

For Mussolini himself, his non-intervention was an anti-climax. He had been expelled from the Socialist Party of his youth for advocating intervention in World War I, and he had made his career on the precept that a day as a lion was better than a hundred years as a sheep. Now here he was, almost the only man in Europe without a drawn sword. For a month he grappled with his conscience, but by the end of October he had decided to hasten his preparations and get into the war as soon as possible.

Two factors finally decided Mussolini to abandon his neutrality. The first was the Soviet attack on Finland on November 6, 1939. Mussolini's mistrust of Bolshevism had not diminished throughout Hitler's treaty negotiations. The Soviet Union as a trading ally was one thing; the Soviet Union on the march westward through Europe was another. Mussolini began to think his idea of a Soviet-German Pact was a mistake. Hitler and Stalin might even do a deal and attack him! He knew that, for Hitler, Bolshevism was just a word; that a soldier was a soldier regardless of the red star on his hat. Even worse, provided Stalin was not a Jew, he was preferable to an unarmed Italian as a friend. The second factor was the success with which Hitler's campaigns everywhere were meeting—even the Finns held the Red Army until March 12th, whereas the British and French were already showing signs of weakening, of the chaos, confusion and demoralization which was to end in Dunkirk.

Mussolini gave orders for partial mobilization, for the building-up of reserves, for "discipline." He sacked Starace from the secretaryship of the party and appointed a war hero, Muti, instead.[28]

On May 10, 1940, Hitler started his big advance in Western Europe. On May 12th he sent a message to Mussolini—to quote Ciano: "For the first time Hitler asks Mussolini to consider that it might be wise for Italy to intervene."

Mussolini did not need asking twice. After a month of agony of indecision, frantic phone calls and martial music, he telephoned the office of his paper and alerted the staff.

On June 10th Mussolini's Ministers were called to Palazzo Venezia. Bottai noted in his diary: "The Square is packed by a crowd sometimes silent, sometimes in a tumult. We are aware of the efforts made by a few lively elements who try to work up shouts of acclamation. There is a sense of stupefied discipline, the sort of discipline the Party has never been able to achieve with its orders of the day. It is war."

8

VIA SENZA USCITA

NO WAY OUT

World War II had little to do with Fascism. Italy's intervention, on June 10, 1940, merely marked the formal end of a process which had formally begun with Mussolini's advocacy of intervention in 1914. If all cats are grey at dusk, then all countries are the same in time of war. It is absurd to speak of a war of Fascism against democracy, of Communism against capitalism. The various "isms" may, in their different ways, make war inevitable, but once declared, it becomes the business of the non-political amateur rather than that of the political professional. In time of war the political, economic, even moral organization of one country closely resembles that of another. In time of war there is little to choose between one belligerent and another; more or less efficiency, more or less bestiality, more or less jingoism, more or less success—these are the criteria which distinguish the victor from the vanquished, not their ideologies.

World War II is important to a history of Fascism only because it brought about a cohesion of discontent with the régime, and this discontent showed itself in a tremendous anti-war effort.

However, a sketch of the background to this discontent would not be out of place. The war began with the usual successes for the aggressor. France, already humbled by the German Army, was attacked in Haute-Savoie and soon capitulated. Mussolini is supposed to have enjoyed nothing more than entertaining the French plenipotentiaries, rubbing in the "extraordinary coincidence that the armistice with the Reich has been signed in the same railway coach in which the German surrender agreement was signed in 1918." At a meeting with Hitler on June 19, 1940, at Munich, Mussolini accepted the responsibility for war in the Balkans and the Mediterranean, while Hitler was to concentrate on the "security of the north." In October 1940 Mussolini invaded Greece, and in April 1941, Yugoslavia. The diplomatic pretexts were now virtually non-existent—all that mattered to the Axis was that the Balkans should be neutralized as far as Turkey. The German armies consolidated their hold on Western Europe, as far as the Pyrénées (confident of the neutrality of Franco and Salazar). The Soviet Union annexed the Baltic and the Bessarabian provinces of Rumania. In North Africa Graziani drove into Western Egypt as far as Sidi Barrâni, before being pushed back through Cyrenaica. On February 12, 1941, at Bordighera, Mussolini and Franco conferred about the war, especially about the embarrassment they both felt at Germany's war bond with the Soviet Union. A further exchange of notes, a conference between Hitler and Mussolini on June 2, 1941, and the embarrassment was removed. On June 22, 1941, the armies of the Reich invaded the Soviet Union, joined by volunteers from Finland, Rumania, Hungary, Slovakia, and Croatia, and eventually by the Spanish "Blue Division," the French "Charlemagne" and "Joan of Arc" divisions, Swiss, Norwegian, Baltic and Ukrainian units, the last-named under the command of General Vlasov. On December 7, 1941, the Axis took on another opponent, the United States, when the Japanese Air Force made what Mussolini called "the most intelligent declaration of war of our time," sinking the U.S. Fleet without warning in Pearl Harbour.

The counter-offensives of Britain, the United States and the Soviet Union, were mildly successful, only to be eclipsed by the 1942 spring offensives of the Axis. In the Soviet Union the armies of Von Paulus and his colleagues drove the Red Armies out of the Crimea (Italian troops took Sabastopol by storm), the Don Basin, the Lower Volga steppe, as far as Stalingrad in the south. There were even reconnaissance units on the banks of the Caspian Sea. In Western Europe, apart from neutral Spain, Switzerland, Portugal and Sweden, every country was in Axis hands—Finland, Norway, Denmark, Poland, Czechoslovakia, Belgium, Holland, Luxembourg, France, Yugoslavia, Albania, Hungary, Rumania, Bulgaria, Greece, the Baltic—even the Channel Islands. In Africa the German-Italian offensives led by Rommel and Graziani, after some to-ing and fro-ing about Tobruk, succeeded in driving the British and allied armies out of Libya, and invading Egypt as far as the line of El Alamein. The Suez Canal was almost within sight, and Alexandria a short drive away. Afraid of being bottled up in the Mediterranean, some British and Allied warships were withdrawn to other theatres of war, where they were sunk. In 1942 the Japanese were as successful, controlling, at the autumn "accounting": Korea, Manchuria, Mongolia, most of China, Indo-China, Siam, Burma, Malaya, Indonesia, the Philippines, part of New

Guinea and most of the American colonies in the Pacific. Like the armies of the Reich, those of Japan were reinforced by volunteers, from China (under Wang Chin-wei), Siam, Indo-China, India and the Philippines.

The fall of 1942 was the high-water mark of Axis military success. From then on defeat for the Tripartite Axis of Italy, Germany and Japan was assured, with or without the use of nuclear weapons. Germany and Japan fought on until 1945. In July 1943 Sicily was invaded and Mussolini deposed. On September 8, 1943, Mussolini's successor Badoglio changed sides, and on the Italian peninsula a civil war broke out between Badoglio with the Allies, and Mussolini, in a new Republic (called Saló) supported by the Reich. From September 8th until Mussolini's death in 1945, the Italians lost interest in the issues at stake in World War II, and got on with the business of settling old scores and paying old political and personal debts of honour.

It is generally agreed by most people who took part that only the 1943–1945 civil war was fought with any enthusiasm. Italy, in part and then as a whole, stopped believing in a man in whom she had wanted to believe, and the result was fratricidal disaster. It has been said that the Fascist régime was the greatest confidence trick of the century. It has also been said that sometimes a situation needs a good confidence-trickster, and certainly, for a time, the trick worked in Italy. But when confidence in the trick and trickster failed, the régime failed, Mussolini and the confusion of guilt, shame and betrayal left behind, had to be expurgated in blood.

At what point did confidence fail? For the interested minorities —the party, the King, the Regular Army, the Church, business— Mussolini had lost his charm before he intervened in the war between Hitler and the democracies. For the people—the broad mass of the people who formed the crowds beneath the balconies—the deluge came later.

In theory, the election of the particular new Pope in 1939 ought to have reinforced the régime. It is always important to remember that, without the regular weekly exhortation in the pulpit, the Duce might not have led for so long. The women of Fascist Italy were particularly susceptible to appeals for support for Mussolini in his hours of triumph, even during the Ethiopian sanctions crisis. The men in Mussolini's day felt their wives tranquil, yet felt, too, that Mussolini "had the priests under control," and was not "under the orders of the Pope." Certainly Pius XI had helped to consolidate the régime. Why should Pius XII not do so, especially since he was a Germanophile, and Mussolini was being driven, by the time of his coronation, steadily into the arms of the Reichfuehrer? Pius XII, as Nuncio to Germany, had been assured by the German Catholic aristocracy that Hitler would "end the peril of Bolshevism," just as Mussolini had done in Italy (just how real the Red threat was is immaterial). Von Papen, the Catholic closest to Hitler, had proposed a concordat, which was signed only seven months after Hitler's rise to power. Nuncio Pacelli, later Secretary of State, saw his road to the Papacy paved with a second series of Lateran Pacts. Not even the murder of the Catholic Action leader, Klausener, in 1934, was sufficient to disillusion him. He even showed mild disapproval of the Papal Encyclical of March 14, 1937, in which Pius XI accused Hitler of breaking faith with the concordat, and on the day of his coronation, on March 12, 1939, urged "patience and moderation" in the Vatican's dealings with Hitler.

Pius XII lost his patience for the first time, according to all reports, when his special appeal for peace on May 4, 1939, was cavalierly treated by Ciano and the Italian Foreign Ministry, though it had been intended as a gesture of goodwill to reinforce the prestige of the "great peacemaker of Munich." By that time, of course, Mussolini was on the brink of signing the Pact of Steel, with a Soviet-German treaty in embryo. Like most political gestures of the thirties, it came too late. On August 31st Pius's direct appeal to the statesmen concerned in the Polish crisis, fell on equally deaf ears, for which again he blamed Mussolini, "*l'ingrato*".

Pius XII's rebukes, never delivered personally to Mussolini, but always filtered through the Vatican bureaucracy, increased in strength from that day on. The Vatican bureaucracy did nothing to diminish them. There were new men in the Papal State, men who felt no gratitude to Mussolini for having brought it into being. The Curia Cardinals, who had praised the Duce at the time of the great Conciliation, were nearly all dead—20 died during the thirties alone. The new Curia, especially strong in French membership, was passively—then actively—hostile to the régime. Their subordinates, the many monsignori, were a new generation, too, most of them men ordained since the coming of the Duce. Their resentment was specific. The war saw the emasculation of Catholic Action, and these "young men" realized that there was nothing to put in its place. They blamed Mussolini for the extinction of the Popular Party, which might have provided the régime with an Opposition. They even blamed Pius XI for his part in extinguishing the Popular Party, the exile of Luigi Sturzo (now in America) and Angelo

Roncalli (in Turkey). They began to discuss, with former Popular Party "young intellectuals" like de Gasperi—still living in frustration in Rome—a post-war Europe which would be dominated by a Catholic, Christian Democratic bloc from Denmark to Sicily, a Paris-Rome-Berlin Axis with priests as wheels and the Pope in the chariot driver's seat. Such a renaissance of the political power of the Church needed a defeat for Hitler and Mussolini if it was to even see the midwife.

The frustration of Pius XII and the discontent of his bureaucracy found many grievances, some of them not new, with which to show the régime their feelings. They protested at the reissue, during the North African campaigns of 1940 and 1941, of photographs showing Mussolini waving the Sword of Islam. If the Duce was to make sense of his claim to be fighting a Holy War, then, as a Catholic, his holiness ought to be Christian. When Japan declared war on the United States, the Vatican hinted that it was being expected to bless a war in alliance with Muslims and Shintoists against millions of faithful Catholics. Again, the habit of referring to the date as so many years of the Era Fascista, with "the Year of Our Lord" as an afterthought, irritated those who were looking for legitimate sources of irritation—especially when, after 1939, "the Year of Our Lord" began to be dropped altogether. To the Vatican's eternal credit, it was genuinely grieved about the idea of civil persecution of the Jews, which it could fairly describe as medieval (the last Jew was tortured by the Inquisition in 1623). Racism it regarded as reactionary and likely to turn world opinion against the Vatican, situated as it was in an officially racist peninsula (the idea of moving the Holy See was mooted in 1941, but dropped).

The Church's attitude to the régime was, after 1940, first one of reproval, then of opposition. In the first year of the war, after the invasion of the Soviet Union especially, many of Mussolini's critics in the Vatican would have been satisfied to see him mend his ways, widen the base of the government, stop flirting with Islam, and generally behave like a good Catholic. This first period was characterized by a determined effort to reverse Fascist policy on racial questions, an effort which met with some success. As late as October 1941 Mussolini was able to respond with a statement to Yvon de Begnac that: "I have had affectionate relationships with many Jews—there were Jews among the founders of Fascism [Renzo Ravenna, Podesta of Ferrara, Remo Pontecorvo, Bolaffi, Mussolini's librarian Foa, Mussolini's doctor and dentist Piperno, Malaparte, Margherita Sarfatti, Aldo Finzi] and Jews have sustained it.

General Pugliese, a Jew, is still on active service. Jews have never represented any danger to Italy . . . they have been loyal and have supported the régime, to a greater or less degree of sincerity, serving its interests as well as their own."[1]

This statement caused a furore in Berlin, and is indicative of the weight the Duce attached to Church opinion (while always remaining himself a sceptic)—on the assumption that any régime which had endured for 1,900 years had something to teach the others.

However, as the war went on and came increasingly under the political and military direction of the Reich and the Fuehrer, Mussolini became deaf to hurt noises from the Church, as indeed he became deaf to all appeals to reason. At this point the Church went into active opposition to the régime. It began by harbouring the enemy, helping Allied prisoners escape (Monsignor O'Flaherty ran an escape ring from the Vatican's chief notary's office). Under the influence of British Minister Sir Darcy Osborne, it began to re-establish political contacts between Balkan political leaders (especially in Croatia and Greece) under cover of aid to refugees. It became more ambitious and set to work to perfect its own plans for political resurgence, a Catholic post-war European bloc, using even discredited Nazis like von Papen for the purpose. Angelo Roncalli (Pope John XXIII), then Apostolic Delegate to Turkey, acted as a liaison officer with both the Greek resistance and German Catholics, visiting Greece himself to traffic in person, and receiving von Papen in Istanbul and Ankara. Mussolini was not unaware of this "unpatriotic" activity, and even appointed Ciano to be Minister, and Bastianini to be Under-Minister to the Holy See, in an attempt to restore the Vatican to diplomatic neutrality (February 5, 1943), but by then it was too late (Ciano's loyalty was, in any case, doubtful).

It is perhaps significant, and an indication of the width of the gulf which had opened between Mussolini and the Church, that when, in 1945, the defeated Duce—on the run from partisans, and the Allied armies within shellshot of the city—appealed to Cardinal Schuster for sanctuary, it was refused. In March 1938 Schuster had been one of the most pro-Fascist cardinals. By March 1945 he had come to regard Mussolini as a murderer and cheat.

The *volte-face* of the King and royal family was not, perhaps, so extreme as that of the Church. With the death of the Queen Mother in 1926, Fascism was left with only one uncritical enthusiast inside the palace, the Duke of Aosta. When he died, before the Fascist Decennial, his sisters and brothers regarded the régime with something of the tolerance with which a home-owner tolerates an expert but nasty-tempered gardener who is given to familiarity and contempt. There was no doubt about the popularity of the conciliation between Church and State, and the King was willing to give Mussolini credit where credit was due. Neither his father nor his grandfather had had a minister capable of bringing about such a brilliant compromise. The paeans of praise from foreign statesmen also impressed the King. Here was a Prime Minister who had raised Italy's prestige to an all-time high, and had forced the world to take his country almost at its own valuation. The King, a small man who had to sit on three cushions to be able to see over the edge of the state landau, was always afraid that the world found both him and his country faintly ridiculous, and he appreciated greatly Mussolini's abuse of "some foreigners who think this is a country riddled with the picturesque."

Victor Emmanuel was doubtful about the wisdom of Mussolini's new institutions, the Grand Council of Fascism, and the corporations, but gave in on the Duce's insistence that the basic institutions of the State had not changed in substance, only in outward form. The King certainly liked becoming Emperor of Ethiopia, and relished Mussolini's diplomatic defeat of the King of England's government. Perhaps the first major point of disagreement between the King and the Duce was over the creation of the title Marshal of the Empire. All the members of the royal family were sensitive to encroachments on the prerogative, and this new rank which Mussolini created for himself seemed to deny the King the right to be Supreme Commander of the Armed Forces. When, in 1939, Mussolini abolished Parliament and created instead a "Council of *Fasci* and Corporations," Victor Emmanuel was vociferous in his complaints that the Constitution (*lo Statuto*) he had sworn to protect had been, if not abrogated, then altered out of all recognition. Henceforth all the "elected members" were to be nominees of the Duce, and the King had no "eyes and ears" (Senate and Lower House) through which he could watch over his subjects' democratic rights. Victor Emmanuel finally broke with Mussolini over his alliance and war game with Hitler, a man he detested, fighting a war for which he knew his country was not prepared.

It was, however, characteristic of the King that he did nothing about it until it was too late, condemning his country to a useless, self-destructive war in the process. He did send emissaries to London and Paris just before the war broke out in September 1939, but they were not well received, largely because the King's powers, eminence and authority, were doubted. Had the King appealed to the nation in the spring of 1940 to preserve Italy's neutrality, it is difficult to see what he might have achieved, but *something* might have happened to stop Mussolini in his tracks. As it was, in 1940, the King started to receive dissident elements from inside the Fascist Party, and from among the former passive supporters of the régime, and laid himself open to an accusation of betrayal of his pledges to his Prime Minister. In any case, his attitude was so ambiguous that there was no doubt in most people's minds that if the régime fell, he would have to abdicate.

All the King could do to oppose Mussolini was to encourage factions in the Regular Army which were jealous of the Duce's claims to direct the course of the war (and so deprive them of loot and glory). The Regular Army conspiracy seems to have begun in the late autumn of 1940.

On October 27, 1940, the Duke of Pistoia made a speech at Turin, in which he pledged himself to "the Duce of all the Victories, the Leader of a Revolution not yet completed." It was in no way a remarkable speech for a royal prince to make at the outset of a war in which his country was involved, but it is significant that it was the last to be made by any member of the royal family in which there was any mention of loyalty to the régime and its leader. Future speeches were to be narrowly patriotic.

Crown Prince Humbert is believed to have been the instigator of the royal family's "boycott" of the régime during the war and to have encouraged those generals who conspired to replace Mussolini by one of themselves, Marshal Badoglio. Humbert, who disliked the Duce, had spent much of his life in Turin, where enthusiasm for the régime was considerably less than in Imperial Rome. Badoglio, after wheedling out of Mussolini titles, estates, a state pension, medals and every order but two in the Italian calendar of chivalry, decided that Italy needed a new king—Humbert—and a new Leader, himself.[2]

According to Galbiati, Badoglio had his conspiracy well under way by the spring of 1941, and had recruited a number of generals to the "Badoglio clan." On June 4, 1941, General Visconti-Prasca presented a memoir to the King in which he hinted that the first stage of the conspiracy entailed the substitution for loyal generals of generals loyal only to the person of Badoglio, irrespective of their ability. Visconti-Prasca was an able man who knew the Greek-Yugoslav-Albanian countryside well and had fought over part of it. He wrote an account of "ambitious generals and their clients," which is almost musical comedy in the atmosphere it recreates. It seems that Mussolini appointed Visconti-Prasca, on August 13, 1940, to be in charge of the forthcoming campaigns in the Balkans, a choice determined by his experience. The appointment did not please Badoglio, who was not anxious that a general loyal to Mussolini should acquire popularity and prestige in what seemed likely to be a quick, decisive campaign.

As Chief of Staff of the Army, Badoglio promptly (September 4th) ordered General Roatta, the then Commanding General for the area, to give Visconti-Prasca only an army corps, instead of the Army, to lead. Roatta's reason was that "if you take command of an Army you will be jumping your seniors in the Army List, especially General Rossi." Visconti-Prasca then protested to General Soddu, Minister for War under Mussolini, who confirmed Mussolini's original instructions. This did not dismay Badoglio and Roatta, who promptly emasculated his command and forbade him to communicate directly with the Ministry of War. When Visconti-Prasca threatened to leave his troops and fly to Rome, this ban was lifted. On November 6th Soddu flew to see Visconti-Prasca in Albania and promoted him to Army General, and they both sent a telegram to Mussolini, expressing their profound satisfaction. On November 10th the new Army General was given authority to wear his new badges of rank. But on November 11th two more Army Generals—above Visconti-Prasca in the Army List—arrived in Albania and forcibly took over command. Visconti-Prasca protested in a letter to Soddu, on December 13th, at this "betrayal," and pointed out that his initial successes in Epirius were being thrown away by two ambitious generals whose competence was questionable and whose loyalty to the régime extremely doubtful. Eventually Mussolini himself had to sort out the situation, removing Badoglio from his post as Chief of Staff and confirming the marshal in his determination to do away with the Duce. By June 1941, when Visconti-Prasca wrote to the King, the whole situation in the Balkans had deteriorated, due to quarrels at Command Headquarters about who was responsible for what, and more particularly who was entitled to enter captured cities first and receive their surrender. Greece was conquered, but at the cost of an army disorganized, demoralized, frozen, and badly fed because supplies were left to rot while the generals bickered. General Visconti-Prasca urged the King to see to it that the rest of the cream of the Italian Army was not destroyed in the same way. He was to be disappointed.

Badoglio, by playing on generals' jealousy of each other and on their dissatisfaction with Mussolini's "political interference," created a climate in which efficient operations were impossible. From there it was only a short step to treason. It was not Badoglio's loyalty to the Crown which urged him to "rid the country of Mussolini." To a lawyer friend, Cassinelli, he said in 1942 (November 11th) that, "we will get rid of all this with or without the monarchy," and seems to have been in touch with the Allies from about that date.

Badoglio was ideally placed for his activities, having planted a friend, General Ambrosio, as Chief of the General Staff, who reported to Mussolini in the mornings and to Badoglio in the evenings. In order to bring about the downfall of Mussolini, Badoglio did not hesitate to put the lives of his fellow-countrymen in danger by betraying to the Allies the battle plans of all three services. Admiral Jachino, who lost the cruisers *Zara*, *Pola* and *Fiume*, and two destroyers, with 3,000 men, at Matapan, commented in his memoirs that "the enemy was immediately informed of any operation we planned in the Eastern Mediterranean." One of Badoglio's admirals, who supplied this information—Admiral Maugeri, Chief of Naval Intelligence—even wrote a book about it—*From the Ashes of Disgrace.* He was tried for treason after the publication of the book, and on June 3, 1950, heard the Court of Cassation comment that: "sufficient proof exists that before September 8, 1943, Maugeri had intelligence with powers with whom Italy was at that time in a state of war." Admiral Maugeri even went so far as to state that "he doubted very much whether there were many English spies in Italy, because there was no need for them. The Admiralty was informed by high-ranking officers of the Italian Military Marine of any imminent move of significance, and eventually of the imminent plot against Mussolini, so that the surrender of the Fleet could be arranged." The Army was involved not only in petty squabbles and espionage, but also in the sabotage of its own supplies. According to an entry in Rommel's diary for July 9, 1942: "Difficulties of supply are increasing. Petrol cans coming from Italy are two-thirds full of water. We made inquiries, and after a thorough investigation concluded that this was habitual—a real example of sabotage. . . ." And on July 18, 1942: "Secret transmitters are all over Italy and the enemy is criminally and systematically informed of every movement at the ports, and for this reason air and sea escorts are now useless—the routes are known to the British before even the Commanders of the convoy ships know them. . . ."

An English Guards battalion refused to surrender at Tobruk, because "this is a manœuvre we have not practised in peacetime, hence it is impossible in time of war." Badoglio and his friends, intent on the destruction of Mussolini and the régime, practised manœuvres which had been habitual in time of peace—deceit, intrigue and the satisfaction of personal vanity. Unfortunately, in time of war these manœuvres cost Italy the lives of many of her best troops, and lowered the morale of the rest to such a point that the "Eyeties" became a standing joke. It is debatable that there are cowards in all armies, and that the number called to the colours in Italy was large because Italians lack the temperament for sustained sacrifice. It is indisputable that a soldier with water in his petrol, nothing in his canteen, boots which have worn out in a month, no letters from home, and officers betraying him to the enemy, is not likely to show much martial prowess.

The only units under arms to fight bravely and well for Mussolini—and to go on fighting after Mussolini's substitution in July 1943 and retirement to the hills—were the units of the militia. There is an element of irony in this. Mussolini had created a formal militia in 1922–1923 as part of his programme of normalization. He had, so some militiamen said, another motive, and that was to weaken the Black Shirts, who had created the latter stages of confusion which had urged him to power. Mussolini, for no apparent reason, doubted the loyalty of the Black Shirt militia, suspecting that it might be used against him if he failed to do what was expected of him. He had "done without" the march on Rome to make himself less dependent on, and obliged to, the Quadrumvirs, and prided himself on having confined its triumph to a participation in his. It was for this reason, it has been suggested, that he starved the militia of money and supplies from 1923–1925. In 1924, during the Matteotti crisis, it is significant that he did not mobilize the militia—perhaps he was afraid its leaders would depose him. He was certainly startled by Tarabella and Galbiati, when they insisted, on January 1, 1925, that he restart the revolution, that he would have the militia 100 per cent behind him. According to Galbiati, Mussolini had not realized until that moment that in the ranks of the militia there were largely "men who had espoused his cause, not because of any fascination for a new political doctrine (because such a doctrine scarcely existed) but because only he, at that moment, in Italy knew how to speak with virile, clear and resonant words to those who had won the war." During the rise of the dictatorship the militia "was a vital instrument for his policy as head of the government, and Mussolini, realizing this, began to strengthen it and give it a certain importance in the life of the country. However, Mussolini never took the militia as seriously as his opponents did."[3]

From 1939 to 1943, and in its reconstituted form from 1943 to 1945, the militia was the most loyal and possibly the most efficient part of the Armed Forces, and certainly the one which gave Mussolini fewest headaches. It was used by Badoglio and his generals as a spearhead unit, kept in the line for twice as long as regular units, and repeatedly milked of its best men for service in the Regular Army. On May 25, 1941, Mussolini appointed Galbiati to be Chief of Staff of the militia and created the only political instrument which remained loyal to him during the crisis of July 24 to 28, 1943. It is perhaps not surprising that Mussolini again found himself unable to test its strength and loyalty because of his innate suspicion.

The Fascist Party organization ought to have been even more loyal than its rowdy brother, the militia. The party was, after all, Mussolini's. Michele Bianchi might have worked out the details of its early organization, but the Duce himself coined many of its slogans and led it during its "democratic" parliamentary life. The militia was a formalization of "*squadrismo*," a phenomenon for which Mussolini had not been responsible. Even its organization (by Balbo) and early leadership were not in his hands, but in the hands of potential rivals. But the party, as he himself said, "is the Duce."

How could the Duce lose the confidence of the party? It is perhaps necessary to be more specific about "the party." By the time Mussolini was impelled to go to war, it had been made compulsory to join if one had any sort of state employment in prospect. The "semi-automatic" membership cannot be taken seriously, nor should it be confused with the hard core of volunteers, most of whom were not careerists. This hard core of the party—the party, say, of 1921—was divided into "interest groups." The largest and most important group had identified its interests with those of Mussolini and offered him a personal loyalty, which, when it was not blind, was certainly uncritical. Some members of this group had resisted the change from "movement" into "party," but their defeat by vote in 1921 did not turn them into anti-Fascists overnight. The second "interest group" was that formed by the so-called "Fascist intellectuals," whose aim was to create a body of Fascist doctrine and propagate it in the name of Mussolini. There was a third group, which saw in Mussolini and Fascism a logical development of its own ideas, and joined the party after the Duce had consolidated it.

Perhaps the most representative of the first group—the group with the blind loyalty if limited intelligence—was Starace. The longest-serving secretary of the party, he was an institution and wore out many jokes at his own expense. He tried to interpret the Duce's pronouncements as best he could, but more often than not reduced near-philosophy to clowning. When the Duce spoke of stiffening the spine of the nation, of increasing its virility, eliminating softness, Starace reacted by compelling party officials to do gymnastics, even jumping through hoops of fire himself to show an example of virility and vertebrate steel. Starace tried to enhance the "virile appearance" of the Italian male by putting him into uniform, but his uniforms always went too far toward a comic-opera effect. He tried to encourage "manly sports" like riding (because the Duce rode), but only succeeded in looking ridiculous himself as, booted and spurred, he rode his bicycle through the streets of Rome (his physical training instructor had recommended bicycling as a way of keeping down his weight). Poor Starace—as Bottai, no friend of his, said: "The man was better than his work." For all his ridiculousness in search of a practice for the Mussolinian doctrine virility, Starace did represent a reaction against the idea of softness current at least among foreign visitors to Italy. He certainly stayed with Mussolini to the end, dying with him and being savaged after death by the Duce's side. When Mussolini dismissed him from the party secretaryship at the outbreak of war, he alienated a substantial section of the party membership of "little Staraces," and kicked away one of the props of his own myth. Starace's successors—Serena, Vidussoni, Scorza—were no better than he and, if anything, less human in their failings.

Typical of the second "interest group" of "Fascist intellectuals" was, of course, Bottai. Bottai believed in Mussolini, firmly believed him to be the only man capable of restoring order in post-1918 Italy, and of keeping order for an indefinite period of time—at least for long enough for a new body of political doctrine to be evolved and applied. Bottai created Fascism, just as Mussolini created Fascists. The idea of the corporate State was to Bottai neither medieval nor absurd. The creation of national economic, political and moral unity, was, he believed, a necessary precedent to the restoration of stability. The Church, for one reason or another (mostly because of its attitude to the reunification, but also because it was incapable of resisting the onset of Socialism), had ceased to be universal. Bottai wanted to create something new and universal to take its place, and offered Fascism to the Duce, ready-made. Bottai was prepared to be patient with the Duce, who was not so taken with the doctrine as its creator. He was rewarded when the first corporate legislation was introduced, when eventually the basic structure of the corporate organization of capital and labour was completed in 1933. Bottai was even prepared to be patient when the Duce stopped work on the corporate State to meddle in international affairs, accepting the explanation that they needed external as well as internal stability for growth. He tolerated men like Ricci who became fanatical P.T. instructors, though he criticized him for becoming "rigid and dogmatic." He had to tolerate Starace. What Bottai would not tolerate, and what eventually alienated his sympathies from the Duce, was what he called the "betrayal of the Revolution." The betrayal, according to Bottai, began with the German alliance, the *passo romano*, the "reform" of Italian grammar to approximate it to German (the use of the third person "*lei*" for "you" was forbidden and replaced by "*voi*", "*sie*"), the persecution (if often nominal) of the Jews. Bottai was not impressed by the hodgepodge of Nazi theory, even if it had the academic merit of antedating their revolution. Hitler could only drag them out of their studies, away from their plans and into a beerhouse brawl. Hitler, then—after 1939—Mussolini, represented to Bottai the enemies of unity, stability, advance. By 1942 he had come to the conclusion that Mussolini would have to go if Fascism was to be saved and the revolution completed.

The third category of party member is perhaps typified by Luigi Federzoni.[4] Federzoni merged his Nationalist Party with the Fascist Party in order to get Nationalist policies adopted by his new colleagues. He was extremely valuable to Mussolini in the early days of normalization, representing as he did the upper-middle-class Right, and he was even more useful in keeping order, as Minister of the Interior, at the time of the Matteotti murder. During the Matteotti crisis he was accused of ill-advising the Duce against the mobilization of the provincial militia and Galbiati, for one still considers this to have been a mistake (which had to be remedied by the consuls' trip to Rome). In fact, his tact may well have prevented the outbreak of a major riot. He was certainly highly regarded by Mussolini. Sure evidence of this is the fact that as soon as the dictatorship had been established and the myth of Mussolini rooted, Federzoni, like Bottai, was put "backstage" where he could not build up a personal following. Federzoni and his fellow Nationalists were not, however, primarily interested in Bottai's doctrinal experiments. Their policy was "Make Italy Great," and they believed Mussolini to be the man to do this, with or without new ideologies. The adventures in Spain and Ethiopia reinforced their loyalty to the régime. The subsequent failures in North Africa, then the Balkans, weakened it. For them, Mussolini had simply ceased to be the best

Nationalist leader available, and their loyalty, therefore, had to be transferred elsewhere, in the interests of Italian greatness.

It is sometimes said that "Big Business" put Mussolini into power, kept him there, and was responsible for his misadventures and his downfall. This is far from the truth, just as it is useless for the Italian middle class to plead apathy as an excuse for their support of the régime. If it can be simplified, part of the explanation of Mussolini's rise to power is rather one of a desire on the part of the middle class—especially the lower middle class—to see order restored, the shops open, and no more windows broken. The help of the Church was valuable. The money contributed by Italian industrialists was considerable, but the "guts" of the régime was the middle class—the middle-class Royalists, the middle-class Nationalists, the middle class who staffed the party and officered the militia. Certainly the businessmen and industrialists kept up their support to the end—as late as April 29, 1943, Giovanni Balella was confirmed in charge of the Confederation of Industry, with the sole task of reorganizing the war effort behind the régime. But by then the war was lost, and the régime which "capital" had espoused too late to dominate could not be saved by anybody, rich or poor, who rushed in with last-minute offers of aid.

In order to understand the final collapse of the régime, it is necessary to trace the steps by which Mussolini lost the confidence of the masses and of the non-Fascist intellectuals who supported him for want of anything better to do. Had the people en masse remained loyal, then Mussolini could have defied the Church, the King, Badoglio, and the dissident elements in the party. After all, the régime was based on popularity, almost on a family relationship between the Duce and the crowd beneath his balcony. The crowd had seen Italy rise from the mud in the gutter to stand astride the main streets of Europe and stop the traffic. This was gratifying, and compensated for the sacrifices they were called upon to make. Until 1933 these sacrifices were made to a visible end, the restoration of stability, and this end seemed to have been achieved—stable prices, a stable relationship with the Church, no strikes, a rising standard of living. The wars in Ethiopia and Spain were at first unpopular (Italians are not warlike), but when they "came off" and Italy's prestige seemed to be still further reinforced, the grumbling ceased. It was when they were asked to make the enormous effort of not only rivalling the democracies, but conquering them, that the first loss of confidence occurred.

The conditions under which the rank and file were expected to fight made matters worse. The disorganization and poor, unenthusiastic leadership lowered morale and convinced the ranker that the régime was "on the way out," and he did not want to be on the losing side. Italians, in uniform and out, protested that they had been asked to make "supreme efforts" for twenty years and had nothing in reserve. They had been cheering for twenty years and their voices were hoarse. They had been wearing uniforms for twenty years and the martial novelty had worn off. Had they been sufficiently articulate, they might have commented that totalitarian states lack the stamina of democracies. They have to go to war under the same dictators who waged the peace, whereas democracies sweep away their peacetime leaders into senates and recruit a new, rested leadership in time of war. The man in the street was bored with roaring like a lion at Mussolini's bidding and wanted to be left alone to graze like the sheep the Duce despised. The man in the street was tired, after twenty years of exhortation and reconstruction. It never occurred to him to wonder if Mussolini, too, might be tired. By 1942 the Italian under arms was still capable of individual acts of heroism—the mining of warships by suicide midget submariners, piratical Mediterranean air sweeps and splendid assaults—like the one on Tobruk—but he was short of breath. He no longer felt he had anything to shout about.

At home, rationing and the usual wartime shortages did not improve morale. Though the vast majority of the peasants remained loyal to the Duce to the end, the urban population began to weaken during the hard winter of 1942. The last public demonstration of unlimited confidence in the Duce took place on December 11, 1941. A crowd was "ordered" and assembled beneath his balcony. It was rumoured that he had called for them to tell them that he had declared war on the United States, but his spell was still so strong that a Swedish journalist, moving among the crowd, reported that "most people honestly believed that the Duce was about to announce the Allied surrender and yet another 'Imperial triumph'." From that time on confidence slackened and the war effort with it.

However, a slackening of confidence is not the same thing as opposition. There have been few occasions in history when the mob has been capable of generating its own thoughts and slogans, and this was not such an occasion. It was only when the old opposition leaders, who had stayed on instead of fleeing to Paris (often collaborating with the régime), and a new generation of intellectuals realized that the crowd was discontented that an effective opposition was formed. This was the opposition which was to move from sullen discontent to armed resistance on a scale unique in the Axis or Axis-occupied territories, eclipsing every effort of the French maquis or Communist underground movements in Eastern Europe.

The old opposition—liberal, Catholic, Communist and Socialist—came to life during 1942, as if it sensed the decay of the régime. Possibly it was far more generally known than he believed that Badoglio was conspiring to overthrow the régime and set up a personal dictatorship of his own. The fear of a Badoglio-Humbert diarchy, which would certainly be even worse than the Mussolini-Victor Emmanuel diarchy they knew, may have urged the opposition out of its inert, passive hostility. The Communist Party, of course, still existed.[5] Its organization had been remade underground, with the help of money from Moscow and a blind faith in the certainty of proletarian victory. Its confidence in the mutual destruction of the "capitalist elements" in both the Allies (except, of course, the Soviet Union) and the Axis, gave it a special arrogance, and its leaders always behaved as if they were the Chosen Few. The Communist Party had the great advantage of an absence of traitors, which reinforced its external prestige, and of a martyr in Antonio Gramsci, who died in a Fascist prison after ten years of confinement, mostly solitary. Gramsci's letters from prison, now published in book form, are a moving contribution to the literature of patient, non-heroic martyrdom. Faith in Gramsci, Marx and the inevitability of the true revolution, kept the Communist Party organization glowing with enthusiasm.

The Communist Party's most serious rival was the old Popular Party, now secretly reformed as the Christian Democratic Party. It was, like its rival, international. The Church, acknowledging its mistake in not encouraging the Popular Party and its German opposite number as alternatives to Fascism and Nazism, was preparing for a Catholic coup. Catholic Action, used as a neutral alternative to organised Catholic politics by Pius XI, was reformed as the framework of a national party organisation. Many priests were pro-Fascist, so this organisation was of necessity mostly lay. The purge of priests would come later.[6]

The Socialist Party was not, in 1942, as well-organized as the Communist Party, nor did it have the auxiliary organization of the new Christian Democrats. It did, however, have tradition. Its roots were still deep in the working class, especially in the north-west of Italy, even if not much life showed above ground. While the Communist Party was suspect because of—real or rumoured—control from Moscow, and the Christian Democratic Party was suspect because it was "in the hands of priests," the Socialist Party was respectable. Only its own incompetence could fail to give it the lead when the time came to make a move.

The fourth of the old opposition parties, the Liberals, had neither organization, mass support, nor respectability. Many of its leaders had joined the Fascist Party; others had compromised themselves to a less extent. What the Liberal Party did have was a handful of men with experience of office in the far-off days before Fascism—Solari, Casati, Einaudi—and they had Benedetto Croce, still editing *Crìtica* and saying what he pleased about the régime. These men had access to the King.[7]

A new opposition came from a new party, which was formed and led by the younger generation. These young men mistrusted Socialists, Liberals and Christian Democrats, because they all three seemed to be backward-looking, anxious only to put the clock back and start again where they had gone wrong in 1919. There were even some young men who mistrusted the Communist Party because Marx had been dead for some time. The new party, called the Action Party, was an ideological mess. One wing was "Liberal-Socialist" and proposed to carry out a Liberal revolution on the lines suggested by Gobetti in 1924. The fact that Gobetti had died before he was thirty, and could, by stretching a point, be considered a martyr to Fascism, increased his value as a point of reference. Nobody had ever put any of Gobetti's ideas into practice, so they could not be considered old-fashioned. There was not much Socialism about Liberal-Socialism. The theory was, in substance, that the masses were the key to construction and reconstruction, but had to be led by an elite of liberals. There were elements of Fabianism, elements of Leninism, elements even of neo-Nazism, in the published programme of this wing of the Action Party. The other wing derived its supporters from the sons, nephews and younger followers of the Founders of Justice and Liberty, a movement started in 1929, which proposed to liberalize the revolution instead of revolutionizing Liberalism. Socialism was to be the aim and the banner, but Socialism without the class struggle, without "Marxist fatalism." In essence, the "Justice and Liberty" programme was similar to that adopted by the German Social Democratic Party in 1960, described impolitely as "not so much liberalizing the revolution as castrating it."

Both wings of the Action Party, like some members of the early *Fasci*, were reluctant to convert their "movement" into a party. They felt at first that it ought to be possible to make such a clean sweep in Italy that parties would no longer be necessary. They would invent an alternative. Unfortunately they were unable to invent anything, and formed themselves into a party like any other.

The four traditional parties, and the new one, established contact with each other during the latter part of 1941. It was at first a tentative exchange of views, rather than an invitation to co-operation. The Catholics and Communists were, understandably, reluctant to sit too close to each other at the conference table. The Action Party breathed fire and made the older Socialists feel uneasy. The Liberals exuded dignity. For a time the five opposition groups acted independently. The Left organized "abstentions from work." The Christian Democrats went to work on the women and the peasants. The Liberals plodded in and out of audience with the King. By the end of 1942, however, it was evident that some more drastic concerted action was necessary if they were to prevent Badoglio from replacing Mussolini with another, even less efficient, bellicose dictatorship.

The only course of action they could agree on (ideological agreement, the drafting of common long-term policies, was for obvious reasons impossible) was the "two-pronged attack." The first prong was to be the spread of disaffection among university students (who were disgruntled at being cut off from non-Axis culture and were too young to remember the chaos out of which Fascism had been created) and industrial workers (who felt a faint twinge of shame at twenty years of inactivity under the régime). The other prong, to be thrust necessarily by the Liberals, who enjoyed his confidence, was to be directed at the King. He was to be shown that only he, according to the Constitution he had sworn to protect—and even according to the Fascist law of the Grand Council—could dismiss Mussolini and provoke the fall of the régime. Once there was no Duce to blind the mob with science, they would listen, strike more easily, and see "reality."

In the spring of 1943 Italy stank of conspiracy. The Armed Forces were being betrayed by their generals and admirals, in the interests of Badoglio and Prince Humbert. The militia was being sucked dry, and the skin thrown into the front line to be punctured by Allied bayonets. Catholic Action and the Vatican bureaucracy were undermining morale. Dissidents in the Fascist Party passed old Liberals in the King's antechambers, both come to urge him to dismiss the head of the government at a crucial stage of the war. The war effort on the land was being sabotaged by peasants hoarding food. The war effort in the factories was being sabotaged by the reborn clandestine trade unions. And the Allies, Britain and

America, profiting by it all, were steadily driving the Italo-German armies out of North Africa toward Tunis and a landing on Italian soil.

Mussolini knew very well what was happening. He may have been blind to his own faults for many years, but he was not stupid. As far as he could see, the only loyal friend he had was his faithful mistress Clara Petacci. He did not trust Galbiati, whom he had once expelled from the party, and so failed to recognize his one potentially powerful source of support. All he knew was that Galbiati was tiresome about the difficulties of recruitment, especially for the building of a new Commando force—the Armoured M Division. Mussolini knew his time had come, and did not see what he could do about it. He saw that the war had been a mistake—he had hoped for a quick victory, as in Ethiopia, and it had not come. Now his forces were disunited and no longer to be relied upon. Above all, he realised that the heart had gone out of his people, who, like him, did not know whom to trust. One of the phenomena of Italian life is the readiness with which Italians volunteer for war, or to serve in any crisis, if the issues at stake are clear and worth while. They volunteered en masse to liberate the Italian peninsula of the Austrians, the Spanish and the French—it is estimated that about 65 per cent of the men under arms during the fight for the reunification of Italy were volunteers, irregulars. Italians volunteered en masse, too, during World War I—even in 1918, after three years of disheartenment—and drove the Austrian Army back across the Dolomites, avenging Caporetto. But there were no volunteers to be had after three years of World War II. People did what they were told to do, at home or in the front line, as best they could, without enthusiasm. Then they sat back and waited for it all to end.

The end was not long in coming. From the King, Mussolini learned that there were movements of Fascists behind his back. Though he was tired and dispirited, he could deal with these. On February 5th there was a Cabinet reshuffle. There was another on the 12th, another on the 13th, another on the 27th. In March 1943 the various opposition parties organised a wave of strikes, the most extensive being in Turin, which virtually paralysed the economy of the country for a week. This was followed by more reshuffling—of the party, of the High Command, of the Cabinet, on April 19th, 24th and 29th.

On June 2nd the King received Bonomi, the man appointed to lead the united non-Fascist Opposition. After a long argument, he agreed in principle to send for Mussolini on July 26th, to ask for his resignation and for the list of alternative ministers which the Grand

Council was supposed to have always on hand. In the meantime, the various groups which formed the non-Fascist Opposition were to organize a succession of strikes and demonstrations culminating in a general strike on July 26, 1943. The general strike was to last until all the Fascist names had been rejected by the King, who would then call on the united Opposition to prepare an alternative government. A caretaker government of "technicians and specialists," led by Badoglio, was to bridge the gap between the fallen régime and the new Democracy.

The war did not allow the King to carry through this plan—or rather, it saved him from collaboration with Bonomi, whom he disliked, and enabled him to turn only to Badoglio.

On July 10, 1943, the Allied Army landed in Sicily. The impossible, according to Mussolini, had happened, Democratic boots were trampling on Fascist imperial soil. Before the King had time to dismiss Mussolini on the part of Badoglio or the non-Fascist Opposition, the dissidents inside the Fascist Party decided to get rid of Mussolini themselves. On July 13th Party Secretary Scorza called for Bottai. At Scorza's house he found Albini, Bestianini, Chierici. He was told that Grandi had refused to speak at a Fascist rally at Bologna the following Thursday, and other party leaders had shown reluctance to appear on public platforms in other parts of Italy. How could they speak? How could they explain away the failure of the régime? Bottai told Scorza that he would not try to persuade his colleagues to speak lies when what was needed was an open meeting with the Duce at which every man could really speak the truth. No more charades. The Duce must authorise the calling of such a meeting. The Duce was reached by phone and agreed. He had no alternative. He was too tired to argue. As Navarra says, "It was easy to see he was fed up with it all—he stopped sticking coloured flags in his war map." [8]

For the next ten days there was a great coming and going of members of the Grand Council as the conspirators discussed two basic alternatives—a refurbishing of Fascism, with more power to the Grand Council, diminution of Mussolini's powers proportionately, a reintroduction of freedom to criticise, advise; or, the other alternative, "a solution without Mussolini, once unthinkable." On July 16th another plotters' meeting was called. Giurati, Farinacci, Teruzzi, de Cicco and Bottai, discussed the deteriorating military situation and the civil situation, which could not be worse. Farinacci, for the first time, proposed "a solution with Mussolini apart." There was no explicit agreement on the part of his small audience (he spoke, says Bottai, as if he were addressing a meeting), but it was understood from then on that Mussolini had to go.

The meeting of the Grand Council, on the evening of July 24th, came almost as an anti-climax to the conspirators.[9] They were not even elated. Most of them were not conscious of the irony of the situation, of having defeated the democratic parties, so to speak, by getting in first with the removal of the Duce. Almost certainly Mussolini knew what was going to happen. Five days previously he had met Hitler at Feltre to discuss future plans and "had returned humiliated, angry and irresolute, perhaps only too pleased at the prospect that somebody else would soon be making the decisions." Mussolini had, in fact, seen a motion which was to be presented by Grandi to the Grand Council which "invited the Head of the Government to beg His Majesty the King . . . to assume command of the Armed Forces for as long as he thinks fit . . ." It may be that Mussolini hoped he could escape with the surrender of Supreme Command. The meeting had not lasted long, however, before he realised that he was finished as both a military and civil power. The meeting opened at five o'clock. The only important man who was not in the conspiracy, Major-General Galbiati, commanding the militia, arrived last. He was astonished to find the Palazzo Venezia unguarded. Mussolini, perhaps fearing that Galbiati would have all the other Grand Councillors arrested as soon as their motions of no confidence were presented, had ordered that there should be no musketeers on duty.

Mussolini opened the meeting himself, with a survey of the situation, civil and military, including a bitter denunciation of the conspiracy and sabotage which had weakened the Armed Forces. He was followed by de Bono, who spoke briefly in defence of the honour of the Army. De Vecchi spoke briefly too. As Galbiati says: ". . . to no great point, but the absurdity relaxed the tension a little." Farinacci, for want of something better to say, suggested that General Ambrosio be invited to give a detailed account of the situation in Sicily, since he, conspirator or not, was Chief Executive of the Army. Nobody thought this was a good idea. Then Grandi got up to speak. First he read out his motion, ending with the invitation to the King to assume Supreme Command. But this was just the beginning. According to Galbiati: "Grandi, explaining his motion, launched into an angry, spiteful and often naïve attack on Mussolini, accusing him of formal dictatorship and of the inconstitutionality of all his acts of Government." He was followed by those members of the Grand Council who had already agreed to support him, all of them bitter. Farinacci then read out a motion of his own, not differing much from Grandi's, again inviting the head of the government to ask the King to assume Supreme Command. As Galbiati said: "It was not that there was any essential disagreement between the two men—but both wanted to go down in history as the man who had deposed the Duce."

At eleven o'clock Galbiati decided that he had had "enough treason and disloyalty for one evening." He had, after all, three militia units within fifty miles. If he could only adjourn the Grand Council meeting for a day, he could fill the streets with Black Shirts and arrest Grandi and his friends. The same thought had occurred to Grandi. When Scorza proposed that the meeting adjourn, the proposal was voted down. At midnight Mussolini adjourned the council for ten minutes, so that the men who were plotting his downfall could have a smoke (having given up smoking himself he had forbidden it in his presence).

When the Grand Council reassembled at ten minutes past midnight on July 25th, Farinacci, Grandi and Ciano spoke first. Farinacci's bitterness had not passed. He launched into a diatribe against Mussolini, accusing him of incompetence, especially in the choice of his advisers: "It seems impossible, but every time you have had to choose between several people, you have always chosen the worst." Grandi, who followed Farinacci, surprised his friends by being less critical of Mussolini's person than he had been a few hours before, perhaps to differentiate between himself (the "cultured diplomat") and Farinacci (the chronic thug). He said that he was not proposing to "dethrone" Mussolini—"You will always be our Chief, our Duce." Bottai, Rossoni and Federzoni shouted, "*si, si!*" at this.

This sign of "weakness" encouraged Tringali-Casanova to state baldly that he would not vote for Grandi's motion. Ciano hovered between his disappearing past and his uncertain future. Galbiati made a speech (later described by Mussolini as "that of an old soldier and Black Shirt"), in which he, too, declared himself opposed to Grandi's motion, which would really solve no problems at all. What the country needed was a new sense of unity. The only man who had been able to give it a sense of unity in eighty years had been Mussolini, and it was stupid to remove him from the post of command. What was really needed was a clean-up of the party. Somehow a gulf between Fascism and the people had opened up, and this had to be closed.

The discussion proper on the real question at issue—whether or not Mussolini should go—opened at about 1 a.m. Nearly every member of the Grand Council spoke, some with pain, most with anger in their voices. At 2.30 a.m. the vote was taken. Nineteen voted in favour; seven voted no.

Mussolini sat impassive as the vote was taken. It was all but the end. For the first time in history a dictator had been democratically removed from office by an institution which was a tombstone over the body of the Parliament which had first elected him to power. It was a situation not without irony.

Galbiati and his friends, who had voted against Grandi's motion, stayed behind to discuss the situation, to speculate. They eventually agreed to meet again in the early morning, and put themselves at Mussolini's disposal, to do whatever he thought fit. Twenty years of service was a long time. As Galbiati said: "The Duce often reminded us that Christ had twelve disciples, one of whom betrayed him for thirty pieces of silver, one denied him, one doubted his Divinity, and all but two fled at the first sign of danger. The Grand Council was not unlike the Twelve Apostles."

None of the handful of loyal Councillors knew why Farinacci and Suardo had abstained from voting, unless it was "headsmen's spite", jealousy that somebody else's axe had been used to decapitate the régime.

The reasons for the about-face by the nineteen who had voted for the Grandi motion have already been suggested. Grandi was voting to avenge his defeat in 1921, in the struggle for the leadership of the party, to avenge his years of exile in London. Federzoni and the Nationalists were voting against a leader who had failed on the battlefield. Balella was expressing the opinion of the industrialists that "the Régime is suddenly worn out." De Stefani was bitter at the waste of the resources of the economy he had created out of chaos; Bottai at the "betrayal of the Revolution." The remainder threw in their lot with what was obviously the "winning side." Of the 19, Ciano, de Bono, Marinelli, Gottardi and Pareschi, were shot six months later by Mussolini, and Cianetti was sentenced to thirty years of imprisonment. The remaining 13 "faded out of sight," all condemned to death in their absence from the trial. Grandi eventually became a salesman, with conspicuous wealth in South America. Balella went back to business. The only one of the 19 to show anything of the spirit of 1921, was, not unexpectedly, Bottai, who went off, muttering about the betrayal of the revolution, to join the French Foreign Legion.

Farinacci, ironically, was shot by partisans who did not appreciate his anti-Mussolini-ism.

On July 25th, after a short sleep, Galbiati set off for the Palazzo Venezia. There he found Mussolini at work as usual, receiving Grand Councillors and discussing his future with them. Grandi was nowhere to be found. Albini and Buffarini were in the antechamber when Galbiati arrived. The general had brought with him a proposal, which he put before Mussolini at noon, that the Duce declare a renewal of their intention to fight on Hitler's side, for good or evil, as they had promised to do. Galbiati himself proposed that he should leave for Germany immediately to see Himmler. The 19 Grand Councillors who had voted the Grandi motion could be disposed of by calling them up (they all held either Army or militia ranks) and sending them off to fight. Refusal to go would be legal (as opposed to their former moral) treason and they could be shot.

Mussolini, tired and dispirited, said No. He would go to the King and discuss the situation with him. An hour later Galbiati saw Mussolini again. By this time the Duce had recovered some of his spirits and told the general that he thought he could make a fight of it. He would go to the King, explain to him what had happened at the Grand Council meeting, and urge him to denounce the "conspirators."

Mussolini arrived at the palace in the late afternoon. The King had been told of the Grand Council meeting by one of the 19 and had summoned up all the courage of his father and grandfather. In his memoirs he wrote spitefully that he had put Mussolini in his place, insisting on accepting the Duce's resignation not only as Supreme Commander but also as head of the government. "This man Mussolini, who had showed such contempt for the Law, pleaded with me that his Grand Council had behaved unconstitutionally." But the King had not only summoned up the courage to dismiss Mussolini—he had made arrangements for the ex-Duce's arrest.

As Mussolini left the palace he was forced into a car, after the manner of Chicago gangsters abducting an obstreperous politician, and driven off into the unknown.

The King and Badoglio were now "in power." Badoglio was proclaimed head of the government, and moved troops to key positions in the city of Rome, ordering all local authorities in the provinces to "take precautionary measures," lest there should be a counter coup on the part of men loyal to the fallen idol. In fact, the only man in Rome who could have made a move to arrest Badoglio and restore Mussolini to power was Galbiati. Galbiati did nothing, allowed himself to be removed from his office, and a few days later arrested and imprisoned. Many of Galbiati's friends and all of his enemies wondered, even for years after the end of the civil war, why Galbiati had done nothing to show his loyalty more forcibly.

Galbiati himself eventually outlined in detail the events of July 25th and 26th. He explained his "immobility," in reply to accusations of cowardice from the former German Commander in the area (in 1944 a German-language paper even predicted, inaccurately, that Galbiati would be shot for desertion and cowardice). Galbiati wrote that first of all he could not bring off a counter coup, because he had insufficient forces at his disposal. There was only one division in the city and the remainder of the militia was either thousands of miles away (sent out of the way by Badoglio as part of *his* conspiracy in 1942) or so far outside Rome as not to be on call. His own Command Headquarters, with an effective garrison, was surrounded by Badoglio's troops, and he had three 75 mm. guns pointing at his office window. He would have risked a move, he said, if he had known where Mussolini was, but without the Duce's presence he could not guarantee to rally the civil population (who were prematurely celebrating the end of the war).

Mussolini was being kept on the move to prevent Galbiati from reaching him. He was taken from the palace and hurriedly put on board the corvette *Persefone*, then landed on the island of Ponza (an isolation centre for *anti*-Fascists). On August 7th he was moved again to La Maddalena, and from there a fortnight later to Gran Sasso (during this last move there was an attempt to rescue Mussolini, by four Italian airmen, but this failed and the rescuers were shot).

By the beginning of August the situation seemed to be "stable." Mussolini was gone. His most powerful friends had either fled or were in prison. The Grand Council had vanished into thin air, and the whole Fascist apparatus was in a state of suspended animation, not knowing how to function without its head. The nineteen conspiring members of the Grand Council had been taken by surprise by the King's coup and could not figure out what to do next. Their reaction was to sit down and wait until Mussolini reappeared, as they felt he was one day bound to do. The habit of twenty years dies hard.

Badoglio and the King were highly satisfied with their coup. They had banked on at least some fighting—a token resistance by the militia—but instead there had been a passive acceptance of the change of command, as if there had been no overtones of betrayal.

They felt so confident of their position, even if the military situation did not inspire confidence, that they treated the delegations from the five opposition parties, now thronging the ante-chambers, with lofty contempt. After all, their efforts had not been necessary. A sharp word and the Duce had been dismissed. Badoglio's refusal even to talk to the Communist members of the five-party "Liberation Committee" did not improve their tempers. When Badoglio did talk to Bonomi, a pleasant moderate, he was polite but firm. There could be no question of elections or political controversy until more pressing problems had been solved. Bonomi was not helped by the intransigence of the leaders of the "Action Party," who were already urging the proclamation of a republic. The main point of contention, however, concerned the denunciation of the Pact of Steel. With the fall of Facism the pact no longer had any validity, being essentially a joint manifesto by two régimes, rather than a "normal treaty." Both Badoglio and Bonomi agreed that the denunciation must be made—but who was to do the denouncing? Badoglio, as head of the government appointed by the King, insisted on his right to do so. Bonomi insisted that this was breaking an "understanding" of June 10th, which envisaged a return to normal political life as soon as possible. The denunciation of the Pact of Steel ought to be signed by all the political leaders of the anti-Fascist front.

Both Bonomi and Badoglio, of course, were, at the same time—separately and without consulting each other—negotiating with the Allies. Bonomi was discussing surrender terms in Switzerland; Badoglio in Sicily. Vice-emissaries who had once met by chance at a meeting of a minority plot in Rome.

On August 13th Bonomi and his colleagues issued a manifesto dissociating themselves from the "technical government of Badoglio." For the next three weeks there was a neck-and-neck race to see who could make an effective denunciation of the Italo-German alliance first—who could persuade the Allies to accept their form of surrender. This race was won by Badoglio, who could at least prove to the sceptical Eisenhower that he was the effective head of government, and, as a soldier, seemed able to understand simple and direct orders. The armistice was signed on September 3, 1943, and it was agreed that it should be proclaimed simultaneously in Rome, London and Washington.

Badoglio wanted a delay so that he could be sure he had the principal cities under law and control, and some sort of administrative programme drafted. Five days later, when the Allies had still heard nothing from Badoglio, they sent General Taylor to Rome to discuss the situation with the Marshal and ask him if he was waiting for some military action on their part. Should they parachute a division into the city? This was the last thing Badoglio wanted—he was looking forward to liberating Rome himself and trying the German officers he would arrest. He assured General Taylor that, with the Germans now in control of the airports and suspecting an Italian capitulation, such a parachuting would be suicidal. On September 8th Intelligence Officers at Allied Headquarters began to suspect that the Italians, political and military, were up to no good, and Eisenhower broadcast the news of their surrender himself.

Taken by surprise, on the morning of September 9th, the King and Badoglio fled Rome and set up the headquarters of their government at Brindisi. They left behind a recording with a message from Badoglio on it, and this was played over and over again during the morning.

The King and Badoglio had just left the city limits when German armour moved in.

During the six weeks from July 25th to September 3rd Hitler had followed the misadventures of his "master and friend" with some incredulity. The idea of the Fuehrer being forced to hand over even a minimal part of his power as the result of a vote in council was laughable. What opposition there was to Hitler was well hidden, and manifested itself in the plots which had fascinated Attolico in the thirties. What was Mussolini up to? Where was he, anyway? German Intelligence reported him a prisoner, but in a prison unknown. Whenever they traced the Duce's guards, they had already handed him on to others. It was not until the end of August that he was traced to the Campo Imperatore in the Abruzzi.

Mussolini's lack of success as a wartime leader had stunned the Fuehrer. His "master and friend" had told him he was short of war material, and this the Fuehrer would appreciate—Italy had no minerals of any value. But what had happened to the Army which had whistled through Ethiopia and demolished the Internationale in Spain? And what were all these reports of plot and counterplot? What had happened to the 100 per cent loyalty and confidence in their leader which the Italians had shown ever since he, the Fuehrer, could remember?

Perhaps poor old Mussolini was too old for war? For a few weeks Hitler toyed with the idea of approaching Badoglio and asking him for a renewal of the alliance. Hitler needed Italian troops, if only to hold down Allied divisions—he had twenty-six in Italy and wanted to transfer some to the Eastern Front and reinforce his garrisons in France.

When Badoglio's recording proclaimed the armistice on the morning of September 9th, this line of wishful thinking came to an end. Badoglio was now a traitor. The Pact of Steel had specified that neither ally was to surrender or make any sort of treaty independently of the other. There was only one possible leader for the Italians—Mussolini. Hitler gave orders that wherever he was he had to be found, rescued and brought to Germany. The Duce was rescued on September 12th by Otto Skorczeny, who flew a small aeroplane right into Mussolini's jailers' arms (almost literally, landing on the lawn beneath the Duce's bedroom).

On September 12th Mussolini met Hitler, discussed the whole situation on the peninsula with him, and proclaimed the Italian Social Republic. For the next week Mussolini's voice was beamed at Italy from Munich and Milan, the monarchy declared at an end. A new call to arms, under a single head of state, reached ears which had grown so accustomed to that voice that the instinct to obey it was overwhelming.

For four days Italy had been, in theory, at peace. It had been an uncertain peace. The King and Badoglio were at Brindisi, acknowledged by the Allies to be some sort of government. There were also five assorted political groups, occasionally united under Bonomi, who considered themselves to be the government. Contradictory orders came from every side during the "peace." Part of the "armistice bargain" had been an understanding that Italian volunteers should be allowed to join the fight against Nazi Germany, and this further confused the man in the street. He could understand a *coup d'état* and Badoglio taking the Duce's place—this was an occupational hazard of politicians, after all, even if it had all seemed too easy. He could even understand Badoglio's changing his mind about fighting on, though it had never occurred to World War I generals to surrender. What he could not fully appreciate was the ethics of changing sides, fighting the Allies one day and the Axis the next. The man in the street was almost relieved when the familiar voice of the Duce came through his loudspeaker, telling him that the war against the Allies was on again.

For the next two months, almost ignoring World War II, Italians of all shapes and sizes regrouped, as during the interval of a football match. Marshal Graziani was named Commander in Chief of the Armies of the new Social Republic. This popular soldier did all he could to get together some sort of army, navy and air force with which (according to his lights) to save Italy's honour. The Italian units in Italy which had been billeted with Germans had continued to fight from the morning of the 9th and had ignored the call to armistice. This was a good nucleus. The "Nembo" parachute regiment had stayed loyal to the Duce, as had several battalions of his old regiment, the *Bersaglieri* and some services (engineers, supply units). After Graziani had appealed for recruits, the Army grew to four divisions, with the militia reformed into the National Republican Guard (this had, however, primarily the functions of a security police force—Galbiati, who had rejoined the Duce, refused to command it).

Graziani had been too late to catch the Navy, most of whose officers were in the Badoglio clan, and this had surrendered, almost in its entirety, at Malta. Some of the younger naval officers with commands of their own (men born during Fascism), mostly torpedo-boat commanders, had refused to sail with the Fleet, and put themselves at Graziani's disposition. A number of aircraft (torpedo-carrying light planes) which had been on airfields in the north of Italy, fell into Republican hands, and their pilots remained loyal (on June 5, 1944, ten of them made a successful raid on Gibraltar, sinking several ships of the Royal Navy). In all, some 800,000 men were under arms, acknowledging Mussolini's political leadership —a not inconsiderable number.

The Allies stopped their advance for the year along a line from the Garigliano (north of Naples) to the Adriatic, south of Pescara. This, the so-called Gustav Line, was a defensive position hurriedly prepared by Hitler and Mussolini, and actually did hold until the spring. South of the Gustav Line, Badoglio was proclaimed Prime Minister of a military government (October 1st), then of the first post-war civil government of Italy.

There were, then, in that fall of 1943, two Italys, and the situation was "clear" again. To the north, Mussolini's new republic, with its four divisions—reinforced by twenty-six German divisions under overall German military command and overall German political direction—but nevertheless, a Fascist Italy under the same old Duce, fulfilling its obligations under the Pact of Steel. To the south—Badoglio. There was also a third government, the Committee for National Liberation (C.L.N.), which wanted no part of either Badoglio or Mussolini. Their "partisans" had liberated Naples three days before Allied troops had arrived there, and the C.L.N. thought this entitled them to special consideration as the political leadership of a nation-wide organization of irregulars. The

Allied authorities did not appreciate the point. As far as Eisenhower was concerned, Italy had surrendered. The defeated government was at Brindisi and was carrying out the terms of the armistice. North of the Gustav Line, the Germans were an occupying power and had to be shifted as quickly as possible. Some British generals interpreted the situation differently, suggesting that the legal position was that there had been a *coup d'état* which had failed. Mussolini was back in power again. The Allied-occupied territory had been simply "liberated," and there had been no valid surrender, no valid armistice.

But whatever the legal interpretation of the situation, nobody would give legal recognition to Bonomi and his five opposition parties. What the Action Party wanted was an agreement with the Allied Armies by which the C.L.N. was appointed at least custodian of the Constitution and arbiter of post-war forms of government. It was not enough for Italy to surrender and be dealt with as a defeated country. The Action Party wanted to convince the Allies that a great many Italians had been anti-Fascists, active or passive, and only wanted to be given a chance to show their anti-Fascism on Italian soil. They pointed out that they had fought in Spain on the Republican side, though few of the actual fighters were at that time on the Italian mainland. They did not want to be treated as volunteers in the Allied Armies as much as they wanted to be an independent force with as much honour and authority as the Free French. After all, part of France was Fascist, too, and under German "protection", and the Allies would soon drive the Germans from the rest. The Action Party stressed that it and its colleagues in the C.L.N. were concerned with the political structure of Italy in the post-war era, as well as with the immediate task of defeating the Republican and German Armies.[10]

To the Allies, Bonomi and his colleagues—and in particular his Left-Wing Action Party colleagues—were a nuisance. It was not a nice clean surrender. Here were these politicians, who had been passive for twenty years, asking for rights as co-belligerents, with their own independent civil and military authority. Not only that—there were Bolsheviks among them, and the word was already going around that in the post-war period there would be trouble with a victorious Soviet Union.

Perhaps the most frustrating thing for the C.L.N. was that it really did have an organisation, military and civil, in Italy, north of the Gustav Line, and north of that line Badoglio and the King were not popular. The anti-Fascists in the big cities of the north—

Turin, Milan, Genoa—owed their loyalty to one or other of the C.L.N. leaders, and where there was any sort of control of the partisans—now fighting the Republican troops and Germans indiscriminately north of the line—it was held by the C.L.N. It was vitally important for C.L.N. pride and prestige that some sort of acknowledgement from the Allies be received. Whatever their motives for zealous anti-Fascism (purely political, shame, desire for loot), the "military" forces of the C.L.N. represented an Italian attitude which ought to be taken into consideration. If encouraged, the C.L.N. believed it could treble its fighting strength behind the lines, destroy the Mussolini republic, as well as expel the German Army, by itself. But nobody south of the Gustav Line took any notice of the C.L.N. The partisans had a hard winter. The politicians nibbled their nails.

As the winter drew on, the political leaders of the resistance grew more and more impatient. It became imperative for them to get rid of the King and Badoglio. If both were still in the seat of authority at the end of the war, it would be hard to find a place in the government for the Left Wing, at least, of the five opposition parties.

From January 28 to 29, 1944, the five parties held an anti-Fascist congress at Bari. It was an occasion for many speeches, and the first anti-Fascist rally to be held in Italy for twenty years. The speeches were long, and seventeen politicians scheduled to orate were unable to reach the microphones. Three motions, previously approved on October 16 and November 16, 1943, were presented to the congress. They all demanded the resignation of Badoglio and the abdication of the King. There was some difference of opinion about when these events should take place. The Liberals in general, and some of the Christian Democrats, were for waiting until the war was over. They realised that the Allies did not want to be bothered with elections at this stage, in territory which already enjoyed a national government, signatory of the armistice, and an Allied military government which was just beginning to trust it. Significantly, the Communists did not insist on an immediate abdication either. It would not have suited them to have elections in the south, while the cities—and Romagna—where their strength was greatest were still battlefields and unable to register a vote. The Action Party and the Socialists, however, were for an immediate change—at least for some sort of national government other than the appointees around Badoglio.

The Allies took no notice of representations made to them after the Bari Congress. The King and Badoglio showed their distaste for the delegates by moving their government to Salerno (February). This double snub infuriated all the delegates. The Allied advance had come to a halt and the only people doing any fighting north of the Gustav Line were Italian partisans not loyal to the King. At least some sort of courtesy was due to their political leaders and representatives in the south. It was decided to organize a massive strike for March 1st, which would paralyse the north and draw the Allies' attention to the fact that the C.L.N. must be taken seriously. The strike was called, and for a few days everything was as the C.L.N. hoped it would be. Then it was repressed in part by German and Fascist troops, who urged people back to work at gunpoint; in part by employers who gave the strikers a holiday and refused to recognize that a strike was on.

The March 1st strike did impress the Allied commanders, and, even more important, it impressed Badoglio. But it also showed both that the C.L.N. was far from being in control of even the areas best disposed to it. Allied Commander-in-Chief General Alexander also knew that it would be some time before his troops could link up with the partisans. Mussolini, with his German troops and German generals and Graziani, looked as if he would fight every inch of the way, and the Italian peninsula had become very much a secondary theatre of war. The front opening in France and the Eastern Front were occupying both Hitler and the Allies far more than the Italian "diversion," and both the German and Allied high commands looked on the Gustav Line and its successors as "troop consumers." Hitler and the Allies drew divisions out of Italy when reinforcements were needed elsewhere as though they were in the House of Commons, making pairing arrangements between Government and Opposition. This did nothing for the self-esteem of either Mussolini or the C.L.N.

The next move was made by Stalin. He had appraised the situation and come to the conclusion that nothing was to be done about Communizing Italy until the war was over. On March 13, 1944, the Soviet Union formally recognised the Badoglio government.

This Soviet move infuriated everyone. The Allies were hurt to think that they had been beaten to this recognition. They were still treating Badoglio as a "temporary," a defeated general who had signed an armistice. The Italian Communist Party was placed in a dilemma and thereafter never trusted by its four political allies. The Action Party, which contained a number of extreme Left-Wingers, violently pro-Soviet, found itself at a loss to know what to do—its idol Stalin had recognised the government it had just sworn at Bari to depose. Even the King was embarrassed to find himself ruling by the Grace of God, and with the consent and full approval of Moscow. On April 12th the King tired of the situation, even after recognition by the Allies. He issued a statement, promising to hand over the affairs of State to Humbert as Lieutenant-General of the Realm, as soon as Rome was liberated. On April 21st Badoglio took the first members of the opposition parties into his government. On June 1, 1944, Rome was freed, and not long afterwards Bonomi became first Prime Minister of the first fully recognised post-Fascist civil government.

This "Rome solution" did not satisfy the Action Party, which had the loudest voice in the C.L.N. in the north-west. They, too, realized that it would be at least a year—at the rate things were going—before they were officially "liberated." By that time there would be a Christian Democrat government, under the Regency of Humbert, and then where would the Left be? The Communist Party had no comment to make, as none was forthcoming from Moscow. Its orders were to fight on, as partisans, and take no political action until further orders were received. The Socialists agreed with the Action Party that an "internal struggle" should start immediately. The Liberals and Christian Democrats, on the other hand, saw things "moving back to normal" (i.e., to 1921). They were prepared to praise partisans, but for them the political aspect of "resistance" was already more than satisfactory. The Pope was Protector of Rome again (this pleased the Christian Democrats), and Croce was making pronouncements about the new Constitution (which pleased the Liberals).

The Allied offensive in the late spring of 1944 carried them as far as the Appenines, where again, in the autumn, they were halted by a prepared position. It came as something of a shock to find that the best troops along this line were under the command of Graziani, who had been given two new German divisions to reinforce his own four. The realization that the Social Republic was still effective, and could count on the loyalty of hundreds of thousands of fighting men, did not help to clarify the political situation or to reinforce the claims of the C.L.N. to be the true Italian government in the north. Nevertheless, the farther north the Allied Armies moved, the more impressed they were by the military resistance, even if they despised the politicians. It is estimated that some 250,000 partisans were actively engaged in fighting in one sort of formation or another.

Seventy-two thousand, five hundred people were killed, including civilians shot for helping partisans or harbouring them. Some

39,000 were wounded. Over 125,000 people were later officially recognized as having consistently helped to sabotage the Social Republic and the German installations in its territory. In addition to the non-belligerent helpers and the fighting partisans (organized in bands, brigades, and commands), there were the Communist "murder squads" (G.A.P. in the towns and S.A.P. in the country) whose job was to "execute traitors" (they shot Gentile, the old philosopher and president of the Italian Academy, though it is difficult to see what danger he represented).

A political breakdown of these resistance formations is interesting. The majority were Communists, again weakening the political bargaining power of the Action Party majorities inside the C.L.N. These Communist brigades numbered 575, called the "Garibaldi Brigades" as they had been during the Spanish Civil war. Next (255) came the so-called "autonomous formations"—without political affiliations, often without any *raison d'être* other than loot. Only third in number (198) came the Action Party's military units, called "Justice and Liberty" (after Roselli). There were 153,600 "Garibaldi" partisans in all, out of the total of over 250,000, and over half the casualties were Communist. In the post-war period they were awarded 387 gold medals (for valour), 217 in silver. The preponderance of Communist units inside the resistance gave their commanders good reason to claim that they "directed" the underground war, and certainly the major insurrections (ending with the last, and finally effective, one of April 25, 1945) occurred when the Communist Party gave the word. It was incomprehensible to the Allies that the Communists should be politically inactive and leave all the political wrangling to an "Action Party" which had no equivalent in their experience.

The effectiveness of the Fascist Republican and German defence and the steady "milking" of the Allied Armies in Italy for use in France, halted General Alexander on the "Gothic Line," and he settled down to spend the winter consolidating his position. The various partisan formations, not unnaturally, were disappointed at the check, but offered to carry on the civil war. They needed arms. Deserters from Mussolini's Army (not so much men who had run away as those who had not answered the call-ups of May and July, 1944) had joined the partisans, but had no guns. The imminent end of the war, and civil war, had attracted thousands of men of little political value, but found everywhere as "strong finishers." There were not enough rifles and ammunition to go round, and the partisans approached the Allies to ask for more. But General

Alexander had no intention of dropping unlimited quantities of arms to the partisans. He knew that many of them were Communists, and this was enough to make him reluctant to draw on his limited supplies. Events in Greece, where Communist partisans were making ready for an armed coup as soon as Liberation was complete, made him suspect that the Action Party leaders ("crypto-Communists") were contemplating something similar in Italy. The behaviour of the C.L.N. leaders did nothing to reassure him. They flatly refused to collaborate with the government in Rome, and even issued a memorandum to the leaders of "Justice and Liberty" unit commanders, urging them to make it clear to their men that they must only receive and obey orders from the C.L.N. and not from the "so-called government in Rome." The C.L.N. memorandum, which was secret, but fell almost immediately into Allied hands, stressed that the forces of the C.L.N. constituted a "new revolutionary Army." To soldiers of Alexander's generation, who had failed to suppress the Soviet State by force of arms, this was a clear warning. On November 13, 1944, Alexander issued an instruction to all partisans to "cease large-scale operations." He also informed them that there would be no arms forthcoming for the time being, and urged them to go to their homes.

General Alexander's instructions caused consternation and increased the political frustration of the C.L.N. Ever since the Armistice it had been treated lightly, or so it felt, and the Allies, while taking advantage of its willingness to risk lives in a war behind the main lines, refused to concede it political recognition. This fact, and the amount of pro-Fascism its units found, especially among the peasants—*and* the fact that 500,000 Italians were under arms against it—produced a frustration among C.L.N. leaders which caused many of them to lose their heads. The frustration had a natural outcome. It increased the ferocity with which the military units (who refused to go home) fought Germans and Fascists alike and started a reign of terror which often obliterated the heroism of earlier partisan campaigns. There were already a large number of partisan units roaming about without any other scope than to live off the land and shoot Germans as they might shoot hares—men for whom the civil war was "fun." They alienated a great deal of sympathy, especially among the peasants whose hens, calves and wine went down partisan throats. When "Justice and Liberty" units, under instructions from their frustrated political leadership in Turin, started to murder and requisition as recklessly, the whole partisan movement earned a bad reputation which it did not deserve.

The anxiety of Italians to play their part in avenging their years of passive hostility to Fascism, to help the democracies to victory, gave way in the minds of the leaders of the C.L.N. to a not always creditable desire to show themselves so powerful that the Allies would be *forced* to show them political recognition. In the long run, of course, it was political suicide, and the Action Party, associated in the minds of many people with reckless partisans, shooting wild, was extinguished at the first real free election of the post-war Italian Republic.

On December 6th the C.L.N. sent a delegation to Rome to see if it were not possible to change the minds of the Allies about laying down their arms for the winter, to try to make some sort of political impact. The attempt was an almost complete failure. In return for an Allied promise to resume supplies of arms and ammunition, the delegation had to sign (December 7th) an agreement (signed for the Allies by Maitland-Wilson) by which it accepted the Italian Regular Army General Cardona as Supreme Commander and surrendered its military autonomy. Maitland-Wilson also extracted the written promise that as soon as Allied troops arrived in a town or city it would be immediately turned over to the military government. No "soviets" were to be set up.

On December 26th the C.L.N., in the areas north of the Gothic Line, lost its political autonomy, too. By the terms of an agreement signed with Bonomi in Rome, it agreed to consider itself only the delegate of the government in Rome, and its forces at that government's disposal. There was no more talk of "new and revolutionary forces." On January 17, 1945, the C.L.N. made a lame apology for its abdication, that "independently of the Rome solution, the C.L.N. maintains its own right to political action" but no one was deceived.

For the last four months of the war—now for the C.L.N. virtually only a civil war—the forces of "Justice and Liberty" pursued their anti-Fascist campaigns with the desperation of men "doomed to respectability in the hands of others." They knew that political power would not be theirs when the war ended, so there was no cause for discretion or moderation. The war became the outlet for their frustration, and the massacres and cruelty on both sides increased accordingly.

Mussolini's headquarters were on Lago di Garda. There he sat, surrounded by members of what was in effect a "Shadow Cabinet," with German guards and German advisers his real authorities.

There was so little to do that he even had time to write a book and prepare himself for the "reckoning" he would have to pay when the inevitable Allied victory arrived. Hitler, after the bomb plot of July 20, 1944, treated him with the respect due a fellow sufferer from the disloyalty of subordinates. Both men knew that the end was in sight. Their only hope for survival lay in the "super weapons" which Hitler's scientists were hurrying to perfect—the rocket, and the atomic device which might be attached to it or dropped from an aeroplane. To Hitler, Mussolini and his men were valuable because they helped him to gain time, and his scientists needed time. If the old admiration for his "master and friend" had gone, at least he conceded to the Duce that he was the only wall which could be erected in Italy. On December 16, 1944, the last Axis offensive was mounted—in France, against the Americans at the Ardennes, in Italy against the Americans at Garfagnana. On the same day Mussolini made his last major speech, in the Teatro Lìrico, Milan.[11]

Perhaps one point of the speech is worth quoting: "Communism represents the gravest threat to Western civilization there has ever been, and I cannot understand why England and America have not understood this . . . England and America persist in the grave mistake of not recognizing the sacrifice being made by Germany for their salvation—they must not be surprised if one day they are made aware of the consequences of this mistake."

The speech, described not quite truthfully by the local Fascists as "Mussolini establishing direct contact with all his people," was not one of the Duce's best. It was noticeable that he was tired. He was reported to be suffering from an acutely painful stomach-ache, and was drugged to cope with the pain. He did not make his speech conversationally, exchanging compliments with the crowd which came to hear him. He read from notes.

Nevertheless, if the long speech on December 16th was not great oratory, it did serve to inspire the Social Republic's last offensive, and the temporary success of that offensive even sparked off some Fascist, anti-Allied, resistance in the south. Lieutenant Rino Corzarini succeeded in getting together 700 men, mostly ex-Black Shirt militiamen, and set up his own "Liberation Movement" in the Calabria-Lucania area. Other "black partisans" operated in the Abruzzi, Puglia and Florence. A young student, Carla Costa, ran a pro-Fascist messenger service from Rome, crossing and recrossing the Allied lines. Another young woman at Rimini, who had been raped by some Australian troops, led them into a minefield and killed seventeen of them. The Allied military governments, their troops and political advisers, continued to fail to realize the extent to which many Italians felt anxious to participate in the "anti-Fascist struggle." Everything the Allied troops did seemed designed to add to this humiliation, without offering an outlet. It was extremely embarrassing to a people, who had been told for twenty years that they were the lineal descendants of Caesar, to find their children used only as shoeshine boys and their women bought and sold for cigarettes and coffee. It is understandable that many of them became, if not pro-Fascist again, at least hostile to the occupying troops, and ceased to regard them as liberators. The psychological incompetence of the Allied military government could have had grave political consequences in the post-war period.

The resurgence of Fascism in the winter of 1944–1945 did nothing to diminish the bitterness of the partisans in the north. They still smarted over their "double defeat" in Rome in December, and it did not help matters to have Allied officers joke about "Mussolini's resistance" in the south. Atrocities on both sides became more frequent.

Mussolini grew more and more despondent. Still the only human being he could trust was Clara Petacci, who meant love and medicaments to him. Graziani, though he fought to the end, was already talking about the necessity for "an honourable surrender in the spring." When, in February 1945, General Wolff, the German Commander who was supposed to be the "liaison commander" with the Fascist Social Republic, started to negotiate with the Allies for an independent armistice, the former Founder of the Empire knew that the "revolution" was finished.

At the end of March Graziani gave the order for a general withdrawal of the parachute regiments on the French frontier, and the *Bersaglieri*, who were holding off Tito in the east. They were to be concentrated in the "last ditch," la Valtellina, where the "armies of the republic" would fire off all their ammunition and then surrender to the Allies. By the evening of April 25, 1945, what was left of the civil and military administration of the republic was at Como. The Germans had signed the form of surrender outside Milan. Archbishop Schuster had refused to grant Mussolini asylum there, and could only suggest that he find some refuge until a strong British or American detachment (strong enough to hold off the partisans howling for Mussolini's head) reached the city.

Mussolini, Graziani, Barracu, Bombacci, Vittorio Mussolini and his wife, and General Bonomi, held a council of war in the prefecture. The Duce's last political act was to speak to the news desk of the *Corriere della Sera* and confirm the fact that the paper was not to appear the next day. Then he walked out with seventeen men and two women and told his friends to "*sauve qui peut.*"

Mussolini and his friends were captured by partisans as they and their German escorts were checked at a road block at Dongo. He and Clara Petacci were taken to a peasant's house at Giulino di Mezzagra, to await an escort. The escort was, they were told, to make sure that they arrived safely at the Headquarters of the Allied Commander-in-Chief. To Mussolini, his destination seemed immaterial. He was convinced that either he would be shot by Russian Bolsheviks in Berlin, side by side with his old pupil, or he would be shot by Communists in Italy, on orders from Moscow. The Allies, he was sure, would make no move to save him. Until he had left Como he had had a faint hope of survival, hoping to barter his life for a truckful of "historical documents," and a briefcase full of letters from Churchill and other former admirers. But the truck had been lost. Nobody knows what happened to the briefcase, though documents which were supposed to have been in it turned up many years later almost 150 miles away.

At two o'clock on the afternoon of April 28th "Colonel Valerio," an accountant whose real name was Walter Audisio, arrived at the house at Giulino with an order to hand over Mussolini to him. One and a half hours later the Duce and his silly, devoted schoolgirl mistress were put up against the wall of the near-by Villa Belmonte and shot.[12]

Many Allied Commanders and their advisers were astonished to hear that Mussolini had been shot. They had been told that it was unlikely that the Duce would commit suicide—he was too tired and drugged to be desperate. But it had been assumed that whoever captured him would want to see him tried by the war-crimes tribunals the Allies intended to set up. If the Italian people really wanted to show the world that they were essentially anti-Fascist, what better condemnation of the "repressiveness" of the régime could they expect than one out of the Duce's own mouth? Surely an exposé on the grand scale would substantiate the opposition's contention that it had been ineffective because they had had to flee, or exist in a "police state"?

Certainly the Action Party had given instructions that the Duce was to be taken alive and kept alive. Their partisans had been briefed to this effect. Lesser members of the hierarchy could be shot after summary jurisdiction, but "the big fish must be kept cool." Not even the frustration felt by the Action Party in the C.L.N. at the refusal of the Allies to take it seriously politically had changed this general line of conduct, approved by the whole C.L.N. It had even been foreseen that some partisan with a personal grudge to settle (or past to hide) might dispatch the Duce on his own initiative. All units in the Como area had political officers with them to guard against this danger. The Action Party wanted to use Mussolini as a bargaining counter, to sell his live body for the key ministries in the post-war government. They were willing to horse-trade him with the Allies. They were especially anxious to get him to sign terms of surrender, as if the armistice which ended the hot war had been negotiated between the C.L.N. (as the lawful government) and Mussolini (as the surrendered rebel). Some leaders of the Action Party believed that the physical possession of a live Mussolini would so reinforce them, compared to the other parties in the C.L.N., that their political demands would be met, in return for "a share of the trial."

Alas for the Action Party, the Communist Party wanted Mussolini as dead as he could be, as soon as possible. It was correct in assuming that an Axis dictator on trial would say embarrassing things about Soviet-Axis relations in the past (as Hitler's Ribbentrop did at Nuremberg). The Communist Party did not care for the idea of a statement in court by Mussolini that Fascist Italy had enjoyed good relations with the Soviet Union for twenty years (just as Churchill was relieved that his past eulogies of Mussolini were never put in as evidence in any post-war trial of the Duce). Too many people had too much to hide—Churchill's letters, pictures of Eden with Fascist friends, Lenin's and Gorki's praise. It was unfortunate, perhaps, that the Duce had to die. It was extremely unfortunate that he fell into the hands of Communists, the people most anxious to see him dead. No documents of any sort were found on his body. The two letters from Churchill and Stalin he was said to have sewn into his shirt were never found. His will vanished, though the Italian journalist Montanelli claimed to have been given it later "by a priest."

On the morning of the 29th Mussolini, Petacci, Pavolini, Bombacci, Gelommini, and the faithful Starace were hanged upside down, their corpses mutilated, from the roof of a petrol station in Piazza Loreto, Milan.

So ended the day of the lion. Twenty-four hours later, in the bunker in Berlin, his pupil and friend committed suicide to avoid a similar fate. For Mussolini, his "friend's" fate came thirteen years too late.

EPILOGUE

A NEED FOR NEW HEROES

For several weeks after the death of Mussolini men and women vied with each other to show the strength of their anti-Fascism. The ineffectiveness of the opposition during the régime was forgotten. The exiles became heroes. Those who had stayed at home, sullen but passive, rushed about with hammers and chisels, stripping public buildings of their Fascist statuary (generally better done away with) and insignia. Those who did not strip and chip away took huge buckets of whitewash and painted out the slogans on the walls.

The whole nation, seized with paroxysms of guilt, set to work to cancel out the visible impact of twenty years of Fascist rule. This of course was not possible. Hitler may have risen to power with the consent of the German people, but he was not a German, and his power, from the start, drove only a war machine. Mussolini was no foreigner. He was about the most typical of a certain type of Italian that even Italians could imagine—a local boy from the heart of Italy, Romagna, who had made good. He had also been part and parcel of Italian public life for at least thirty-five years. Not all the whitewash and chisels in the world could remove the traces of such a man, even though his régime had crumbled. Mussolini may often have been stupid—his stupidity relieved in later years only by occasional flashes of genius—but he was not an evil man. In this, too, he was unlike Hitler. It is fair, as Shirer has done, to spend most of the time devoted to a history of Nazism to a history of World War II. But Fascism did not lead inevitably to war, though it may be argued that the personalities of many Fascists made war, at some stage, a likely adventure.

Perhaps the word "adventure" is the key to the essential relationship between Mussolini and war. Armed conflict, even on the grand scale, was to Mussolini merely an enlargement of the duel, fought, ideally, for reasons of "honour," but also, ideally, brief and to the point. For all his talk of "centuries of imperial endeavour," the Duce at the height of his power never really believed himself or the Italian people capable of incessant struggle. His two successful wars, in Ethiopia and Albania, were over quickly, to his intense relief. The war in Spain dragged on too long, and lost his interest. He believed that World War II would be quick and decisive from the moment of his entry. Not exhausted, and rich with booty, he could then placate Bottai and get back to the business of building a Fascist Corporate State.

But the nature of Fascism and Mussolini-ism—and the differences in form and substance from Nazism—were for the man in the mob too academic to be discussed in a bar. There was only time to refill the wineglass, then go out to spit on statues of the Duce, whitewash hammers and sickels on the walls, and deny ever having shouted "*Duce—a noi!*"

The sense of guilt at finding themselves accused by the world of failure or inertia in the face of the advance of a now fallen régime—this was a human failing. It was also understandable that many Fascists felt the armistice had been in vain, if changing sides had brought with it only the same sort of treatment being meted out to the Germans, who had fought to the end. Reports from Berlin told of Allied troops busy handing out chocolate to children and buying their wives and sisters for cigarettes. Reports from Rome told of Allied soldiers bribing and corrupting on the same scale. The Allied military government treated Bonomi and his government no better than the temporary civil administrations were treated in West Germany. Perhaps, felt many young people who had never known anything other than the régime, it would have been better to be vanquished heroes than members of a nation which had bought itself an equivocal status at the cost of a bloody, bitter civil war.

The psychology of the deserter is well known. Punishment for desertion has veered from death to some sort of treatment which will make complete rehabilitation possible. It is not beyond the scope of this epilogue to ask if the experiences of Fascism, Mussolini-ism and war have taught the Italian people anything; if much good and/or evil have been left behind; and in what sectors of the economy and society these remainders predominate. The answer to these questions can provide the best summing-up of the Duce's success or failure as an innovator, purgative or "Fascist beast."

It is perhaps logical to ask first the question: What have the parties learned from this misadventure of the super-party?

It might be expected that, of all the parties, the Socialist would have learned the most valuable lesson. It was the rigidity and theoretical obsolescence of the Socialist Party which forced Mussolini out of it toward a political agglomeration of his own. The Italian Socialist Party, in 1914, was pacifist and internationalist (the two words ought to be synonymous, but are not). And yet they professed Marxism, and Lenin (in spite of Khrushchev's attempt to distinguish the concept) preached the inevitability of war for as long as the world held both capitalists and the rest, at least until the rest reached the goal of Socialism and outnumbered the capitalists. There was nothing pacifist about Lenin, and if foreign workers had to die in the interests of Marxism-Leninism, then this was their fate and the price they paid for being the "sacred proletariat." Italy and the Italians in 1914 wanted war—war against the Kaiser. The Socialist Party opposed the people and lost their support. It also lost the editor of its newspaper, *Avanti*, and eventually he threw the Socialists out of Parliament and the country. The Italian Socialist Party ought to have learned its lesson in 1914, but it did not. It ought to have learned that flexibility is the cement of unity; that doctrinal squabbles are a luxury a party in power can afford—a party in opposition never. And yet argument must be not only condoned but encouraged in a party which is not conservative. The best brains in the post-1918 Socialist Party, oppressed by the antique rigidity of the executive and its obsolete ideas, broke away and formed the Communist Party. A mind like Gramsci's might well have been able to lead a united Left into the lists against Mussolini's *Fasci*. A disunited Left got nowhere. This lesson at least—that of outward unity and internal flexibility—the Socialist Party ought to have learned from its twenty years of Fascism. But it did not. In 1945–1946 it had every advantage. The administrative and general elections showed the Left to have well over half the support of the voters, with polls higher than ever before recorded. In Piedmont, Lombardy, Trentino, Umbria, Lazio, the Abruzzi and the south (excepting Sardinia, Puglia and Calabria) the Socialist Party received more votes than the Communists, whose organization was better and richer. Milan, the birthplace of Fascism, had a Socialist administration. It seemed like the best and most appropriate revenge for those humiliating defeats at the Fascist polls.

By 1949 the Socialist Party had once again thrown away its chances of government and jeopardised the future of the whole of the Left. Even before the elections of 1946, two "wings" of the Socialist Party had grown. The one, led by Nenni, was pro-Communist and pro-Popular Front, yet not so far Left that Nenni himself was willing to sacrifice his personal position as leader of the party on the altar of Left unity. The Right Wing of the Socialist Party, led by Saragat, suffered less from any lust for power by Saragat himself, but leaned toward alliance with the Christian Democrats.

Saragat, a realist, assumed correctly that the Church would play an important part in political life from now on, would somehow preserve the gains it had made during Fascism (the Lateran Pacts), and yet make up its losses, all without seeming undemocratic. Nenni refused to compromise, either with the Right or with the Left. At the party congress in April 1946 he said as much. He had obviously learned nothing. In October 1946, in spite of all he had said about "priests' parties," he accepted the post of Foreign Minister from Christian Democratic Prime Minister de Gasperi. In January 1947, unable to put up with Nenni, his policies or his person, Saragat walked out of the Socialist Party, taking almost half Nenni's parliamentary following with him, and formed the Socialist Party of Italian Workers. In January 1948 Lombardo, Silone, Garosci and their friends left to form the "Union of Socialists." In May, 1948, Romita "deviated," too, and took away more of Nenni's nominal followers to form the "Autonomous Socialists." In December 1949, the "Unified Socialist Party" was formed, anything but unified and as disorganized as the rest.

In three years—from a position of strength, popular support and apparent unity—Nenni and his Socialist Party had degenerated into a whole complex of factions. Unable to control, sometimes even permit, discussion inside the party and so preserve the façade of unity cherished by the electorate, Nenni had destroyed his party's chances as effectively and in exactly the same way as they had been destroyed in 1921. Perhaps it is only fair to add that not all the fault was Nenni's. Those who broke away from the party before it had had a chance to consolidate and make a serious bid for parliamentary majority were as guilty, and had obviously learned as little during the twenty years of Mussolini's "super-Socialism."

The Italian Communist Party was accused, in 1921, of having weakened the Left by quitting the then Socialist Party, thereby helping to pave the way for the march on Rome. There is, as Gramsci said, "some truth in this accusation, but not much." The Socialist Party was already dead before the C.P. was formed. It is to the credit of the C.P. that, during the long years of Fascist rule, it did not lose heart or faith in the future, but kept some sort of organization intact, and always kept hope alive. Had Gramsci survived imprisonment, he might have led it to victory in the post-Fascist era. Unfortunately for the party, Gramsci died in prison, and his successor Togliatti, though intelligent and physically brave, was not half as competent, not a quarter as politically shrewd. Togliatti was handicapped in the years of "possibility," 1945–1949, by a succession of directives from Moscow. Stalin was, in his way, an even bigger nuisance than Nenni. It was a mistake for Stalin to recognise the Badoglio government and so halt the natural reaction against Fascism in the liberated south before that reaction had gone far enough to the Left. The Communist Party in Italy, though it may well achieve the majority vote in the towns, will not rise to power democratically until it has won over the peasants south of Rome. Of course it is possible that the party, if it finds a new leader, may attempt a coup—a Red march on Rome.

The Action Party had disappeared by 1947, lacking any sort of electoral support. It had learned nothing from Mussolini. Had the Action Party's partisans moderated their passions after the fall of Fascism, had they been transformed into the "new and revolutionary army"—as Mussolini had transformed the *squadristi* into the party and militia—then an Action Party revolution might have succeeded. It might well have succeeded in the north, and the south would have followed the lead of the north, as it has done, without acknowledgement, for a hundred years. Unfortunately, the party lacked leadership, was afraid of dictatorship in means or ends, and slowly disintegrated, losing its supporters to Socialist and Communist parties which were neither new nor revolutionary.

The Liberal Party learned nothing from the years of Fascism. It ought to have learned the importance of mass organisation and not to rely solely on the personalities of its leaders at election time. Its lack of any sort of popular support made its elimination by Mussolini easy. By 1949, like the Republican Party, it was merely a quaint survival from the past, and not even the formation of a radical wing in 1957 saved it from attrition.

A similar fate soon befell the party which represented the most "genuine" reaction against the Duce, Starace and the "supermen." Founded by the writer Giannini, the "Man in the Street's Party" was a sort of anti-political grouping of men and women tired of policies, programmes, speeches, the ambitions of northern reformers and demagogues. It was especially successful in Rome, even won thirty seats in the 1946 Parliament and ran a newspaper which was a cross between the British *Punch* and the *New Daily*. It was not so much a party as a protest against parties. By 1948 the man in the street had been submerged, as he always is, and both Giannini and his paper turned their attention to other forms of protest.

The party which really did learn every sort of lesson from its failure to halt Mussolini at the start was the Church Party, now called the Christian Democratic Party. Its organisation, in 1945, was rudimentary but efficient. It consisted of a network of sympathetic priests and officials of Catholic Action. Every pulpit was an election office. The priests themselves were delighted to be able to do some of the work thought "improper" not so long ago. The older clergy remembered the time when it had not been "expedient" for Catholics as Catholics to take part in any political activity whatsoever. The quality of the Catholic priest may be lower—at the lowest levels of the hierarchy, than that of his Protestant colleague—but there was no doubting his political enthusiasm in 1945. The Vatican, by urging Catholics to make themselves heard as often as atheists, showed itself aware of the changing nature of the political struggle; from a mere scramble for seats to a major conflict of ideologies. Men who had preached political action and ideological warfare for years, and had been exiled to placate Mussolini, were either brought home or put to work encouraging Catholic politicians elsewhere in Europe, laying the foundations for a "European Catholic bloc." The most rebellious of the younger monsignori of 1922, Angelo Roncalli, was whisked out of Turkey and made Nuncio to France, surely the fastest promotion ever enjoyed by any prelate.

The Christian Democrats, confident that the Church itself had learned its lesson, were able to involve Catholicism politically to a much greater extent than even men like Roncalli thought desirable. They were fortunate in having able leaders who watched very carefully to see that whenever enthusiasm ran to excess it was checked. There were to be no Staraces in the C.D.P. De Gasperi, who first became Prime Minister on December 10, 1945, on the fall of Parri, the only Action Party man ever to reach high office, was a heaven-sent political tactician. His methods of destroying the Opposition were oddly similar to those Mussolini had used during the period of normalization. In the 1946 elections (for Parliament, and to decide whether or not Italy was to become a republic) the Christian Democrats won 207 seats out of 556, with 35.2 per cent of the vote. De Gasperi allowed the Right Wing of the party to have its head and counsel a vote for the monarchy, so discrediting it for years. Then, realizing that if the Communists (104 seats) and the Socialists (115 seats) formed a Popular Front, they would vote him out of office, he invited Nenni to become Minister of Foreign Affairs. He then managed to persuade Scoccimarro, a Communist, to become Minister of Finance, and lo! . . . his government was one of national concentration—a "reconstruction coalition."

As soon as the Socialist Party split, out went Nenni—there was now nothing to fear from the Left. De Gasperi "tranquilised" the Republicans by giving their leader, Count Sforza, the Foreign Ministry. Confident that the Left was too divided to retaliate, he sacked Scoccimarro in January 1947, and gave the Finance Ministry to one of his friends, Campilli. In May 1947 de Gasperi got rid of the last Communists and Socialists from the "coalition," recruiting some Liberals (most important—Einaudi) and keeping the Republicans. This alliance increased his parliamentary strength sufficiently to be able to keep the squabbling Left at bay while he prepared for new elections (the new Constitution, in which de Gasperi wanted the electorate to show a vote of confidence, had been approved at its most difficult point on March 25th).

At the general elections on April 18, 1948, the Christian Democrat vote went up from over 8,000,000 to over 12,000,000, from 35.2 per cent to 48.5 per cent. The number of C.D.P. seats increased from 207 to 306 (now out of 574), an absolute majority. Like Mussolini, de Gasperi played on the middle-class fear of Communism at home and abroad (the Czech coup by the Communists overshadowed the election). Like Mussolini, he played on Italian Nationalism, persuading the Allies to hand back Trieste at election time and not concede it to Yugoslavia. He showed even more subtlety when he came to form his government, not only including Republicans and Liberals (who represented no sort of threat, but were "respectable," the "traditional element"), but also inviting Saragat to join his Cabinet. De Gasperi had made a bargain with Saragat before the election, just in case he should not secure an absolute majority. He kept the bargain to keep the Left divided. From that day on the Christian Democrats settled down to "govern forever." De Gasperi had not spent the twenty years of Fascism watching Mussolini at work for nothing. What there was to learn, he learned.

The Christian Democratic Party (or rather its most intelligent members, there being still many sub-standard politicals among them) also devoted a great deal of time and energy to youth. Mussolini was perhaps the first politician to organise youth efficiently in the service of a party. Both Hitler and Stalin learned a great deal from the Opera Natzionale Bàlilla. De Gasperi always prided himself on learning his lessons thoroughly. He not only encouraged the Church to multiply its youth organizations—which gave him a C.D.P. youth at no cost to the party—he also encouraged the brighter young men to become members of Parliament, start newspapers of their own, make recommendations to him—generally make it easy for him to pick their brains, while at the same time "stifling rebellion by participation."

De Gasperi's real successor, Fanfani, who first built up a party organisation parallel to that of the Church's auxiliary, carried on the policy of encouraging youth, aided by La Pira, the mayor of Florence (Fanfani's Bottai). He also created a party organisation and found financial help independent of the Church, which enabled him to deny charges of being dependent on the Vatican.

It would be agreeable to conclude that political apathy had vanished through the efforts of post-Fascist politicians, that a new maturity had come to the whole Italian people together with an instinctive appraisal of democracy. This is not the case. Mussolini did not solve the problem of illiteracy. In 1961 there were still 5,000,000 illiterates (10 per cent of the population) in Italy, most of them in the south. Mussolini did not get far with his programme for the economic unification of the peninsula and the modernisation of Sicily. His "adventures" stopped his work of natural land reclamation before it had come within sight of completion. And of course Mussolini and Starace did nothing to encourage the man in the street to believe that "the government," the inhuman "They in Rome," the "authorities," were flesh and blood and at the service of those who paid taxes and cast votes. The idea of the Member of Parliament as the servant of his electorate is laughable to most Italians, who still tremble and wheedle in the presence of Members and Senators as they did in the presence of Starace. Similarly, the bureaucracy has not realised, or helped toward a general appreciation of, its function as a "public service." The general public feels impelled to genuflect to the bureaucrat, and often tries to obtain services due it as a right, by offering bribes.

If anything, government has become more remote and impersonal than it was in the days of Mussolini. At least you could always see Mussolini here, there and everywhere, apparently doing good. You could hear him speak, and read his speeches. Most members of Parliament in Italy never make a speech worth publishing in any newspaper, and have no power to compel publication. Mussolini may have been a politician of doubtful morals, but he was at least readable. It is probably this dissatisfaction with what has taken Mussolini's (rather than Fascism's) place, which is responsible for the number of *nostalgici*, or neo-Fascists. The neo-Fascists, or Italian Social Movement, are the heirs to the Social Republic, and hanker after the "good old days" when Italy at least made the headlines in Europe (if for the wrong reasons). The government of "faceless bureaucrats and nameless priests" is not to their liking. Its achievements in the economic field may be considerable, but these men do not look like leaders. There is no Starace around to design uniforms. There are, of course, simple *nostalgici* who are not neo-Fascists, who take no part in politics because the Duce is dead.

Perhaps typical of these men are Buronzo and del Giudice, and it is interesting to note that both of them devoted themselves during the years of Fascism to its "positive side," to the economic sphere of the corporations. Del Giudice's attitude (he is now a professor of law at Rome University) is that those twenty years under Mussolini "could have been the finest in the history of Italy, but finished, instead, in catastrophe." Those Fascists who take no further part in politics tend to ascribe Mussolini's failure to "his uncertainty about the corporative reform," emphasizing the difference between Mussolini and Fascism, between the Duce and the theories to which, for a time, he gave his support (it is interesting to note that del Giudice accuses Mussolini of "Leninism" in his attitude to the party).

It is not, however, likely that there will be a return to dictatorship in Italy. A return to Fascism is, by definition, impossible—the Duce is dead, and without his support Fascism could never take root. From time to time there are nostalgic demonstrations. In 1960 Right-Wing Christian Democratic Prime Minister Tambroni offered to collaborate with the neo-Fascist minority in Parliament to avoid continuing his alliance with the Left Centre. Riots in Genoa, in protest against Tambroni's granting permission for the neo-Fascists to hold a rally there, brought down the government. The feelings of bitterness on the one side, regret on the other, are still there, but with time they will fade.

Mussolini tried to solve the problem of Italy's racial minorities as (in another way) he tried to solve the same problem for the rest of Europe. When he signed his Pact of Steel with Hitler, he made provision for the "repatriation" of those Germans who had been settled in Alto Adige for many generations. There was a mass exodus which lasted until the spring of 1940. When Italy entered the war, however, this exodus stopped. Since the war, Austria has appointed herself champion of the German-speaking majority in Alto Adige, which once belonged to the Austro-Hungarian Empire. Several attempts have been made to secure autonomy in the real sense for the German-speaking inhabitants of the region, and a neo-Nazi "Nationalist People's Party" blew up a number of bridges in 1962, almost like old times. The lack of success of the fanatical neo-Nazis, however, would seem to indicate that this issue is not now a live one, except to the eccentrics in Vienna and Bolzano.

There has been little attempt to interfere with the considerable body of legislation achieved by Mussolini, though, in theory, all "notable acts" ceased to be valid in 1945. In fact, the substance of Italian law is as it was devised by Mussolini's lawyers. The work of codification (1930) remains virtually intact, and though some clauses (for example, those restricting the liberty of the press) are now anachronistic, the codes are on the whole in conformity with contemporary notions of justice. The laws regulating collective bargaining, discipline at work, and establishing the norms of social security, are all still intact, though they have been elaborated and disguised in accordance with the unwritten rule that Mussolini must not be given credit for anything.

One of the notions which remained stuck to Mussolini's skull in 1944, when most others had fled, was that of a United Europe. In his speech on December 16, 1944, speaking of "moving toward a European Community," he said: "I must say a word about Europe . . . not what is Europe, its geographical, historical, oral and economic limits, nor whether an attempt at unifying it would enjoy more success now than on preceding occasions—this would take me too far and would take too long. . . . I will limit myself to saying that the constitution of a European Community is desirable and realizable. . . ." He even, in the same speech, enunciated the idea of the Europe des Patries, with the comment: "We do not feel Italian because we are European, but rather we feel European in so far as we are Italians."[1] Neither General de Gaulle nor the leaders of the Common Market have even given Mussolini credit, either for sustaining these ideas as far back as 1923, or for remaining faithful to the idea (one of the few) almost to his deathbed.

In fairness to the Duce, it is perhaps important to stress that for all his belief in the virtue of "off-the-cuff" decisions and his contempt for eulogists who listed him in their works as having read almost every indigestible philosopher, Mussolini placed a great deal of reliance on his statisticians. He issued the regulations of the new Central Office of Statistics, and encouraged academic statisticians to use their initiative and make "other enquiries (than those specified in the regulations) of a general character, especially into the administration of the State apparatus." Mussolini was unfortunate in the incumbents of the highest posts in the statistical office, but he did at least sponsor some research.

In spite of the evident prosperity of Milan and the industrial north it is questionable whether Italians in general are better off in the post-Fascist era than they were during the golden years of Fascism (before the Ethiopian adventure)—i.e., whether the rate of growth of the economy is higher. Certainly one of Mussolini's greatest assets was his ability to convince the man in the street, and even the housewife, that their standard of life was improving, even though at times this resulted in many people showing gratitude for something which they had not received. As the modern state is largely sustained by bluff as a substitute for policy and information, and the economy by credit as a substitute for a real exchange of goods, this asset of Mussolini's was not inconsiderable. Certainly in the agricultural sector—until the "Green Plan" of December 1961—most peasants were convinced that they had been better off under Mussolini's rule, when they had had free issues of farm clothing, guaranteed prices, and markets, and large subsidies.

But it is impossible to measure the legacy of Fascism in terms of goods and services, just as it was always impossible to evaluate it except by its own criteria. Its legacy is considerable, and Italians make a mistake when they pretend—as many of them do—that "it never happened." Even the whitewash has faded from the slogans, and these are visible once more, to the irritation of Italian-speaking Socialist visitors.

Perhaps the most significant and positive legacy of Mussolini-ism is the unacknowledged realisation that the age of empires is past. Perhaps it took the Ethiopian adventure, and all the absurdities of Mussolini's latter-day Caesarism, to convince the nineteenth-century imperial powers of this. Certainly the Italians are now convinced. Many Italians hope they have a political part to play in international organisation and inside the European Community, but the days of white horses and the Via oleff' Impero are past, and they know it. It is never acknowledged except in the excellence of Italian craftsmanship, the excellence in particular of design and finish. In the words of an anti-Fascist, American poet Leslie Woolf Hedley, now the Duce is dead the Italian in the street has realised that:

> Somewhere men live poetry with their lives . . .
> Coming on this earth for a simple space,
> Never to kill never to plunder never to destroy;
> Men like flowers
> Have no other purpose
> But to make beautiful.

Mussolini would not have fully appreciated that as an epitaph. It smacks too much of the "picturesque Italy of the tourist." But perhaps it is a better epitaph than he deserves. "Mussolini," he once wrote of himself, "rose so fast that, like a meteor, nobody saw him coming until it was too late. He deserved a better audience. . . ."

SOURCES OF NOTES

CHAPTER 1

1. *Mussolini dal Mito alla Realta*, Mergaro (*IEI*, Milano, 1947); also Monelli. *P. Mussolini Piccolo Borghese* (Garzanti, 1950).
2. Proceedings of O.G.W.A., 1926.
3. Monelli, *op. cit.*, and Mergaro, *op. cit.*, autobiography issued as part of *Opera Omnia* (La Fenice Firence, 1951, etc.).
4. Police reports on Mussolini are filed in the Questura and Prefettura, Forli, and Rome at Ministry of Interior. Police reports on his father in Questura only, Forli. In both cases copies of most reports are available in Municipio, Predappio.
5. Edvige's biography of her brother quoted in *Mussolini: L'Uomo e L'Opera*, Pini (La Fenice, Firenze, 1954).
6. Mussolini's school reports, extensively quoted, are to be found in the original at the school.
7. Headmaster's letter quoted in Mergaro, *op. cit.*
8. *Opera Omnia, op. cit., Autobiography.*
9. Y. de Begnac, *Vita di Benito Mussolini* (Mondadori, Milano, 1936), for Mussolini's letters, also filed in *Opera Omnia*; letters are dated in the text.
10. Margherita Sarfatti, *Dux* (Milano, 1936). Para. 3, quoted in P. Orano, *Il Fascismo*, and Monelli, *op. cit.*
11. *Opera Omnia, Autobiography.*
12. Edvige Mussolini, *op. cit.*
13. For this and other reports of Mussolini's syphilis, see Monelli, *op. cit.*
14. *La Lotta di Classe*, September 1911.
15. Mussolini reported his own speeches in *La Lotta di Classe* for July–August, 1912.
16. Sarfatti, *M. Dux, op. cit.*

CHAPTER 2

1. Mussolini's speech in *Scritti e Discorsi* (Hoepli, Milano, 1934).
2. Author's conversations with Mussolini's brother-in-law, Buronzo, 961.
3. Meeting reported with speeches in *Scritti e Discorsi*, vol. 1.
4. *Orlando V.E. Discorsi per la Pace e la Guerra* (Campiteli Foligno, 1923).
5. *Futurist Manifesto.*
6. *Dal Fascismo alla Resistenza*, A. Satta (*La Nuova Italia*, 1961).
7. *Il Popolo d'Italia*, May 19, 1915.

8. Mussolini's *War Diary* was published in *Il Popolo d'Italia* and later reproduced as an integral part of *Scritti e Discorsi*, vol. 1, *op. cit.*

9. Monelli, *op. cit.*

10. The war was conducted verbally in the Italian Parliament without reserve or discretion; see *Discorsi Parliamentari*, vol. 3 and vol. 4 (Parl. Printer), covering the period, and *Discorsi Extraparlamentari* (Einaudi, Torino, 1952, n.b. introductory remarks by Valeri).

11. The Pope's appeal for peace was widely published in the Italian Press, including the Socialist Press.

12. The story of Mussolini's wound, convalescence, etc., is reported in *Scritti e Discorsi*, vol. 1.

13. See *Scritti e Discorsi*, p. 304, *op. cit.*

14. Text of Charter of Fasci in Satta, *op. cit.*, p. 47, *et seq.*

CHAPTER 3

1. *Primo Libro del Fascista* (Mondadori, 1939).

2. Fascist Programme in Satta, *op. cit.*, p. 49, *et seq.*

3. Chabod, F., *l'Italia Contemporanea*, 1918–48 (Einaudi, 1961).

4. Also author's interview with Ada, widow of Gobetti, 1961, for details of "revolutionary Liberal programme" not in *Una Battaglia Liberale* (Torino, 1924).

5. Mussolini's speech in *Scritti e Discorsi*, *op. cit.*, vol. 2.

6. Correspondence between author and Luigi Federzoni, 1961–2.

7. For recollections of atmosphere in which returning officers were immersed Maj.-Gen. Galbiati and Gen. Giovanni Passerone, for their interviews with the author, deserve his thanks and acknowledgements.

8. D'Annunzio's letter in *Opera Omnia*, first published in *Il Popolo d'Italia*, first edition, June 19th, then withdrawn for reasons unknown.

9. D'Annunzio's letter, see *Opera Omnia* and other publications, including Monelli, *op. cit*; Pini, G., *Mussolini l'Uomo e l'Opera*, etc.

10. See Sarfatti, *Dux*, and Monelli, *op. cit.*

11. *Critica Fascista* (Bottai ed.).

12. Salvemini *Diario*, extract from *Il Mondo*, October 14th, 1958.

13. Bottai's articles in *l'Ardito* were later collected in *Pagine di Critica Fascista* (Rome, 1930).

14. See Farinacci, *Squadrismo, dal mio Diario della Vigilia* (Ardita, Rome, 1933).

15. See I. Bonomi, *Dal Socialismo al Fascismo* (Garzabti, Milano, 1946).

16. See Bottai, G., *op. cit.*

17. See *Il Popolo d'Italia.* Generals Galbiati and Passerone, in their talks with the author, were sarcastic about Mussolini's conception of the role of the militia.

18. See my *Life of Pope John XXIII* for para. 3, *et seq.* (Cassell, 1961, and *Sunday Express*, February–March, 1950).

19. Several versions of the *Manifesto of Fascist Womanhood* exist, some obscene, rewritten by militia officers ved. Passerone.

20. Mussolini's brother-in-law says M. was in close touch with the German Right via Milan businessmen from 1920 on.

21. See *Il Popolo d'Italia* and *Il Corriere della Sera* for 23rd–25th September, 1922.

22. Passerone says that at the Torre Pellice meeting "The whole question of the loyalty to the Movement of the Italian Royal Family was discussed including possible intervention by countries with relatives of the Savoys on their thrones."

23. When the King received the telegram he was virtually surrounded by Fascist sympathising cavalry officers invited to San Rossore by the Queen Mother, see Passerone, *op. cit.*

24. *The Times* Correspondent of the day was very well informed about Mussolini's plans, deliberately misinformed about the dates of their execution. See Pini *Filo Diretto dal Palazzo Venezia.*

25. Federzoni's account of these days, correspondence with author, *op. cit.*

CHAPTER 4

1. See *Gazzetta del Popolo*, October 28th–31st, 1922.

2. For the reluctance of the militia to be demobilised see Galbiati, E., *Il 25 Luglio e la M.V.S.N.* (Bernabo, Milano, 1950, pp. 16 and 17, *et seq*).

3. For the story of Torre and the engine-driver, the author is indebted to Senator Buronzo.

4. For behaviour of the Queen Mother at this time the author is indebted to Senator Buronzo, *sopra cit.*, and Baron Carlo Emmanuele Basile, in conversation.

5. For other speeches in Parliament during Fascist era see *Discorsi Parlamentari, op. cit.* (memo: there are two Parliamentary Printers, one for each house), and *Deliberazioni, op. cit.*

6. For the Lausanne anecdote see Monelli, *op. cit.*, and others.

7. The first London *Fascio* was, in fact, largely composed of waiters, some genuine, some planted by the Italian Secret Service; the Secret Service at this time, see Leto, *Ovra Fascismo Antifascismo* (Cappelli, Bologna, 1951) was still "controlling" Fascists should the new régime fall.

8. For these and other comments on the militia's early "legal days" see Galbiati, *Il 25 Luglio*, etc., *op. cit.*, and conversations with the author.

9. For the position of Catholics at the time and in retrospect see *Politica*, autumn 1961, N. Pistelli (ed. Florence).

10. For the transition from Balilla (Youth Movement) under Buronzo, to Balilla—Ricci's para military pre-service training corps on which the Hitler Youth was modelled—the author is indebted to Senator Buronzo himself in their conversations, 1961–2.

11. For the debate between the various Fascist intellectuals see *Critica Fascista* (1923–5, vols. 1, 2, 3).

12. For the groundwork of economic reform the author is indebted to De Stefani himself in his correspondence, 1961–2. Cf. Chabod, *op. cit.*, p. 84, *et seq.*

13. For "cronaca piccola, spicciola" of the first years of the régime see *Il Corriere della Sera*, slowly becoming hostile and still "free".

14. See E. Ward Price, *Extra Special Correspondent* (London).

15. Kahn and Heidenstam are quoted in Orano, *op. cit.*

16. For the beginnings of a Fascist foreign policy the author is indebted to Ezio Maria Gray himself, during conversations in Rome and in correspondence.

17. Matteotti's letter to the *Statist* was published June 7th, 1924.

18. For the story of the Matteotti murder the author is indebted to Senator Buronzo, *op. cit.*

19. Federzoni to the author, *op. cit.*

20. For reports of speeches of cardinals slowly warming to Fascism see the *Osservatore Romano*, contemp.

21. For the reaction of the militia, the author is grateful as above to Gen. Galbiati, who went to see Mussolini at this time to "give him courage". See also *Il 25 Luglio*, etc., *op. cit.*

CHAPTER 5

1. See Galbiati, *Il 25 Luglio*, etc., *op. cit.*, p. 44, *et seq.*

2. For Mussolini's speeches, etc., see *Scritti e Discorsi*, *op. cit.*, vols. iv, v.

3. For the conversation with Federzoni the author is indebted to Senator Federzoni himself.

4. For the behaviour of intellectuals in general during, especially, the early years of the régime see F. Flora, *Ritratto di un Ventennio*; the author is indebted to the late Professor Flora for additional comments made during their conversations in Bologna.

5. See Galbiati, *op. cit.*

6. See Bottai, ed., *Critica Fascista*, *op. cit.*

7. See Salvatorelli in *La Stampa*, January 2nd, 1923.

8. Federzoni, *sopra cit.*

9. Author's conversations with Buronzo, *sopra cit.*

10. See *Scritti e Discorsi*, *op. cit.*

11. Churchill quoted in *Il Popolo d'Italia*, January 16th and 17th, 1927.

12. For a hostile admission of partial success see Salvemini, *Sotto la Scure del Fascismo* (Torini, 1948, *La Nuova Italia*), p. 220, *et seq.*

13. See Bottai, ed., *Critica Fascista*, *op. cit.* Bottai's suggestions were later part incorporated in *La Dottrina del Fascismo* (*Hist. Encyclopedia Italiana*, Rome, 1935, vol. i) and attributed to the Duce himself, the *Work Charter* being converted into a statute.

14. See Salvemini, *op. cit.*, for the competition to cut one's wages.

15. For this "foreign policy" the author is indebted to Ezio Maria Gray, in conversations, etc., *sopra cit.* Gray invented this policy.

16. Bottai, *Critica Fascista*, *op. cit.*

17. For Church–State relations at this time see A. C. Jemolo, *Stato e Chiesa in Italia Negli Ultimi Cento Anni*, especially chapters v, vi, vii (Einaudi, Torino, 1955). The *Osservatore Romano* at this time is also interesting as a study in cautious optimism.

18. See the article "La Pupilla del Duce", *Il Mondo*, March 26th, 1957, by Mangini.
19. Leto, *op. cit.*
20. See Gray, *sopra cit.*
21. Maraini quoted in Orano, *op. cit.*
22. See *Scritti e Discorsi*, vol. vii, *op. cit.*
23. *Vita di Arnaldo*, in *Opera Omnia*, *op. cit.*
24. See Gray, *sopra cit.*
25. This report is in *Scritti e Discorsi*, *op. cit.*

CHAPTER 6

1. Cf. the *Daily Mail* and *Pravda* for September–November, 1933, for an amusing unconscious debate on the merits of Nazism and Fascism contra Bolshevism.
2. Cf. Shirer, *Rise and Fall of the Third Reich* (Cassell, London), p. 283, *et seq.*
3. Gray's conversations with the author, *sopra cit.*, on the Hitler visit.
4. *Scritti e Discorsi*, *op. cit.*, vol. ix.
5. For the Stresa Conference, an "inside report", the author is indebted to Baron Basile, *sopra cit.*, who acted as host-interpreter.
6. *Scritti e Discorsi*: the "Empire" speech was later published (January 1936) as a pamphlet by the Partito Nazionale Fascista.
7. Galbiati, *Il 25 Luglio*, *op. cit.*
8. See *La Guerra d'Ethiopia*, Pietro Badoglio (Mondadori, 1936), and Badoglio's correspondence with Signora Ferrero, in edit, seen by author at her home in Grazzano Badoglio.
9. See *Il Popolo d'Italia* for December 19th, 1935, and later Pini, *Filo*, *et seq.*, *op. cit.*
10. Gray, conversations with author, *sopra cit.*
11. See Orano, *op. cit.*
12. For an account of the "docile Press" see Bortone, *Il Ponte*, October 1952.
13. The *Memoirs* of Mussolini's usher Navarra are full of "cronaca spicciola", and timetables of the Duce's activities (Rome–Milan, 1946, 1947).
14. For the latest revelations about Mussolini's girl friends see *Epoca* and *Eva* for September, 1962.
15. Cf. Shirer, *op. cit.*, p. 300, *et seq.*
16. *Scritti e Discorsi*, *op. cit.*, also Pini, *op. cit.*
17. The Autarchy speech was also published as a pamphlet by the *PNF*, May 20th, 1937.
18. *Il Popolo d'Italia*, September 5th, 1937.
19. Ciano, *Diario Segreto*, and Pini, *op. cit.*
20. *Scritti e Discorsi* for a garbled, edited version of the speech dictated by Mussolini to Pini that night, see *Il Popolo d'Italia*, December 12th, 1937.

CHAPTER 7

1. For the "self destruction of Fascism and the consolidation of Mussolini-ism" the author is indebted to Senator Buronzo, *sopra cit.*, and his exchange of correspondence with Bottai at this time.

2. Bottai, *Veint'anni e un Giorno*, *op. cit.*

3. For the Mediterranean survey the author is indebted as above to Ezio Maria Gray.

4. See Pini, *op. cit.*

5. See Shirer, *op. cit.*, p. 322, *et seq.*

6. Bottai, *Veint'anni*, etc., *op. cit.*, diary at end of volume.

7. Gray, *sopra cit.*, for the "horizontal Axis" plan.

8. See *Documents on British Foreign Policy*, Third Series, vol. iii, at p. 312, *et seq.* Also Second Series, end volume (H.M.S.O.).

9. See Extract from Foreign Office Memorandum on Anglo-Italian Relations, R 7966/23/22, in *D.B.F.P.*, *op. cit.*, vol. iii.

10. See Shirer, *op. cit.*, p. 357, *et seq.*

11. See *D.B.F.P.*, *op. cit.*, pp. 314–16, for the Ciano–Perth exchange.

12. See *Il Popolo d'Italia* for the "Zion proposals", and Orano and Pini, *op. cit.*-

13. See Missiroli, *La Politica Estera dalla Marcia su Roma a Monaco* (Milano, 1939).

14. See *D.B.F.P.*, *op. cit.*, vol. iii, p. 318.

15. Cf. Pini, *op. cit.*, kept informed directly by Mussolini at his desk at *Il Popolo d'Italia* with Shirer's sources (Cap. 12, *op. cit.*). Pini's *Filo Diretto con Palazzo Venezia* at this point is in diary form and events can be referred to under the appropriate date.

16. See Shirer, *op. cit.*, p. 380, footnote.

17. See letter from Sir E. Phipps, printed as (ii) in Appendix II of *D.B.F.P.*, *op. cit.*

18. See *Hansard* for September 27th, 1938, *et seq.*

19. Anfuso, F., *Memorie* (Milano, 1948).

20. See *Il Popolo d'Italia*, September 14th, 15th and 16th, 1938, for the Munich proposals already a fortnight old when made.

21. See the Phipps letter, *op. cit.*, *D.B.F.P.* Appendix II, (ii) and (iii), vol. iii.

22. See p. 319 *et seq.*, *D.B.F.P.*, *op. cit.*, vol. iii.

23. See *D.B.F.P.*, vol. ii, *op. cit.*, p. 356, for beginnings of talk of a British P.M.'s visit to Rome after implementation of Anglo-Italian Agreement.

24. For Lord Perth on the "existing situation in Italy", see *D.B.F.P.*, vol. iii, *op. cit.*, p. 496, *et seq.*

25. See Federzoni, the author, *sopra cit.*, for death of Pope and political impact.

26. For an amusing olde worlde summary of the situation in Albania by the Foreign Office representative in Durazzo see *D.B.F.P.*, vol. v, p. 168 *et seq.*

27. For the Perth report see *B.D.F.P.*, vol. v, *op. cit.*, p. 262, *et seq.*

28. See Bottai, *Veint'anni*, etc., *op. cit.*, diary at end of volume, and Pini, *op. cit.*

CHAPTER 8

1. Y. de Begnac, *op. cit.*, for Mussolini on the Jewish question at this late stage.

2. See Galbiati, *op. cit.*, for the conflict between the Militia and Regular Forces, p. 108, *et seq.* See also Badoglio, *L'Italia nella 2nd Guerra Mondiale* (Mondadori, 1946).

3. Galbiati, *op. cit.*

4. Federzoni—author, *sopra cit.*

5. See Togliatti, *P. per la Salvezza del Nostro Paese* (Einaudi, Torino, 1946).

6. Edizioni Avanti, especially *Documenti del Psi Dal* 1943 *al* 1948.

7. See L. Valliani, *Tutte le Strade Conducono a Roma* (La Nuova Italia, 1947).

8. Navarra, *op. cit.*

9. For the Grand Council conspiracy see Galbiati, *op. cit.*, especially p. 218, *et seq.* According to Signora Ferrero in an interview with the author, the conspiracy on the King and Badoglio's side was complete by March 1943 and contact had already been made with Grandi. See the Badoglio letters, etc., at Grazzano Badoglio.

10. The author is indebted to Ada Gobetti and to On. Walter Audisio for their sketches of the C.L.N. and Resistance in action, during conversation in Turin and Alessandria, 1961–2.

11. The speech was published in all the national dailies, most of which print in the north; see especially *Gazzetta del Popolo* for Sunday, December 17th, 1944, for the speech and comment.

12. For the debate on whether or not Mussolini should die I am indebted to On. Walter Audisio, who shot M. himself. Audisio, an accountant in charge of the Communist Party Secretariat of the Resistance, was more or less drawn out of a hat; this was ironical because his last employment was at the Borsalino hat factory, Alessandria.

EPILOGUE

1. For Mussolini's speech see *Gazzetta del Popolo*, December 17th, 1944.

BIBLIOGRAPHY

Abshagen, K. H.: *Canaris, Patriot und Weltburger.*
Acerbo, G.: *I primi tre anni della Rivoluzione Fascista.*
Alatri, P.: *Le origini del Fascismo*; *Nitti, D'Annunzio e la questione Adriatica.*
Albertini, A.: *Venti anni di vita politica—L'Italia nella Guerra Mondiale.*
Albrecht-Carrié, R.: *Italy at the Paris Peace Conference.*
Aldrovandi Marescotti, A.: *Guerra diplomatica* (1914–1918); *Nuovi ricordi.*
Allason, B.: *Memorie di un antifascista.*
Amendola, A.: *Una Battaglia Liberale.* Discorsi politici (1919–1923): "La Democrazia Italiana contro il Fascismo"; "La Democrazia nel Mezzogiorno".
Arena, C.: *La Politica Sociale.*
Azzari, A.: *L'Ossola nella Resistenza Italiana.*
Bachi, R.: *L'Italia Economica.* Annuario della vita commerciale, industriale, etc.
Badoglio, P.: Africa: *La Guerra d'Etiopia*; *L'Italia nella Seconda Guerra Mondiale*; *Rivelazioni su Fiume.*
Balabanoff, A.: *Ricordi di una Socialista.*
Balbo, I.: Diario 1922.
Barbagallo, C.: *Napoli contro il terrore nazista 25 aprile. La resistenza in Piemonte.*
Basile, Carlo Emmanuele: *Marciando; Il gallo e la lupa.*
Basso, L.: *Il principe scenza scettro:* Democrazia e sovranità popolare nella costituzione della realtá italiana.
Battaglia, R.: G. Garritano: *Breve storia della Resistenza Italiana*; *La Seconda Guerra Mondiale.*
Baumont, M.: *La faillite de la paix.*
Belforte, F.: *La Guerra Civile in Spagna.*
Bellonci, G.: *La rinàscita nazionale.*
Belluzzo: *Economia Fascista.*
Bergamo, C.; de Falco, G.; Zirbotti, G.: *Il Fascismo visto da Repubblicani e Socialisti.*
Bernotti, R.: *La Guerra sui Mari.*
Bertolotto, G.: *La Dottrina del Fascismo.*
Biagi: *Scritti di politica corporativa.*
Bissolati, L.: *La politica estera dell'Italia dal 1897 al 1920.*
Bollati, A.; del Bono, G.: *La Guerra Civile di Spagna.*
Bonomi, I.: *Diario di un anno* (2 giugno 1943–10 giugno 1944); *Dal Socialismo al Fascismo.*
Borghese, G. A.: Golia. *Marcia del Fascismo.*
Borghi, A.: *Mezzo secolo di anarchia.*

Bottai, G.: *Pagine di Critica Fascista*; *Vent'anni e un giorno.*
Braunthal, J.: *La tragedia dell'Austria.*
Brenan, G.: *The Spanish Labyrinth.* (An account of the social and political background of the civil war.)
Buozzi, B.: *Scritti dall'esilio.*
Cadorna, R.: *La riscossa. Dal 25 luglio alla liberazione.*
Caedana, M.: *Figlio del Fabbro.*
Calamandrei, P.: *Uomini e città della resistenza.*
Cancogni, M.: *Storia dello squadrismo.*
Cantalupe, R.: *Fu la Spagna.*
Caporilli, P.: *Il Fascismo ed i Giovani*; *Spagna Rossa.*
Caracciolo, A.: *L'intervento italiano in guerra e la crisi politica dal 1914–1915.*
Carceri: *esperienze e documenti*; Ed. il Ponte.
Carli, F.: *Problemi Nazionali e Sociali.*
Carli, R.: *Ballila*: *Storia della Resistenza.*
Carocci, G.: *Storia del Fascismo.*
Catalano, F.: *Storia del C.L.N.A.I.*; *Dalla crisi del dopoguerra alla fondazione della Repubblica.*
Catalucco, F.; *La nostra guerra.*
Cavallero, V.: *Comando Supremo.*
Caviglia, A.: *Il complotto di Fiume.*
Caviglia, E.: *La dodicesima battaglia.*
Orsoloni-Cencelli, V.: *Le paludi Pontine.*
Cessi, R.: *La resistenza nel Bellunese.*
Ceva, B.: *1930—Retroscena di un dramma.*
Chiurco, G. A.: *La storia della Rivoluzione Fascista.*
Churchill, W.: *The Italian Campaign*; *Discorsi Segreti.*
Ciano, G.: Diario (1937–1938); Diario I° (1939–1940); II° (1941–1943).
Cilibrizzi, S.: *Badoglio.*
Cilombi, A.: *Nelle mani del nemico.*
Cione: *Storia della Repubblica Sociale Italiana.*
Compagna, F.; de Caprariis, E. V.: *Geografia delle Elezioni Italiane dal 1946 al 1953.*
Compagna, F.: *La lotta politica italiana nel secondo dopoguerra e il Mezzogiorno.*
Conti, G.: *La Costituente.*
Corradini, E.: *L'Unità e la potenza della Nazione*; *Scritti politici.*
Crespi, S.: *Alla difesa dell'Italia in guerra ed a Versailles.*
Crouzet, M.: *L'Epoque contemporaine.*
Curato, F.: *La Conferenza della Pace*—1919–1920; *La storiografia delle origini della Prima Guerra Mondiale*; *Prima Guerra Mondiale.*
Daffina, O.: *Mussolini ed il Fascismo.*
De Begnac, Y.: *Vita di Benito Mussolini.*
Degli Espinosa, A.: *Il Regno del Sud*—1943–1944.
Degli Occhi, C.: *Che cosa ho pensato del Fascismo quando ero popolare.*
Degrass, J.: *The Communist International*—1943; Documents, Vol. II, 1923–1928.
del Bono, E.: *La Conquista dell'Impero.*

del Bono, G.: *La Guerra di Spagna.*
delle Piane, M.: *Funzione Storica del Comitato di Liberazione Nazionale.*
di Nolfo, E.: *Mussolini e la Politica Estera Italiana.*
Documents on British Foreign Policy—1919–1939—Vols. I–V; 3rd Series.
Donati, G.: *Gli scritti politici.*
Donosti, M.: *Mussolini e L'Europa. La Politica Estera Italiana.*
Dorso, G.: *La Rivoluzione Meridionale*; *Mussolini alla conquista del potere.*
Dumini, A.: *17 colpi.*
Fabbri, L.: *La Controrivoluzione preventiva.*
Farinacci, R.: *Squadrismo. Dal mio diario della Vigilia*; *Storia della Rivoluzione Fascista.*
Fascismo—"Inchiesta socialista sulle gesta del Fascismo in Italia"—ed.: *Avanti!*
Favagrossa, G.: *Perchè perdemmo la guerra.*
Federzoni, L.: *Il Trattato di Rapallo.*
Ferrari, F.L.: *Le Régime Fasciste Italien.*
Ferrero, G.: *Da Fiume a Roma. Storia di quattro anni* (1919–1923).
Fiore, T.: *Un popolo di formiche.*
Flora, F.: *Ritratto di un ventennio.*
Galanti, F.: *Socializzazione e sindacalismo nel R.S.I.*
Galbiati, E.: *il 25 luglio e la M.V.S.N.*
Galli, G.: *La Sinistra del Dopoguerra*; *Storia del Partito Comunista Italiano.*
Gallian, M.: *Ventennale.*
Garin, E.: *Cronaca di Filosofia Italiana.*
Garosci, A.: *Storia dei fuoriusciti.*
Garosci, G.: *Intellettuali e la Guerra di Spagna.*
Gavagnin, A.: *Ventanni di resistenza al fascismo*; *Una lettera al Re.*
Gentizzon, P.: *Difesa d'Italia.*
Giannini, A.: *Documenti per la storia fra l'Italia e la Jugoslavia.*
Gianpoli, M.: *1919.*
Gigli, G.: *La Seconda Guerra Mondiale.*
Giolitti, G.: *Memorie della mia vita*; *Discorsi parlamentari; Discorsi extra-parlamentari.*
Giovanazzi, G.: *La scuola di Baleilla.*
Giudice, P.: *Storia d'Italia.*
Giva, M.: *Ricordi di un ex-detenuto politico.*
Gobetti, A.: *Diario Partigiano.*
Gobetti, P.: *La Rivoluzione Liberale.*
Goebbels, J.: *Noi Tedeschi ed il Fascismo di Mussolini.*
Gorgolini, P.: *Il Fascismo nella Vita Italiana.*
Gramsci, A.: *Scritti giovanili*; *Lettere dal Carcere*; *Sotto la Mole*; *L'Ordine Nuovo.*
Grandi, D.: *Le Origini del Fascismo e la missione del Fascismo.*
Gravelli, A.: *Canti della Rivoluzione.*
Graziani, A.: *Ho difeso la Patria.*
Graziani, R.: *Fronte Sud.*
Grifoni, P.: *Il capitale finanziario in Italia.*
Gualerni, G.: *La politica industriale fascista.*

Guariglia, R.: *Ricordi* (1922–1946).
Guarneri, F.: *Battaglie economiche fra le due grandi guerre.*
Guerrin, D.: *Fascismo e Gran Capitale.*
Harris, C. R. S.: *Allied Military Administration of Italy* (1943–1945).
History of the Communist Party of the Soviet Union (F.L.P.H., Moscow).
Hitler-Mussolini: Lettere e documenti.
I Documenti Diplomatici Italiani. I.S.T.A.T.: Dal Censimento dell'Unità al Censimento del Centenario.
Jachino, A.: *Gaudo e Matapan.*
Jacometti, A.: *Ventottene.*
Jemolo, A. C.: *Stato e Chiesa in Italia negli ultimi Cento Anni.*
Kesselring, Field Marshal: *War Memoirs.*
Kogan, N.: *Italy and the Allies.*
Labriola, A.: *Le due Polemiche—Fascismo e Riformismo.*
L'Europa Verso La Catastrofe: 184 colloqui con Mussolini, Hitler, Franco, ecc. verbalizzati da Ciano.
Lazagna, G. B.: *Ponte rotto, Storia delle Divisione Garibaldina "Pinan Cicchero"*; *Lettere di Condannati a Morte della Resistenza Italiana.*
Leto, G.: *O.V.R.A., Fascismo—Antifascismo.*
Levi, C.: *Cristo si è fermato ad Eboli.*
Levi, P.: *Cavaglione—Guerriglia nei Castelli Romani.*
Lodolini, A.: *La Storia Sociale del Lavoro.*
Lombardo-Radice, L.: *Fascismo e Anticomunismo—Appunti e Ricordi* (1935–1945).
Ludwig, E.: *Colloqui con Mussolini.*
Luraghi, R.: *Il Movimento Operaio Torinese durante la Resistenza.*
Lussu, E.: *La catena; Diplomazia Clandestina*; *Un Anno sull'Altopiano*; *Marcia su Roma e Dintorni.*
Lussu, J.: *Fronti e Frontiere.*
Mack-Smith, D.: *Italy—A Modern History.*
Magistrati, M.: *L'Italia e Berlino.*
Malagodi, O.: *Conversazioni della Guerra.*
Malatesta, E.: *Gli Scritti.*
Malgeri, A.: *L'Occupazione di Milano e la Liberazione.*
Mangeri, F.: *Dalle Ceneri della Disfatta.*
Manzocchi, B.: *Lineamenti di Politica Economica in Italia (1945–1955).*
Marston, F. S.: *The Peace Conference of 1919—Organisation and Procedure.*
Matteotti, G.: *Discorsi e Scritti.*
Mattioli, G.: *Aviazione Squadrista, Anviazione Legionaria in Spagna.*
Megano, G.: *Mussolini in the Making.*
Ministero Della Guerra Italiana—Documenti.
Mira, G.: *Autunno 1918.*
Missiroli, M.: *il Fascismo e la Crisi Italiana; Date a Cesare—La Politica Religiosa di Mussolini*; *Monaco*; *Una Battaglia Perduta.*
Modigliani, V.: *Esilio.*
Mondaini, G.: *L'Assetto Coloniale del Mondo dopo la Guerra.*
Mondolfo, R.: *Sulle Orme di Marx*; *Per la Comprensione Storica del Fascismo.*
Monelli, P.: *Mussolini: Piccolo Borghese.*

Montagnana, M.: *Ricordi di un Operaio Torinese.*
Montanelli, I: *il Buonuomo Mussolini*; *i Rapaci in Cortile.*
Monti, A.: *Realtà del Partito d'Azione.*
Morandi, R.: *Lettere al Fratello*; *La Pupilla del Regime*; *Una Spia del Regime*; *La Democrazia del Socialismo* (*1923–1937*); *Lotta di Popolo* (*1937–1945*).
Mortara, G.: *Prospettive economiche.*
Mosca, P.: *Documenti Diplomatici Italiani*, Serie VI (1918–1922).
Mussolini, B.: *Discorsi e Scritti*, Vol. 1–8; *Tempo del Bastone e della Carota*; *Vita di Arnaldo*; *Opera Omnia*; *Il mio diario di Guerra.*
Note: The books by members of Mussolini's family seemed to me to be of dubious objectivity and are not included in this bibliography.
Natale, G.: *Le "Giornate Radiose" del Maggio 1915.*
Nenni, P.: *Storia di quattro anni*; *Pagine di diario; Taccuino 1942.*
Nicoli, M.: *La Resistenza Italiana.*
Nitti, F. F.: *Le nostre Prigioni e le nostre Evasioni*; *Rivelazioni Dramatis Personae*; *Scritti Politici*, Vol. I e II; *il Maggiore è un Rosso.*
Olivetti, A.: *Storia Critica dell'Utopia Communitista.*
Omodeo, A.: *Libertà e Storia—Scritti e Discorsi politici*; *Momenti della Vita di Guerra.*
Opera del O.N.B. e. del P.N.F.
Orano, P.: *Il Fascismo.*
Orestano, F.: *Verso la Nuova Europa.*
Orlando, V. E.: *Su alcuni niei Rapporti di Governo con la Santa Sede*; *Discorsi per la Pace e per la Guerra*; *Memorie.*
Ottaviani, G. B.: *La Politica Rurale di Mussolini.*
Pacciardi, R.: *il Battaglione Garibaldi.*
Panorami delle Realizzazioni del Fascismo.
Pantaleo, P.: *Il Fascismo Cremonese.*
Panunzio, S.: *Diritto—Forza—Violenza.*
Papa, E. R.: *Storia di due Manifesti—Il Fascismo e la Cultura Italiana.*
Paposogli, E.: *Fascismo.*
Parri, F.: *La Malfa V.: Lezioni sull'Antifascismo.*
Pascazio, N.: *La Rivoluzione di Spagna.*
Pellizzi, C.: *Una Rivoluzione Mancata.*
Perticone, G.: *La Politica Italiana nell'Ultimo Ventennio.*
Pesce, G.: *Soldati senza Uniforme* (*Diario di un Gappista*).
Pieri, P.: *L'Italia nella Prima Guerra Mondiale.*
Pini, G.: *Filo Diretto dal Palazzo Venezia*; *Mussolini, l'Uomo e l'Opera*; *Storia del Fascismo.*
Pischel, G.: *Che cosa è il Partito d'Azione. Dottrina ed esperienza Storica di un nuovo Partito e sue Direttive per l'Avvenire.*
Pitt, R.: *La Spia Timida.*
Raggianti, C. L.: *Disegno della Liberazione Italiana.*
Reale, E.: *La Politique Fasciste et la Société des Nations.*
Renouvin, P.: *Histoire des Rélations Internationales. Les Crises du XX Siecle.*
Riccardi, R.: *Pagine Squadriste.*
Ricci, B.: *Avvisi.*

Ricci, M.: *Balilla in terra lontana.*

Roatta, M.: *Otto milioni di baionette. L'esercito italiano in guerra dal 1940 al 1944.*

Rocca, M.: *Il trattato di Rapallo.*

Romita, R.: *Dalla Monarchia alla Repubblica.*

Rosen, E. R.: *Italiens kriegseintritt in jahre 1915 als innen politisches problem der Giolitti aera ein Beitragzur vergeschichte Zur Fascismus.*

Rosenstoch-Franck, L.: *L'économie corporative fasciste en doctrine et en fait*; *Les étapes de l'économie fasciste italienne.*

Rosselli, G.: *Socialismo liberale*; *Oggi in Spagna domani in Italia*; *Scritti politici ed autobiografici.*

Rossi, E.: *Lo Stato industriale*; *Settimo: non rubare*; *NO al fascismo.*

Rossi-Doria, M.: *Dieci anni di politica agraria nel mezzogiorno.*

Rossini, G.: *Il fascismo e la resistenza.*

Saitta, A.: *Dal fascismo alla resistenza*; *Saggio bibliografico sulla seconda guerra mondiale a cura dell'ufficio storico del ministero della Difesa, Roma 1949* (Supplemento, 1951).

Salandra, A.: *La neutralità italiana*; *L'intervento*; *Memorie politiche.*

Salvadori, E.: *Resistenza ed azione*; *Brief History of the Patriotic Movement in Italy* (1943–1945).

Salvatorelli, L.: *Nazionalfascismo*; *Storia del novecento*; *Il fascismo nella politica internazionale*; *La politica della Santa Sede doppo la guerra.*

Salvatorelli, L., Mira, G.: *Storia d'Italia nel periodo fascista*; *Storia del fascismo L'Italia dal 1919 al 1945.*

Salvemini, G.: *Giolitti e il patto di Londra*; *Dal patto di Londra alla pace di Roma, documenti della politica che non fu fatta*; *Memorie di un fuoriuscito*; *The Fascist Dictatorship in Italy*; *La terreur fasciste*; *Sotto la scure del fascismo*; *Mussolini diplomatico*; *L'Italia economica dal 1919 al 1922*; *Tendenze vecchie e necessità nuove del movimento operaio italiano.*

Salvemini, G., La Piana, G.: *What to do with Italy.*

Sapegno, N.: *Figure del primo antifascismo.*

Sarfatti, M.: *Dux.*

Savino, E.: *La Nazione operante.*

Schiavi, A.: *La vita e l'opera di Giacomo Matteotti.*

Secchia, P.: *I communisti e l'insurrezione.*

Secchia, P., Moscatelli, C.: *Il monte Rosa è sceso a Milano. La resistenza nel Viellese, nella Val Sesia, nella Val d'Ossola.*

Serant, P.: *Le romantisme fasciste.*

Sereni, E.: *Il mezzogiorno all'opposizione*; *Vecchio e nuovo nelle campagne italiane.*

Serra, E.: *Camille Barrère e l'intesa Italo-Francese.*

Settemelli, E.: *Sassate.*

Sforza, C.: *Jugoslavia*; *Pensiero ed azione di una politica estera italiana*; *L'Italia dal 1914 al 1944 quale io la vidi.*

Silvestri, C.: *Matteotti—Mussolini.*

Skorczeny, O.: *Missioni segrete.*

Spriano, P.: *Torino operaia nella grande guerra* (1914–1918).

Starace, A.: *La marcia di Gondar.*

Stato e Chiesa (scritti di Salvatorelli, Pittazoni, Basile, Falconi, ecc.).

Sturani, L.: *Antologia della resistenza.*
Sturzo, Don. L.: *La liberta in Italia*; *Il partito popolare italiano*; *La mia battaglia a New York*; *Italy and fascism*; *L'Italia ed i nuovi ordini internazionali.*
Tamaro, A.: *Vent'anni di storia*; *Due anni di storia* (1943–1945).
Callan-Tansill, C.: *Il gioco diplomatico fra le due guerre.*
Tasca, A.: *La naissance du fascisme. L'Italie de 1918 à 1922.*
Thomas, H.: *The Spanish Civil War.*
Thomson, D.: *The Era of Violence, 1898–1945.*
Tittoni, T., Scialoja, V.: *L'Italia alla conferenza della pace.*
Togliatti, P.: *Per la salvezza del nostro paese*; *Il partito communista italiano.*
Torre, A.: *Versailles. Storia della conferenza della pace.*
Toscana, M.: *Le origini diplomatiche del patto d'acciaio*; *Il patto di Londra. Storia diplomatica dell'intervento italiano.*
Trabucchi, A.: *I vinti hanno sempre torto.*
Trenti, S.: *Le fascisme à Genève.*
Treves, C.: *Quello che ci ha fatto Mussolini.*
Trotski, L.: *My life.*
Turati, F.: *Le vie maestre del socialismo*; *Una rivoluzione ed un capo.*
Turati, F., Kuliscioff, A.: *Dopoguerra e fascismo* (1919–1922); *Il delitto Matteotti e l'Aventino* (1923–1925).
Valeri, N.: *Storia d'Italia; Da Giolitti a Mussolini. Momenti della crisi del liberalismo*; *La lotta politica in Italia dall'unità al 1925. Idee e documenti.*
Valliani, L.: *Recenti pubblicazioni sulla prima guerra mondiale*; *Tutte le strade conducono a Roma*; *L'avvento di de Gasperi.*
Valori, A.: *La guerra Italo-Austriaca.*
Villari, L.: *Affari esteri.*
Viterbo, M.: *Il mezzogiorno e l'accentramento statale.*
Wiskemann: *L'asse Roma-Berlino. Storia dei rapporti tra Mussolini e Hitler.*
Zachariae, G.: *Mussolini si confessa.*
Zerboglio, A. Grandi, D.: *Il fascismo.*
Zibordi, G.: *Critica socialista del fascismo.*
Zuccaro, D.: *Vita del carcere di A. Gramsci.*
And the following pamphlets published by the Fascist Press: "Ora e lavora nelle nuova econmia"; "Gli otto punti"; "La tecnica della guerra attuale"; "Ragione di questa guerra"; "La crisi dell'Impero Britannico"; "Le materie prime"; "L'Imperialismo degli Stati Uniti"; "Plutocrazia e Bolscevismo"; "Prigioniera nel mare"; "Frate T.: I problemi del Baltico."

INDEX

Abyssinia: *see* Ethiopia
Academy, the Italian, inaugurated, 200–1
Acerbo, G., 141, 150, 155
Action Party: formation of, 331–2; tentative co-operation with other opposition parties (*1941*), 332; activities after the armistice, 344; at the Bari conference, 345; attitude to Russia's recognition of Badoglio, 346; and the Bonomi government, 347, 349; the partisan units, 348; hopes to keep Mussolini alive, 353–4; eclipse, 359
Adam, Gen., 280
Agriculture: the battle for wheat, 187–8, 194, 209–10
Air Force, the Italian: condition in *1915*, 62; Pinedo's "show the world" flight, 179; Balbo's Flying Circus, 194, 205; unreadiness in *1939*, 306; divided loyalties in *1943*, 343
Albania: early Italian designs on, 80; nationalist rising (*1920*), 110; treaty with Italy (*1927*), 193–4; occupied by Italy, 304–5
Albertini, Luigi, 164, 167, 179
Albini, 334, 338
Alexander, Gen., attitude to the partisans, 346, 348–9
Alfonso XIII of Spain, visits Italy, 153–4
Altobelli, Argentina, 112
Ambrosini, Luigi, 131
Ambrosio, Gen., 323
Amendola, A., 165, 177
Ancona mutiny, 110
Anti-Comintern Pact, 250–1
Aosta, Duke of: military success (*1916*), 71; a possible alternative king, 128; last days, 204
Arditi, 69, 83
Army, the Italian: lack of equipment in *1915*, 62–3; Caporetto, 76–7; improved morale, 79–80; and success, 82–5; the ex-officers leaning to Fascism, 97–8; collaboration with Fascists, 109, 115; uneasy relations with Militia, 139–40; the fighting in Ethiopia, 228–9, 231, 234, 236–7; unreadiness in *1939*, 306; jealousies of generals exploited by Badoglio, 321–3; sabotage of supplies, 323–4; divided loyalties in 1943, 342–3
Ascolo, 282
Asquith, Lord, 69
Astakhov, Georgi, 308
Attolico, 279, 284, 291
Audàcia (leader by Mussolini in *il Popolo d'Italia*), 51
Audisio, Walter ("Col. Valerio"), 353
Austria: the assassination at Serajevo, 46; relations with Italy (*1915*), 56; at war with Italy, 61; record of the air force, 69; the *1916* offensive, 70; the Caporetto campaign, 76–7; the last offensive, 83; asks for armistice, 85; the Fascist and Nazi factions in *1934*, 219–20; murder of Dollfuss, 221; international diplomacy before the German occupation, 262–7; the *anschluss*, 267–9
Avanti: supports Mussolini (*1908*), 34; edited by Mussolini, 42–8; reaction to *il Popolo d'Italia*, 52; offices burnt down (*1919*), 99–100; suspended, 170, 179
Aversa, 106
Avvenire del Lavatore, edited by Mussolini, 34

Bacci, 41
Badoglio, Marshal Pietro: derides the idea of the march on Rome, 124; adjusts his ideas after it, 130; decides to work with Mussolini, 135; Chief of General Staff, 178; warns Mussolini against a clash with Britain, 226; takes over command in Ethiopia, 231, 233–4; finishes the campaign, 236–7; receives dukedom, 238; his conspiracies and treacheries, 321–4; dismissed as Chief of Staff, 322; proclaimed head of the government, 338; friction with Bonomi, 340; signs armistice with Eisenhower, 340; leaves Rome for Brindisi, 341; disliked by opposition parties, 345; moves to Salerno, 345–6; recognized by Russia, 346; co-operates with the opposition, 347
Balabanoff, Angelica, 24, 25, 42, 43, 48, 52
Balbo, Italo: an early violent Fascist, 114; organizes Fascist formations, 115; occupies Ferrara, 121; and Parma, 122; work for the march on Rome, 124, 125; during the Freemasonry crisis, 141, 142; during the Matteotti affair, 163; his Flying Circus, 194, 205; Minister for Air, 200; his work in Libya, 251; attends funeral of Pius XI, 302

Baldini, 185
Balearic Islands, 241, 253
Balella, 337
Bálilla: *see* Youth movements
Balilla, Giovanni, 328
Banfi, 106
Bari conference, 345
Barone, Professor, 192
Barracu, 352
Bartolomasi, Mgr., 233
Barzilai, 57
Barzin, 172
Barzini, Luigi, 148
Baseggio, 106
Bastianini, 236, 319
Battisti, Cesare, 35
Baudouin, M., 307
Beck, Col. Jósef, 275, 280
Beck, Gen., 279, 280
Bedeschi, 22, 23
Bellinato, 106
Benedict XV: attitude to World War I, 66–7; appeals for peace, 72; attitude to the Popular Catholic Party, 108; death, 119
Bensa, 103
Bentini, 40
Bercholdt, 56
Bianchi, Camillo, 106
Bianchi, Michele: an early Fascist, 96; opinion before the *1921* election, 114; works for Nationalist-Socialist truce, 117; and for the march on Rome, 124, 126; for the *1924* election, 155; Minister of Public Works, 200
Bissolati, L., 41, 94, 97
Blomberg, F.-M., 262
Bocchini, Arturo, 184
Bolaffi, 318
Bolzon, 106
Bombacci, 82, 352, 354
Bonacorsi, Count, 241
Bonacossa, Count, 82
Bonardi, Carlo, 133
Bonar Law, A., 138
Bonnet, P., 312
Bonomi, Ivanoe: expelled from the Socialist Party (*1912*), 41; on Trent and Trieste, 57; becomes Prime Minister (*1921*) and ignores the Fascists, 117; resigns, 121; plans with the king for the overthrow of Mussolini, 333–4; friction with Badoglio, 340; negotiates with the allies, 340; tries to gain their recognition, 344; becomes Prime Minister, 347; signs agreement with C.L.N., 350
Boris, King of Bulgaria: admires Mussolini, 148; a Balkan pawn, 193; marries Giovanni of Italy, 203–4; friendship for Mussolini, 242; brings goodwill message to Britain, 282–3
Boselli, Paolo, 71, 72
Bottai, Giuseppe: an early Futurist collaborator with Mussolini, 95; proposes an ex-service *coup d'état*, 101; urges violence, 102–3, 104; attitude to occupation of Fiume, 105; opinion before *1921* election, 114–15; urges Mussolini to become Prime Minister (*1921*), 116; suggests peaceful assumption of Fascist power, 122; on the lack of a Fascist philosophy, 148–9; on international Fascism, 172; his rôle as party critic, 174–6; campaign against opposition leaders, 176–7; economic theories expressed in the Work Charter, 188–91; on the Party as the Nation, 194; Minister of Corporations, 200; out of favour, 244; criticizes Italy's approach to Germany (*1936*), 250; his premonitions of war, 252; on German intervention in Spain, 253; on the isolation of Mussolini, 258; on the Austrian *anschluss*, 269; goes to Cologne, 276; and reports to Mussolini, 278–9; on the declaration of war, 313; typifies the Fascist intellectuals, 326–7; his revulsion from the Nazification of Fascism, 327; instrumental in calling the final meeting of the Grand Council, 334; at the meeting, 336–7; eventual fate, 337
Braida, 82
Britain: sends troops to the Italian front (*1917*), 79–80; supports Yugoslav territorial integrity, 91; and claim to Fiume, 104; approves Mussolini as the only stable element in Europe (*1923*), 145–6; negotiates over Fiume, 146–7, 155; regard for Italy in *1926*, 186; suspicious of a Mediterranean bloc (*1927*), 193–4; the Four Power Pact, 216; reaction to the Dollfuss murder, 221–2; appeasement and attempted *rapprochement* with Germany, 225; warns Mussolini against intervention in Spain, 236, 241; Mediterranean agreement with Italy (*1937*), 251; seen by Mussolini as indecisive and decadent, 260; policy with Italy and Germany before the Austrian *anschluss*, 264, 265, 266; reaction to the *anschluss*, 268; fresh attempt at understanding with Italy, 269, 270, 271; agreement breaks down over Spain, 276–8; rejects Italy's solution of the Jewish problem, 281–2; military moves before Munich, 290; failure to appreciate

Britain—*contd.*
value of Italian friendship after Munich, 295–9, 300–2; rejects Soviet alliance, 309; declares war on Germany, 312
Bufferini, 338
Bukharin, 112
Buozzi, Bruno, 161, 185
Burian, Baron, 56, 59
Buronzo, Vincenzo: organizes Youth Movements, 142, 147; attitude today, 363
Buvoli, Orsola, 243

Cabrini, 41
Cadogan, Sir Alexander, 283
Calderara, 28, 29, 30, 31
Calvi, Count Carlo, 143
Campagni, 118
Campilli, 361
Caneva, 103
Capello, Gen., 77
Caporetto, 76–7; enquiry into, 84–5, 103, 104
Cardona, Gen., 70–1, 76–7, 78
Carducci, Valfredo, 21
Carli, Mario, 104
Carnazza, Gabriello, 133
Carrocci, Cesira, 183
Casalini, Armando, 165
Casati, 163, 331
Castelnuovo, 282
Catholic Action: attempted opposition to Mussolini, 205–6; loss of prestige during the war, 317; post-war political activity, 360
Cavachiocchi, Gen., 77
Cavazzoni, Stefano, 133
Cavour, his political legacy, 90–1
Ceccherini, Gen., 141
Ceccheti, Dr., 30
Cecil, Lord Robert, 152
Ceresa, 82
Chabod, Professor, 91
Chamberlain, Sir Austen, 178
Chamberlain, H. S., 178
Chamberlain, Neville: attempts at *rapprochement* with Italy (*1938*), 264; hesitates between Italian and French friendship, 270; advocates Sudeten plebiscite, 279–80; more hesitation on Italy's offers of friendship, 282–3; first flight to see Hitler, 285, 286; agrees to the cession of Sudetenland, 286; the Godesberg agreement, 287; announces Hitler's invitation in the Commons, 292; at the Munich conference, 294–5; his appreciation of Mussolini's efforts, 296; abortive visit to Rome, 301; "guarantees" Poland, 304
Charles, Sir Noel, 307
Cheledi, Giovanni, 35
Chiang Kai-shek, 208, 238
Chierici, 334
Chigi, 255
Christian Democrat Party: its position in *1942*, 330; tentative co-operation with other opposition parties, 332; at the Bari conference, 345; attitude to the Bonomi government, 347; rise to power under de Gasperi, 359–62
Church, the: negotiates over the Law of Guarantees, 67; first negotiations with Mussolini on reconciliation, 140–2, 143–5; during the Matteotti affair, 163; further hopes of reconciliation, 187; the achievement of the Lateran Pact, 195–9; the Bulgarian marriage affair, 204; crisis over the Òpera bàlilla and Catholic Action, 205–6; satisfaction over the Ethiopian campaign, 239; decorates Mussolini, 242; attitude on occupation of Czechoslovakia, 303; growth of opposition to Fascism, 316–19; deplores discrimination against Jews, 318; post-war political activity, 360
Churchill, Sir Winston: visits Mussolini—his views, 186; approves Mussolini's firmness over Dollfuss crisis, 222; warns Mussolini of gravity of the Czech crisis, 288–9; reaction to Munich, 295
Chvalkovsky, Frantisek, 296
Cianetti, 337
Ciano, Count Galeazzo: marries Edda Mussolini, 203; his qualities, 248–9; his policy of "enlightened neutrality", 249; difficulty in interpreting Mussolini's wishes, 249; inconclusive visit to Britain, 249–50; his views on the German hierarchy, 250; negotiates Mediterranean agreement with Britain, 251; and approaches Germany, 252; cautious over a German alliance, 255; diplomacy before the Austrian *anschluss*, 264–7; diplomacy before the Godesberg agreement, 284–7; negotiations for British-Italian agreement, 296; warns France against intervention in Barcelona, 302; attends funeral of Pius XI, 302; discusses Soviet-Axis pact with Ribbentrop, 308, 309; signs the Pact of Steel, 309; fears precipitate German action, 310; Minister to the Holy See, 319; at the final meeting of the Grand Council, 336; death, 337
Cimmatura, Capt., 222–3
Cipriani, Amilcare, 54, 57
Cittadini, Gen., 126, 129

Civelli, 126
Clark, Ectin, 91
Clemenceau, Georges, 81
C.L.N.: *see* Committee for National Liberation
Codignola, 172
Committee for National Liberation: frustrated by lack of allied co-operation, 343–6; calls the strike of *March 1944*, 346; agreement with Bonomi and loss of influence, 350; its hope to keep Mussolini alive, 354
Communist Party: break-away from the Socialists at Livono, 112; the bomb outrage at the Teatro Diana, 113–14; position after the *1924* election, 156; position in *1942*, 330; tentative co-operation with the other opposition parties, 332; at the Bari conference, 345; attitude to Russia's recognition of Badoglio, 346; and to the Bonomi government, 347; the murder squads, 348; responsible for Mussolini's death, 354; development to its present position, 358–9
Compagni, 113
Confederation of Industry: early support for Mussolini, 100–1
Contarini: deals with the Corfu affair, 152; views on Stalin, 155; Balkan and Mediterranean policy, 193
Coppola, 172
Coptic Church, welcomes Italians in Ethiopia, 230
Corfu, bombardment of, 151–2
Corporations, 200, 204, 239
Corrandini, E., nationalist leader, 57, 61, 63, 97, 204
Corriere della Sera, 148, 179, 231, 353
Corsi, 165
Corsica, 299
Corzarini, Rino, 351
Costa, Andrea, 15–16
Costa, Carla, 351
Crispi, 93
Crìtica Fascista, 148, 174, 189
Croce, Benedetto: anti-Fascist ideas, 172; lingers in opposition, 185; position in *1942*, 331
Cuardi, 58
Curzio, 141
Curzon, Lord, 137
Czechoslovakia: Mussolini's warning to Hitler, 273; the beginning of the Sudeten question, 273; the May (*1938*) crisis, 274–6; reactions to Hitler's speech (*Sept. 1938*), 285; capitulates, 287; but rejects Hitler's ultimatum, 288; the Munich conference, 293–5; disintegration, 295; final occupation by Germany, 303–4

Daily Mail, on Mussolini, 138, 180
Daily Telegraph, on Mussolini, 135
Daladier, E., 285, 294
Dalmatia: early Italian designs on, 80; as a *casus belli* (*1915*), 59; anti-Italian riots (*1918*), 86; discussed at Peace Conference, 91
D'Annunzio, Gabriele: an interventionist (*1915*), 58, 59, 60; wartime activities, 69; recruits a private army, 101; occupies Fiume, 104–5; evicted, 111; prefers violence to "respectability", 114; views on a march on Rome, 123; coolness with Mussolini, 123; armistice day speech, 125; his nuisance value, 146, 151; Prince of the Snowy Mountains, 156; during the Matteotti affair, 165; final allegiance to Fascism, 170–1; his economic ideas, 188
Danti, Paolina, 27
d'Arzago, G. de C., 132
Day of Intervention (*1915*), 59
de Begnac, Yvon, 318
Debenedetti, 382
de Bernadi, 194
de Bono, Gen. Emilio: work for the march on Rome, 124; dealings with the Queen Mother, 125; views on Lenin, 155; during the Matteotti affair, 158, 159, 166; Governor of Libya, 183; Minister for the Colonies, 200; commands the Ethiopian campaign, 228, 230; relieved of command, 231; at the final meeting of the Grand Council, 335; death, 337
de Cicco, 334
de Felice-Giuffrida, 55
de Gasperi, Alcide, 35; support from the Church, 318; includes Nenni in his government, 358; builds the power of the C.D.P., 360–1
Degrelle, Léon, 208
Del Giudice, 289, 363
Delser, Ida, 35–6
del Vecchio, 172
de Magistris, 106
Democrats, 132–3
de Nicolo, 117
de Orestis, Ragni, 103
de Pinedo, F., 179
de Preto, 194
de Stefani, Alberto: Finance Minister, 134, 139; his financial skill, 149; balances the budget, 156; his brilliance concealed as a "Fascist success", 189; economic report (*1932*), 208–10; advises Chiang

de Stefani, Alberto—*contd.*
Kai-shek, 238; at the final meeting of the Grand Council, 337
de Vecchi: work for the march on Rome, 125; dealings with the Queen Mother, 125; inspires riots in Turin, 139; Governor of Somalia, 152–3; at the *1925* Congress, 174; at the final meeting of the Grand Council, 335
Diaz, Gen. Armanda, 78, 79, 128, 134
di Cesaro, G. C., 133
di Giacomo, 172
di Giorgio, Gen., 163
di Revel, Admiral, 128, 134, 142
Dirksen, H. von, 263
Djibouti, 299, 307
Dollfuss, E.: political position in *1934*, 219; warns Mussolini of Hitler's intentions, 221; murdered, 221
Drummond, Sir Eric: *see* Perth, Lord
Duca, Mgr. B., 242
Dudan, 141
Dumini, 160
Duse, Eleonora, 139

Eden, Sir Anthony: at the Fascist Exhibition, 208; receives assurances from Hitler (*1934*), 219; approves Mussolini's firmness in Dollfuss crisis, 222; tortuous diplomacy before German rearmament, 223–4; fails to dissuade Mussolini from Abyssinian adventure, 225–6; urges sanctions against Italy, 230; efforts to ensure their application, 232; suspects Mussolini's interest in Middle East (*1937*), 252; resignation over *rapprochement* with Italy, 264; accused of rejecting Italy's Jewish policy, 282
Educational reform, 154
Einaudi, 172, 331, 361
Eisenhower, Gen., announces armistice with Italy, 340–1
Ekrem Bey, Col., 242
Electoral reform (*1923*), 150
Enriques, 282
Ethiopia: Mussolini's attitude in *1923*, 151; the Regent visits Italy, 163; attacks on Italian nationals, 222–3; the Italian attack, 228; progress of the campaign, 231, 234; defeat, 236–7
Evans, Sir Arthur, 81

Fabbri, L., 106
Facta: Prime Minister, 121; attempted resignation, 122; efforts to negotiate with Mussolini, 123–9
Faenza, the Salesian College, 20–1
Falche, 109
Fano, 282
Fara, 124
Farinacci, R.: an early violent Fascist, 114, 116; escapes assassination, 119; occupies Cremona, 122; accuses Mussolini of inaction, 123; work for the march on Rome, 127; during the Freemasonry crisis, 142; during the Matteotti affair, 157, 163; Secretary of the Party, 171; foils opposition plan to commemorate Matteotti, 174; distrust of Bottai, 175; attacks Freemasonry, 179; dismissed, 182; becomes anti-semitic, 282; refuses to attend funeral of Pius XI, 302; instrumental in calling final meeting of Grand Council, 334; at the meeting, 335–7; death, 337
Fascism: the early interventionist groups, 54–5, 57; the *Fascio* for national defence (*1917*), 80; formation of the *Fasci di Combattimento*, 86–7; the vagueness of Fascist objectives, 88–9; support of the anti-Socialists, 95–8; unorganized violence in *1919*, 103–4; growth of membership after occupation of Fiume, 105; defeated in the *1919* election, 105–6; beginnings of military organization, 109; increased membership after the "revolution of the Soviets", 111; further violence (*end of 1920*), 111–12; shows influence of army training, 115; strength before the *1921* election, 115; which it wins, 116; abortive truce with the Socialists, 117–18; birth of the National Fascist Party, 118–19; further violence in *1922*, 120–2; conflicting views on how to achieve power, 122–3; the march on Rome, 123–9; the *1922* Naples congress, 125; formation of the Grand Council of Fascism, 138–9; first clash over Freemasonry, 141–2; its lack of a philosophy, 148–9; electoral reform (*1923*), 150; the *1924* election, 156; the Matteotti crisis, 159–68; further attack on Freemasonry, 173–4; Party Congress of *1924* and concept of "devotion to the Leader", 174–6; the prefects, 187; its vague philosophy contrasted with Nazism, 188; "the Party is the Nation", 194–5; the Corporations, 204; the "Ten Years of Fascism" Exhibition—foreign imitators, 208; strength in *1932*, 210; and after the Ethiopian campaign, 238; growth of discontent with the régime: in the Church, 316–19; in the royal family, 319–21; in the army, 321–5; in the Party, 325–8; among the masses, 328–33; the removal of Mussolini and the suc-

Fascism—*contd.*
ceeding vacuum, 334–9; the last flame in the north, 351–2; influence on the development of Italian political parties, 356–63; the neo-Fascists of today, 362–3; no chance of revival, 363; the legacy remains, 365
Federzoni, Luigi: Nationalist Party leader, 97, 98; his blue-shirt army, 103; the link between Facta and Mussolini, 128–30; Minister for the Colonies, 132; becomes a National Fascist, 139; during the Matteotti affair 162, 163; on Mussolini and dictatorship, 171; attack on Freemasonry, 179; intrigues against Farinacci, 181–2; relegated to the Academy, 201; attends funeral of Pius XI, 302; eventual loss of faith in Mussolini, 327; at the final meeting of the Grand Council, 336–7
Feltre, 335
Feltrinelli, 82
Fermi, 282
Ferrandini, F., 96
Ferrari, Enzo, 96, 106
Figaro, Le, on Mussolini, 180
Filippelli, Filippo, 159, 161
Finland, attacked by Russia, 313
Finzi, Aldo, 146, 158–61, 318
Fiume: occupied by Italy (*1918*), 85; discussed at Peace Conference, 91; pro-Italian riots (*1919*), 103, 104; occupied by D'Annunzio, 104–5; the "bloody Christmas", 111; reoccupied by Giunta, 113; annexed to Italy, 155
Foa, 318
Forlinopoli, the Royal Normal School, 21
Four Power Pact (*1933*), 216
France: sends troops to the Italian front (*1917*), 79–80; supports Yugoslav territorial integrity, 91, 104; occupies the Ruhr, 145; strained relations with Italy and treaty with Yugoslavia (*1927*), 192–3; reaction to the Dollfuss murder, 221–2; the Four Power Pact, 216; approach to Mussolini through Laval, 216–17; anti-Italian feeling (*1938*), 259; attitude to Austria before the *anschluss*, 266–7; during the *anschluss*, 268; averse to British agreement with Italy, 270, 277; attitude to Czechoslovakia before the Godesberg agreement, 285–7; military moves before Munich, 290; reaction to Munich, 295; post-Munich policies driving Italy into the arms of Germany, 299–300, 306–8, 312
Francini, A., 131
Franco, Gen., 241–2, 259, 277, 278, 293
François-Poncet: interview with Hitler before Munich, 291; far-sighted views on the future of Europe, 295
Frauenfeld, A., 221, 222
Frans Ferdinand, Archduke, assassination of, 46
Freemasonry, Fascist antagonism to, 141–2, 173–4, 179
Fubini, 282
Futurism, 95–6

Galassi, 54
Galbiati, Maj.-Gen. Enzo: an early Fascist, 98; opposes creation of a Fascist Party, 119; on Army and Militia, 139, 140; organizes the Consuls in the Matteotti crisis, 166–7; on Mussolini's speech of *Jan. 3, 1915*, 169; misgivings on the strength of Mussolini's position, 173; expelled from the party, 174; his description of the Ethiopian campaign, 229; appointed Chief of Staff of Militia, 325; his unswerving loyalty, 333; at the final meeting of the Grand Council, 335–7; his plan to reinstate Mussolini, 338; imprisoned, 338–9; reasons for his inactivity, 339
Galimberti, 106
Gandhi, Mahatma, 208
Garber, Josef, 15
Garibaldi family, 57
Garinei, 74
Garosci, G., 358
Gasparri, Cardinal: begins to support Mussolini, 122; negotiates on reconciliation, 141–2, 143–5; during the Matteotti affair, 163, 165; negotiates Lateran Pact, 196–7
Gelommini, 354
Gemelli, B., 163
Gentile, G., 134, 154, 172
Germany: invades Belgium (*1914*), 46; at war with Italy, 72; financial and political chaos (*1923*), 145; the Four Power Pact, 216; leaves the League of Nations, 218; rearms, 224; occupies the Rhineland, 235: signs Anti-Comintern Pact, 250; leaves the Committee of Non-intervention in Spain, 253; occupies Austria, 267; occupies Czechoslovakia, 303–4; the Pact of Steel, 309; the Soviet pact, 311; invades Poland, 312; occupation of Rome, 341; *see also* Hitler
Giannini, A., 359
Giampoli, M., 96, 142
Gibson, Violet, 182
Giolitti, G.: attitude to war (*1915*), 60, 61; political ideas in *1919*, 93–4; Prime

Giolitti, G.—*contd.*
Minister, 109; offers Mussolini a place in the "National Bloc", 110; claims to have provoked Socialists to abortive rising, 111; signs treaty of Rapallo and evicts D'Annunzio from Fiume, 111; restricts export of capital, 112; plans for the *1921* election, 115; resigns, 116; accepts Fascism, 121, 131; position after the *1924* election, 156; on the Matteotti affair, 164, 165, 166; as the last of the opposition, 170, 185
Giovanna, Princess, 203–4
Giraldi, Gen. P., 108
Giuliani, 74
Giunta, F., 113, 155
Giurati, G., 205, 206, 334
Giustizia, suspended, 170, 179
Gnecchi, Cdr., 82
Gobetti, P.: the "Liberal Revolution", 93; on the inevitability of Fascism, 148; but becomes anti-Fascist, 155; during the Matteotti affair, 165; persecution and exile, 176–7; death, 185; his legacy to the Action Party, 331
Godesberg agreement, 287, 288
Goebbels, J.: studies Fascism, 211, 214; views on Ciano, 248; at Mussolini's state visit, 254
Goering, H.: shelters in Italy (*1923*), 153; enthusiasm for Fascist Italy, 192; studies Fascism, 211, 213–14; at Mussolini's state visit, 254; speech on Czechoslovakia, 284; military consultations with Mussolini, 305; and on a Soviet pact, 308
Gothic Line, the, 348
Gottardi, 337
George V, visits Italy, 145–7
Gramsci, A.: revolutionary activities, 93; leads the "revolution of the Soviets", 110; arrest, 185; influence as a martyr, 330; views on the Socialist-Communist split, 358
Grand Council of Fascism: formation, 138–9; fuses Army and Militia, 139; debates electoral reform, 150; during the Matteotti affair, 162; integrated with the constitution, 194; the final meeting, 335–7
Grandi, Dino: an early violent Fascist, 112, 114, 116; reaction to the massacre of Sarzana, 117; defies the truce with Socialism, 118; fails to become leader, 119; praised but distrusted by Mussolini, 121–2; position after the march on Rome, 130; during the Freemasonry crisis, 142; during the Matteotti affair, 163; abandons the idea of leadership, 176; Minister for Foreign Affairs, 200; liking for Britain, 203; Ambassador in London, 265; instrumental in calling final meeting of the Grand Council, 334; at the meeting, 335–7; eventual fate, 337
Gray, Ezio Maria: influences policy on Spain, 154; favours a Latin Federation, 193, 201; but is foiled by the Spanish revolution, 207; return to the idea, 211; negotiates with Metaxas on sanctions, 231
Graziani, R.: "frees" Libya, 142; in the Ethiopian campaign, 228, 231, 234, 236; as C.-in-C. of the new Social Republic, 342–3, 347; surrenders to the allies, 352; last meeting with Mussolini, 353
Gronchi, G., 133, 144
Gruhn, Erna, 262
Guidi, Anna, 33
Guidi, Augusta, 33
Guidi, Rachele: *see* Mussolini, Rachele
Gustav Line, the, 343–7

Habicht, T., 222
Hácha, Dr. A., 304
Haile Selassie: supported by Italy for League membership, 223; defeat and exile, 237
Halder, Gen., 291
Halifax, Lord: offers concessions to Hitler (*1938*), 261; attempts at *rapprochement* with Italy, 264; hesitates between French and Italian friendship, 270, 271, 282–3; and over agreement with Italy after Munich, 296–9; abortive visit to Rome, 301; hopes of Italian neutrality, 310–11
Hassan Pasha, 183
Hassell, U. von, 252, 263
Hedley, Leslie Woolf, 365
Heidenstam, V. von, 153
Hemingway, Ernest, 77
Henderson, Arthur, 162
Henderson, Sir Nevile, 275, 297, 309
Henlein, Konrad, 273
Herald Tribune, on Mussolini, 180
Herlitska, 282
Hesse, Prince Philip of, 268
Himmler, 293
Hitler, Adolf: his political development compared with Mussolini's, 28–9; emerges politically, 145; the Nuremburg *putsch*, 153; *Mein Kampf*, 178; early approaches to Mussolini, 192; becomes Chancellor, 211; publicly praises Mussolini, 214; and copies him, 214–15; leaves the League and signs Polish pact,

Hitler, Adolf—*contd.*
218; soothes Britain, 219; first meeting with Mussolini, 219–20; the bloodbath of *1934*, 220; first threat to Austria, 220–1; checked by Mussolini, 221; decrees compulsory military service, 224; attitude to the Ethiopian campaign; 235; occupies the Rhineland, 235; intervention in Spain, 242; Mussolini's first state visit, 254; genuine admiration for Mussolini, 261–2; prelude to the occupation of Austria, 262–4; interview with Schuschnigg, 264–5; orders the occupation of Austria, 267; gratitude to Mussolini, 268; visits Mussolini and is cautioned, 271–3; foiled by Mussolini in his first attempt on Czechoslovakia, 273–6; but fixes date for invasion, 278; again cautioned by Mussolini, 279–80; threats to Czechoslovakia leading to the Godesberg agreement, 284–7; reaction to European military moves before Munich, 290–1; invites Chamberlain to see him, 291; accepts the Munich conference, 292; at the conference, 294; anxiety for military alliance with Italy, 298; opens negotiations for the Pact of Steel, 302; final occupation of Czechoslovakia, 303–4; annexes Memel, 304; tells Mussolini of the impending attack on Poland, 311; and rejects Mussolini's appeals, 311–12; asks Italy to join the war, 313; meets Mussolini at Feltre, 335; reaction to the fall of Mussolini, 341–2; attitude to him at the end, 351; death, 354
Hoare, Sir Samuel: approves Mussolini's firmness in Dollfuss crisis, 222; the Hoare-Laval pact, 232
Holy See: *see* Church
Horthy, Admiral, 100, 208, 280
Hotzendorf, Marshal, 70
Humbert I, 22
Humbert, Crown Prince: popular in *1912*, 41; marriage, 203; encourages Badoglio's conspiracies, 321; prospective head of the Realm, 347
Hyndmann, 57

Igliori, 124
Illiteracy, 362
Istria, as a *casus belli* (*1915*), 59
Italy: feelings on Trent (*1909*), 35; the Libyan war (*1911*), 38–9; the strikes of *1913* and *1914*, 43–4, 45; varying political views on World War I, 46–7; growth of support for intervention, 56–61; the Interventionist Declaration, 58; breaks with Austria, 59; at war with Austria, 61; unprepared for war, 62–3; war position at end of *1915*, 64; chaotic war administration, 68–9, 70; naval disasters, 71; declares war on Germany, 72; Caporetto, 76–7; corruption in *1918*, 82; eventual military success, 82–5; political and economic conditions in *1919*, 90–6; strikes and riots of *1919*, 102–5; and early *1920*, 108; the chaos of *1920–21*, 111–14; the *1921* election, 115–16; political and social chaos before the march on Rome, 116–30; the longing for a settled country, 131–2; lack of modern development (*1923*), 149–50; reaction to Mussolini's reforms (*1925–6*), 180–1; the coming of the police state, 185; foreign opinion in *1926*, 186; international relations (*1926*), 192–4; economic position in *1932*, 208–10; international position in *1933*, 213; the nation during the Ethiopian campaign, 227–8, 229–31, 233; exuberance after victory, 237–40; withdraws from Committee of Non-intervention in Spain, 253; joins Anti-Comintern Pact and leaves the League, 255–6; foreign opinion (*1938*), 259–61; strength of her position after the Austrian *anschluss*, 269–70; pacifist feeling before Munich, 289; the Pact of Steel, 309; reluctance to enter the war, 312; enters the war, 313; gradual lowering of morale during the war, 328–30, 333; the state of decay in *1943*, 332–3; the armistice of *1943*, 340; and the ensuing confusion, 342; division of the country, 343; the post-war reaction against Fascism, 355–6; the post-war political parties, 356–63; modern political apathy, 362; the end of imperialism, 365

Jachino, Admiral, 323
Japan, signs Anti-Comintern Pact, 250
Jews: Fascist attitude to, 199; early reactions to Hitler's anti-semitism, 215; Italians revolted at Nazi policy, 238; a Zionist appeal to Italy, 259; the proposed Italian Jewish home, 281–2; discrimination against Jews in Italy, 282; attitude of the Church, 318
Jolanda, Princess, 139, 143
Joza, 200
Justice and Liberty Movement, 331, 349

Kahn, Otto, 153
Keitel, F.-M., 293
Klausener, 317

Kordt, T., 294
Krassin, 137
Kulishchoff, Anna, 42

Lanzillo, 106
Lateran Pact: signing of, 198; reactions to, 198–9
Lausanne conference (*1922*), 136–7
Laval, Pierre: discusses Europe and the Mediterranean with Mussolini, 216–17; secret treaty with Italy on Abyssinia, 223; rebuffed in London; 223; the Hoare-Laval Pact, 232
Lavoro, suspended, 170
Law of Guarantees, 67
Lazzari, 82
League of Nations: and the bombardment of Corfu, 152; votes for sanctions against Italy, 230; orders them to be applied "fully", 232
Lenin, 24, 49, 90, 112, 155
Leto, G., 200
Levi-Gibita, 282
Liberal Party: position in *1919*, 93–4; congratulates Mussolini on accession to power, 132; attacks Mussolini after the Matteotti murder, 165–6; its collapse, 169–70; position in *1942*, 331; tentative co-operation with other opposition parties, 332; at the Bari conference, 345; attitude to the Bonomi government, 347; eclipse, 359
Libya: the *1911* war, 38–9; "freed" by Graziani, 142; visit by Mussolini, 182–3
Lima, La, Mussolini's open letter to the police, 31
Lissia, Pietro, 133
Litvinov, M., 217, 308
Lloyd George, D., 80, 81
Locarno conference, 178
Lombardo, 358
London Naval Conference, 203
London, Treaty of (*1915*), 59, 81, 85
Loraine, Sir Percy, 307, 310
Lotta di Classe, La, edited by Mussolini, 37
Lucetti, Gino, 183–4

Macchi, 106
MacDonald, Ramsay, 162
Malacria, 160
Malaparte, 148, 178, 318
Malato, 57
Mallarmé, Camille, 201
Maltoni, Rosa: *see* Mussolini, Rosa
"Man in the Street Party", 359
Manstein, F.-M. von, 268
Maraini, N., 202
March on Rome, the, 123–9; Mussolini's later version of it, 288
Marconi, G., 205
Margaria, Mgr., 233, 239
Maria José, Princess, 203
Marinelli, 158, 159, 160, 337
Marinetti, E.: Futurist leader and interventionist, 58; war service, 63; supports Mussolini, 95–6; an expert in violence, 100, 103, 114; attitude to occupation of Fiume, 105; stands in the *1919* election, 106; relegated to the Academy, 201
Marpillero, D., 30
Mary, Queen, visits Italy, 145–7
Masaryk, 178
Matapan, battle of, 323
Matteotti, G.: denies Fascist economic recovery, 157; speech in parliament, 157–8; background and position, 158; disappearance and death, 159–60; the consequent crisis for Fascism, 160–8
Maugeri, Admiral, 323
Maurano, S., 282
Mazzini, his political legacy, 90–1
Mazzuccato, 106
Mein Kampf, 29, 178
Memel, 304
Meraviglia, C., 96
Merlin, U., 133
Merry del Val, Cardinal, 186
Metaxas, J., 231
Milani, F., 133
Militia: uneasy relations with the army, 139–40; during the Matteotti affair, 166–7; Mussolini's debt to it, 173; its unswerving loyalty, 324–5
Misiano, 117
Missiroli, M., 121
Modigliani, 185
Mola, Gen., 81
Molotov, 308
Mondo, il, suspended, 170
Monelli, P., 25, 28
Montenegro, Italian designs on, 80
Morning Post, on Mussolini, 136, 180
Mosley, Sir Oswald, 208, 225
Munich conference, 293–4, 295
Mussert, 208
Mussolini, Alessandro: socialist activities, 17, 19, 23, 24; courtship and marriage, 18; influence on Benito, 20, 21, 23; on the assassination of Humbert I, 22; attacks the Church, 25; life in Forlì, 26–7, 28, 33; death, 38
Mussolini, Anna Maria, 243
Mussolini, Arnaldo: birth, 19; edits *il Popolo d'Italia*, 136; death, 206

Mussolini, Benito:

1883–1914

birth, 15, 18; ancestry, 16–18; childhood and schooldays, 19–22; elementary teacher—socialist activities, 22–3; goes to Switzerland, 23; socialist activities there, 24–6; military service in Italy, 26; further teaching and studies—watched by police, 26–31; his political development compared with Hitler's, 28–9; his alleged syphilis, 30; imprisoned for attack on sharecroppers, 32; woos Rachele Guidi, 33; lives with her, 36–7; edits *La Lotta di Classe*, 37; opposes the Libyan war, 38; organizes the strikes in Romagna, 39; imprisoned with Nenni, 39–41; success at the XIIIth Socialist Congress, 41–2; editor of *Avanti*, 42–7; defeated in the Forlì election, 45; interventionist in *1914*, 45–7; clashes with Socialists and leaves *Avanti*, 47–50

1914–1919

starts *il Popolo d'Italia*, 51–4; final break with the Socialists on intervention, 54–5; organizes interventionist *fasci* and propaganda, 57–61; strength of his position in *1915*, 62; his call-up delayed, 63–4; war service, 64–5, 66, 70; marries Rachele, 65; attacks the Papacy, 67–8; and the wartime administration, 68; renewed attacks on Papacy, 72–3; accident in the field, 73–5; further attacks on Church and socialism, 75–6; reaction to Caporetto, 77–8; distrust of the coming peace terms, 80–2; speech on the future policy of Italy—ceases attacks on the Church, 83; his post-war position, 85; forms the *Fasci di Combattimento*, 86–7

1919–1921

political thought in *1919*, 89–90; his idea of extra-parliamentary influence by *fasci*, 95, 102; support from Nationalists and ex-officers, 95–8, 101–2; conducts a "menace of Bolshevism" campaign, 100–1; defeated in the *1919* election, 106; courted by industrialists, church leaders and the army, 108–9; accepts place in Giolitti's National Bloc, 110; policy before the *1921* election, 114; wins in it and sees the king, 116; manœuvres for power—makes and unmakes the truce with Socialists, 117–18; confirmed as Duce of the National Fascist Party, 118–19; political manœuvres with king, government and party, 120–9; meets German industrialists, 121; orders demobilization of Militia, 122; promises the march on Rome, 123; his prevarications with the Party, 124–5; asked to form government, 129

1921–1925

announces policy of normalization, 131–2; distribution of government offices, 132–4; first steps in home affairs, 134–6; at the Lausanne conference, 136–7; tentative approaches to Russia, 137; at the London Reparations conference, 137–8; negotiates reconciliation with the Church, 140–2, 143–5; work on party unity, 142–3; receives George V, 145–7; signs treaty with Russia, 146; asks British help over Fiume, 146; growing popularity and weakening opposition, 147–9; public works, 149; orders bombardment of Corfu, 151–2; shelters Goering, 153; influence on Primo de Rivera, 153–4; views on Lenin, 155; annexation of Fiume, 156; the quarrel with Matteotti, 157–9; reaction to his disappearance, 159–60; and to his murder, 160–1; his position shaken, 162–3; but rallied by support, 163–5; threat of impeachment, 165–6; the support of the Consuls, 167; speech of *Jan. 3, 1925*, 167–8

1925–1932

collapse of the opposition, 169–70; orders revision of the constitution, 171; initially averse to dictatorship, 171–2; support from intellectuals, 172; his debt to the Militia, 173; suppressing the opposition, 174–8; at the Locarno conference, 178; attempts on his life and national reaction, 178, 182, 183–5; administrative and constitutional changes, 179–81; his increasing aloofness, 183; and popularity, 184; decrees for the defence of the State, 185; agricultural and industrial policy, 187–91; the Pontine Marshes, 191; initial indifference to Hitler, 192; Mediterranean policy (*1927*), 192–4; "tidying-up" the constitution, 194–5; the Lateran Pact, 195–9; cautious approach to a Latin bloc, 201–2; but woos Britain, 202–3; failure to achieve proposed alliances, 207–8; growing isolation, 210–11; professed loyalty to League of Nations, 211

1933–1937

ignores resurgence of Germany, 212, 213; returns to the idea of the Latin bloc, 213; checks Pilsudski's move against Hitler, 215; negotiates the Four Power Pact, 216; tentative approaches

Mussolini Benito—*contd.*
to Laval, 216–17; non-aggression pact with Russia, 217; reactions to the German-Polish pact, 218; first meeting with Hitler, 219–20; armed reaction to the Dollfuss murder, 221; resultant international prestige, 221–2; which he consolidates before attacking Ethiopia, 223–4; at the Stresa conference, 224–5; snubs Eden in Rome, 226; ignores Britain and the League, 226–7; orders mobilization for Ethiopia, 227; speech to the nation, 227–8; dealing with the campaign and with sanctions, 228–35; contemplates intervention in Spain, 235–6; victory in Ethiopia—the "rebirth of the Roman Empire", 237; the height of popularity at home, 237–40; and prestige abroad, 240; decides on intervention in Spain, 240–2; loaded with foreign honours, 242; his private life and the myths surrounding it, 243–5; his tours, 245–6; his reading, 245; his casual women, 247; takes to Clara Petacci, 247; still lukewarm to Germany, 249; speaks of a *rapprochement* with Britain, 250; which he achieves, 251; but hovers between German and British friendship, 251–3; accuses Britain of misunderstanding, 253–4; pays state visit to Berlin, 254; and is overwhelmed, 254–6

1937–1940
his exalted isolation in Italy, 257–8; and prestige abroad, 258–61; foreign policy (*1938*), 261; temporizes with Hitler over Austria, 262–7; deserts Schuschnigg on the question of the plebiscite, 267; European policy after the Austrian *anschluss*, 269–70; refuses military pact with Germany—urges caution over Czechoslovakia, 272–3; dissuades Hitler from attacking, 275–6; rejects British proposals on Spain, 277–8; again cautions Hitler on Czechoslovakia, 278–80; proposed solution to the Jewish problem, 280–2; further offers of friendship with Britain, 282–4; diplomatic moves leading to Godesberg agreement, 284–7; military and diplomatic action before Munich, 289–91; arranges the Munich conference, 291–4; at the conference—his credit for it, 294–5; frustrated efforts to turn to Britain rather than Germany, 295–302; opens negotiations for the Pact of Steel, 302; refuses to attend funeral of Pius XI, 302; occupies Albania, 304–5; further reasons for pact with Germany, 305–8; suggests Soviet-Axis pact, 308; authorizes the Pact of Steel, 308, 309; but hopes to postpone war, 309–11, tries to dissuade Hitler from attacking Poland, 311–12; factors deciding him to enter the war, 312–13

1940–1945
decay of his relations with the Church, 316–19; and the king, 319–21; and the army, 321–5; and the Party, 325–8; and loss of confidence of the masses, 328–33; conscious of growing opposition, 333; agrees to calling of the Grand Council, 334; meets Hitler at Feltre, 335; deposed by the Grand Council, 335–7; after the meeting, 338; dismissal by the king and arrest, 338; subsequent prisons, 339; rescue by the Germans—proclaims the new Republic, 342; last days and final speech, 350–1; capture and death, 353–4
contrasted with Hitler, 355; his attitude to war, 355–6; his policy for national minorities, 363; his legacy to Italian law, 364; his idea of a united Europe, 364; his work on statistics, 364; his political persuasiveness, 365
Published books: Man and Divinity, 25; *The Cardinal's Mistress*, 35; *The Life of Arnaldo*, 207
Mussolini, Bettino, 16
Mussolini, Bruno, 243
Mussolini, Edda, 37; marries Ciano, 203
Mussolini, Edvige: on the infant Benito, 19–20; on his love affairs, 33
Mussolini, Luigi, 17
Mussolini, Rachele: wooed by Benito, 33–4; lives with him in Forlì, 36; marriage, 65; baptised, 143; persuades him to hand foreign affairs to Ciano, 242
Mussolini, Romano, 192, 243
Mussolini, Rosa: marriage, 18; as wife and mother, 19, 20, 21; illness and death, 25–6
Mussolini, Sandro, 204
Mussolini, Troilo, 16
Mussolini, Vittorio, 68, 243, 352
Muti, 313

Naldi, F., 52–4
Nanni, T., 28
Nationalist Party: first notices Mussolini, 36; early alliance with Fascism, 96–7; position in the *1921* election, 116; offices in Mussolini's first government, 132; merges with the Fascists, 139; its

Nationalist Party—*contd.*
contribution to Fascism, 181–2; eventual loss of faith in Mussolini, 327
Nava, 163
Navarra, Quinto, 135, 160, 162
Navy, the Italian: heavy losses in *1916*, 71; unreadiness in *1939*, 306; treachery of high-ranking officers, 323; divided loyalties in *1943*, 343
Nenni, Pietro: imprisoned with Mussolini (*1911*), 39–41; returns to socialism, 112; fails to reach agreement with Mussolini, 120; in and out of jail, 143; during the Matteotti affair, 157, 161; duel with Malaparte, 178; position in *1949*, 357–8; Minister for Foreign Affairs, 360
Neurath, Baron von, 242, 263
Nitti, F. F.: Prime Minister, 101; fails to control D'Annunzio in Fiume, 105; or disorders at home, 108, 109; in exile, 185

O'Duffy, Gen., 208
O'Flaherty, Mgr., 319
Ojetti, U., 172, 231
Olivetti, A., 58
O.N.B.: *see* Youth Movements
Orlando, Vittorio: Prime Minister, 78; in the pre-armistice peace negotiations (*1918*), 81–2; attends Peace Conference, 86; a traditionalist, 90; resignation, 101; support for Mussolini as Prime Minister, 128
Osborne, Sir Darcy, 319

Pact of Steel, 309
Pagani, A., 119
Palzani, L., 119
Pantaleoni, 163
Panzini, 172
Papacy: *see* Church
Papen, Franz von, 263, 264, 317, 319
Pareschi, 337
Parri, F., 360
Partisan activities, 343, 344–5, 346, 347–50, 352
Passerone, G.: an early Fascist, 98; leads ex-officers, 111; opposes creation of a Fascist Party, 119; in the Militia, 143; during the Matteotti affair, 166–7
Pavolini, 354
Pau, Gen., 57
Pellizzi, C., 172
Pende, 172
Perro, Gen., 67
Perrone, 141
Perth, Lord: warns Mussolini against intervention in Spain, 236; on Ciano, 248; negotiates on British-Italian agreement, 270, 271, 276–8, 281, 296, 297–8; his report on the dangers of an Axis alliance, 300–1; and on French diplomacy, 307
Pettaci, Clara, 247–8, 262, 333, 352, 353, 354
Phipps, Sir Eric, 277, 285, 291, 306–7
Pieraccini, 111
Pilsudski, Gen.: suggests Franco-Polish move against Hitler, 215; checked by Mussolini, 215–16
Pincherle, 172, 282
Pini, G., 62, 77
Piperno, 148, 318
Pirandello, L., 172
Pius XI: his anti-political Church policy, 119–20, 143; dealings with Mussolini over Catholic Action, 206; death, 302
Pius XII: as Papal Nuncio at Munich, 264; attitude to occupation of Czechoslovakia, 303; early Germanophile tendencies, 316–17; growth of his opposition to Fascism, 317–19
Pizzetti, 172
Plekhanov, 57
Podrecca, 106
Poincaré, R., on Mussolini, 137, 138
Poland: takes its share of Czechoslovakia after Munich, 295; pact with Germany, 218; invaded by Germany, 312
Police: the work of the O.V.R.A., 199–200
Pontecorvo, R., 282, 318
Pontine Marshes, reclamation of, 191–2
Popolo d'Italia, il: founding and early finances, 51–4; early progress, 55–6; its offices attacked (*1919*), 99–100; edited by Arnaldo Mussolini, 136; during the Matteotti affair, 158; Mussolini's "peacemaking" article on Czechoslovakia, 285–6; the revised version of the march on Rome, 288
Popular Catholic Party: position in *1919*, 94–5; out of favour with the Cardinals, 108, 114; position in the *1921* election, 116; loses influence under Pius XI, 120; split over Mussolini's first government, 133–4; loss of government offices, 143–4; during the electoral reform debate, 150; decline in *1923*, 151; position after the *1924* election, 156; its extinction a later cause of Church antagonism to Fascism, 317; *and see* Christian Democrat Party
Porro, Gen. C., 57, 77
Postiglione, 126
Poveromo, 160
Powell, Maj., 208
Pozzi, 106

Prefects, 187
Press, the: attitude to World War I, 59; control of, 170; suppression of, 185
Primo de Rivera, Gen., 153–4, 240–1
Proletario, il, employs Mussolini, 24
Pugliese, Gen., 319

Queen Mother, the: intrigues in support of Mussolini, 125, 126; relations with Mussolini, 135; urges reconciliation between Church and State, 140–1; her help over Fiume, 147; influence on the death duties law, 154; during the Matteotti affair, 162; death—her value to Mussolini, 180–1

Racah, 282
Raimondo, 103
Ramperti, M., 55
Rapallo, treaty of, 111
Ratti, Achille: *see* Pius XI
Ravenna, R., 318
Reichman, Gen. von, 267
Republican Party: position in *1919*, 93–4; after the *1924* election, 156
Rhineland, occupation by Germany, 235
Ribbentrop, J. von: hopes for an Anglo-German alliance (*1936*), 242; diplomacy before the Austrian *anschluss*, 264–7; diplomacy over Czechoslovakia, 274, 275, 286, 287; in Rome before the occupation of Czechoslovakia, 303; discusses Soviet-Axis pact with Ciano, 308, 309; signs the Pact of Steel, 309; works for the Soviet pact, 310; signs it, 311
Ricci, B., 172; in charge of Youth Movements, 205–6
Rinaldi, G. B., 20
Rivoluzione Liberale, la, 155
Roatta, Gen., 322
Rocca Gorga, 43–4
Rocca, M., 47
Rocco, A., 132
Roehm, 220
Romanini, 106
Roncalli, Angelo (John XXIII): First War service, 67; in the Popular Catholic Party, 120; in Bulgaria, 192, 204, 239; in Turkey, 317–18, 319; Nuncio to France, 360
Roosevelt, President, appeals for European moderation, 291, 305
Rossi, E., 282
Rossi, T.: Minister of Industry and Commerce, 133; in the Freemasonry crisis, 141, before the *1924* election, 155; during the Matteotti affair, 159, 161, 165; imprisoned for treason, 199
Rossoni, 336
Ruberti, G., 243
Runciman, Lord, negotiations in Czechoslovakia, 279, 286, 290
Russia: wavering war effort in *1915*, 56; the revolution, 75; supports Italian Communists, 112, 113; treaty with Italy (*1923*), 146; and non-aggression pact (*1933*), 217; admitted to League of Nations, 222; influence in Spain, 240–1; attitude to Italy in *1938*, 260; and to Austria before the *anschluss*, 266; reaction to the *anschluss*, 268; the pact with Germany, 311; attacks Finland, 313; recognizes the Badoglio government, 346
Ryan, Sir Andrew, 305, 308
Rygier, Maria, 24, 58

Saar plebiscite, 223
Salandra, Antonio: wavers on intervention (*1915*), 60; forced to resign, 70–1; supports Mussolini for Prime Minister, 128; last days, 204; death, 206
Salazar, A., 216
Salvatorelli, L., 172, 176–7
Salvemini, G., 111, 172, 176–7
Salvolini, Virginia, 27
Sanctions against Italy: voted by the League, 230; their effect in Italy, 230–1, 233; ordered to be applied "fully", 232; half-heartedly applied, 232, 233, 235
San Giuliano, 52
Sagarat, 185, 361, 357–8
Sarfatti, Margherita, 28, 42, 107, 137, 148, 149, 247, 318
Sartrocchi, 163
Sarzana, massacre of, 117
Schacht, Dr. H., 263
Schleicher, Gen. K. von, 220
Schnurre, Dr. J., 308
Schobert, Gen. von, 267
Schuschnigg, Kurt von: takes over after Dollfuss, 222; relations with Hitler and Mussolini before the *anschluss*, 263–4; interview with Hitler, 264–5; announces a plebiscite, 267
Schuster, Archbishop: during the Ethiopian war, 233; admiration for Mussolini, 251; refuses him sanctuary, 319, 352
Scoccimarro, 360
Scorza, 334, 336
Segato, Gen., 77
Serajevo, 46
Serao, Matilde, 162
Seyss-Inquart, A., 268
Sforza, Count, 116, 135
Sharecroppers, 32, 92
Sheridan, Clare, 135

Shirer, 28, 294
Sicily, allied landing in, 333
Silone, 358
Simon, Sir John: suggests arms parity for Germany, 219; approves Mussolini's firmness in Dollfuss crisis, 222; tortuous diplomacy before German rearmament, 224; alarmed at Stresa, 224
Skorczeny, O., 342
Social Democrats, in Mussolini's first government, 132–3
Socialist Party: appoints Mussolini to Trent (*1909*), 34; Milan Congress (*1910*), 37; opposition to Libyan war (*1911*), 39; XIIIth Congress—expulsion of seven members, 41; appoints Mussolini editor of *Avanti*, 42; attitude to World War I, 47; clashes with Mussolini, 48–50; reaction to founding of *il Popolo d'Italia*, 51–4; remains neutralist and attacks Mussolini, 63; anti-war demonstrations, 67; appeals for peace, 72; reaction to the Russian revolution, 75; volte-face after Italian victories, 84; its strength and weakness in *1919*, 94; post-war anti-militarism, 97–8; beginning of a Leninist-Social Democrat split, 107–8; the revolution of the Soviets, 110–11; the Livorno conference and the breakaway of the Communists, 112; losses in the *1921* election, 116; abortive truce with Fascists, 117–18; declining influence, 121; during the electoral reform debate, 150; position after the *1924* election, 156; reaction to the Matteotti murder, 161; position in *1942*, 330; tentative co-operation with other opposition parties, 332; at the Bari conference, 345; attitude to the Bonomi government, 347; its failure to learn from Fascism, 356–8
Soddu, Gen., 322
Soffici, 172
Solari, 331
Sonnino, 56, 58, 90, 91, 101
Sotelo, C., 241
Spain: becomes a republic, 207; the civil war and Italian intervention, 240–2, 253, 259, 277–8, 299, 302
Stalin, 155, 346
Stampa, La: applauds Fascism, 148; suspended, 170
Starace, Achille: an early Fascist leader, 121; during the Matteotti affair, 157; General Secretary of the Fascist Party, 206; encourages Mussolini's isolation, 210; announces mobilization for Ethiopia, 227; makes the Ethiopian campaign, 232, 233–4, 236; organizes Hitler's visit to Rome, 272; refuses to attend funeral of Pius XI, 302; dismissed, 313; typifies the blindly loyal Fascist, 325–6,; death, 354
Statist, The, 157
Statistical services, 149–50, 365
Stephen, the Patriarch, 204
Stojadinovitch, 255
Stoppato, 103
Stresa conference, 224
Sturzo, Don Luigi: leader of the Popular Catholic Party, 94; bad relations with the Cardinals, 108, 114; and with Giolitti, 110; not supported by Pius XI, 120, 143; vetoes Giolitti as Prime Minister, 121; reluctantly supports Mussolini, 144; opposition to electoral reform, 150; resigns as secretary of the Popular Party, 151; during the Matteotti affair, 166; exile, 317
Suardo, 337

Tagore, Rabindranath, 183
Tamburini, 141
Tangorra, 139
Tarabella, 166–7, 173, 174
Taylor, Gen., 341
Tecchio, V., 281
Teruzzi, 124, 334
Terzaghi, M., 133
Times, The, on Mussolini, 151
Tittoni, T., 128, 206
Tiso, Mgr., 303
Todt, Dr., 280
Togliatti, P., 358
Tommasi, 103
Torre, R., 134, 147
Toscanini, Arturo, 106
Trade unions: proclaim general strike (*1911*), 39; and in *1914*, 45; dissolution under the Work Charter, 189; suppression of, 179
Trent, as a *casus belli* (*1915*), 57, 58
Treves, C., 41, 93, 185
Trieste: as a *casus belli* (*1915*), 57, 58; riots in *1919*, 103
Tringali-Casanova, 336
Trotsky, 112, 155
Trumbic, 81
Tunis, 259, 299
Turati, A., 182, 185
Turati, F., 112
Tuvati, 93

Ungaretti, 172
Unita, suspended, 179
United States of America, attitude to sanctions, 232

"Valerio, Col." (Walter Audisio), 353
Valéry, Paul, 208
Vansittart, Sir Robert, 274
Vecchi, F., 96, 99–100
Victor Emmanuel III: marriage, 21; attempted assassination of, 41; opts for war (*1915*), 58–9; visits Mussolini in hospital, 74–5; first consults Mussolini, 116–17; attempts to deal constitutionally with him, 121–9; asks him to form government, 129; during the Matteotti affair, 163, 165; position under the new constitution, 180, 181, 183; distrust of the new law of *1928*, 195; as Emperor, 238–9; entertains Hitler in Rome, 271–2; warns Mussolini to "avoid" Germany, 276; his initial acceptance of Fascism, 319–20; and growing opposition to it, 320–1; encourages dissident factions in the army, 321; agrees to ask for Mussolini's resignation, 333–4; dismisses and arrests Mussolini, 338; leaves Rome for Brindisi, 341; unpopular with the opposition parties, 345; moves government to Salerno, 345–6; promises to hand over to Humbert, 347
Visconti-Prasca, Gen., 321–2
Vittoria Colonna, Princess, 142
Voce, la, suspended, 170
Volpe, 172
Volpi, 160
Volterra, 282

Waterhouse, Col., 138
Weizsaeker, E. von, 294
Weizmann, Dr. Chaim, 259
Wilson, Sir Henry Maitland, 350
Wilson, Sir Horace, 290
Wilson, President, his fourteen points, 80
Wolff, Gen., 352
Work Charter, the, 189–91
World War I: Serajevo, 46; Germany invades Belgium, 46; situation in *1915*, 56; pre-armistice diplomacy, 80–2
World War II, summary of, 314–16

York, Duke of (George VI), 203
Youth Movements, 142, 147, 187, 205–6, 361–2
Yugoslavia: old Italian claims on, 80–1; proposed as a new state, 81–2; gains Porto Baros from Italy, 116; cedes Fiume, 155

Zaniboni, Tito, 178
Zammerini, 185
Zibordi, G., 63
Zog, King, 304–5
Zupelli, Gen., 69